WOMEN'S health & WELLNESS 2005

Real Life Solutions from the Editors of *Health* Magazine

Oxmoor
House®

Women's Health & Wellness 2005

©2004 by Oxmoor House, Inc.

Book Division of Southern Progress Corporation

P.O. Box 2463, Birmingham, Alabama 35201

Published by Oxmoor House, Inc.

Hardcover ISBN: 0-8487-2820-3

Softcover ISBN: 0-8487-2832-7

ISSN: 1537-4394

Printed in the United States of America

First Printing 2004

The articles in this book were printed in *Health* magazine and prepared in accordance with the highest standards of journalistic accuracy. Unless otherwise noted, these articles have not been updated since their original publication in 2004. Readers are cautioned not to use information from this book as a substitute for professional health care and advice.

To order additional publications,
call 800-765-6400.

For more books to enrich your life,
visit **oxmoorhouse.com**

Cover: Photography by David Martinez

health

Editor-in-Chief: Doug Crichton

Executive Editor: Lisa Delaney

Design Director: Paul Carstensen

Managing Editor: Jerry Gulley II

Deputy Editor: Lisa Davis

Senior Editors: Nichele Hoskins (*Fitness*), Adam J. Martin (*Body*), Abigail M. Walch (*Mind*)

Beauty and Fashion Editor: Colleen Sullivan

Editorial Coordinator: Christine O'Connell

Associate Editors: Alisa Blackwell (*Food/Nutrition*), Su Reid-St. John (*Fitness*), M.A. Woodbury (*Mind*), Leah Wyar (*Beauty/Fashion*)

Assistant Editors: Eric Steinmehl (*Body*), Amanda Storey, Karina Timmel (*Beauty/Fashion*)

Photography Director: Denise Sfraga

Associate Art Director: Kevin de Miranda

Graphic Designers: Christen Colvert, Jenn McManus

Photo Editors: Jeanne Dozier Clayton, Angie Wilson Kelly

Copy Chief: John R. Halphen

Copy Editors: Tanya M. Hines-Wright, Courtney Roush

Research Editors: Joseph O. Boone, Gregory Cosby

Contributing Copy Editor: Lady Vowell Smith

Contributing Researchers: Shana Aborn, Walter E. Dunnavent, Aimee Lichtman, Martha Yeilding Scribner, Holly Ensor Smith, Bernadette Sukley

Production Manager: Faustina S. Williams

Production Assistant: Laine Williams

Health.com Editor: Laurie Herr

Office Manager: Stephanie Wolford

Editorial Interns: Carly Cardellino, Rebecca Lanthorne, Paulette Perhach, Ginny Temple

OXMOOR HOUSE, INC.

Editor-in-Chief: Nancy Fitzpatrick Wyatt

Art Director: Cynthia R. Cooper

Copy Chief: Allison Long Lowery

Editor: Suzanne Powell

Copy Editor: L. Amanda Owens

Senior Writer: Patricia Wilens

Editorial Assistant: Terri Laschober

Senior Designer: Emily Albright Parrish

Publishing Systems Administrator: Rick Tucker

Director of Production: Phillip Lee

Production Manager: Theresa L. Beste

Production Assistant: Faye Porter Bonner

Contributors

Indexer: Sandy Charles

Editorial Interns: Leighton Batte, Jessica Lynn Dorsey

Contents at a Glance

Table of Contents

Discover how alternative medicine could affect your child (page 44).

Turning 40 isn't what it used to be. Learn why (page 138).

Say goodbye to your usual burger. Get the
most out of your meat (page 196).

V. Fitness: The Best Exercises for a Healthy Body

VI. Healthy Looks: Secrets to Looking and Feeling Your Best

Female friends are a valuable part of a woman's life. Here's how to find more of them (page 324).

VII. Relationships: The Keys to Success for Love, Family, and Friendship

VIII. Mind & Spirit: How to Release Stress and Enhance Emotional Well-Being

Editors' Picks

Take a peek at some of our favorite articles appearing in this year's edition of *Women's* Health *& Wellness*.

THE YEAR'S TOP 10 MEDICAL BREAKTHROUGHS

A healthier future can be yours. Find out the latest scientific discoveries that are most likely to make it happen.

Modern medicine is making a huge impact on how you live your life. From vaccines against cancer to healthier meals at McDonald's, learn about all of the fascinating changes that lie ahead (page 12).

JEAN'S JOURNEY WITH CANCER

We all know life doesn't last forever—we just act as if it does. Discover what one woman gains by no longer pretending.

For most people the phrase "take it one day at a time," is helpful advice. For Jean Miller, it's a way of life. She savors every moment as she battles ovarian cancer. Her story will touch your heart and may even give you a new perspective on your own life (page 120).

ENERGY FOOD: WHAT YOUR BODY COULD BE MISSING

Banish blood-sugar highs and lows. Learn the right way to welcome carbohydrates back into your diet.

A lack of energy affects many Americans, and they don't realize how easy it is to get a boost. The candy bar in the snack machine may seem like the perfect quick fix, but there is a smarter, healthier way to get the lift you need without crashing later (page 150).

THE <u>5 BEST BODY-SHAPING MOVES</u>
Say good-bye to workout angst. These exercises are sure to shape you up!

With all of the exercise trends around today, it's hard to know what *really* works. It turns out that some of the basics are the best. Here's how you can crunch and lunge your way to a better body (page 267).

YOUR PERSONAL <u>ANTISTRESS STRATEGY</u>
Learn to cope, using a plan tailored to your personality type.

How you handle stress depends on your personal characteristics. For example, if you're the "take charge" type you may get especially upset when dealing with chaotic situations. Discover which personality profile best describes you, and then take advice from our experts on the best ways to handle your daily stress (page 350).

EXTREME <u>MAKEUNDER</u>
There's nothing radical about the new less-is-more beauty philosophy—except for the results.

It doesn't take much to make the most of your beauty routine. Just look at our five candidates  after their make*under*. With the help of makeup artist, Bobbi Brown, these women learned how to bring out their best features without overdoing it (page 298).

Editor's Note

How healthy are you? That can be a loaded question—its answer sometimes equally loaded with rationalizations. But the bottom line is that everyone can be healthier than they are today. And that's why we've compiled *Women's* Health *& Wellness 2005*, to help you along the road to enjoying better health. The fourth in the series, this book provides exciting and informative updates about nutrition, exercise, and medicine. It also offers realistic approaches to the day-to-day stresses most women face.

Here, you'll find expert advice to help you live your life to the fullest. From comprehensive reports on medical breakthroughs to entertaining stories about family life, we've covered all the topics most important to you and packed a year's worth of knowledge into this one volume. We've made it easy to access the health information you want by organizing everything into eight chapters: Breakthroughs in Women's Health, Everyday Wellness, Female Body, Nutrition, Fitness, Healthy Looks, Relationships, and Mind & Spirit.

You'll learn which foods are most likely to help you age gracefully (page 146), as well as how you can build a better memory (page 97). Or you can keep up with the latest advances in ovarian cancer (page 116). You'll also find articles to help you enjoy your everyday life, such as "Wanted: More Female Friends" (page 324) and "Take the Fear Out of Fitness" (page 226). So whether you're looking for tips about using supplements (page 36) or ideas for quick workout routines (page 260), you can trust this book to deliver the latest news and the smartest advice concerning just about anything to do with your well-being.

I hope you enjoy this 2005 edition of *Women's* Health *& Wellness* and that it helps you enjoy a happier, healthier life.

Best regards,

Doug Crichton
Health Editor-in-Chief / Vice President

chapter 1

breakthroughs

in women's health

**the latest advances in medical
and alternative care**

The Year's
Top 10 Medical Breakthroughs

A healthier future can be yours. Here are the latest scientific discoveries most likely to make that happen.

BY BOB HOLMES

It sometimes seems that breakthroughs are a dime a dozen. Week after week, medical journals are full of important studies. Month after month, researchers present their latest results at scientific meetings. Day after day, reporters describe those findings in the media. But which discoveries really matter? We consulted experts at major research institutions to come up with this list of the year's developments that have the potential to make the biggest difference in your life and the lives of those you love.

1 A HEART THAT HEALS ITSELF
Stem cells offer the hope of regrowth to protect heart-attack victims from deadly damage.

If you have a heart attack tomorrow, you'll probably pull through, thanks to modern therapies. But then what? Most people don't realize that the real danger period is the months *after* a heart attack, when the undamaged part of the organ tries to compensate for the muscle tissue that died. The added stress often starves healthy cells of oxygen, leading to further deterioration. Eventually, your damaged heart may no longer be able to pump properly. This—not the heart attack itself—is now the leading cause of death after a coronary.

But in 2003 doctors got their first real glimpse of a way to prevent this cascade of disaster. The secret? An injection of bone-marrow extract into the part of the heart bordering the dead zone. This marrow contains stem cells, the body's raw material; they are able to develop as needed into many bodily structures, including blood vessels and heart muscle. The idea is that injected stem cells might transform into heart tissue, rebuilding the blood supply and averting further damage.

In a test in 2003, doctors infused bone-marrow extract into the hearts of 14 Brazilian patients with severe cardiac failure. Four months later, the subjects' hearts were beating almost 50-percent better and had better blood flow to damaged regions than the hearts of comparable patients who had not received the bone marrow. "Some patients who had been limited before—could not work, could not walk—were significantly better," says James Willerson, M.D., chief of cardiology at Texas Heart Institute and one of the leaders of the research team. "Some of them were able to resume doing things that they hadn't been able to do for a long time."

Government approval for general use is still several years off. But if all goes well in more extensive tests of the therapy in the United States, the technique could become frontline therapy for heart-attack patients—and postcoronary heart failure could become much less of a worry.

DISARMING A KILLER
A new drug starves deadly tumors and keeps them from spreading.

Earl Woodard was sailing through life. He had a great job as a pilot for US Airways, a happy marriage, and a 5-year-old son. But one day, Woodard (then 51) went to the doctor for a minor leg problem—and discovered that he had advanced colon cancer, with a baseball-sized tumor and signs that the disease had spread to other parts of his body. Woodard could read the death sentence in the look on his doctor's face.

A new kind of cancer drug may turn the disease into one you can live with for a long, long time.

Normally, Woodard could have expected to live only another 15 months or so. But he got lucky. His oncologist referred him to nearby Duke University for a clinical trial of a new anticancer drug called Avastin. Today—three years later—Woodard is still alive. And for more than a year, his doctors haven't been able to find any trace of his cancer.

Only a few of the nine hundred–odd patients in the trial have done as well as Woodard, but the numbers are impressive nevertheless. The patients

were randomly assigned to receive the usual regimen of chemotherapy plus either a dummy drug or Avastin, a so-called angiogenesis inhibitor. That term means the medication prevents the growth of the new blood vessels a tumor needs to thrive and spread. Most of the patients in the study have died, but those who took Avastin lived about a third longer than those taking a placebo; the drug added almost five months to survival time.

There have been promising results with angiogenesis inhibitors in animals before now. But when Herbert Hurwitz, M.D., the Duke oncologist who led the study, presented his findings to cancer researchers in summer 2003, it was the first clear proof that the drugs can make a difference. Hurwitz's results set everyone abuzz, recalls Judah Folkman, M.D., of Children's Hospital Boston. "It was pretty stunning," says Folkman, who is widely seen as the father of anti-angiogenesis research.

Preliminary studies suggest that Avastin can also slow the progression of prostate and kidney cancers. At least 30 angiogenesis inhibitors are being tested; the drugs are unlikely to cure most people with aggressive cancer, but they may someday turn the disease into one that people can live with for a long time.

As for Woodard, he celebrated his 20th wedding anniversary in summer 2003, and he's busy getting on with life. His son is now 8½, he says, "and this evening we went outside and played a little baseball. That's wonderful to be able to do."

BYPASS WITH A BEAT
Now, doctors can stitch up a beating heart—and prevent damage to the brain.

Surgeon Jeffrey D. Lee, M.D., will never forget a patient he treated five years ago. The man was just 50, but the arteries that supplied blood to his heart were so badly clogged that he needed a coronary-bypass operation. The cutting and stitching went flawlessly, but despite the best efforts of his surgical team, tragedy struck. "He had a massive stroke and never woke up," says Lee, of the University of Hawaii School of Medicine. The death of such a young patient hit the surgeon hard. "It really shook me," he says. "It's no use doing a beautiful bypass if they don't wake up."

That patient's death spurred Lee to try an experimental new bypass technique. In 2003, Lee and others proved that the new approach dramatically reduces the risk of strokes in high-risk patients.

In most cardiac bypasses, a heart-lung machine circulates the patient's blood while the heart is stopped for surgery. But attaching the machine to the patient's aorta can dislodge debris, which can cause a stroke if it travels to the brain. Stroke occurs in up to 10 percent of bypass patients at the highest risk for the problem: older patients who have high blood pressure or who've had prior strokes, together with other risk factors. But as Lee's aforementioned patient showed, youth doesn't guarantee protection. Even bypass patients who escape full-blown strokes often suffer less-obvious damage; nearly half experience some decline in their mental abilities in the years after the surgery.

That's why Lee and others have begun doing bypass operations while the patient's heart is beating, using a special clamp to hold part of the heart still while they cut and sew. In 2003, this "off-pump" surgery proved its worth. In a study of 30 on-pump and 30 off-pump patients, Lee showed that the new procedure reduces the amount of debris lodging in the brain by 97 percent and keeps blood flowing to the brain better. That's probably the reason for the striking results that came a few months later: Another group of researchers reported that off-pump surgery halves the chance of stroke in high-risk patients. Lee suspects that going off-pump may cut the risk of subtler damage as well.

As you'd expect, operating on a beating heart is trickier than using the conventional method, and no one knows yet whether bypasses done this way will hold up as well 10 or 20 years down the road.

But a third study out in 2003 found no difference in failure rates within the first year.

Certainly Lee is convinced of the benefits. "Many patients, I feel, are living now because of off-pump surgery," he says.

DIABETES: HITTING THE RIGHT NUMBERS
Watching your blood pressure may be the most important thing you can do.

For a person with diabetes, what's the most important thing to keep an eye on? Blood sugar, right?

Wrong. If you're one of the 16 million Americans with Type 2 diabetes (the kind that tends to strike in adulthood), the right answer is blood pressure.

For years, doctors have focused on keeping blood sugar steady in their diabetes patients to avoid such complications as blindness and kidney damage. But a recent study in Britain showed that stabilizing blood sugar doesn't help prevent heart disease, the biggest killer of people with diabetes. What *does* help is keeping blood pressure low.

There's a new message in diabetes control: Blood sugar counts, but blood pressure counts more.

New guidelines issued in April 2003 by the American College of Physicians say people with diabetes should aim for a blood pressure of 135/80 or below, several points lower than the target for nondiabetics. Even a 4-point rise in the bottom number can double the risk of heart disease for someone with diabetes. That's big, according to Sandeep Vijan, M.D., a co-author of the guidelines and a diabetes researcher at Veterans Affairs Health Services Research and Development in Ann Arbor, Michigan. "It's so enormous that we think people should be focusing on this as the major thing they think about in diabetes," he says.

Vijan and other experts have known for a few years that blood pressure is an important part of diabetes treatment, but the message hadn't been getting out. A recent survey of 35 medical-review articles about diabetes—the kinds of articles that family physicians read to keep up with the latest research—found that less than half considered blood-pressure control important. More than two-thirds of people who have diabetes don't even realize that they run an increased risk of heart disease, according to a recent survey by the American Diabetes Association (ADA).

"People weren't paying enough attention to this—both patients and physicians," says ADA president Eugene Barrett, M.D., Ph.D. With the new guidelines, doctors are saying it's time for that to change.

DAMAGE CONTROL FOR MS
A new drug targets the inflammation that destroys nerves.

You could say Stacey Hughes is one of the lucky ones. Though she'd had multiple sclerosis (MS) for five years, the disease was more annoying than debilitating. "Mostly just tingling and numbness," she recalls. "And vertigo. I'd have to hang onto things walking down the hall." Still, when her doctor mentioned an experimental medicine, Hughes wanted in.

The Plano, Texas, resident became one of 213 patients who received injections of either a new drug, Antegren, or a placebo every month for half a year. Hughes immediately suspected she was getting the real thing. The annoying tingling faded, as did her other symptoms. "I felt so much better," she says.

The results of the study, reported in early 2003, bear Hughes out. MS usually progresses in fits and starts, with good times interrupted by periods of worsening. During relapses, inflammation strips the insulation from nerve cells, leaving lesions in the brain and spinal cord that interfere with the patient's ability to control muscle movements. Those who took Antegren suffered half as many relapses, developed one-tenth as many new brain

Changing Lives Now
For some people, cutting-edge research means a richer life today.

In medicine, gains are often incremental: a bit less pain here, a little more oomph against disease there. But for Earl Woodard, 55, of Carthage, North Carolina, an experimental

Earl Woodard

drug called Avastin made all the difference in the world—the difference between an early death from colon cancer and the life he's now enjoying with his wife and son.

For Stacey Hughes, 40, of Plano, Texas, a medication called Antegren cleared up the numbness caused by her multiple sclerosis and allowed her to walk without stumbling or hanging onto a wall for support.

Stacey Hughes

Sara Davis

And although Sara Davis, 77, of Los Angeles, California, has never had high cholesterol, drugs to lower her levels are cutting her risk of death from heart disease.

lesions, and generally felt better than those who got the placebo; they also reported few side effects. Indeed, Antegren appears to work considerably better and faster than the therapies now in use, which reduce relapses by about a third. (Current drugs have so many side effects that many patients, like all of those in the study, choose not to take them.)

Antegren blocks a key molecule that white blood cells use to leave the bloodstream and cause the nerve-damaging inflammation. The same approach could work against other inflammatory diseases, such as rheumatoid arthritis and inflammatory bowel disease, says William Sheremata, M.D., director of the MS center at the University of Miami and one of the leaders of the trial. (Antegren helped people with Crohn's disease shake some of their diarrhea, pain, and fatigue in another clinical trial whose results were released at the same time.) "The principle has great promise," says Ulrich von Andrian, M.D., Ph.D., an immunologist at Harvard Medical School.

Before Antegren receives government approval, researchers need to confirm its power in larger, longer studies. But Hughes, now age 40, has already made her judgment: She wants to resume treatment. "Now I'm just impatient," she says.

A VACCINE AGAINST CANCER
The best way to prevent cervical cancer is to block the virus that causes it.

The Pap test is one of medicine's great success stories. Since screening became widespread in the 1950s, the death rate from cervical cancer has dropped to a quarter of what it once was. Even so, the disease still strikes nearly thirteen thousand American women each year. But perhaps not for much longer.

In 2003, Laura Koutsky, Ph.D., an epidemiologist at the University of Washington, and her colleagues announced remarkable success with an experimental vaccine against a sexually transmitted virus known as HPV-16—the human papillomavirus that is the leading cause of cervical cancer. Koutsky's team gave

either the vaccine or a placebo to over two thousand young women and then followed them for 17 months. Not one of the vaccinated women contracted an HPV-16 infection, while the unvaccinated ones were infected at a rate of about 4 percent per year.

"I'm excited about this," says Doug Lowy, M.D., a virologist at the National Cancer Institute. "But we have to temper our excitement with a good deal of caution." While HPV-16 is to blame in half of all cervical cancers, he points out, other viruses in the same family cause the rest. Drug companies are in the final phase of testing compound vaccines that cover both HPV-16 and HPV-18, which together account for about 70 percent of cervical cancers, but even that leaves a dozen or so bit players.

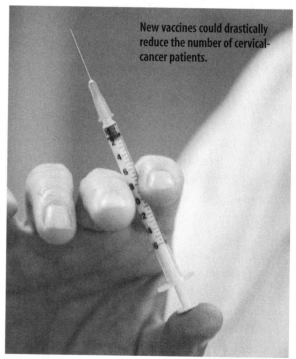

New vaccines could drastically reduce the number of cervical-cancer patients.

The HPV-16 vaccine won't hit clinics for several years. When it does, the first recipients are likely to be adolescents, the group just entering the highest risk period for HPV transmission. So in the short term, most women won't be able to escape the inconvenience of regular Pap tests. In the long run, those tests will become less crucial, as the vaccine wards off one of the major causes of cervical cancer.

A REALLY HAPPY MEAL
Chicken raised without antibiotic growth enhancers can make drugs work better for everyone.

Chicken McNuggets don't often make good news in medical circles, but they did in 2003. The occasion? McDonald's announced it was phasing out the routine use of antibiotics as growth enhancers in some of the animals that wind up as meals in its fast-food empire. That could help slow or reverse the increase in antibiotic resistance in bacteria, which has already rendered many of the crucial drugs useless against certain diseases in people.

Doctors who overprescribe antibiotics—and the patients who demand them even when they're not needed—are part of the problem. Even more at fault is the beef and poultry industry, which laces animal feed with these chemicals to speed growth and fend off diseases that would otherwise flash through crowded henhouses and feedlots. So when McDonald's pledged to stop buying meat from suppliers that use antibiotics as growth promoters by the end of 2004, advocacy groups cheered.

"I've been working in this area for over 30 years, and a move by a company like McDonald's makes a big statement," says Stuart Levy, M.D., a microbiologist at Tufts University, who heads the Alliance for the Prudent Use of Antibiotics. The nonprofit group gave McDonald's its Annual Leadership Award in fall 2003.

> Advocacy groups cheered when McDonald's pledged to stop buying meat from suppliers that use antibiotics as growth promoters by the end of 2004.

The new policy is only a first step, though. While it bans the use of antibiotics to promote growth, it still allows veterinarians to prescribe the drugs for healthy animals that are at risk of becoming ill.

Because of this loophole, antibiotic use will likely drop by only about 10 or 15 percent. Furthermore, the policy applies only to producers who sell exclusively to McDonald's. That means it will cover most chicken, but no beef or pork. There's also the question of whether the company will follow through on its promise. In 2002, McDonald's announced to great fanfare that it would cut back on unhealthy trans fatty acids in cooking its French fries, only to quietly backtrack in spring 2003.

But Levy hopes this time will be different. "I think they're serious about it," he says. Lobbying groups will keep an eye on the company's actions, he says. After that, it will be up to consumer pressure to hold McDonald's to its word.

DIALYSIS GETS LESS RISKY
For people who need this lifesaver, a new drug helps fix a deadly flaw.

Dialysis can be a boon to people with kidney failure, but it doesn't guarantee survival—almost a quarter of patients who receive the treatment die each year. But kidney patients recently got good news: A new drug cuts the risk of death by more than 40 percent.

It's not the kidneys that get most dialysis patients. "Heart disease is by far the major cause of death," according to Brian Pereira, M.D., a kidney specialist at New England Medical Center and president of the National Kidney Foundation. That's because kidney failure jacks up blood levels of a host of cardiac risk factors.

One of the most significant dangers comes from high levels of phosphorus, a mineral common in many foods, which dialysis does a poor job of removing from the bloodstream. Excessive amounts of phosphorus increase the likelihood of mineral deposits in blood vessels, which leads to heart disease. Today, kidney patients can choose between two drugs to pull phosphorus from the bloodstream. One is calcium, which can cause mineral deposits itself when used for this purpose. A drug called sevelamer (Renagel) has fewer side effects but is so expensive that most patients don't use it.

A new kid on the block—a simple compound called lanthanum carbonate—is looking great. The drug has not yet been approved for general use in the United States, but in an early analysis of a two-year study led by William Finn, M.D., a nephrologist at the University of North Carolina, patients on lanthanum were 43-percent less likely to die than patients on other phosphate binders. Deaths from heart disease showed the greatest drop. That's a welcome change for kidney patients with plenty of other things to worry about.

STROKE: THE GENDER GAP
A new recognition of women's symptoms can speed help and save lives.

Despite its reputation as a man's disease, stroke kills many more women than men. And every minute counts when you're having a stroke. So the discovery in 2003 that women are less likely than men to show textbook symptoms could save many lives.

Lewis Morgenstern, M.D., director of the stroke program at the University of Michigan Medical School, and his colleagues reviewed the charts of 467 men and 658 women hospitalized with strokes to see what they had complained of when they came to the emergency room. Men, they found, tended to describe classic symptoms, such as imbalance or one-sided weakness. Women were more likely to report vague symptoms, such as pain and a generalized sense of debility, symptoms that don't automatically make doctors think "stroke." The differences aren't huge—28 percent of women and 19 percent of men reported atypical symptoms. But with 600,000 Americans annually suffering strokes, even little differences add up to a lot of misery.

Obviously, most pain and malaise have nothing to do with stroke. But Morgenstern thinks that when a

woman who is having one notices those sensations, she probably has the familiar symptoms, too. It's just that women may be less likely to pay attention to them, unlike men, who may be more attuned to the strength and balance of their bodies, he says.

More women than men actually die of strokes; one reason is the common misdiagnosis of strokelike symptoms in female patients.

Morgenstern suggests that when a woman suddenly feels ill, stroke should be one possibility that crosses her mind. Then she should ask herself whether she has any of the well-known symptoms of stroke as well—and call 911 if the answer is yes.

A STATIN A DAY?
Cholesterol drugs may lengthen your life even if your numbers already look good.

When Sara Davis's physician prescribed a statin to help treat her heart disease, she was surprised. "I do not have high cholesterol," says the 77-year-old Southern California woman. "I never have." But Davis had suffered a small heart attack. Because

Some doctors believe statins can reduce the risk of heart disease for just about anybody who eats a typical Western diet.

of new findings, that was enough to make her doctor pull out his prescription pad.

In recent years, doctors have begun to realize statins aren't just for high cholesterol, explains Robert Bonow, M.D., chief of cardiology at Northwestern University and past president of the American Heart Association. In 2003 came proof that the drugs can reduce your risk of heart attack and stroke not only if you have high cholesterol, but also if you've had a heart attack or stroke, or if you have diabetes or high blood pressure. In one study, more than ten thousand people with low to normal cholesterol levels and high blood pressure controlled by medication were randomly assigned to receive a statin or a dummy pill every day. After a little more than three years, the group taking statins had experienced 36-percent fewer heart attacks and 27-percent fewer strokes—an effect so dramatic

that researchers stopped that part of the study early to give everyone a chance to switch to the statins.

No one knows yet just how many people would benefit from taking one of these drugs daily. "If you ask, many doctors are taking statins even if they don't have any risk factors," says Neil Poulter, head of preventive cardiovascular medicine at Imperial College London and one of the leaders of the blood-pressure study. Indeed, Poulter thinks statins could reduce the risk of heart disease for just about anybody who eats a typical Western diet.

Of course, no drug is perfect. Though statins are among the safest drugs around, they do carry a slight risk of serious side effects, including liver damage, muscle problems, even (very rarely) death. These could tip the balance against statins in people who run little risk of heart disease. And no one should rely on a pill alone to keep his or her heart healthy, Bonow advises. "As important as statins are, they work a lot better in someone who's exercising, losing weight, and eating the right diet," he says. ■

Bob Holmes is a correspondent for New Scientist.

Q + A

New Alzheimer's Drug Offers Big-time Benefits

My mother has Alzheimer's disease, and I've heard about a new medication that sounds promising. What is it, and is it better than what's currently available?

The drug that researchers are currently so excited about is memantine (Namenda), which was approved by the Federal Food and Drug Administration in October 2003 as a treatment

for moderate to severe Alzheimer's. Several recent studies have shown that memantine helps with the ABCs of the disease: activities of daily living, such as eating, dressing, and bathing; behavioral complications; and cognitive decline. The drug seems to work particularly well at controlling problem behaviors, such as wandering off and lashing out, a finding that could

ease some of the stress on caretakers. Only mild side effects, such as headache and dizziness, have been noted so far.

Migraine Update: It's Time to Get to the Heart of the Matter

A simple type of heart surgery may cure the worst kind of headache. Up to half of people who suffer from migraines have a common heart defect—a hole between their two upper chambers known as a patent foramen ovale (PFO). Patching the hole by snaking a catheter through the groin and into the heart to insert a tiny repair device brought noticeable relief to four out of five sufferers in a recent Swiss study involving 200 patients. The results, which support earlier findings, were reported at a European Society of Cardiology meeting.

Experts think PFOs may lead to migraines by allowing some substance, perhaps a tiny blood clot that impairs circulation or a chemical that irritates blood vessels, to reach your brain. Yet you may not know you have a PFO unless a doctor goes looking for it as a possible explanation for stroke. (PFOs are believed to be conduits for clots that travel to the brain and cause stroke.) All the study subjects were victims of stroke or had related symptoms. Because two-thirds had headaches (mostly migraines) as well, researchers wanted to find out whether patients' PFOs were linked to their headaches.

About twenty-eight million Americans suffer from migraines. One-third may have a PFO that contributes to their pain, says study author Bernhard Meier, M.D., chairman of cardiology at the Swiss Cardiovascular Center in Bern, Switzerland. But experts say it's too soon to screen or treat all migraine patients for PFOs. Researchers at Swedish Medical Center's Cardiovascular Research Program in Seattle are hoping to get federal approval for a large clinical trial on the value of closing PFOs.

Say Goodbye to Pills and Hello to Microchips?

Pill popping may soon be a thing of the past. Researchers at the Massachusetts Institute of Technology have developed a tiny implantable microchip that can deliver drugs over weeks or months, even for people who need a combination of drugs every day. What happens to the microchip when the medicine is gone? In testing on rats and mice, the animals simply absorbed the device, while experiencing no side effects. Human trials are expected to begin around 2006.

How This Brain Scan Can Detect a Deadly Disease

Diagnosing Alzheimer's disease is difficult—an autopsy is required for certainty. But new findings from the University of California, Los Angeles, show that positron-emission tomography (PET) scans can help greatly. In the study, 167 people with mild cognitive problems were given PET scans and then followed for an average of three years. Participants whose brain scans showed abnormalities associated with an Alzheimer's-like illness but who were diagnosed as stable were 18 times more likely to suffer worsening mental abilities than those with normal scans.

Why You Could Be Affected by a Recently Discovered Brain Disorder ... and Not Know It

If a middle-aged or older person has tremors and difficulties with balance, a number of explanations are likely to occur to a doctor—Parkinson's disease, for instance. Now it seems that men (and women who want to keep the men in their lives healthy) should keep another possibility in mind. A new study suggests such problems may actually indicate a previously unrecognized brain disorder.

Named fragile X–associated tremor/ataxia syndrome (FXTAS), the illness can cause symptoms in men who are carriers of a genetic defect. (For reasons that are not completely understood, the disorder is much more common among men than women.) The disease is caused by the same gene (FMR1) responsible for fragile X syndrome, the leading cause of inherited mental retardation. In both cases, problems crop up when the gene becomes abnormally large, which happens because part of the DNA repeats itself, much the way *cat* can become *cccaattt* if the buttons on a computer keyboard get stuck. If the gene is bigger than normal but not large enough to cause fragile X, people are said to be carriers. Until recently, that was not thought to cause disease, although some women carriers may experience premature menopause.

But at the University of California, Davis, School of Medicine, developmental pediatrician Randi Hagerman, M.D., began to notice an odd pattern: Many mothers of children who had fragile X disease told her of their own fathers' trouble with balance at relatively young ages. Hagerman alerted her husband, biological chemist Paul Hagerman, M.D., Ph.D., who started a study. Sure enough, carriers of the mutation were 13 times more likely to have arm tremors, poor balance, and difficulty walking than those whose genes were normal.

Because 1 in 813 men is considered a carrier of the mutation, Paul Hagerman suspects that FXTAS may be a common cause of tremor and balance problems in those over age 50. Awareness of FXTAS is key to avoiding misdiagnosis, which can lead to mistreatment, even unnecessary surgery, he says. There's no cure for the ailment, but therapy can help with some of the symptoms. A DNA blood test can determine if someone has FXTAS.

Medical Search at Your Service

You can actually pay someone to scour the Web for the latest remedies. But is it worth it?

BY TIMOTHY GOWER

When Angela Scalpello was diagnosed with a rare form of hepatitis in 2001, her first thought was, "I've got to learn more about this disease." Her second thought was, "How?" The busy human resources executive, then 46, lacked the time and know-how to track down more information. So she hired an Internet search service called The Health Resource (www.thehealthresource.com). For $295, Scalpello received a comprehensive report that included details about novel treatments. Her physician was so impressed that he asked for a copy. "It was totally worth the money," says Scalpello, who lives in New York.

More and more medical-search companies like The Health Resource are popping up on the Internet. What they offer is attractive. With the rapid pace of change in medicine, doctors may not be current on the latest therapies, even for serious conditions. But are the searches worth the $200 to $500 cost? More importantly, can you trust the results?

There's no question that you can get reams of information this way. The Health Resource and Schine On-Line Services (www.findcure.com), for instance, deliver reports that

can run up to 300 pages. They include names of leading doctors who treat the condition, information about the therapies, and lists of clinical studies involving experimental treatments. But neither company offers advice about which therapies are best—and they might not be qualified to do so. For instance, Gary Schine, founder of Schine On-Line, has no medical training. So if you don't feel confident about your ability to make sense of the literature and your physician isn't willing to dig through the data with you, these bulky reports may be overwhelming.

At the other end of the spectrum are services like CanHelp (www.canhelp.com) that issue concise and highly opinionated reports. While that may sound useful, it worries oncologist Jay Brooks, M.D., chairman of hematology and oncology at Ochsner Clinic Foundation in Baton Rouge, Louisiana. "If they're offering advice, they're sort of practicing medicine," he says.

At least one medical-search service, Cancer Advisors (www.canceradvisors.org), does employ physicians to review reports, but the majority of services don't. And be forewarned: Not every so-called doctor has a medical background. The founder of one site, The Moss Reports (www.cancerdecisions.com), identifies himself as "Dr. Moss," but his Ph.D. is in the classics. Moss frequently recommends alternative therapies, which raises another potential concern: Some search services tout remedies that have not been put to the test by reputable researchers; these treatments include ones flagged by the National Institutes of Health as unproven.

So these services can't give you all the answers. Then again, you may not need their help. An M.D. or Ph.D. isn't required to learn about cutting-edge therapies; you just need to know where to look. Much of the information sold by these services is at public-access Web sites operated by the National Library of Medicine (www.nlm.nih.gov) and the National Cancer Institute (www.cancer.gov). If you're clueless about how to get started, CancerGuide (www.cancerguide.org), a site run by cancer survivor Steve Dunn, offers tips for patients who want to conduct their own searches. It's a great tool for people who don't want to become their own doctors—but who do want the best medical care their doctors can give. ■

You don't need an M.D. to learn about cutting-edge therapies—you just need to know where to look for the most reliable information.

Talk to the Virtual M.D.

Here's a novel way to cut down on time spent in the waiting room: Talk to a cyberdoc. Researchers at the University of California, San Francisco (UCSF), recently tested reactions to a "video doctor"—a computerized, personalized message delivered by an actor. The virtual M.D. asked patients about their smoking and drinking habits; patients used the computer keyboard to spill the beans. The software then offered individualized comments based on their answers. Patients were more likely to fess up when interacting with the computer than with a flesh-and-blood doctor, a finding that supports earlier research. Many also said they were ready to change their unhealthy ways.

The UCSF team, led by Barbara Gerbert, Ph.D., plans to develop virtual-doctor videos aimed at educating pregnant women about what drugs, alcohol, and smoking do to a growing fetus. We wonder: Is it too much to ask for virtual OB-GYN checkups, too?

The Return of

SHOCK THERAPY

Is it a miracle or a form of abuse?

BY ANNDEE HOCHMAN

Charles H. Kellner, M.D., likes to blame Jack Nicholson for the stigma surrounding electroconvulsive therapy (ECT). After all, it was Nicholson's searing performance as a psychiatric patient in the 1975 film *One Flew Over the Cuckoo's Nest* that gave many people an image of ECT as a brutal, brain-zapping treatment applied to patients against their will.

Kellner, a psychiatrist who ran the ECT service at the Medical University of South Carolina for 18 years and now chairs the department of psychiatry at New Jersey Medical School in Newark, says ECT doesn't deserve its bad rap. He's not the only one who thinks so. After falling out of favor for several decades, the therapy has reemerged as an effective—though still controversial—tool for treating severe depression, mania, and other serious mental disorders.

"When you see patients so depressed they've lost their jobs, they're not eating, not drinking, wasting away, it's a miracle to see them up and ready to go back to work after just two weeks of ECT," says C. Edward Coffey, M.D., chair of psychiatry at Henry Ford Health System in southeastern Michigan.

In the '40s and '50s, ECT was sometimes used not to heal but to control troublesome patients. During treatments, people suffered fierce convulsions, bit their tongues, or even broke their bones. Studies show that the gentler, safer ECT used today, applied only with patient consent and under general anesthesia, offers relief to the most desperately ill patients, including those who have tried medication without success and those who are so ill that they can't wait the six to eight weeks that it typically takes for drugs to work.

"ECT is not like it was 50 years ago," says Sarah H. Lisanby, M.D., associate professor of psychiatry at Columbia University and a depression researcher. "It has been modernized. It is the most effective and rapidly acting treatment we have for severe depression."

According to the American Psychiatric Association, ECT will help lift an acute episode of depression for 80 to 90 percent of people who receive it, compared with a 40- to 50-percent improvement rate for those who take antidepressants. But that success comes at a cost.

During the procedure, electrical pulses are delivered to a patient's brain—enough to make a 100-watt bulb flicker, and enough to set off a seizure in the brain as large fields of neurons fire simultaneously. No one knows exactly why ECT benefits mood. But practitioners and critics alike agree that the therapy can cause headaches and confusion immediately following treatment, as well as memory loss in subsequent days and weeks.

There's still debate over how big a problem those side effects pose. ECT's most vocal critics (in many cases, not psychiatrists) dub it a crime against humanity. A recent review in the *British Medical Journal* fueled the fire when it reported that at least one-third of ECT patients describe persistent memory loss. In the United States, the National Mental Health Association, a nonprofit research and advocacy group, recommends ECT be presented to patients "with extreme caution" as a last resort. The National Council on Disability, an independent federal agency, described ECT in a 2000 report as "unproven and inherently inhumane" and urged its elimination.

> **ECT is not like it was 50 years ago. It has been modernized. It is the most effective and rapidly acting treatment we have for severe depression.**
>
> —Sarah H. Lisanby, M.D.

Medication offers no cure either, ECT supporters point out. By its nature, depression tends to recur, says David Miller, M.D., head of the ECT service at Friends Hospital in Philadelphia. Getting follow-up care after the initial course of shock therapy lessens the likelihood of recurrence, according to the National Institute of Mental Health.

Lisanby and others are currently researching alternatives to ECT—methods involving magnetic stimulation of the brain—in the hope that they will be as effective without impairing memory. In the meantime, there's a growing consensus that, for a certain group of patients, shock therapy's benefits outweigh its risks. "ECT erases a chunk of recent memory," Kellner says. "Some of it comes back, some of it doesn't. But the trade-off is this: Do you want to be suicidally depressed and unable to function? Or do you want to lose some memory in return for becoming healthy again?"

ECT is far from perfect, Miller acknowledges, but it can be an immense aid. "If initially successful and then used for maintenance treatment," he says, "it allows people to get back to being themselves." ∎

Anndee Hochman is the author of Everyday Acts & Small Subversions: Women Reinventing Family, Community and Home.

ECT is far from perfect, but it allows people to get back to a healthy life again.

SHOCKED BACK TO LIFE

I was living in a bleak and wintry world.
Electroconvulsive therapy brought spring back.

BY SUSAN MAHLER

The drugs weren't working. Not that they'd never helped; they had—at times spectacularly—during the six years I'd battled severe depression. Overnight, my world would be transformed from a barrage of persecutory images to a benign landscape rife with possibilities. But, always, my newfound serenity would fade, my thoughts becoming increasingly constricted, self-incriminating, hopeless.

By April 2001, as I was nearing the completion of my psychiatry residency, my doctor was recommending electroconvulsive therapy (ECT). I hesitated. I knew the treatment was not supposed to cause long-term memory problems. But, I thought, what about the unmeasurables? What about creativity, the subtle capacity for self-expression?

Susan Mahler recommends ECT for severe depression, but only when other medications have failed.

I didn't want to emerge from the treatment happier, yet a stranger to myself.

I decided I was in no position to argue.

The ECT clinic at Boston's Beth Israel Medical Center consisted of a series of spare exam rooms, each occupied by a single long steel table and partially obscured by a curtain. As I crossed the threshold, a nurse approached, handing me a frayed white gown and blue pajama bottoms.

An anesthesiologist inserted an intravenous catheter into my arm. Cold gel was slathered over the right side of my head; adhesive pads were slapped onto the skin.

I awoke with a searing pain on that side of my head. I reached for my clothes—or rather the clothes I presumed to be mine, though I barely recognized them. Likewise, the image

of my friend Yvette standing in the doorway evoked the memory of her name, but not who she was; our history together was obscured. We drove home along the Charles River. Though I had made this drive only hours earlier, it seemed that in the interim, spring had suddenly ensued. How could I have failed to notice the magnolias, the apple blossoms? I rolled down the window and breathed in warmth, possibility.

The next treatment was scheduled for Wednesday. Again the shutter-click, the instant displaced reawareness. This time, I awoke in tears. A spasm of sadness washed through me, shattering for its utter lack of context. I could not remember my life, my identity. I returned home to find rooms that I did not recognize, strange toiletries in the bathroom, unfamiliar foods in the fridge.

I completed three ECT sessions that spring. By the third, I had emerged from despondency. I could go to work;

conversation did not seem an overwhelming effort. Suddenly I could enjoy dressing, the lightness of spring cotton on my arms and legs. And then there were other pleasures: a joke in the staff room, the taste of orange juice, a meaningful exchange with a patient, the heady smell of hyacinth on my back porch. A million tiny satisfactions heretofore denied me.

But quirks of memory and attention lingered. I could not account for the activities of several days, and I made uncharacteristic mistakes in writing. I had trouble with vocabulary; it was not as though I'd forgotten words, rather that they were hidden by some dense fog.

These days, I do recommend ECT to my patients when medications have failed them. But I do not recommend it lightly. I tell them this can help, maybe quickly, maybe dramatically. I warn them about short-term memory problems and the possibility for subtler cognitive changes. And if they are worried, I reassure them: You will still be yourself.

Susan Mahler is a psychiatrist and writer in the Boston area.

MRIs: The Latest Mood Medicine?

Sometimes, new treatments pop up when researchers aren't looking. Scientists at McLean Hospital in Belmont, Massachusetts, recently stumbled upon the finding that a new form of magnetic resonance imaging (MRI) seems to help lift the moods of some depressed folks.

The serendipitous discovery occurred when the researchers were investigating medications in a group of people with bipolar disorder. The studies used a type of MRI scan that picked up chemical changes in their brains after treatment with the drugs, and the researchers noticed that after the patients underwent the scan, many reported mood improvements.

So Michael Rohan, an imaging physicist at McLean, and his colleagues began another study to put their finding to the test. The bet paid off: Mood boosts were reported by 77 percent of the 30 bipolar patients who underwent the scan. Of the 11 patients not on medication, all improved.

This treatment is still in the early stages of research, years away from clinical use if all goes well. But this is not the first time electromagnetic fields have been used to treat depression, Rohan says. Researchers have also had success with a technique called repetitive transcranial magnetic stimulation (rTMS), but its electric fields are quite strong; they not only can cause discomfort, but also can carry a slight risk of seizures. The field produced by the rTMS is 500 times stronger than that of the MRI used in the McLean study.

Rohan's MRI differs in significant ways from the kind used to make diagnostic pictures. The timing of the electromagnetic pulses may be crucial, Rohan says. He suspects those pulses may affect the firing of nerve impulses in the brain, and that, he speculates, may somehow raise a person's mood.

Fight Your Phobias with Virtual Reality

Does the sight of a spider make your flesh crawl? Or the thought of a plane flight send you into a tailspin? Standard treatment for common phobias is exposure to the panic provoker in the company of a therapist—effective, but time-consuming and expensive. Now, researchers at the University of Quebec in Outaouais have turned three popular home-computer games (Half-Life, Max Payne, and Unreal Tournament) into treatment tools. If you buy one of the games, you can download therapeutic adaptations at www.uqo.ca/cyberpsy—but you'll also need a head-mounted display unit. If you don't want to shell out the bucks, you can find a virtual reality–savvy therapist in your area at www.virtuallybetter.com.

27

How an Alternative Treatment

IBS

for

Is Changing Lives

New research shows that undergoing hypnotherapy is an effective way to help people with irritable bowel syndrome.

BY ALICE LESCH KELLY

Court reporters have little flexibility when it comes to taking work breaks. If they need to use the restroom, they wait until the judge declares a recess. But Barbara Andersen, a court reporter who lives on the West Coast, couldn't always wait. When she got the urge one day in 1991, Andersen had no choice but to tell the judge she had to go. "He had the jury and everyone in the courtroom waiting for me to come back from the bathroom," Andersen remembers. She was mortified. Yet the reason Andersen excused herself was infinitely more painful.

For more than a decade, Andersen, 62, has suffered from irritable bowel syndrome (IBS), a maddeningly common disorder that afflicts people of all ages. Nearly forty-five million Americans, or almost 20 percent of the population, have it. Women get it more than men, although the reason isn't clear. Sufferers live with debilitating diarrhea, constipation, cramping, and, very often, severe pain. There's no cure, no obvious cause, and no simple treatment.

Fortunately, there is hope. An alternative remedy—hypnosis—is proving to be especially effective for a growing number of people, and it's working wonders for Andersen.

Fed up with ineffective medications, she began listening to hypnotherapy audiotapes three years ago. The tapes were made available to IBS sufferers as part of a University of North Carolina study. Andersen had never been hypnotized, but after just a few weeks, she noticed she was having fewer accidents and feeling less like she had to go all the time. About three months into her treatment, something happened that was—for her—amazing: She had an experience in the bathroom most people take for granted. Now, Andersen thinks she's about 80-percent better. "Most of the time I have normal days," she says.

It's easy to understand why people with IBS might try hypnotherapy—or just about anything. The symptoms are awful and can have a huge impact on their quality of life. Sufferers are known to miss work nearly twice as often as people without IBS, and they often avoid travel, social events, and sex. Andersen even missed part of her daughter's wedding. Plus, no one treatment seems to work for everyone—or for very long.

British researchers pioneered hypnotherapy as a treatment for IBS in the '80s. In small studies, Peter J. Whorwell, M.D., and a team of researchers at the University Hospital of South Manchester showed that hypnosis significantly reduced symptoms and the need for medication. Today, the guidelines of the British Society of Gastroenterology say hypnotherapy, although time-consuming, is effective for severe cases of IBS that seem resistant to other treatments.

Hypnotherapy has been slow to catch on in the United States, perhaps because Americans' general view of it has been shaped largely by stage hypnotists who, at the snap of a finger, may have audience members involuntarily quacking like ducks. A 2003 review of alternative IBS treatments published in the *Archives of Internal Medicine* did find that patients showed significant improvement during hypnotherapy trials. But the authors noted that the studies were highly subject to bias. Similarly, after reviewing virtually all research on IBS, a task force of the American College of Gastroenterology found in 2003 that hypnotherapy and other behavior-based remedies did help reduce individual symptoms. But the panel criticized the studies for being poorly designed.

Still, the latest research is convincing. In 2003, nearly all of the first 250 patients treated for IBS at a British hypnotherapy clinic saw improvement in pain severity, pain frequency, bloating, bowel habits, and quality of life. (The only people not helped, for reasons that aren't clear, were men with diarrhea.) The study, run by Whorwell, was published in *The American Journal of Gastroenterology*.

A recent longer term study, co-authored by Whorwell and published in the journal *Gut*, showed that the benefits of hypnotherapy appear to last at least five years.

The treatment isn't a quick fix: Patients attend 12 sessions over a three-month period at Whorwell's clinic. Therapists use relaxation techniques to induce a hypnotic state and then offer suggestions about how to slow down the movement of waste through the colon, for example. Between sessions, subjects in Whorwell's study also listened to tapes like the ones that helped Andersen.

Researchers aren't sure why hypnotherapy has an impact, but it could be that the treatment taps into brain-gut connections. Your upstairs and downstairs plumbing are linked by huge networks of nerves, neurotransmitters, and hormones. They send signals back and forth constantly. "In a person with IBS," says Arnold Wald, M.D., professor of medicine at the University of Pittsburgh Medical Center and a researcher on IBS drug studies, "those signals may be magnified or processed differently." A psychological therapy such as hypnosis, which tends to reduce stress and lower anxiety and depression, may alter these signals in a beneficial way.

Experts say hypnotherapy may be helpful for more than 70 percent of people who are afflicted with IBS.

It's possible that the treatment has an effect on serotonin levels in the body. Despite the fact that this chemical is commonly associated with the brain and mood, 95 percent of the body's serotonin is actually in the bowel. Studies suggest that in IBS sufferers, serotonin receptors in the intestines malfunction, interfering with the chemical's ability to speed up or slow down colon contractions. This can result in diarrhea or constipation—or both. The link between serotonin and IBS may also explain why antidepressant drugs known as SSRIs, or selective serotonin-reuptake inhibitors (such as Prozac), help some people with the condition.

Can hypnotherapy aid only certain kinds of people? Not necessarily. Olafur S. Palsson, Psy.D., a licensed clinical psychologist and associate professor in the Division of Digestive Diseases and Nutrition at the University of North Carolina at Chapel Hill School of Medicine, says it can bring relief to more than 70 percent of those with IBS. Palsson and his colleagues have found success with a three-month program modeled after Whorwell's.

If you want to try hypnotherapy, it may take some work to find a practitioner. The treatment is most effective when a therapist has had experience with IBS patients. But just 120 clinicians nationwide are using methods developed in Palsson's clinic. That's one for every 375,000 people with the condition.

Using audiotapes, as Andersen has, may be a smart alternative. They're not available to everyone yet, but Palsson and his colleagues showed in a recent pilot study that more than half of sufferers found them helpful. Andersen is amazed at what the tapes did for her. "I used to feel imprisoned," she says. "IBS pervades your whole life. I still have bad days, but it's nothing like it used to be. I can rebuild my life now." ■

Medications Worth Trying

People with irritable bowel syndrome (IBS) use a variety of medicines to control their symptoms, but there are no cure-alls. So what works well? Scientific evidence favors just a handful of drugs.

THE DRUGS	THE EVIDENCE	THE SIDE EFFECTS
TEGASEROD **Brand name:** Zelnorm **Purpose:** Relief of symptoms in women who have IBS-related constipation. Not approved for use in men because of minimal testing	In four controlled trials, tegaserod performed better than a placebo. It's structurally similar to serotonin, a naturally occurring chemical that affects pain sensitivity and the movement of substances through the intestines, among other functions.	Diarrhea occurred in 9 to 10 percent of people using tegaserod in studies; 1 to 2 percent of subjects stopped using it for this reason.
ALOSETRON **Brand name:** Lotronex **Purpose:** Relief of severe IBS-related diarrhea in women	In five controlled trials, alosetron performed better than a placebo. It slows the movement of waste through the colon and lowers water secretion.	Constipation is not uncommon. Maker pulled it off market after it was linked to a handful of deaths. But after a public outcry, it was brought back in 2002.
LOPERAMIDE **Brand name:** Imodium A-D **Purpose:** Relief of diarrhea and urgency	Most trials involving IBS patients have been small and poorly designed. In general, this drug does control diarrhea and improve stool consistency. But it doesn't touch such IBS symptoms as pain or bloating.	A task force of the American College of Gastroenterology says it doesn't have enough data to comment about side effects.
DICYCLOMINE, HYOSCYAMINE **Brand names:** Bentyl, NuLev **Purpose:** Relief of cramps; meds are known as antispasmodics	One controlled trial showed that dicyclomine worked better than a placebo on IBS symptoms. But in two other controlled studies, antispasmodics proved ineffective.	Constipation and dry mouth. The American Academy of Family Physicians says chronic use may reduce the drugs' effectiveness.
LOW-DOSE ANTIDEPRESSANTS **Brand names:** Adapin, Elavil, Paxil, etc. **Purpose:** Relief of IBS-related abdominal pain	Tricyclic antidepressants, such as Adapin and Elavil, seemed to help IBS patients in several small, flawed trials. Paxil, a selective serotonin-reuptake inhibitor (SSRI), appeared to help in a recent uncontrolled trial in the United Kingdom. Evidence on SSRIs is minimal.	Tricyclics may cause drowsiness and constipation.

How Hypnosis Can Help You Heal

Discover why doctors are using the power of the mind like never before.

BY PETER JARET

When Claire Frederick, M.D., a Harvard psychiatrist, is stuck in a slow lane at the grocery-store checkout counter, she doesn't get irritated. She gets relaxed. Very relaxed. Calming and focusing her mind, she slips into a brief trance and concentrates on a knee she injured while skiing. "Lately I've been using hypnosis to ease the pain and encourage healing," Frederick says.

Preposterous? A few years ago, most doctors thought so. Now, even many doubters are convinced that hypnosis is powerful medicine. "I was one of the skeptics," says Frederick, immediate past editor of the *American Journal of Clinical Hypnosis*, "until I began to see first-hand what hypnosis could do. Now I'm on something of a crusade."

When most people think of hypnosis, they picture a mysterious figure swinging a pocket watch and repeating, "You're getting very sleepy." In fact, hypnosis is somewhat of a mystery. Solid science is showing it can improve your health in surprising ways: It's powerful enough to help relieve the often-excruciating pain associated with serious burns, for instance, and it can make breathing easier for people with respiratory illnesses.

The most astonishing evidence comes from research on healing. In a pilot study published in 1999, Harvard University psychologist Carol Ginandes, Ph.D., showed that hypnosis can help broken bones heal faster. In a follow-up experiment published in 2003, Ginandes and her research team found that women who'd had breast-reduction surgery recovered more quickly after undergoing hypnosis. During the sessions, the women were encouraged to think of pain as "sensations of healing" and to

> We're not just talking about people feeling better. We're talking about structural tissue healing.
>
> —Carol Ginandes, Ph.D.

visualize their incisions "knitting together rapidly and becoming strong, smooth, and elastic." An independent team of surgeons and nurses later examined the women and reviewed photographs of their incisions taken one week and seven weeks after surgery. The group's judgment: Patients who had received hypnosis were farther along the road to recovery. "We're not just talking about people feeling better," Ginandes explains. "We're talking about structural tissue healing. Hypnosis, our results suggest, can influence the body to heal itself."

No one understands how—yet. Some researchers speculate that hypnosis alters levels of brain chemicals that influence the nervous system, hormone production, and the immune system. Hypnosis may even affect how particular genes in cells express themselves, turning certain functions on and others off. Current studies using brain scans and other imaging technologies may begin to piece together an explanation.

Scientists have no shortage of potential test subjects, because almost anyone can be hypnotized. Only about 5 percent of people are not responsive, and roughly the same percentage are exceptionally so. Most score in the middle of a hypnotizability scale developed at Stanford University. Studies show that with practice, people can learn to become more responsive, according to Timothy Carmody, Ph.D., clinical professor of psychiatry at the University of California, San Francisco. Carmody is conducting a study to see if hypnotherapy can help smokers kick the habit.

Hypnosis can't make people do things they don't want to do. It can't turn people into automatons.

But it does make them unusually receptive to suggestions. "A hypnotic trance is really just a form of deep relaxation, which allows people to block out distractions and focus their minds," Carmody says. Patients who suffer from panic attacks, for example, can be encouraged to think of frightening situations in new and less alarming ways. Pain sufferers, meanwhile, can move their perception of pain from the foreground of their minds to the background, explains University of Washington psychologist David Patterson, Ph.D.

Hypnotizing someone is surprisingly simple. "Most people can reach a hypnotic trance simply by staring at a spot on the wall and listening to a soothing voice telling them to relax," explains University of Tennessee psychologist Michael R. Nash, Ph.D., a leading expert. In one widely used approach, subjects visualize themselves walking down a staircase, becoming more relaxed with each step. In another variation, people imagine themselves in a relaxing place: on a beach, say, or at a cabin in the mountains. Taking slow breaths, the subjects fall into a state of deep relaxation.

"To test whether someone has reached a deep trance, we may tell them they're so relaxed and their eyelids are so heavy that they don't want to open them," says psychologist Sally Cernie, Ph.D., a hypnotherapist in Riverside, California. "When they don't, then we know they're in a deep trance." Therapists then offer carefully phrased suggestions to help solve problems or change behaviors.

FIND AN EXPERT

For more information on hypnosis and referrals to qualified practitioners, contact one of the following organizations:

- American Society of Clinical Hypnosis
  630-980-4740 or www.asch.net
- Society for Clinical and Experimental Hypnosis
  617-469-1981 or ijceh.educ.wsu.edu/sceh/scehframe.htm
- Society of Psychological Hypnosis
  202-336-6013 or www.apa.org/divisions/div30

It's true that hypnosis remains a hard sell with many doctors because of the ongoing mystery behind it. "There's still a lot of skepticism out there," Harvard's Frederick admits. Yet as more studies are published offering evidence of the benefits, a growing number of psychologists and physicians are embracing it as a healing tool.

If you're interested in giving hypnosis a try, experts recommend finding a therapist or doctor certified by the American Society of Clinical Hypnosis, which seeks to ensure that practitioners are appropriately trained. Talk to your doctor first if you plan to use the therapy for a medical purpose, such as controlling pain or anxiety. And remember that hypnosis isn't a panacea. People with acute pain who use hypnosis, for example, typically still need medication, just less of it.

Books and audiotapes offering advice on self-hypnosis may work, Carmody says, but no scientific studies have documented their effectiveness.

Self-hypnosis can be used, Frederick says, as a way to relax and reinforce hypnotic suggestions made by a therapist. And once you get the hang of hypnosis—it might take a single session under the guidance of a trained practitioner, or as many as 10—you can do it almost anywhere: during a break at work, between commercials on TV, even when you're stuck in the checkout line. ■

Award-winning writer Peter Jaret is a contributing editor.

Mindful Medicine

Hypnosis appears to have a wide range of benefits. Studies suggest it can ease pain, speed healing, and more. Here are the highlights:

PROBLEM	PROOF
HOT FLASHES	A preliminary study showed that hypnosis significantly reduced the frequency, duration, and severity of hot flashes in menopausal women, Canadian researchers reported in 2003.
PAIN	A 2003 review concluded that hypnosis can be more effective than conventional pain treatments for such conditions as burns and such uncomfortable medical procedures as spinal taps.
SURGICAL SIDE EFFECTS	In 2000, a Harvard University study of 241 patients found that those who underwent hypnosis before surgery required less pain medication, experienced fewer complications, and were discharged from the hospital sooner than patients who went without.
WARTS	Some studies suggest that hypnosis can help make common warts disappear. It may work for as many as 55 percent of patients who undergo the therapy.
WEIGHT LOSS	Dieters who tried hypnosis lost almost twice as much weight as those who didn't, according to a 1996 analysis by University of Connecticut scientists.

Peace Palaces Pledge a Less-Stressed World

Need a refuge from the big, bad world? The Maharishi Mahesh Yogi wants to help. The man who brought Transcendental Meditation (TM) to the West some 50 years ago recently announced plans to open 100 Peace Palaces across the United States. The centers will be urban oases, he says, offering training in TM as well as health programs that use antistress techniques. In addition, the daily practice of meditation by 100 or more experts at each site will further world peace, the Maharishi says. It should be noted, though, that the Peace Palaces opened so far (in Bethesda, Maryland; Lexington, Kentucky; and Fairfield, Iowa) haven't made an obvious dent in global unrest.

New Sleep Aid Promises You Better Z's

For the 40 million Americans dogged by sleeplessness, no one medicine is best—but that may change soon. In a controlled study, researchers at Duke University and other medical hubs recently found that insomniacs who took a new drug called Estorra fell asleep faster, slept longer, and woke up feeling more refreshed. Just as importantly, they kept it up consistently over six months (most sleeping pills tend to become less potent the longer you take them). Also, there was none of the grogginess, dependency, memory and coordination problems, or irritability associated with most sleep aids. The new drug, made by Sepracor, is a modified version of zopiclone, a sleep med available in Europe. The U.S. Food and Drug Administration is expected to OK prescription Estorra in mid-2004.

The Shot That Can Stop You (or Your Hubby!) from Snoring

Is there anything possibly more irritating than snoring? Roughly 45 percent of Americans do it, which means that there are millions of partners being kept awake by it out there. That may explain why more than three hundred so-called cures are currently registered with the U.S. Patent and Trademark Office. But the sheer ubiquity of the problem seems to suggest that no previously touted remedy is winning any popularity contests.

Fortunately for snorers—and their bedmates—that all may change now that injection snoreplasty is widely available. It's a quick, affordable procedure that turns off the snoring "speaker," so to speak.

Snoring occurs when the roof of the mouth in the back of the throat collapses during sleep, which narrows the airway. Tissue in this area flutters and vibrates when a snorer breathes, producing those log-sawing sounds.

In snoreplasty, which takes only about 10 minutes and requires only local anesthesia, a doctor injects plain old alcohol into the tissue. After about a month, the tissue hardens, and that stops the vibrations—and the snoring. Brief swelling is common, and a blister often forms at the injection site. But any discomfort lasts only about three weeks. No serious complications have been reported.

In early trials the procedure helped 92 percent of test subjects to stop snoring, and experts seem to be on board about snoreplasty's effectiveness.

Snoreplasty does have limits, though. For example, it isn't likely to help overweight folks with bulky throat tissues and people with stuffy nasal passages, who together comprise about 20 percent of snorers, says Eric Mair, M.D., an ear, nose, and throat doctor at Wilford Hall Air Force Medical Center in San Antonio and one of snoreplasty's creators. Also, the treatment might hide the symptoms of sleep apnea, a dangerous condition in which breathing actually stops for brief periods during sleep. Therefore, Mair advises snorers to be evaluated before seeking the procedure.

Though most insurers do not cover the procedure, snoreplasty (at about $300) costs much less than other invasive remedies. To find a doctor in your area who performs the procedure, go to www.talkaboutsleep.com/sleepdisorders/Snoring_apnea.htm and scroll to the "Injection Snoreplasty" section.

The Latest Twist on
MASSAGE

Find out why these therapists are actually letting their feet do the rubbing.

BY MICHELE BENDER

I never thought I'd say this, but I want to get walked on. Between sitting at my computer for long periods of time, carrying my 2-year-old daughter, and working out regularly, I've always got a tight, achy back.

That's why I was excited when I heard about Ashiatsu Oriental Bar Therapy, a type of massage that uses feet, not hands, to apply pressure. Experts in the field say that this method allows therapists to get more deeply into the muscles than they can with their hands, so it better relieves stress and tension and improves posture and flexibility.

Still, I was nervous. My first concern: It would hurt. My second: I'd have a stranger's bare feet on my back—what if they were, well, gross? And finally: Was this dangerous? Specifically, would this person crush me?

After undressing completely, I lay facedown on the table. Melissa, my masseuse at Sunpoint Spa in New York, slathered her feet (which, by the way, were in pristine condition) with lotion and sat on a tall stool at the same end of the massage table as my head. She leaned back a bit and then dug her heels into my upper back, generating just the right amount of pressure to untie the knots. Next, she stood on the

This technique isn't for someone who likes a light touch. It's all about serious pressure.

table and, holding onto bars suspended from the ceiling, began massaging my spinal area, lower back, butt, and legs, using her feet to create strokes that pushed and pulled my muscles. (After 5 minutes, I stopped worrying that she would come crashing down on top of me.) It never felt as if there were a pair of feet working on me. In fact, it was by far the best massage I've ever had. For two days afterward, I was sore—a normal result of Ashiatsu therapy—but every inch of me felt more relaxed and flexible.

The technique isn't for someone who likes a light touch: It's all about serious pressure. To be sure it was safe, I checked with an orthopedic surgeon. "If you're healthy, with no back problems, it's probably fine," says Edward Toriello, M.D., a spokesman for the American Academy of Orthopaedic Surgeons. "But for women past menopause, it's important to make sure you don't have osteoporosis or other back problems before you have this done, or you could risk a fracture." Others who shouldn't get walked on include people with heart conditions, those with high blood pressure, and pregnant women (go figure). Of course, you shouldn't let just anyone slip-slide along your spine; find a certified therapist at www.deepfeet.com. ∎

Get Smart About
Supplements

Keep yourself and your family healthy by staying informed about alternative medicine. Here's the lowdown on 15 popular all-natural remedies.

BY MICHAEL CASTLEMAN

Alternative medicine has gone the way of alternative music: mainstream. Popular, however, doesn't necessarily mean good. Complementary remedies don't have much scientific research behind them, and the findings from existing studies flip-flop faster than a gymnast. That's why we decided to put 15 holistic treatments for several common women's health problems under the microscope. We took a critical look at roughly two hundred and fifty studies and interviewed international experts on the cutting edge of alternative medicine to come up with your guide to the most effective supplements and herbs for 10 top conditions.

Colds

VITAMIN C

Since 1970, when Nobel laureate Linus Pauling first touted it as a cold remedy, vitamin C has been passionately championed—and reviled. Some studies support it, but others cast doubt. According to Finnish researcher Harri Hemila, Ph.D., a leading international authority on vitamin C, the negative studies generally used low doses (less than 1,000 milligrams daily) for too short a time (only 24 to 48 hours after the subjects first noticed that their throats were sore). Hemila reviewed 21 studies in which cold sufferers took at least 1,000 milligrams of vitamin C per day from the moment they felt a scratchy throat until they recovered. In all these studies, compared with a placebo treatment, the vitamin helped soothe sore throats, reduce nasal congestion, relieve runny noses, and get people on their feet faster. "Vitamin C is not a miracle cure, but it makes colds milder," says Mary Hardy, M.D., medical director of the Integrative Medicine Program at Cedars-Sinai Medical Center in Los Angeles.

Dosage: Take 500 milligrams or more four times a day, from the moment you realize you're coming down with a cold until you feel like yourself again.

Caveats: Loading up on more than 5,000 milligrams of vitamin C per day is useless at best, because your body cannot absorb that much; at worst, megadosing is harmful because it can cause you to have an upset stomach.

ECHINACEA

For reasons that escape scientific explanation, this daisylike flower seems to charge up the immune system. Many studies show that echinacea lessens cold symptoms and speeds recovery by a day or two. In a study that was published early in 2004, Canadian researchers gave the herb or a placebo to 128 people coming down with colds. The echinacea group reported milder symptoms (enough to make a difference in the number of cough drops that they downed and tissues that they blew through) than the placebo group. "As soon as I feel a cold coming on, I take it. My colds are mild and brief," says James Duke, Ph.D., retired chief of the U.S. Department of Agriculture's Medicinal Plant Laboratory in Beltsville, Maryland, and the author of many books about herbal medicine, including *The Green Pharmacy* and *Dr. Duke's Essential Herbs*.

> **What works well for you may not work for your kids: A recent study showed that echinacea does not help relieve cold symptoms in children.**

Promising, yes, although even the researchers admit more-standardized trials are needed in order to confirm this supplement's effectiveness. While echinacea is helpful in treating colds, it doesn't do much to keep them away, contrary to the wishful rumors (and sometimes sneaky marketing). Also, what works well for you is not necessarily effective for your kids: A recent study at the University of Washington showed that echinacea does not help relieve cold symptoms in children.

Dosage: Bruce Barrett, M.D., lead author of the most comprehensive investigation of echinacea's cold-fighting power to date, suggests taking the herb in tea or capsule form several times a day from the moment cold symptoms appear until you feel

better. Doses vary depending on the form, so follow the label instructions.

Caveats: To lower the risks of side effects, take the pills. Liquid products may upset your stomach or cause temporary, harmless numbing or tingling of your tongue.

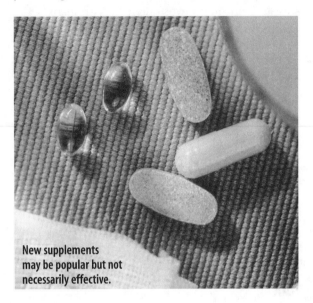

New supplements may be popular but not necessarily effective.

Depression

SAINT-JOHN'S-WORT

Many well-designed studies agree that for mild to moderate depression, Saint-John's-wort works—often as well as the widely prescribed drugs Prozac and Zoloft. "We recently concluded a comprehensive review of the scientific literature on Saint-John's-wort," says Mark Blumenthal, executive director of the American Botanical Council (ABC), the nation's leading independent organization for herb education. "Twenty-one of 23 studies show that it's effective for mild to moderate depression."

One of the most recent studies determined that the herb is as effective as Prozac, but with fewer side effects. In the drug group, 23 percent reported agitation, upset stomach, dizziness, fatigue, anxiety, and sex problems. However, among those taking

Saint-John's-wort, only 8 percent described side effects, most often an upset stomach. Similar results have been found in a study comparing the herb with the drug Zoloft.

Dosage: In most studies showing benefits, people were given 900 milligrams of the herb per day.

Caveats: Saint-John's-wort interacts with many medications—including birth control pills, possibly reducing their effectiveness—so talk to your physician or pharmacist before mixing meds with this or any other herb. Also, as with other life-threatening illnesses, don't self-medicate depression; talk to your doctor first.

> Studies show that Saint-John's-wort is effective in treating mild forms of depression. But you should always talk with your doctor to be sure it's the right treatment for you.

SAM-E

Your body naturally produces small amounts of S-adenosylmethionine, more commonly known as SAM-e ("sammy"), which plays a critical role in the synthesis of mood-regulating neurotransmitters in the brain. Many studies over the past decade have shown that, as a supplement in doses higher than the amounts the body produces, SAM-e is an effective antidepressant. In one of the more recent studies, an Italian team gave 281 depression sufferers either SAM-e (1,600 milligrams daily) or the pharmaceutical Tofranil (125 milligrams daily). After six weeks, both groups reported the same relief from depression, but SAM-e caused fewer side effects.

Dosage: Researchers recommend starting with 400 milligrams three times a day and gradually increasing the dosage as needed to as much as 1,600 milligrams daily.

Caveats: Some people experience stomach problems, including nausea and diarrhea.

High Blood Pressure

POTASSIUM

Potassium (primarily found inside all the cells in the body) and sodium (which is found mainly outside the cells) must exist in balance to keep your blood pressure at healthy levels. A salty diet can throw this delicate balance off-kilter, which can result in hypertension. "Potassium supplementation has been shown to lower blood pressure, while salt restriction is not as significant as a therapy," says Shari Lieberman, Ph.D., a New York clinical nutritionist who has researched the topic extensively. (Even so, potassium does not give you free rein over the saltshaker. Keep your sodium intake down to obtain the best results.)

One of the most comprehensive reports, which appeared in *The Journal of the American Medical Association* (JAMA), analyzed 67 studies of potassium's effects on blood pressure. Every one of the reports indicated that supplementing your diet with potassium is an effective way to keep blood pressure under control.

Dosage: Lieberman recommends up to 300 milligrams per day.

Caveats: Extremely high doses of potassium—more than 1,800 milligrams per day—may cause muscle fatigue, irregular heartbeat, and, in rare cases, heart failure.

FISH OIL

Reputable studies have shown that the omega-3 fatty acids in fish oil reduce blood pressure. A Harvard analysis of 31 studies concluded that as fish-oil intake increases, blood pressure decreases. "Fish oil not only reduces blood pressure," Hardy explains, "but also may make blood less sticky, a factor which contributes to stroke and heart attacks."

The supplement doesn't work as well as some blood pressure drugs, so if you already have hypertension, medication may be a better option. But if your stats are normal and you've got a family history or other factors that put you at risk for high blood pressure, fish oil may keep the numbers from creeping up.

Dosage: The recommended daily amounts differ from one product to the next, depending on what type of oil (that is, which fish) is used, so follow the label directions.

Caveats: Sometimes fish oil's ability to block blood clotting works too well; if you notice increased bruising, stop taking it and consult your physician. It's especially important for pregnant and nursing women to talk with their doctors before using this supplement because some fish contain high levels of mercury, which can harm a developing fetus.

Safety First

The recent push by the U.S. Food and Drug Administration to crack down on questionable supplements highlights the need to be picky about the alternative remedies you buy. These two organizations can steer you to solid information and quality products.

American Botanical Council (ABC): Established in 1988, ABC is the foremost independent nonprofit organization that promotes the responsible use of herbal medicines. ABC publishes books and the quarterly magazine *HerbalGram*. The group also has a Web site, www.herbalgram.org.

ConsumerLab.com: CL leads the nation in the independent testing of vitamins, minerals, and herbs. It publishes test results online at its Web site (www.consumerlab.com), naming brands that actually contain what their labels say they do, as well as brands that don't.

Garlic supplements can help if your cholesterol is mildly elevated, but you may want to try statins if your levels are really high.

High Cholesterol

GARLIC

Skeptics point to a highly publicized 1998 *JAMA* report that showed garlic is useless for reducing cholesterol. But Blumenthal contends that you need to take a closer look at that study's design before you write off this pungent bulb. The researchers tested not whole garlic but steam-distilled garlic oil, a semisynthetic product created by a process that removes most of the herb's cholesterol-lowering compound called allicin, he says. Thirteen other studies, published in respected journals, such as the *Annals of Internal Medicine* and the *Journal of the American College of Nutrition*, used garlic that contained allicin and found that it does reduce cholesterol slightly, but often significantly. "Garlic doesn't work as well as statin drugs to lower cholesterol, so if your cholesterol is really high, you may need medication," Blumenthal says. "But if your cholesterol is just mildly elevated, garlic supplements definitely help."

If you'd rather not have to eat cloves of fresh garlic, Blumenthal says that over-the-counter garlic supplements, including deodorized ones, have a similar cholesterol-lowering effect. The catch: So far, scientists have only looked at results over a few weeks; studies still need to determine garlic's effectiveness over the long haul.

Dosage: Look for products that contain allicin, such as Kwai and Kyolic, and follow label directions.

Caveats: Garlic may impair blood clotting, so if you start bruising more easily than usual, stop taking the supplement and call your doctor.

Insomnia

MELATONIN

Since the mid-1990s, a laboratory version of melatonin, a sleep-inducing hormone produced in the brain, has been a popular insomnia remedy—and for good reason. In a review of eight studies of the substance published around the world, Spanish researchers found that 60 percent of the participants reported melatonin helped them fall asleep faster and stay asleep longer. And unlike sleeping pills, the supplement is natural and nonaddictive. "I'm impressed with the research on melatonin," Duke says.

Dosage: Studies have shown effectiveness with doses ranging from 0.3 to 3 milligrams per day. Duke suggests starting with a low dose and increasing it as necessary.

BEFORE YOU BUY

If you're pregnant or nursing, or if you take medication for a chronic condition, talk to your physician before popping natural supplements (as well as drugs of any kind). And once you start taking them, if your initial symptoms last for more than 10 days or get worse, call your doctor.

Caveats: At very high doses (6 to 12 milligrams daily), some people have complained of headaches and morning sluggishness.

VALERIAN

Valerian's centuries-old reputation as a sleep aid was scientifically validated in 1981, when research showed that the plant contains sedative compounds. German researchers gave 202 chronic insomniacs either valerian or Serax (oxazepam), a drug similar to Valium. After six weeks, both treatments had equally successful results. Since then, additional studies have shown that valerian puts insomniacs to sleep, often as well as pharmaceutical sleep aids. And, like melatonin, valerian is nonaddictive. "The research is compelling: Valerian works," Blumenthal says.

Dosage: Products vary, so follow the label directions.

Caveats: A single dose of valerian doesn't knock you out the way other sedatives might. "You have to take it nightly for two weeks or more," Hardy says. Side effects may include stomach upset and headaches.

Osteo-arthritis

GLUCOSAMINE AND CHONDROITIN

In 1997, the best seller *The Arthritis Cure* argued that two then-new supplements, glucosamine and chondroitin, could "cure" joint pain. For the record, neither glucosamine nor chondroitin cures arthritis. But they (especially glucosamine) do help alleviate pain. Over the last 20 years, five studies have compared glucosamine head-to-head against ibuprofen (Advil, Motrin). All five trials showed that the supplement works as well as the drug to relieve joint pain and stiffness, but with less stomach distress.

Osteoarthritis develops when the natural wear and tear of aging breaks down the shock-absorbing cartilage inside joints. Glucosamine helps repair this cushioning by improving its ability to hold water, while chondroitin draws water into cartilage. The more water that cartilage contains, the better the shock absorption for your joints. The studies are not unanimous, but most show that both supplements diminish osteoarthritis pain, particularly in the knees. "The research is compelling, especially for glucosamine, which has been better studied," Blumenthal says. "Both supplements have a solid safety record."

Dosage: Most of the studies used 1,500 milligrams per day of glucosamine and 1,200 milligrams per day of chondroitin.

Caveats: None.

PMS

CHASTE-TREE BERRY

Loading up on chaste-tree berries will not make you more virtuous, but it could make premenstrual syndrome (PMS) more tolerable. Studies find that the berries help balance levels of estrogen and progesterone, thereby reducing the mood swings, breast tenderness, and bloating associated with your period. In some recent research pitting the herb against two other popular PMS treatments—vitamin B_6 and Prozac—chaste-tree berry worked as well as the popular antidepressant and considerably better than the vitamin. "I recommend chaste-tree berry to women complaining of PMS," Duke says. "It's safe, and the studies are convincing."

Dosage: The amount used depends on the form that you take it in (pills, capsules, or tincture), so follow the label directions.

Caveats: Be patient—it can take three months of daily use for you to experience benefits. Some women report stomach problems, headache, and increased menstrual flow.

Menopause

BLACK COHOSH

For 48 years, Europeans have been using black cohosh to treat menopausal discomfort; during the past decade, it has become popular stateside. Some studies question its benefit, but scientists generally agree that the herb can relieve hot flashes safely and effectively. "Black cohosh is in the 'yes' column," Blumenthal says. "The vast majority of studies show benefit."

In one of the most often cited studies, German researchers gave 60 women one of three treatments: estrogen, a Valium-like tranquilizer, or black cohosh (two tablets of the over-the-counter remedy Remifemin twice a day). Women who took the herb reported the greatest relief from hot flashes, sleep problems, irritability, and depressed mood. How it works is still a mystery, but scientists are confident that it does not act like estrogen, so it's safe for women who should avoid the hormone (those who are at risk for breast cancer, for instance).

Dosage: Products vary, so follow the label directions.

Caveats: Side effects are rare, although some women have reported stomachaches, dizziness, and headaches. Studies have yet to determine black cohosh's long-term safety record.

SOY ISOFLAVONES

Billed as a natural form of hormone replacement therapy, soy contains estrogen-like compounds known as isoflavones. Loma Linda University researchers analyzed 13 isoflavone studies and concluded that soy supplements do ease hot flashes. Although a few studies show no benefit, Hardy says that "soy provides some women substantial relief from hot flashes. Most get more modest benefits, but they get benefits."

Dosage: Take a daily supplement that provides 50 milligrams of soy isoflavones.

Caveats: While studies have found that eating soy in foods does not increase your risk of breast cancer (some evidence, in fact, suggests that such foods decrease it), the risk associated with taking soy supplements is still up for debate.

Sexual Enhancement

ARGINMAX

Yes, the idea of improving your sex life by popping a pill seems a little too pat, but a double-blind study showed that the blend of ingredients in ArginMax for Women can help. This multivitamin contains several reputed sex-enhancers: ginseng, a mainstay of Asian herbalism with stimulant action; ginkgo, which improves blood flow in the body, including to the genitals; damiana, a Central American plant, as well as a purported aphrodisiac; and L-arginine, a chemical precursor of nitric oxide, which plays a key role in the biochemistry of sex.

> **Boosting your sex life by popping a pill may seem crazy, but one study shows that a certain multivitamin can help.**

Stanford University researchers gave a placebo or the supplement to 77 women with a variety of sexual complaints. After two months, 37 percent of the placebo group reported significant increases in libido, frequency of lovemaking, and sexual satisfaction. But in the ArginMax group, the figure was 74 percent, a significant difference, and the supplement did not cause any major side effects. "I didn't expect ArginMax to be effective, let alone as effective as it was," says researcher Mary Polan, M.D., chief of obstetrics and gynecology at Stanford.

Dosage: Follow label directions.

Caveats: Ginseng and ginkgo slow down blood clotting; if you bruise unusually easily while taking ArginMax, stop taking it and call your doctor.

Varicose Veins

HORSE CHESTNUT SEED EXTRACT

When the walls of veins in your legs weaken because of genetics, aging, or on-your-feet jobs, blood pools in your calves, and fluid leaks into surrounding tissue. The result is unsightly varicosities, also known as spider veins, and in more severe cases, pain and discomfort from swelling. Horse chestnut seed contains a compound called aescin that strengthens vein walls, decreasing fluid leakage.

Several studies have shown that the herb is effective for treating varicose veins that have appeared within the past few months and that it can help relieve feelings of heaviness associated with the condition. In one study, German researchers gave 240 people with varicose veins either compression stockings or horse chestnut seed extract (containing 50 milligrams of aescin twice a day). After 12 weeks, swelling decreased equally in both groups. "Horse chestnut won't eliminate every spider vein," Hardy says. "But it will strengthen the walls of leg veins."

Dosage: Studies have prescribed 50 milligrams of aescin once or twice a day.

Caveats: Off the tree, horse chestnuts are toxic, even deadly. Commercial extracts are detoxified and safe. ▪

San Francisco–based health writer Michael Castleman specializes in alternative medicine.

Q + A

How High-tech Additives Can Give You the Benefits of Soy

I see "soy-protein isolates" listed on energy-bar wrappers. What does this mean, exactly?

It's the technical term for a class of nutrients that isn't just showing up in energy bars. Food makers are using the high-tech additives to infuse cereals, protein drinks, salty snacks, meat substitutes, and even pasta with the goodness of soy. Plus, manufacturers are hoping to take a bite out of the market of people looking to add more lean protein to their diets.

Soy-protein isolates (aka isolated soy protein) are created by extracting the fat and carbs from soybeans. What's left is a flavorless, flourlike substance that consists of 90- to 95-percent protein.

The extraction process involves several chemicals, including hexane, a petroleum solvent commonly used to mill vegetable oil from grains and legumes. (That means most isolates can't be used in certified-organic products.) Once the bean has been milled and the oil drawn out, further washing, drying, and spinning remove all components that might lend a beany flavor.

The U.S. Food and Drug Administration (FDA) has allowed manufacturers to claim that soy protein promotes heart health since 1999. Some studies also suggest that soy might be helpful in preventing certain types of cancer (although the FDA doesn't yet allow manufacturers to label their products as cancer fighters). The recommended 25 grams a day, though, is too much soy for most people to stomach ($1/2$ cup tofu contains 10 grams of protein). That's why fortified foods are so appetizing—eating them is an easy way to get soy without having to nosh on edamame 24/7. Judging by the numbers, people are gobbling up soy-enhanced edibles: In 2004, an estimated one hundred thousand tons of soy-protein powder will be added to foods.

The benefits of isolates most likely lie in isoflavones, plant-based hormones that are similar to human estrogen. "It's the phytochemicals, particularly the isoflavones, that seem to hold the most promise for cancer," says Mark Messina, Ph.D., a nutritionist and adjunct professor at Loma Linda University in Southern California. Some isoflavones are lost in the processing, but enough remain to make eating isolated soy protein a good way to get these substances into your diet, says Messina, who has reviewed current research both independently and as a consultant to the soy-foods industry.

Indeed, some health experts are concerned that soy isolates are such a concentrated source of isoflavones that people who regularly eat products fortified with them might get too much of a good thing. Despite the FDA's endorsement of soy's benefits, the long-term effects of eating isolates in high quantities are still unknown. Conflicting studies indicate that consuming isolated soy protein could have both positive and negative effects on menopausal hot flashes and the prevention of certain diseases, such as breast and ovarian cancers. Because isolates blend easily into many foods, they have become the most common soy ingredient in these studies. No one is sure whether eating whole soy products delivers better overall nutrition or whether they might offer more potential for fighting cancer. Isolates also don't provide any of the fiber of such foods as edamame, which contains 4 grams of fiber in $2/3$ cup. (Tofu and soy milk, on the other hand, have little fiber.)

Until more is known about the pros and cons of eating isolates, it's best to keep tabs on your consumption of soy-fortified foods. Avoid going over the 25-gram-a-day limit to make sure you reap the benefits without overdoing it.

Alternative Care for Children

Safe or Sorry?

Holistic therapies are going mainstream. The results are mixed concerning how it could affect your kids.

BY JACQUELINE STENSON

By the time Kristin Wilinkiewicz was 5, her ear infections were no longer just an occasional problem—they were a recurring nightmare. "She'd be free from medication for two to three weeks and then back on it," says her mother, Phyllis. "This went on for a year." For Kristin, the taste of some of the antibiotic liquids she had to swallow was almost worse than the pain; one made her throw up. And the fluid buildup in her ears interfered with her hearing. On their pediatrician's recommendation, Phyllis scheduled surgery to have Kristin's adenoids removed and drainage tubes placed in her ears, a prospect that terrified the young girl.

Around that time, Phyllis learned that the chiropractor she saw for her back pain, Michael LeRoux, also treated kids with ear infections. So Phyllis brought Kristin in. After undergoing manipulation of her neck and spine a few times each week for three months, Kristin began having fewer infections. Phyllis canceled the surgery.

"The operation wasn't a guarantee of success," Phyllis says, "and this was a lot less painful." It seemed to work, too. Kristin had suffered about seven infections in the year before she started getting chiropractic adjustments; she had only two in the year after.

It isn't clear how—or even if—manipulation helps prevent these infections. LeRoux, of Ocean State Chiropractic in Providence, Rhode Island, thinks the treatment may ease muscle tension and alleviate pressure on pinched nerves, promoting drainage, but there are no studies to prove manipulation actually works. Still, it's an increasingly popular alternative to surgery for children suffering from chronic ear infections. LeRoux says adjustments seem to work wonders for about 60 to 70 percent of his young patients.

But alternative medicine was not so kind to Kelly Wilson (not her real name). Kelly has cystic fibrosis, an incurable genetic disease that is characterized by thick mucus in the lungs and pancreas. The disease, which causes chronic lung infections, takes the lives of many patients by the time they reach age 30. Kelly was 11 when her mother and father stopped taking her to doctors at the University of California, San Francisco (UCSF). Instead, in a desperate attempt to find a cure, her parents decided to try another course of treatment, giving her a variety of herbal medicines and other supplements, including evening primrose oil, co-enzyme Q10, brewer's yeast, lysine, and grape-seed extract.

The next time Dennis Nielson, M.D., saw his young patient, a year and a half later, her condition had deteriorated markedly. "She had lost a tremendous amount of weight, her belly was bloated, and her lung function was so low that she was almost at the point of needing a lung transplant," recalls Nielson, chief of pulmonary medicine at UCSF. Kelly's pancreas had stopped working properly, and she had developed diabetes. She spent three weeks in the hospital. Now 15, she's doing well, but her lung function remains far below that of her peers who have cystic fibrosis. "She's lost years of her life," Nielson says. "There's no way to get them back."

Alternative and complementary therapies are increasingly being used in the youngest of patients, according to the American Academy of Pediatrics. What's more, it's not just parents who are interested in the world of alternatives—so are some mainstream doctors. Various holistic therapies have been integrated into pediatric care at such major medical centers as the University of Minnesota's and Stanford's. A small but growing number of researchers have begun testing these treatments, subjecting them to the same kinds of rigorous trials long reserved for conventional medicines.

When it comes to caring for kids, in other words, alternatives are making remarkable strides into medicine cabinets and hospital wards. That's exciting—and worrisome. While there are plenty of anecdotal reports of success and increasing numbers of preliminary but promising reports from researchers, solid evidence of the safety and effectiveness of many treatments is still in short supply. In the absence of such evidence, as the cases of Kristin and Kelly illustrate, the field holds both promise and peril for children.

It's easy to see why nonmainstream approaches appeal to parents. Holistic practitioners tend to work at a slower pace, be in cozier settings, and promise individualized care.

"We're just swamped," says Timothy Culbert, M.D., medical director of the Integrative Medicine and Cultural Care Program at Children's Hospitals and Clinics, a teaching hospital affiliated with the University of Minnesota in Minneapolis. Referrals to his clinic, which combines mind-body practices with traditional medicine, have boomed over the past two years. Statistics on the use of alternatives vary widely, but a recent nationwide telephone survey of 1,500 parents found that one-fifth used some form of unconventional treatment, such as dietary supplements, for their children, and almost 1 in 10 brought their kids to an alternative provider, such as a chiropractor or homeopath.

Parents are particularly likely to seek out alternatives when their children have serious or chronic illnesses, such as cancer, autism, asthma, multiple sclerosis, or cystic fibrosis. In one recent study, one in three children with autism was treated with vitamin supplements, chelation, or other such therapies. In another, parents of nearly three-quarters of kids with cancer have given alternatives a try, including chiropractic, herbs, and vitamins.

> The greatest risk of using alternatives may be one of omission. Any holistic therapy could pose a threat to children if it is substituted for necessary conventional care.

It's easy to see why nonmainstream approaches appeal to parents. Conventional medicine can be painful and unpleasant, and it has no solutions for some of childhood's worst tragedies. Pediatricians are frequently pressed for time and sometimes use bewildering medical technology. Holistic practitioners, by contrast, tend to work at a slower pace and in cozier settings, and promise individualized care.

Yet the use of alternative medicine is by definition an experiment, regardless of the patient's age. If little is clear about the effects of holistic approaches in adults, far less is understood about their impact on children. Researchers prefer to study people who can give informed consent. Also, scientists—and those who approve their studies—tend to be extremely cautious about even the remote possibility of an experimental treatment harming a child.

Richard Wahl, M.D., found that out when he tried to start a clinical trial on alternative treatments for kids, like Kristin, who suffer recurrent ear infections. "Our goal was to find something to reduce these children's exposure to antibiotics," says Wahl, associate professor of clinical pediatrics at the University of Arizona in Tucson. He wanted to study osteopathic manipulation and the herb echinacea, each the subject of encouraging reports from parents, physicians, and holistic practitioners. (Unlike chiropractic manipulation, which focuses primarily on adjusting spinal alignment, osteopathic manipulation aims to "rebalance relationships" between the skeleton and soft tissues.)

But getting the go-ahead wasn't easy. "The human-subjects committee felt that if there was any risk whatsoever, the research was not worth doing," Wahl says. Eventually, he was able to convince the committee that the risks of osteopathic manipulation were minimal: He could find no cases in which the procedure had harmed a child. Permission granted, Wahl enrolled 90 children ages 1 to 5 to determine whether echinacea taken at the first sign of a cold, along with cranial manipulation, could help prevent ear infections. (His study is ongoing.)

As the number of studies grows, doctors at some of the nation's most well-respected institutions are putting complementary therapies into practice. At Stanford University's pediatric hospital, for example, physicians in the Pain Management and Integrative Medicine Program have been using unconventional remedies to ease the suffering of pediatric patients since the late 1980s. The staff relies on such techniques as acupuncture, biofeedback, hypnosis, and guided imagery to treat conditions ranging from headaches to cancer-related pain and chemotherapy-induced nausea.

The foray into holistic medicine began out of sheer necessity. Pain medicines can cause nausea and other unpleasant side effects, explains Brenda Golianu, M.D., director of the Stanford clinic. Many parents are reluctant to heavily medicate their children, particularly for extended periods. But those aren't the only problems. "Medications sometimes just don't help enough," Golianu says. "Treating pain is good medicine—children heal faster. So you're stuck. What are you going to give?"

Golianu has found that a mix of drugs and alternative treatments sometimes does more for her patients than medicine alone. When premature infants in the neonatal intensive care unit become tolerant to standard pain and sedation medications, ear acupuncture helps ease these babies' pain and keeps them more relaxed while they're on mechanical ventilators. "You can see them calm down," Golianu says. "There are

Getting the Best of Both Worlds

Interested in trying holistic approaches—but don't want to abandon the benefits of medical science? Try these tips for getting started.

Use Your Doctor as a Resource

One of the best places to look for a reliable alternative practitioner is in the office of your pediatrician or family doctor, says Brenda Golianu, M.D., who uses acupuncture and other complementary techniques at Stanford University's Lucile Packard Children's Hospital. Many primary-care doctors have links to the local community of alternative-medicine specialists, she says.

The National Center for Complementary and Alternative Medicine also has a useful guide to help you find a practitioner; go to www.nccam. nih.gov/health/practitioner/index.htm.

If you're looking for an acupuncturist, visit the American Academy of Medical Acupuncture's Web site at www.medicalacupuncture.org, where you'll find a national list of physician-acupuncturists.

Read Up at Home

A good book can help you get your bearings in the world of alternatives. In *The Holistic Pediatrician,* Kathi J. Kemper, M.D., professor of pediatrics at Wake Forest University School of Medicine, provides a thorough guide for parents who are interested in melding the worlds of conventional and complementary medicine.

Another helpful book, says Timothy Culbert, M.D., medical director of the Integrative Medicine and Cultural Care Program in Minneapolis, is *Healthy Child, Whole Child,* by Stuart H. Ditchek and Russell Greenfield.

On the Internet, Holistickids.org is a great resource for reliable information. It's a group project of Children's Hospital Boston, Harvard Medical School, and a number of other institutions.

Keep the Lines of Communication Open

In talking with a practitioner, ask whether he or she treats many children, including some with your child's condition. It's best if the practitioner is willing to have an ongoing conversation—a collaboration—with your child's pediatrician. "Like all good health-care providers," Culbert says, "complementary- or alternative-medicine practitioners should know their limits and when they need to call in support." An ideologue does not make a good healer.

Pay attention to mind-set—that means your own, too. Don't assume a remedy will work for your child just because it worked for you, Culbert says. Remember that what's true for toadstools also applies to treatments: Natural doesn't necessarily mean safe.

fairly fast results." She and her colleagues are also using ear acupuncture to help wean babies off morphine.

When the Stanford doctors started using acupuncture for babies, there were no pediatric studies that proved the approach would work. But it seemed worth a try, Golianu says, because of research showing it could safely help treat pain and addiction in adults. So far, acupuncture seems both effective and safe in infants, she says; the treatment is certainly safer than long-term reliance on drugs.

Low-risk holistic therapies are being used in pediatric care at several other major medical centers, too. At the Integrative Medicine and Cultural Care Program in Minnesota, children with chronic conditions can get acupuncture, therapeutic massage, or aromatherapy, or use guided imagery, biofeedback, or other alternative approaches. "For the kinds of kids we're seeing, with disorders that have a mind-body component, these treatments can be very helpful," says Culbert, the clinic's medical director. Often, he says, the therapies allow doctors to reduce or eliminate pain medicines.

At the Integrative Medicine Service of Memorial Sloan-Kettering Cancer Center in New York City, young cancer patients can partake in music therapy and learn meditation and self-hypnosis to help them manage pain and anxiety. "Many of these children are depressed and isolated, and these are ways of bringing them together and lifting their spirits," says Barrie Cassileth, Ph.D., chief of the program. "All of these activities put more control in the hands of these children. That helps a great deal."

If doctors are cautiously optimistic about some complementary techniques, is research showing equally positive results? In some areas, yes. One study suggests that essential oils of spearmint, ginger, or sweet fennel can alleviate nausea caused by chemotherapy. In another, Thomas Ball, M.D., a colleague of Wahl's at the University of Arizona, has seen promise in guided imagery, in which children think about something that represents their pain, such as fire, and then create an image to help them cope, such as an ocean wave wiping out the flame.

For schoolkids, recurrent stomach pain is a common but misery-making problem, says Ball, an associate professor of clinical pediatrics, and it usually has no known cause and no treatment. Ball and his colleagues taught guided imagery and deep-breathing exercises to children and teens who'd been struggling with the ailment for months or years. The techniques helped ease the discomfort in 9 out of 10 patients: After just two months of therapy, they averaged 67-percent fewer painful days. "It's well-known that the 'brain bone' is connected to the 'intestine bone'—that there are nerve connections," Ball says. Guided imagery appears to help prevent pain messages from traveling that route, he says.

What about ear infections? So far, interim results from Wahl's study have shown no significant benefit from either echinacea or osteopathic manipulation. But other recent research has yielded more intriguing results for manipulation. A six-month study, published in September 2003 in the *Archives of Pediatrics & Adolescent Medicine*, looked at kids ages 6 months to 6 years who had frequent ear infections. Those who received osteopathic manipulation in addition to their regular care had slightly fewer infections than those who didn't get the alternative treatment. More impressive, just 1 of the 25 kids who underwent manipulation ended up getting ear tubes, compared with 8 of 32 youngsters in the other group. Study author Miriam Mills, M.D., clinical professor of pediatrics and osteopathic manual medicine at Oklahoma State University in Tulsa, calls the finding "pretty remarkable." Still, she notes, ear infections typically subside with time. It's also possible that manipulation made parents more willing to wait for improvement instead of taking their children for surgery.

So did the therapy truly help? Or did the kids just outgrow their infections? Did Kristin?

"The research is still young," Wahl says. "There are a lot of unanswered questions."

Meditation and acupuncture. Dance therapy and dietary supplements. Obviously, not all complementary and alternative treatments carry the same potential for risk. Yet it's not always the scary-seeming remedies that worry researchers the most. "In my experience, things like massage, acupuncture, hypnosis, and biofeedback are all

Once children coping with stomach pain learned guided imagery and deep-breathing exercises, 9 out of 10 of them reported feeling less discomfort.

very safe," says Kathi Kemper, M.D., professor of pediatrics at Wake Forest University School of Medicine in Winston-Salem, North Carolina, and author of *The Holistic Pediatrician*. On the other hand, experts express concern over the herbs and dietary supplements that are dispensed so lightly to children by so many parents. These make up the most commonly used alternative therapy in kids.

The worry stems in part from the fact that children are not simply small adults. Pharmacological researchers know that children metabolize some medications differently than adults do, and the same is almost certainly true for the chemicals in supplements. Because most supplements are formulated for adults, the appropriate amount for a child is often a guess. "There's little information available about long-term usage and dosage," says Rebecca Costello, Ph.D., deputy director of the National Institutes of Health's Office of Dietary Supplements in Bethesda, Maryland. "We just don't know."

The fact that organs are still developing during childhood also raises the potential for damage. Just as the antibiotic tetracycline can stain the developing teeth of young children, some herbs may be harmful during certain phases of growth.

Certainly, contaminated supplements can pose a particular risk to children. In 2000, Los Angeles pediatricians reported on a developmentally impaired child whose mother had given him daily doses of an imported herbal preparation. The folk medicine promised to strengthen his brain, but it was tainted with lead and mercury. By the time the contamination was discovered, when the boy was 5, he had ingested a huge amount of lead, pediatrician Robert Adler, M.D., says—enough to greatly exacerbate his original problems. He's had to be hospitalized several times for treatment of the lead poisoning.

More recently, some British researchers described a worrisome situation at their dermatology clinic: Aware that some parents were using herbal creams for their children's eczema—"Parents were even making recommendations to each other while they were in our waiting room!" says dermatologist Helen Ramsay—the doctors decided to run an analysis. Of the 24 remedies tested, 20 contained a potent prescription steroid. Applied all over, as one label advised, the creams could cause serious side effects, including susceptibility to infection, stunted growth, and a shutdown of children's production of natural steroid hormones. " 'Herbal' creams, which work very quickly or produce 'miracle' results, should raise suspicions," says Ramsay, of the University of Sheffield in the United Kingdom.

Beyond the dangers presented by adulterants are the risks inherent in some supplements themselves—as the now-notorious herb ephedra shows. It was promoted as a way to lose weight and boost energy and athletic performance, all selling points apt to grab teens. In December 2003, the U.S. Food and Drug Administration announced a ban on ephedra, but not before it was implicated in 155 deaths. One person who died was a 16-year-old Illinois football player who had a heart attack after taking an ephedra-containing product touted as an alternative to street drugs.

The greatest risk of using alternatives may be one of omission. Any holistic therapy could pose a threat to children if substituted for needed conventional care. That's the mistake Kelly Wilson's parents made when they started using herbs to treat their daughter's cystic fibrosis and stopped taking her to her doctors—and Kelly paid a steep price.

It is crucial that alternative medicine be treated with respect, researchers say. That means recognizing that natural does not necessarily mean benign. Aspirin was discovered in willow bark, penicillin in bread mold. Like these medications, many complementary therapies may have the potential to help as well as harm.

To reduce the risk of harm, say experts like Culbert, parents should talk to their child's doctor about any nontraditional therapies being used—and doctors must educate themselves as much as possible about those therapies' risks and benefits. Communication is essential if the child has a serious medical condition. Children with cancer are likely to be treated with alternative medicine, but high doses of vitamins C and E may reduce the effectiveness of chemotherapy. Some botanical remedies, such as yew needles and essiac, cause the same sorts of side effects as chemo, so combining them with conventional treatments could subject a child to a double hit.

Informed natural practitioners can help prevent problems like these. The operative word, of course, is *informed*. Parents should look for solid credentials: Has the provider earned a certificate or license if that's offered in a given state? Was he or she educated at an accredited school? The practitioner also should be willing to have an ongoing conversation with the child's pediatrician.

When it comes to herbs and other dietary supplements, there are no guarantees—of safety, of efficacy, or even of the bottle containing what the label says it does. But the United States Pharmacopeia (USP), which sets industry standards for pharmaceuticals, recently began issuing a seal of approval for supplements, indicating that tests have found the product to be pure. Look for "USP Dietary Supplement Verified."

A growing number of doctors, like Culbert and Cassileth, believe that holistic remedies hold great promise for children and may in some cases even become mainstream medicine one day. "As opposed to polarizing the model, with conventional medicine on one side and alternative medicine on the other," Culbert says, "people are seeing there's a lot of benefit in getting what's best from both and bringing them together."

When using both traditional therapies and the alternatives that complement them, a healthy dose of skepticism may be the best medicine of all. ∎

Jacqueline Stenson has written extensively on health and medicine for a variety of publications.

You Can Blame a Bad Gene for Dyslexia

Words can be tough to decipher for people suffering from dyslexia. Now, it seems that, at least in some cases, a "misspelled" gene may be to blame for this difficulty. Researchers at the University of Helsinki in Finland recently isolated a mutation in a gene called DYX1C1. Having this mutated gene increases the risk of the disorder. Other genetic glitches that increase vulnerability to dyslexia may also exist, the scientists say. This discovery may eventually lead to a gene test that could help keep affected kids from falling behind in school.

Q + A

I've seen ads for starch-blocker supplements that promise to let you indulge in pasta, bread, and potatoes and still lose weight. Do they work?

Don't count on it. Starch blockers might seem like the must-have accessory for the carb-conscious crowd: They contain a chemical that supposedly shuts down the enzyme your body uses to digest the starch in high-carb foods. The reasoning is that if you don't digest those calories, they won't

Starch Blockers: A Good Choice?

turn up on your thighs. But put down that third plate of pasta, because experts say that you shouldn't expect these supplements to deliver. Most of the studies starch-blocker believers cite as proof that these formulas work were so poorly designed, they didn't even make the medical journals. The few that have been published were conducted on lab rats—and as we've said before, rats aren't little people (although some people are big rats).

Why Olive-Oil Pills Are Worth a Taste

Product: Olivenol is a little-known antioxidant supplement made from the pulp of organic olives. It's manufactured by CreAgri, whose founder is one of the original researchers at San Francisco–based biotechnology company Genentech.

Purpose: The capsules, tablets, and liquid supposedly provide the healthy benefits of the Mediterranean diet, without the fat and calories. Each dose of Olivenol (two pills per day, for instance) is designed to contain the free radical–busting equivalent of approximately $3/4$ cup extra-virgin olive oil.

Proof: In test-tube studies, Italian researchers found that olive oil's active antioxidant—hydroxytyrosol—prevented immune cells from attaching to the lining of blood vessels. That means consuming the oil may slow the development of heart disease. A Spanish study (not conducted on humans) found that hydroxytyrosol appears to prevent DNA damage, which causes cancers to grow.

Expert's take: "Hydroxytyrosol is known as one of the most potent antioxidants around," says Penny Kris-Etherton, Ph.D., professor of nutrition at Pennsylvania State University. "If this product has as much as it says, it could be helpful."

Availability: A 60-capsule bottle sells for $16 to $20 on the Internet (search for "Olivenol"). Also check your local health-food store.

vital *stats*

71
Percent of Americans who say they are optimistic about achieving "the good life"

52
Percentage of Americans who say achieving the good life means owning a second car

29
Percentage of American full-time workers who put in more than 40 hours a week

12
Percentage of Americans who say they take no vacation at all

21 BILLION
Number of dollars in unused vacation time employees gave back to their companies in 2003

1,712
Size in square feet of the typical American primary residence

1
Number of fire extinguishers recommended per 600 square feet

34
Percentage of households with more than one fire extinguisher

78
Percentage of households with more than one TV

48
Percentage of people in the United States who say they would buy mail-order drugs from another country to save money

90
Percentage of mail-order drugs that are found in border screenings to be potentially dangerous

10
Times as likely you are to die or be injured during surgery in a doctor's office as in a hospital or outpatient-surgery center

1.2 MILLION
Number of surgeries that take place in doctors' offices each year

33
Percentage of people who say they buy cell phones mainly to call 911

57
Millions of 911 calls made by cell-phone users in 2001

4
Percentage of cell-phone users who tried to call 911 and couldn't get through, mostly because of a weak signal or other phone problem

77
Percentage of women surveyed worldwide who say beauty products are a necessity, not a luxury

15
Percentage of those women who say their makeup routines take less than 10 minutes

26
Percentage of video-game players who are women over age 18

59
Percentage of self-described happy people who say they work out "a lot"

38
Percentage of self-described unhappy people who say they do

70
Percentage of Americans who say their gym memberships would be the first thing to go if they needed money for a new home

61
Percentage of women who say they dust once a week

25
Percentage of men who say they dust only when they can't see the TV screen

0
Number of human mad cow–related deaths in the United States at press time

5,200
Annual number of deaths from other foodborne illnesses in the United States

3
Pounds of food the average healthy woman eats every day

3
Weight in pounds of *Merriam-Webster's Collegiate Dictionary* (10th edition)

Sources: Roper ASW; Census.gov; Expedia.com; U.S. Centers for Disease Control and Prevention; *Wall Street Journal* Online/Harris Interactive Health-Care Poll; U.S. Food and Drug Administration; Entertainment Software Association; Avon Women's Survey; Sedona Training Associates; Century 21; Archives of Surgery; Hector Vila, M.D., H. Lee Moffitt Cancer Center and Research Institute; Cellular Telecommunications & Internet Association; Procter & Gamble; American Housing Survey/U.S. Census Bureau; Barbara Rolls, Ph.D.—Reported by Lisa Lee Freeman

everyday wellness

smart tips for healthy living

OutSmart

Doctor's Office Jitters

Take the worry out of these six common medical procedures.

BY HILARY BEARD

I f you've put off scheduling a doctor's appointment because you dread baring all to a virtual stranger or you've lost sleep stressing about test results, you know that medical procedures can rattle even the steeliest nerves. Now research indicates that test anxiety can do more than keep you up at night. A study published in 2003 in the journal *Psychosomatic Medicine* found that worrying causes patients to feel more pain, heal slower, and take longer to recover after surgery.

People who arm themselves with knowledge not only debunk frightening falsehoods, but also are more confident when faced with vital health decisions.

Sure, a glass of wine the night before your next trip to the doctor could help, but pretest prep is an even more potent elixir. Physicians tell us that people who arm themselves with knowledge not only debunk frightening falsehoods, but also are more confident when faced with vital health decisions. To help you head off a case of exam-table jitters, here's the inside story on what to expect before, during, and after six common procedures, courtesy of doctors and women who've been there.

SKIN BIOPSY

First, the scary stat: 40 to 50 percent of Americans will get skin cancer at least once by the time they reach age 65, according to the National Cancer Institute. Now, the reassuring news: The disease is nearly always treatable if detected early. If you spot a suspicious mole or lesion—one that has jagged edges or is multicolored, for instance—you can increase your odds of beating any potential problem by scheduling a skin biopsy right away.

What to expect: Your dermatologist will numb the area before she conducts one of four types of biopsies: shave (only the top layers of skin are removed), punch (the tumor is carved out with a cookie cutter–like tool), incisional (a scalpel is used to cut deeply and remove a wedge of skin containing a portion of the tumor), or excisional (a wedge of skin including the entire tumor is cut out). Then she'll stitch and bandage the wound. Expect results of the skin biopsy within 10 days. **What to do before:** Repeat this mantra: "Almost all skin cancers are curable when caught early." Now pick up the phone, and make an appointment. **What to do during:** Show your dermatologist other scars on your body to give her an idea of how your skin heals, so she can sew your wound in a way that reduces the chance of leaving an ugly mark behind.

Lessen the pain of the anesthesia shot by asking your doctor to numb your skin (20 seconds with an ice pack should do the trick) and inject the medicine slowly (taking between 15 and 60 seconds). **What to do after:** You will likely have a mark, but nothing that should cause a fright. "Most of the time it's like a chicken-pox scar," says dermatologist Susan Boiko, M.D., co-chair of the National Council on Skin Cancer Prevention. If the mark really bugs you, ask your dermatologist to refer you to a plastic surgeon. He or she will probably be able to eliminate all but a slight trace of the scar.

If your biopsy results indicate that cancer is present, consider having Mohs surgery to remove the malignancy. This procedure minimizes scarring because it removes only cancerous tissue, layer by layer, preserving normal skin. The best candidates are people with nonmelanoma cancers on the face or neck, or individuals whose cancers have returned, says dermatologist Kishwer Nehal, M.D., director of Mohs micrographic surgery at Memorial Sloan-Kettering Cancer Center in New York. "Fear of having a big scar drove me to find a Mohs surgeon," says Anne Kauffman, a 27-year-old advertising sales representative who lives in Manhattan. "The scar's hardly noticeable, and I had a pretty big area of skin taken from my shoulder." (To find a Mohs surgeon in your area, log on to the Web site of the American College of Mohs Micrographic Surgery and Cutaneous Oncology, www.mohscollege.org.)

COLONoscopy

The thought of having a tiny video camera snake its way up your rectum and into your colon sounds about as unpleasant as it does embarrassing. But don't balk. A colonoscopy can save you from colon cancer, the third most common cancer among women after breast and lung cancers. You should schedule the test once you turn age 50 (earlier if colon cancer runs in your family or if lifestyle factors put you at increased risk). The good news is that depending on your medical history and test results, you may not need another colonoscopy for 5 to 10 years.

What to expect: Your doctor will probably put you on a liquid diet the day before the test and give you a powerful laxative to empty your bowels. (Think of it this way: You'll probably feel lighter than you have in a long time.) Before the procedure, you'll be sedated so that while you'll be conscious of what's going on, you won't remember the details later. Then a colonoscope, a finger-thick tube, will pump air into your colon, inflating it so that a miniature video camera attached to the device can project real-time images of the inside of the organ onto a television monitor. This will enable the doctor to inspect for signs of polyps (noncancerous or precancerous growths) and other irregularities. Most abnormalities will be scraped off on the spot; large ones may be snipped for biopsy. The examination lasts about an hour, plus another 30 to 60 minutes of recuperation time. Ask someone to take you home, because you will probably be quite drowsy from the sedative. You should get results of your colonoscopy in three to five days.

What to do before: Make the day-before purge easier to swallow by chilling the laxative to mask the taste or sucking on an ice cube to numb your tongue.

To ease the irritation of multiple bowel movements, use creams containing zinc oxide (an ingredient that protects young bums from diaper rash) or baby wipes. **What to do during:** Most people say the screening is tolerable, although air bubbles give some people gas. Since holding it in will only cause greater discomfort, go ahead and let it rip. Taking long, slow breaths to relax your ab muscles can also help prevent cramping.

Some people, women in particular, complain of pressure from the probe knocking into the colon wall as it snakes its way through their bodies. "The colon can be curvier in women, especially if they've had prior pelvic surgeries [such as a hysterectomy]," says gastroenterologist Dayna Early, M.D., associate professor at Washington University in St. Louis. The feeling is more uncomfortable than painful, though.

What to do after: Don't plan a dinner party to celebrate the end of your colonoscopy; your body, inside and out, will probably want to rest. Grab a spoon and a straw, and replace lost fluids with plenty of juices and brothy soups (solid foods are out for at least a couple of hours).

MAMMOgram

If you're 40—the age women should have their first exam, most organizations suggest—or older, having this screening is the best way to detect breast cancer in its early—and most treatable—stages.
What to expect: You'll undress above the waist, don a hospital gown, and meet with a mammography technician. She (most mammographers are women) will X-ray each breast twice—once horizontally, once vertically.

> **Take ibuprofen or acetaminophen 45 minutes before a mammogram to reduce breast sensitivity.**

To do this, she'll have to grasp your breast and position it between two plates that close (kind of like a vise) to compress it. When the plates reopen, she will reposition you, take a second picture, and then move on to your other breast. Only the few seconds your breast is between the plates are uncomfortable. Later, a radiologist examines the images. No news is not necessarily good news: You should be notified of your results within 10 days. If you aren't, call your doctor and ask him to follow up with the radiologist.
What to do before: Schedule your mammogram at a large hospital or radiology center. The more experience radiologists have, the less likely they are to diagnose cancer that doesn't exist or overlook cancer that does.

Get the test done three to seven days after your period, when your breasts are less swollen and easier to X-ray.

If caffeine makes your breasts tender, avoid it (or at least cut back) the month before your exam.

Have the results of prior mammograms, biopsies, or breast procedures sent to the mammography center. This will allow the radiologist to compare images of your breasts over time and maximize her chance of accurately reading the film.

Take ibuprofen or acetaminophen 45 minutes before the procedure to reduce breast sensitivity.
What to do during: While most women experience discomfort, only a small percentage of them find mammograms painful, says radiologist Carl D'Orsi, M.D., director of breast imaging at Emory University in Atlanta. "By the time it gets really uncomfortable, it's over," says Claire Lomax, 41, a Philadelphia lawyer who postponed her first screening for 10 months after being told that mammograms hurt.

Let's be honest: Regardless of how gentle the technician is, no woman wants to have a stranger groping her breasts. So think of it as a challenge. "The sense of accomplishment and empowerment you feel when it's over and there's a good result far outweighs the discomfort and awkwardness," Lomax says.
What to do after: While you are waiting for the results of your mammogram, remind yourself that there's only a small chance (1 in 252 for a woman in her 30s) you have breast cancer. Even among postmenopausal women, who have higher rates of the disease, fewer than 1 percent of the ones who are screened receive a positive diagnosis, D'Orsi says.

If you're called back for further testing, remember that 80 percent of those women who require follow-up procedures walk away from them cancer-free.

ON THE HORIZON

- Duke University researchers have created an experimental machine called a breast scanner that detects changes in cells before a tumor has a chance to grow. Doctors hope it will be used in addition to traditional mammograms for women at high risk for breast cancer or whose breasts are tough to X-ray because of their size or density.
- Researchers are investigating confocal microscopy, a noninvasive way of determining if suspicious spots are cancerous.

BREAST BIOPSY

Mammograms are the best tool doctors have to detect irregular breast tissue, but breast biopsies are the only way to tell if that tissue is cancerous or not.

What to expect: Depending on the size of the lump and how skittish you are, your doctor will give you either local or general anesthesia. Technological advances have allowed physicians to obtain tissue samples with a needle in many cases, which reduces scarring. If part or all of the lump (and we stress *lump*, not breast) must be removed, the doctor will probably have to use a scalpel. Depending on the procedure that is used, your breast may feel sore for several weeks; over-the-counter painkillers should relieve any discomfort. Your results should be available within five days.

What to do before: You should ask an additional radiologist—from a large facility that specializes in mammograms and breast-cancer diagnoses—to read your X-ray in order to be sure that the biopsy is absolutely necessary.

Take comfort in statistics: About 10 percent of women will be called for a breast biopsy at some point during their lives, D'Orsi says. More than

80 percent of the time, doctors discover such irregularities as fibrocystic changes, benign lumps, scar tissue, or milk-duct abnormalities—but not cancer.

If you smoke, now's the time to quit. Besides the obvious ill effects cigarettes have on your health, puffing tends to decrease the circulation of nutrients to the skin, increasing the likelihood of scarring.

If you can't avoid having a surgical biopsy, ask your doctor about making a smaller cut or one along a natural crease or fold to make any scarring less noticeable.

What to do during: Breast biopsies hurt, but only a little. "If you've ever had your ears pierced, you've experienced the feeling before," says New Yorker Elizabeth Kirk (not her real name) of the needle biopsy she had at age 36 to sample a lump, which was later surgically removed while she was anesthetized.

What to do after: Even if results show that you're cancer-free, write down the name of the condition identified by the lab and whether it tends to recur or is associated with increased breast-cancer risk.

> Try not to panic. If breast cancer is caught early, the five-year survival rate is 97 percent.

You should also request a copy of the pathology report so that you can keep it in your home health files.

If the test does indicate breast cancer, your doctor will probably recommend surgery. Make sure that you obtain a second opinion before going ahead with it, and also contact the American Cancer Society (800-227-2345) for more information about treatment options and to help you locate support groups in your area.

Finally—this is the hardest part—try not to panic. "Many cancers detected by mammograms are very early breast cancer," D'Orsi says. When the disease is caught early, the five-year survival rate is an encouraging 97 percent.

HYSTERectomy

Many conditions, including fibroids (non-cancerous tumors of the uterus), endometriosis (growth of uterine lining outside of the womb), or uterine prolapse (in which the uterus slumps into the vagina), prompt doctors to recommend hysterectomies.

What to expect: Depending on your condition, your gynecologist will remove only your uterus; your uterus and cervix; or your uterus, cervix, and ovaries through your vagina or an abdominal incision. If your cervix has to come out, your doctor must close up the top of your vagina. Expect to stay in the hospital for two to three days. Once you go home, you'll probably have to lie low for a week or so (sex is off-limits for up to two months). Complete recovery takes time. Anita Clark (not her real name), 37, returned to her job as a drug counselor in Columbus, Ohio, six weeks after her hysterectomy, but she says her energy wasn't back to normal until the three-month mark.

What to do before: Because this is major surgery that will eliminate your ability to bear children, make sure that a hysterectomy is your only choice. Obtain at least one alternate opinion, suggests Hilda Hutcherson, M.D., assistant professor of clinical obstetrics and gynecology at Columbia University. About 10 percent of hysterectomies are necessary—for instance, to save women from such deadly diseases as cervical or uterine cancer. However, the American College of Surgeons estimates that in 90 percent of cases, less-invasive procedures, such as myomectomy to remove uterine fibroids, would also work.

Once you've decided on a hysterectomy, you still have options to reduce its side effects. If you're worried that having the surgery will put orgasms out of your reach, ask about a supracervical hysterectomy, which leaves the cervix in place and makes reshaping your vagina unnecessary. Also, unless your doctor has made a cancer diagnosis, you should be able to keep your ovaries and sidestep instant menopause, which many women say is more jolting than the natural process.

What to do during: Not much. Since you're given general anesthesia, you'll be out cold during this 1- to 2-hour procedure.

What to do after: If you have your ovaries removed and begin to experience menopausal symptoms, temporary hormone replacement, black cohosh, or soy supplements may help. Also, check with your doctor about ways you can keep your heart, bones, and sex drive healthy now that you're lacking protective amounts of estrogen.

TOOTH SCALING AND ROOT PLANING

The idea of winding up with a toothless grin is just one reason you should take periodontal disease seriously. More and more research is linking gum disease with chronic inflammation, which can increase your risks of such serious health problems as heart disease and delivering a low birth-weight or premature baby. Tooth scaling and root planing are the most effective ways of removing tartar, plaque, and bacteria from below the gum line, slowing—and possibly stopping—gum disease before it can further harm your health.

What to expect: What would a visit to the dentist be without having a needle stuck into your gums? After you endure that pesky pinprick, the anesthesia should kick in, enabling the doctor to use a probe to scrape beneath your gum line without your feeling much of a thing. You may experience an occasional twinge of pain if the hook happens to hit a nerve or snag your skin. The procedure lasts about an hour, and you may notice that your mouth will be somewhat sore or sensitive to hot and cold for several days afterward.

What to do before: Ask your dentist to refer you to a periodontist, or gum-disease specialist, who is likely to own the newest equipment and stay up-to-date on the latest procedures.

What to do during: The truth is that having your teeth scaled and planed is no fun, although the anesthesia helps. The pain, however, is not out of line with that of other common dental procedures. "It is uncomfortable," says Alison Suzanne, a 37-year-old account manager in Cleveland, "but I've had much worse pain getting cavities filled."

What to do after: Over-the-counter pain relievers should ease any soreness. Schedule regular cleanings with your periodontist (she can replace your dentist altogether) so she can perform repeat procedures as needed. ■

Hilary Beard is a freelance writer living in Philadelphia.

Discover What's Missing in Your Doctor's Diagnosis

When you're sick, you definitely don't want to be told the problem is all in your head. But a new study shows doctors often can't do any better.

Kurt Kroenke, M.D., and colleagues at Indiana University School of Medicine looked at the records of 289 people who visited a primary-care clinic with such complaints as back pain or headaches. A physical cause was found in only 52 percent of patients. Psychological problems, such as depression or anxiety, were to blame in another 10 percent. The remaining cases were labeled idiopathic—doctor-speak for "I don't know what's wrong."

Many idiopathic cases can indeed be linked to undiagnosed anxiety or depression, Kroenke believes. Previous studies blame these conditions for unexplained symptoms in 50 percent of patients.

But sometimes, Kroenke adds, "symptoms are a diagnosis in themselves; we can do exams or tests, but often all the tests come back normal." Chronic headaches, for instance, often have no identifiable cause but can still be treated effectively.

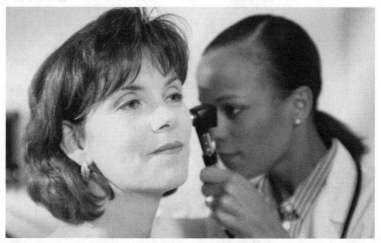

Q + A

How to Talk to Your Doc About Chronic Pain

I've had knee pain for years, and I feel that my doctor has stopped trying to find a solution. What should I do?

Chronic pain can often be tricky to treat, which helps explain why an estimated fifty million Americans live with it (and why one out of four pain patients changes doctors at least three times before finding one who helps). Try starting each doctor's appointment by stating what you hope to achieve with the visit: a diagnosis, a new treatment plan, or quick relief, for instance. If your pain doesn't improve in the time frame your doctor estimates, ask for a referral to a pain clinic—a sort of one-stop shop for acupuncture, physical therapy, medication, and other approaches. The American Academy of Pain Management (www.aapainmanage.org) can help you find a clinic near you.

The Battle over Heart Disease

Some experts believe everyone should start taking common drugs to lower their risks. Not everyone agrees.

BY ERIC STEINMEHL

Two respected doctors claim they've found the ultimate tools for preventing heart disease: For the rest of your life, take a combination of drugs designed to lower your risks.

The medical establishment still says people who want to lower their risks should concentrate on eating healthy foods and exercising. But the maverick doctors, who arrived at their conclusions independently, argue that lifestyle changes should take a backseat. Why? One reason is that most people fail at them. "You can't change 50 years of habits, and even if you do, the impact on your risk is very small," says Jonathan Sackner Bernstein, M.D., director of the Heart Failure Prevention and Treatment Program at North Shore University Hospital in Manhasset, New York. Instead, Sackner Bernstein recommends in his book, *Before It Happens to You,* that people of all ages who show any signs of heart disease take drugs to lower their blood pressure and cholesterol. And his thresholds for such signs—blood pressure above 115/75 and total cholesterol above 160—are much lower than those largely seen as healthy today.

Meanwhile, Peter Salgo, M.D., associate director of the Open Heart ICU at New York-Presbyterian Hospital and clinical professor of medicine and anesthesiology at Columbia University, contends in his book *The Heart of the Matter* that lifestyle changes alone simply won't prevent heart disease. He recommends that people start taking three drugs around age 40: statins to cut cholesterol; aspirin to

Doctors debate over the best way to reduce chances of heart disease: by lifestyle changes or by popping pills.

fight inflammation and prevent clotting that causes heart attacks; and a course of antibiotics to fight the respiratory bug *Chlamydia pneumonia* (not the same as sexually transmitted chlamydia), which infects more than 50 percent of Americans. He points to research showing that the germ, which infects heart blood vessels, causes inflammation linked to heart disease.

These unorthodox strategies may sound familiar. In summer 2003, British researchers proposed a similar idea, dubbed the "PolyPill," and said it could save hundreds of thousands of lives. It would combine a statin with several blood pressure medications, folic acid, and aspirin. Drug companies are mulling the idea.

Mainstream medical organizations, though, are reluctant to de-emphasize preventive strategies. They worry that people might mistake the pop-a-pill approach for a license to overeat or smoke. "We shouldn't give pills until we take care of the lifestyle issues that modify risk," says Robert Bonow, M.D., immediate past president of the American Heart Association. Plus, critics note, the drugs aren't cheap, and there are risks. Bonow says side effects (such as bleeding from aspirin) could kill thousands.

But the authors point out that the risks for any individual are minimal. Simply taking a lot of vitamins, Sackner Bernstein adds, might be riskier.

Look for this debate to heat up as doctors keep searching for new ways to fight heart disease. ∎

Why You May Need a New Kind of Cholesterol Test

It could reveal hidden risks for heart disease.

Are the cholesterol particles in your blood large or small? You probably have no idea, and that may be dangerous. Little ones are more likely to stick to the walls of your arteries and lead to heart disease. But the good news is that an often-ignored test, which is getting some new attention, may reveal your hidden risks.

Routine cholesterol screens measure only the total amount of good (HDL) and bad (LDL) cholesterol in your blood. But the apoB test, developed in the 1990s and named after apolipoprotein B, one of several proteins attached to cholesterol, determines whether the LDL itself is composed of small or large particles. Fragments of apoB are attached to small LDL (other proteins are connected to large LDL), and the test counts these fragments. When that number is high, it means a load of small particles is circulating.

Naturally, it's not healthy people who are most at risk. In a recent study published in *Circulation*, the journal of the American Heart Association (AHA), Allan Sniderman, M.D., professor of medicine at McGill University in Montreal, and his colleagues noted that people with high apoB typically displayed other danger signs, such as insulin resistance and inflammation. But the researchers also showed that 25 percent of people with normal LDL had apoB high enough to need treatment (such as statin drugs). Even people with low LDL may be in danger. "The test is more precise because LDL levels will be misleading in people with lots of small particles," Sniderman explains.

The evidence supporting apoB tests goes back at least five years, and Canada already recommends widespread screening. The AHA is waiting for more research before making any recommendations. For now, Sniderman says, apoB is a useful add-on to traditional tests. If conventional screens reveal low HDL or high triglycerides—either of which suggests that you're not in perfect health, regardless of your LDL level—an apoB test might make sense.

Aspirin: Great for Your Heart (But It Has Its Limits)

An aspirin a day may help prevent heart attacks, but it doesn't work for a surprisingly large number of people. Fully one-quarter of the population, according to Hungarian and Danish researchers, is aspirin-resistant—the medication won't prevent clotting in their blood. The finding, presented at a recent European Society of Cardiology meeting, builds on earlier research showing that people whose blood doesn't respond to aspirin are 3 1/2 times as likely to die of heart attacks as those who aren't resistant. Experts are trying to figure out whether testing for aspirin resistance should become standard.

Discover Whether High Blood Pressure Is in Your Future

Are you at risk for hypertension later in life? If you're 40 years old or younger, here's how to find out: Rest for 5 minutes, then take your blood pressure while sitting (check it twice for accuracy). Now stand and take it again, keeping your arm relaxed and slightly bent, with your elbow at heart level. If your systolic pressure (the top number) rises by at least five points, you might be at risk even if the number is below 120, which is considered normal.

The finding comes from an ongoing study begun in 1983 and funded by the National Institutes of Health. In a sample of nearly three thousand adults ages 18 to 30 who were tracked regularly for eight years, those whose pressure rose at least five points after standing had a 12.4 percent chance of developing hypertension. Not a big deal? Well, those odds are double the expected risk for people in that age range, says lead author Randal Thomas, M.D., a preventive cardiologist at the Mayo Clinic in Rochester, Minnesota. And the greater the rise, the higher the risk.

If your systolic pressure increases using this test, it may mean your blood vessels over-constrict in reaction to stress, a problem linked to high blood pressure. Unfortunately, this method probably won't work for people over age 40, Thomas says, because vessels react differently as you age. Still, you can cut your risks by exercising, losing weight, and going easy on salt.

A Win in the Battle Against Antibiotic Resistance

Some parents are known to shop for doctors who will dole out antibiotics anytime little Jack or Jill comes down with a sniffle. But antibiotic prescriptions for young kids have actually declined—by as much as 39 percent between 1996 and 2000, according to Harvard University researchers. That's good news, because 50 million courses of antibiotics are still prescribed unnecessarily each year, and reports are showing alarming jumps in the numbers of resistant bacteria.

Remember that when your child does need an antibiotic, he or she should take *all* of it. Otherwise, the germs exposed to the medicine may survive, not only prolonging the illness but also passing on resistance to other strains.

Do You Worry About Cancer Too Much?

Cancer is a very real problem, but you may not be doing yourself any favors by going all out to prevent it.

BY ERIC STEINMEHL

A recent Gallup Poll shows Americans are more worried about getting cancer than any other illness. But Veterans Affairs researcher H. Gilbert Welch, M.D., professor of medicine at Dartmouth Medical School, thinks Americans might be better served by thinking less—a lot less—about the disease. In his book *Should I Be Tested for Cancer?* Welch decries today's culture of "medical correctness" for making people feel guilty if they don't faithfully get a whole battery of cancer tests. He points to mainstream studies and statistics showing that the majority of people don't benefit from screening because most will never get cancer (roughly one of three women will get it during her lifetime). "Cancer screening is a two-edged sword," Welch says. "All the focus on early detection may not be in your best interest."

Worry is understandable, of course. Our story about the danger of CT scans (page 66) should give you pause. Plus, you or someone close to you may have the disease, or your risks may be elevated. But experts think Welch's argument is not off base. "Screening is not a silver bullet," says Stephen Taplin, M.D., M.P.H., senior scientist with the Division of Cancer Control and Population Sciences at the National Cancer Institute.

> **A woman who has a mammogram every year for 10 years has a 49-percent chance of getting a false-positive result, which could lead to a needless biopsy.**

"Early detection is only good sometimes. It's only better when it adds to the quality of life."

It often doesn't. Testing, Welch says, is a common match light for invasive, expensive, and sometimes risky follow-up exams and unnecessary treatments. And he says not all experts agree on who has the disease. He points to a study showing that a 15-year-old girl who undergoes a lifetime of Pap screenings has a 77-percent chance of getting a colposcopy (a visual examination of her cervix after an abnormal Pap smear), though 99 percent of such tests won't find cancer. A woman who has a mammogram annually for 10 years has a 49-percent chance of getting a false-positive result. That might lead to a needless biopsy—and false alarms won't do anything for your psyche.

Welch isn't suggesting that people blow off all tests. The problem, he says, is that there are no simple rules for when to get them. Your family history, lifestyle, and overall health should help you decide. But we think it would be foolish to let the availability of cancer testing—or even breakthrough research on cures—trick you into thinking smart behavior, such as eating right, is any less important. Find useful tips on prevention at www.cancer.org. ∎

How to Help Him Prevent
Prostate Cancer

Learn about the latest updates concerning this deadly disease.

BY TIMOTHY GOWER

The average man would rather shop for dish towels than talk about prostate cancer. Just thinking about a certain test used to detect the disease (that would be, uh, the digital rectal exam) makes guys squirm. In other words, when it comes to the second most common form of cancer among men in the United States (after skin cancer), women may need to start the conversation with the men in their lives.

And now's the right time. Recent studies are changing the way doctors think about diagnosing and preventing this disease. Here's what you should know before you have "the talk."

TO SCREEN OR NOT TO SCREEN

New research suggests that the prostate-specific antigen (PSA) test, the standard for detecting this type of cancer, could save more lives if it were fine-tuned. The authors of a recent study published in *The New England Journal of Medicine (NEJM)* estimated that the test, which measures the level of a protein that rises in the presence of prostate cancer, yields normal readings a shocking 82 percent of the time in men under age 60 who actually have the disease. Not exactly a good track record. But one of the study's

co-authors, urologist William Catalona, M.D., of Chicago's Northwestern Memorial Hospital, argues that if doctors were to use a lower PSA threshold to decide which men should receive biopsies, they would detect more potentially deadly tumors.

Catalona's research in the 1980s led to the widespread use of the test in the 1990s. Since then, Catalona points out, deaths from prostate cancer are down 20 percent among white men in this country, even though more men are being diagnosed with prostate cancer these days. (Death rates among African-American men, who get the disease more often than Caucasians or any other group, have diminished, too, but not as much.) Catalona believes the improving survival rates suggest more men are finding out they have prostate cancer before it spreads and becomes deadly, thanks to the PSA test. Still, he stresses that the exam is not perfect. The test only evaluates risk: The higher a man's PSA, the more likely a biopsy will show he has cancer. "It's not like a pregnancy test," Catalona says.

The test's high false-alarm rate, in fact, is the main reason critics don't like it. They point out that some prostate tumors are aggressive and potentially fatal, while others are slow-growing and never become deadly—but the standard PSA test can't tell one from the other. As a result, the skeptics say, too many men who take the test live with needless anxiety and undergo unnecessary invasive medical procedures, including biopsies and surgery, which can cause incontinence and impotence. Catalona believes the potential for saving lives by lowering the PSA threshold outweighs these risks. Still, it may also increase the ranks of men who have to live with debilitating side effects.

For now, the American Cancer Society (ACS) and other health groups encourage all men over age 50 to discuss screening with their doctors, and then decide on their own whether to get tested. That's a conservative, but sound, position. The ACS also recommends screening for any man with an increased risk, including men over 45 who are African-American or who have a close relative (such as a father or brother) who has or had the disease.

Remember, a complete prostate checkup always includes a digital rectal exam. And until a better test comes along, men and their partners need to decide for themselves how much faith to place in PSA screening.

BEAT CANCER—AND BALDNESS?

No one knows for sure how to prevent prostate cancer. But another study published in the *NEJM* in 2003 suggests that a common prescription drug might hold some promise. In landmark research involving more than eighteen thousand men, scientists at the University of Texas found that the drug finasteride (sold as Proscar) reduces prostate-cancer risk by 25 percent. Finasteride is already widely prescribed for urinary difficulties caused by an enlarged prostate, a common noncancerous condition. The same drug is also sold in lower doses (it's known as Propecia) to fight baldness. If the Texas researchers are right, men may be able to beat cancer, feel better, and save their hair at the same time. "Every guy, perhaps, over the age of 45 or 50 may want to consider finasteride," says urologist Ian M. Thompson, M.D., lead study author.

But should every guy in America take the stuff? Most doctors, who are waiting for evidence from ongoing studies, say no. Critics point to a scary finding in the finasteride study: 6.4 percent of the men who took it developed a form of cancer believed to be highly lethal (compared with 5.1 percent of the men taking a placebo). Because finasteride is known to lower PSA, some experts think taking it may mask the presence of deadly tumors. "If it were my brother, I wouldn't recommend finasteride right now for reducing the risk of prostate cancer," says internist Durado Brooks, M.D., director of prostate and colon cancer for the ACS.

DRUG-FREE HELP

Men who aren't ready to start taking drugs can take other steps that may ward off the disease, most of which landing in the "can't hurt, might help" category. For instance, smokers who quit may cut their risk of prostate cancer by as much as 60 percent, according to a study published in summer 2003 by epidemiologist Janet Stanford, Ph.D., of Seattle's Fred Hutchinson Cancer Research Center.

You might already know that consuming ketchup and other tomato-based products, which contain the antioxidant lycopene, may reduce cancer-causing damage to prostate cells. But new evidence indicates that other vegetables may fight off prostate cancer as well. Researchers at the University of California, Berkeley, reported in spring 2003 that a chemical in broccoli blocked the growth of prostate-cancer cells in a test tube. This finding appears to support a 2000 study, published by several of Stanford's colleagues, showing that men who ate three or more servings a week of cruciferous vegetables (broccoli, as well as cabbage and cauliflower) had a 41-percent lower risk for prostate cancer than men who avoided these veggies. Serve this potentially protective produce steamed with lemon juice and a sprinkle of salt, and it—like the new information about prostate cancer—shouldn't be too tough to swallow. ■

Are CT Scans SAFE?

This test is known for detecting cancer, but it could also increase your risk of getting the disease.

BY ERIC STEINMEHL

You might want to think twice if your doctor suggests a CT (computed tomography) scan. The imaging technique can be incredibly useful in diagnosing a host of ailments, including cancer, stroke, and even bone-density problems. But a growing number of experts are concerned about the potential risks—and the fact that many doctors are not telling their patients about them.

CT zaps you with up to 250 times the amount of radiation in one simple X-ray. But in a recent study conducted by Howard P. Forman, M.D., an associate professor of diagnostic radiology at Yale University School of Medicine, three-quarters of emergency-room physicians underestimated the dose. In a larger study, British researchers quizzed 130 doctors to see if they knew the amount of radiation in 16 different imaging tests, including CT. Every one failed.

Without question, the overall risks of CT are low. The U.S. Food and Drug Administration says the chance of developing a fatal cancer from one scan is 1 in 2,000—not worth widespread worry. Still, the risks of simply getting cancer from CT may be closer to 1 in 100. And since 65 million scans are done every year in the United States and use has jumped sevenfold in 10 years, there's a potential public-health problem.

Plus, some researchers point out that if a patient undergoes a handful of CTs—a 2000 study found 30 percent of patients who get a CT scan actually have at least three exams—she absorbs the same amount of radiation seen in some atomic-bomb

Determining the stages of certain cancerous tumors is an essential use of CT, but using it to diagnose kidney stones may not be.

survivors who got cancer. "It doesn't matter if the risks are really small; if you don't need to do a scan, you shouldn't do it," says Donald Frush, M.D., a pediatric radiologist at Duke University who has studied ways to reduce CT radiation.

Frush adds that the scans may be especially dangerous for kids and young adults. Their expected life spans are plenty long enough for radiation-related cancers—which develop over several decades—to become lethal. That's not the case for elderly people.

CT scans have been available since the 1970s. It's commonly thought that doctors order them to show they've gone to all lengths possible to get a correct diagnosis. Indeed, Forman claims M.D.s are increasingly ordering

CT scans when older, lower radiation tests would do just as well.

Determining the stages of certain cancerous tumors is an essential use of CT. But using it to diagnose kidney stones or to check for colon cancer, in a procedure called virtual colonoscopy, may not be. A CT may be faster than older kidney-stone tests, but the convenience might not be worth the risk. And virtual colonoscopy has other drawbacks: It's not clear whether the procedure will

> Some researchers point out that if a patient undergoes a handful of CTs, she absorbs the same amount of radiation seen in some atomic-bomb survivors who got cancer.

Babies and Brain Scans: What's the Cost?

If your tot takes a tumble and hits his or her head, your pediatrician may order a computerized tomography (CT) scan to make sure no serious head trauma has occurred. But a new study raises the question of whether even relatively small doses of radiation to a child's developing brain may affect IQ scores later.

Researchers combed through Swedish hospital records to find thousands of baby boys who received low-dose radiation to treat strawberry birthmarks. Boys who got doses comparable to those used in CT scans today scored slightly lower on learning and logic

tests 18 years later and were 50-percent less likely to attend high school. Further studies are needed to confirm the findings. In the meantime, says Lane F. Donnelly, M.D., chief

radiologist at Cincinnati Children's Medical Center and an expert on pediatric radiation, it's essential to follow your doctor's advice when a serious problem is suspected.

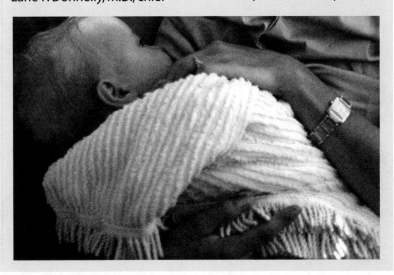

identify tumors at the earliest stages, so it may be right only for people who refuse to have the traditional kind.

Other newfangled uses of CT, such as whole-body scans, are especially controversial. They're popular with "worried well" types—healthy people willing to spend $1,000 for peace of mind. But Forman says the tests are rarely useful enough to justify the large radiation dose or the high false-negative and false-positive rates. Body-scan patients often undergo expensive follow-up procedures that cause needless anxiety. While the radiation threat of a single whole-body screen is small, says Scott Atlas, M.D., professor of radiology at Stanford University School of Medicine, patients need to be fully aware of the risks.

Our advice: If your doctor fails to talk about the dangers of CT, start the conversation yourself. ◼

Fight Cancer with Sleep?

Cancer patients who have strong social networks tend to fare better than those who don't. Researchers at Stanford University Medical Center proposed one explanation: They're more apt to get a good night's sleep. "If you're alone, you might sit and watch TV until 2 a.m.," says David Spiegel, M.D. "But if you're with someone else, you're more likely to decide to turn in together at 11." That could be crucial, he says. One reason: Melatonin is produced during sleep. The hormone is known to have antioxidant properties that can protect cells from cancer-causing damage. Cancer patients who don't have anyone to cuddle with under the covers can join a support group to improve their z's, Spiegel says. Hashing out anxiety during the day can keep it at bay during the wee hours.

WARNING: This Cancer Threat Just Got Bigger

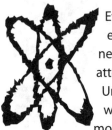

Even the smallest skin cancers need big-time attention. A Duke University study, which followed more than ten thousand melanoma patients for up to 30 years, found that small tumors have a 15-percent chance of coming back or spreading. That's 50-percent higher than previously thought and is similar to the risk with larger early-stage melanomas. Researchers recommend yearly follow-up exams, including a chest X-ray, for at least two decades after the original diagnosis. Every year, more than fifty-three thousand Americans are diagnosed with melanoma, the most dangerous form of skin malignancy.

Your Birth Weight, Your Future?

A baby's birth weight is often a source of pride for parents. It may also be a hint of trouble that'll surface years later. Why? Experts say weight is a clue to how the womb may have influenced a child's organs and hormone balances. Here's what to worry about—and how you (or your kids) might change fate.

PROBLEM	EVIDENCE	PRESCRIPTION
HEART DISEASE **At risk:** Small babies	Infants weighing 5.5 to 7 pounds have a 12-percent higher risk than those weighing 7 to 8.8 pounds, according to a Harvard University study published in 1997. And a recent British study found that each 2.2-pound increase in weight is linked to a 10.7-percent decline in CRP, a blood marker of inflammation associated with heart disease.	Make friends with fruits and vegetables, cut back on saturated fat, exercise often, and check blood pressure and cholesterol regularly.
DEPRESSION **At risk:** Small babies	A new study says infant girls weighing less than 6.5 pounds are 30-percent more likely to be depressed in their 20s than girls who were larger; infant boys who weigh less than 5.5 pounds have even higher depression risks. Being small at birth may be a sign of impaired brain development, which can lead to depression.	If you're feeling blue, get help now.
DIABETES **At risk:** Small or big babies	Small babies tend to have insulin resistance—a precursor to diabetes—for life. In a recent Japanese study, those weighing less than 5.5 pounds were twice as likely to develop Type 2 diabetes. But weighing more than 9 pounds can be bad, too: Diabetic mothers tend to deliver big children who grow up to be big adults; increased heft hikes their risk.	Keep weight in check, and have blood sugar tested. Also, find out if you gained weight quickly after birth; small babies who catch up to normal by age 2 are more likely to be fat adults.
BREAST CANCER **At risk:** Big babies	A recent Danish study of more than a hundred thousand women found that each 2.2-pound rise in birth weight increases risk by 9 percent. In another study, 10-pound babies had triple the risk of girls weighing 5.5 to 7.7 pounds. Faster growth in the womb may program breast cells to multiply faster and raise their odds of turning cancerous.	Get mammograms and clinical breast exams on a regular basis. And go easy on alcohol: Drinking boosts risks.
LACK OF SMARTS **At risk:** Small babies	Babies entering the world at less than 5.5 pounds are known to score lower on intelligence tests. But each additional pound adds about a point to IQ, especially among boys.	Beef up your smarts with brain exercises; try crossword puzzles.

Why You Should Watch Out for These
Household Dangers

Flame retardants in commonplace products could be as harmful to your health as the notorious PCBs. Here's how to protect yourself.

BY LOREN STEIN

Sometimes the cure can be worse than the problem, and scientists fear that may be the case with a class of flame retardants known as PBDEs (polybrominated diphenyl ethers). These chemicals were widely hailed as a public-safety breakthrough in the 1960s, but now experts are concerned that the substances are accumulating in humans in unhealthy amounts. They are so concerned, in fact, that some lawmakers are already taking action: California legislators passed a law in 2003 that will ban two common PBDEs by 2008.

California data indicates that PBDE levels in animal and human tissue in North America are doubling every two to five years.

You can't see, smell, or taste the chemicals, but chances are they surround you. "PBDEs are now measured everywhere; they're a ubiquitous environmental contaminant, just like PCBs and DDT," says Tom McDonald, Ph.D., a toxicologist with the California Environmental Protection Agency. Recent studies have detected the compounds worldwide in indoor and outdoor air, house and office dust, streams and lakes, and even in remote Arctic regions. They've been found in wildlife, including fish that people eat, and—perhaps most troubling of all—in human breast milk. Scientists still don't know exactly how PBDEs—used in such everyday products as sofas, mattresses, computers, hair dryers, and TVs—get into the body, but the theory is that people are breathing contaminated air and eating tainted foods.

Studies to assess the risks in humans have yet to be completed. But if lab results hold true for people, the outlook is disturbing. PBDEs have a chemical composition that is strikingly similar to that of their notorious cousins PCBs (polychlorinated biphenyls), suspected carcinogens that were banned in 1976 and have since been found to alter human development. Like their relatives, PBDEs mimic thyroid hormones, which help regulate the growth of a baby's neurological system. Experiments in the United States and Europe have shown that relatively low levels of PBDEs (less than 1 milligram per kilogram of body weight) disrupt brain development in young rats and mice. If these findings extend to human children, scientists believe they could mean subtle but measurable and irreversible changes in learning, memory, hearing, and behavior.

Luckily, eliminating PBDEs in the environment seems to quickly lower amounts in people. Levels in human breast milk began to drop in Europe almost immediately after the European Union started phasing out the chemicals, in the late 1990s.

Closer to home, Michigan and Massachusetts lawmakers are considering banning the chemicals following the lead of their counterparts in California. "Now that California has taken this historic step, I think there's no question that the issue is on the national agenda," says California State Assembly member Wilma Chan, who authored the state legislation. Congressional action or federal Environmental Protection Agency (EPA) regulation will likely take a while, though, because the studies are so recent that the issue isn't yet a priority on many state EPA agendas.

Meanwhile, the clock is ticking. California data indicates that PBDE levels in animal and human tissue in North America are doubling every two to five years. Of the women studied in another recent international report, levels were highest among those in the United States, primarily because U.S. industries use the most PBDEs; the studies reveal 10 to 70 times as many PBDEs in these women's fat tissue, blood, and breast milk as in the bodies of European women. Researchers warn that unless the substances are uniformly banned, within 10 years the average American may be carrying levels high enough to harm lab animals.

Scientists aren't sure how chemicals used in everyday products—such as sofas, computers, hair dryers, and TVs—get in the human body. But the theory is that people may be breathing contaminated air and eating tainted foods.

For now, no one is urging women to stop breast-feeding, says Linda Birnbaum, Ph.D., director of experimental toxicology for the U.S. EPA. "There's no reason to panic," she says, adding that the benefits of nursing clearly outweigh the risks. But shoppers can take measures now to protect themselves. Look for natural, rather than synthetic, home furnishings (such as wool and down) and products made in Japan, where the chemicals have been voluntarily phased out over the past 10 years. And pay attention to labels: At least a dozen major manufacturers—including Sony, IBM, Intel, Apple, Hewlett-Packard, and Ikea—are switching to safer alternatives. You can put your opinions into action by urging your state's lawmakers to push for the ban of PBDEs in consumer goods. ■

Loren Stein is an award-winning freelance writer based in Palo Alto, California.

When Infection Turns Deadly

Sepsis, a relatively unknown condition,
claims more lives every year than lung and breast
cancers combined. Know your risks.

BY MAUREEN KENNEDY

A few years ago, when Sandra Tiffany went in for routine surgery to treat a blocked kidney stone, it turned out to be anything but textbook medicine. After the surgeons successfully removed the stone, Tiffany's blood pressure mysteriously plummeted, and she struggled to breathe. The 54-year-old Nevada state senator was rushed into intensive care, where doctors hooked her to a respirator. "I was put on a deathwatch," Tiffany says. "My mother, father, sister, and daughter were called to my bedside."

How could a routine procedure spin out of control so suddenly? It turns out that as a result of the stone, Tiffany's urinary tract became infected, and her body's natural immune response to the bacteria went haywire.

Sepsis, the condition that nearly killed Tiffany, can strike anyone—it affects more than seven hundred thousand people annually, in fact. And it's increasingly common; cases have soared 302 percent over the past two decades, according to a recent study in *The New England Journal of Medicine* (*NEJM*). That rise is prompting new research as well as efforts to better educate doctors about sepsis.

The little-known condition turns deadly in about a third of cases, a mortality rate on par with heart disease and higher than that of lung and breast cancers combined. "There are probably about one thousand deaths from sepsis per day," estimates leading sepsis researcher Peter Ward, M.D., pathology-department chairman at the University of Michigan Medical School. "This would be the equivalent of three full 747s going down daily." And until doctors have a better understanding of how and why sepsis occurs in some people while sparing others, the number of cases will likely keep rising.

Normally, when you get an infection, your immune system sends white blood cells called phagocytes to find and wipe out the invading bacteria. Antibiotics speed that process along. But if the medicine isn't given quickly enough or if the bacteria are resistant to the drugs, the bugs can overwhelm the good guys. That kicks into overdrive the production of another kind of white blood cells called mediators, which play a critical role in blocking the spread of bacteria. But when mediators run rampant, they can cause blood clotting, cell damage, capillary leakage, and other serious problems. "When we see mediators in the bloodstream, this means the body has lost control of its inflammatory response, and we know the individual is in trouble," Ward says. Left untreated with antibiotics, sepsis can lead to organ failure or death within a few days or even a few hours.

If it's left untreated with antibiotics, sepsis can lead to organ failure or death within a few days or even a few hours.

People like Tiffany whose immune systems are weakened by illness are more prone to sepsis. In fact, medical advances could be contributing in part to the upsurge in sepsis cases. "There are a lot more surgeries and invasive procedures today that predispose people to infection," says Greg Martin, M.D., the lead author of the *NEJM* study. Doctors speculate that sepsis cases are also rising because of the aging population and, to a lesser extent, a resistance to antibiotics.

While you are most likely to get sepsis during a hospital stay, any exposure to bacteria raises your risk. Though rare, there have been cases caused by something as ordinary as stepping on a rusty nail or having wisdom teeth pulled. Urinary-tract infections are the most common sepsis trigger in women, accounting for about 15 percent of all cases, says Martin, assistant professor of pulmonary and critical-care medicine at Atlanta's Emory University.

Short of preventing infections altogether, doctors are still trying to solve the puzzle of what causes sepsis in the first place. "It's sort of been dubbed 'the Bermuda Triangle,' " Martin says. Researchers in Germany are trying to pinpoint physiological changes in the blood that may lead to an early-detection test, says Ward, who is a member of the research team. They may have results from the experiments within the year.

Tiffany, too, is working to find answers. After 19 days in the hospital, she has now fully recovered and has launched a public-awareness campaign to help researchers coordinate efforts to develop better detection and treatment methods. In 2003 she was behind a resolution that requires the Nevada health board to track sepsis cases and make the information available to scientists. She has also given talks to state legislators across the country, hoping that they, too, will organize awareness campaigns. Tiffany, grateful that she survived the ordeal, says, "I am aware that I was saved and that I have a purpose."

Q + A   Stop Kidney Stones

Not too long ago, I passed a kidney stone, and I'll do anything to avoid going through that again. What precautions should I take?

Some people say that passing a stone is as painful as childbirth, only when the ordeal is over, all you're left with is a jagged mineral crystal instead of a bouncing bundle of joy. Your doctor has probably told you that the most effective way to prevent future kidney stones is to drink plenty of fluids (enough to help you produce 2½ quarts of urine every day) and to make changes in your diet (limit consumption of salt and animal protein—meat, eggs, poultry, and fish). Here's additional advice: Be especially vigilant in your stone-prevention practices during colder weather.

A recent study, which examined urine samples from more than twenty thousand male and female patients, found that for some reason women are at increased risk for developing kidney stones during the early winter months. That's not to say that you can slack off the rest of the year, but you should be extra careful when the temperature starts dropping.

Don't Let Rising
Prescription Prices
Get You Down

As health-care costs rise, restrictions on popular allergy medicines are growing more common. But there are smart ways to get relief.

BY TIMOTHY GOWER

When Kathy Weber walked into a pharmacy in winter 2003 to pick up her Allegra prescription, she was stunned to learn her insurance plan wasn't covering the common allergy medication anymore. She turned to her doctor for help, but her insurer still refused to pay. Instead, Weber was told she'd have to switch to over-the-counter Claritin—and pay for it herself. Months later, she's still wheezing mad about the change in her policy. "I pay an awful lot for insurance to have a choice of which doctors we see," says Weber, of Coto de Caza, California. "I just can't believe we don't have a choice of what medicines to use."

Weber has plenty of company. Many of the nation's 50 million allergy sufferers are struggling to treat their irritating symptoms. Some, like Weber, are wrestling with their health plans over which drugs should be covered. Many others simply find

themselves digging deeper into their wallets to pay for medicine. A 2003 survey by Harris Interactive found that recent changes in how insurance companies pay for prescription drugs had some negative effect on 60 percent of U.S. allergy sufferers.

What's driving these changes? Money. Most major U.S. health plans won't pay for nonprescription medications. So after the popular drug Claritin became available over the counter in December 2002, the majority of insurers stopped covering it—which, according to one estimate, allowed them to save about $500 million in 2003, or one-third of what they would have paid out for allergy medications.

Sure, these savings may get passed along to consumers in the form of lower annual premium increases. "Our clients didn't have to raise rates as much as they would have had over-the-counter Claritin not become available," explains Glen Stettin, M.D., of Medco Health Solutions, a New Jersey–based pharmacy benefits management company whose clients include major insurers. But Claritin's new status has complicated life for some people who take allergy drugs.

Before they will OK coverage for prescription meds, including Allegra and similar drugs Clarinex and Zyrtec, many insurers now require doctors to fill out special forms explaining that a patient tried Claritin and didn't get relief. Patient advocates worry that some physicians will become frustrated with all the paperwork and simply recommend whichever drug is easiest to obtain. "I think some doctors may prescribe drugs that might not be their first choice," says Francene Lifson, executive director of the Southern California chapter of the Asthma and Allergy Foundation of America.

A few insurance companies have stopped covering Allegra, Clarinex, and Zyrtec altogether because they know patients can get Claritin without a

> **With co-pays for prescriptions on the rise, doctors worry you'll switch to over-the-counter medicines that make you drowsy.**

prescription. Most insurers, in an effort to make Claritin the first choice for patients, have simply made the prescription drugs harder to get by requiring the extra paperwork or raising co-payments. In some cases, a monthly co-pay of $5 or $10 has been raised to as much as $40—significantly more than the price of Claritin (a month's supply costs less than $20 at some retailers). But the cheaper drug may not be the right choice, doctors say.

Claritin and its prescription counterparts are all antihistamines. They counteract the itching and sneezing caused by histamine, an immune system chemical that the body churns out when it's invaded by allergens, such as pollen, dust, mold, and animal dander. But antihistamines aren't interchangeable because their chemical makeups differ slightly, explains University of California allergist William Berger, M.D., author of *Allergies and Asthma for Dummies*.

"We all have patients who have not done well on Claritin," Berger says, "but when we switch them over to one of the other medicines, they do really well." As a result, allergists like Berger believe the insurance industry is misleading patients by conveying the message that switching to Claritin shouldn't be a big deal.

The company that makes Claritin, Schering-Plough, received permission from the U.S. Food and Drug Administration (FDA) in 2002 to sell the drug over the counter. The company sought the change because its patent on Claritin (which allowed it to be the sole vendor) was set to expire, and lower priced generics were about to hit the market. Reclassifying the

HOW TO FIGHT BACK

If Claritin doesn't control your allergy symptoms and your health plan has made it difficult to fill a prescription for Allegra, Clarinex, or Zyrtec, consider taking the following steps:

- Ask your doctor to submit a "prior authorization" form to your insurer, indicating that Claritin was ineffective and that you need a different remedy; your physician should have the forms on hand. After that, you'll likely receive coverage for a prescription medication. But keep in mind that you may have to repeat this procedure to get an OK for a different prescription if the first one doesn't work.
- Talk to your doctor about prescription nasal corticosteroids, such as Flonase, Nasacort, Nasonex, or Rhinocort. "They're the drugs of choice for individuals who have mild to moderate allergic rhinitis," says Clifford Bassett, M.D., an allergist at the Long Island College Hospital in Brooklyn, New York, and a spokesman for the American Academy of Allergy, Asthma & Immunology. There's no indication that insurers are putting restrictions on these drugs. But remember that they don't provide relief for itchy eyes, a common allergy symptom, and you'll have to get used to squirting medicine up your nose.

drug made it easier for Schering-Plough to compete with the makers of the generic versions.

The move was good news for uninsured consumers: Paying out of pocket for prescription Claritin used to cost about $80 per month.

But in a 2001 poll by Harris Interactive, most allergy sufferers reported that health insurance covered at least a portion of their medication costs, and half said their co-pays were less than $10. Now, many doctors worry that insured patients who feel

Many allergy sufferers are now forced to try nonprescription drugs before their health plans will pay for pills that may work better.

Claritin isn't effective and are faced with higher co-pays for prescription drugs may switch to older over the counter antihistamines that are cheaper but may cause drowsiness. One big advantage of Allegra, Clarinex, and Claritin is that they don't make you sleepy (Zyrtec has only a mild sedative effect).

One managed-care company, California-based WellPoint Health Networks, has asked the FDA to allow all nonsedating antihistamines to be sold over the counter. WellPoint acknowledges that such a move would save the company $90 million a year, but spokeswoman Lisa Mee-Stephenson says

WellPoint is simply trying to keep its drug plans affordable. Retail spending on prescription drugs rises by at least 10 percent each year in the United States, Mee-Stephenson points out, so removing coverage for medications that treat such ailments as allergies might help insurers keep premium raises in check.

Still, if all of these medicines are available without a prescription, fewer allergy sufferers may bother to see an M.D.—another possibility that worries many physicians. "It promotes people diagnosing and treating themselves, and they may not be their own best doctor," says allergist Michael Schatz, M.D., president of the American Academy of Allergy, Asthma and Immunology.

Kathy Weber finally got relief (with her doctor's help), but it wasn't easy. After she suffered a severe attack of asthma—which can often accompany allergies—her physician petitioned Weber's health plan a second time, reporting that Claritin wasn't working. Eventually, the insurer agreed to cover Zyrtec, and it seems to keep Weber's allergies at bay. But now her co-pay is $25 a month instead of $10. Like many allergy sufferers, Weber simply has to accept that the price of breathing easy is going up.

Timothy Gower is a Health *contributing editor.*

Add Extra Punch to Your Painkillers

Combining ibuprofen with a common arthritis supplement can get you more pain relief. Though it won't fight pain on its own, glucosamine roughly doubled the power of ibuprofen in a recent study on mice. Researchers don't fully understand why, but they're moving forward on patenting an ibuprofen-glucosamine pill that may be available in 2005. The pill would let frequent ibuprofen users take smaller doses, reducing stomach-ulcer risk. Animal studies suggest that taking at least 400 milligrams of glucosamine (most supplements have 500 to 750 milligrams per dosage) for each 200 milligrams of ibuprofen would work best. Combining ibuprofen and glucosamine produced no adverse effects in earlier human studies.

Caveat: Glucosamine actually reduced the effectiveness of aspirin and acetaminophen in the mouse study.

The Common Drug You Shouldn't Mix with Ear Infections

Antihistamines could be harmful for kids who have earaches. The medicines are typically used to control allergy or cold symptoms, such as a runny nose and itchy, watery eyes. The problem comes when parents don't realize an ear infection is also present or when ears get infected soon after a bug or an allergy flare-up seems to be gone.

A recent study of 179 children with a common infection called acute otitis media showed that those who took an antihistamine retained fluid behind their eardrums for an average of 73 days, two to three times as long as those who took a steroid or placebo. The danger: As long as there is fluid in the middle ear, hearing is impaired.

Antihistamines may slow normal drainage in two ways: They might damage cilia, tiny hair-like structures in the middle ear that clear away fluid, says study author Tasnee Chonmaitree, M.D., professor of pediatrics at the University of Texas Medical Branch in Galveston. Or it may be that the medications' drying effect makes the fluid thicker and harder to clear.

Antihistamine products are easy to find at drugstores. Most of them have "allergy" in their names or chlorpheniramine or diphenhydramine among their ingredients. Decongestants, another common medication for respiratory illness, are not known to slow drainage the way antihistamines do, but they won't make ear fluid go away any faster, either.

Future studies might show that steroids can shorten the length of ear infections, Chonmaitree says, but for now the best remedy is still either taking antibiotics or watchful waiting.

How Antacids Are Causing Allergies

Medications designed to fight heartburn and other stomach problems may be unwitting accomplices to an apparent rise in food allergies. Although the medicines may seem harmless—many women take one kind just for its calcium—Austrian researchers have found that people may develop allergies after taking the drugs along with foods that are not normally part of their diets.

The researchers observed this effect in people who used such medicines as Prilosec and Zantac, but they predict that everyday antacids would have a similar impact. By blocking the production of stomach acid or neutralizing it, these drugs inhibit an enzyme that breaks down food proteins. Undigested, the proteins may be absorbed by the gut, where they can trigger an immune response, researchers say.

At a recent World Allergy Organization meeting, the investigators reported similar results from a study on mice that were given unfamiliar fish and hazelnut proteins along with the meds.

Food allergies affect as many as seven million Americans. So if you take antacids or heartburn drugs, stick to familiar foods, warns study author Erika Jensen-Jarolim, M.D., of the University of Vienna.

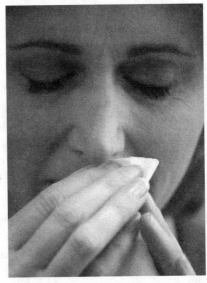

the Sunshine Vitamin

Why You Need More of It

A surprising number of people run low on vitamin D.
Here's what to do if you're one of them.

BY PETER JARET

H ere's a radical suggestion: Catch a few rays before you slather on the sunscreen. Too much sun can be dangerous, of course, but it turns out that not enough may be unhealthy, too.

The sun triggers your skin to make vitamin D, and direct sunlight is one of the main ways to get enough of this essential nutrient. Yet recent findings warn that there might be millions of Americans suffering from vitamin-D deficiency, and the consequences are serious. A shortfall may lead to chronic muscle and joint pain and osteoporosis—or even high blood pressure, colon cancer, non-Hodgkin's lymphoma, and multiple sclerosis (MS). The latest evidence is so alarming that the National Institutes of Health (NIH) organized a conference in fall 2003 to discuss the deficiency issue and how to address it.

Besides direct sunlight, the other ways of obtaining the vitamin are to take a supplement or to consume such fortified foods as milk (see "Getting Your Ds," on page 80). But these days many adults don't drink very much milk because of weight worries, a belief that they're lactose-intolerant, or other diet restrictions.

Vitamin D helps maintain bone strength by aiding in the absorption of calcium. When levels dip too low, bones become thin or misshapen.

And many never go without sunblock because they fear skin cancer or the wrinkles sun damage can cause. Problem is, sunscreen with an SPF of 15 almost completely blocks the body's ability to make vitamin D.

"One reason we may be seeing vitamin-D deficiency is that Americans have become too careful about staying out of the sun," explains Michael Holick, Ph.D., a professor of medicine at Boston University Medical Center and one of the country's leading experts on vitamin D. "The message has been, 'There's no such thing as a healthy tan.' But some sunlight is essential."

The growing worry that deficiency is far more widespread than anyone thought came to light in 2003. A study at Boston University School of Medicine found significant deficits in healthy young women and men tested that winter. A survey in Maine conducted at the same time suggested that young girls may also be at risk for vitamin-D shortages. And in a 2002 study, more than 40 percent of African-American women were found to be deficient (people of color don't make as much vitamin D from sunlight).

Doctors have long known that vitamin D helps maintain bone strength by aiding in the absorption of calcium. When levels dip very low, bones become thin or misshapen, a condition known as rickets in children or osteomalacia in adults. Inadequate levels also increase the danger of osteoporosis, or age-related bone deterioration.

But now doctors have new worries: Gregory Plotnikoff, M.D., a physician at the University of Minnesota, is convinced that vitamin-D deficiency is behind many cases of chronic muscle and joint pain. In a study published in the *Mayo Clinic Proceedings* in 2003, he found that more than 90 percent of patients suffering from unexplained pain had inadequate levels of vitamin D, 28 percent had severe shortages, and five of those patients actually had no detectable sign of the vitamin in their blood. Women were at the highest risk of falling short—perhaps because they tend to be more careful than men about sun protection.

Why vitamin-D deficiency might cause muscle and joint pain isn't fully understood, though researchers have long known that

this kind of discomfort is associated with osteomalacia. A recent study by scientists at the Riyadh Armed Forces Hospital in Saudi Arabia suggests that back pain could be another consequence: More than 80 percent of sufferers were vitamin-D deficient.

Too little vitamin D also appears to be a cause of high blood pressure. In a recent German study, people with moderate hypertension and low levels of the nutrient saw their blood pressure return to normal when they were given supplements. Preliminary findings also show a link between low levels of vitamin D and elevated risks for prostate and colon cancers. Cells in these parts of the body have receptors for the vitamin, which suggests that these organs need it to function properly.

Vitamin-D deficiency may also lead to MS, a debilitating disease in which the immune system attacks and destroys nerves. In 2004, researchers at Harvard School of Public Health found that women who get at least 400 International Units (IUs) of vitamin D—the amount in a typical multivitamin—are 40-percent less likely to get MS than those who don't take multivitamins. That makes a lot of sense to Boston University's Holick. "We've known for a long time that the risk of multiple sclerosis increases with latitude," he says. "The risk goes up the farther you go

There is good reason to enjoy a few rays.

from the equator, where the sun is less intense. The link may be vitamin D."

The nutrient is essential to immune cells. And when they don't have enough of it, the cells can malfunction in ways that are just beginning to be understood. Preliminary evidence links vitamin-D

Getting Your Ds

Here are some expert tips for making sure your body isn't short on the sunshine vitamin.

Catch some unfiltered rays. Dermatologists are reluctant to tell people to bask in the sun for fear of increasing skin-cancer risk. But that worry may be overblown, says Catherine Gordon, M.D., a researcher at Harvard Medical School who has conducted several studies of vitamin-D deficiency. "We need to get across that sunlight is healthy in moderation. During most months, 10 to 15 minutes a day is all most people need." That's enough for your skin to make vitamin D but probably not enough to raise cancer risk. Gordon's advice: Walk from your car to the beach, and then put on sunscreen. (You might also want to stay in the shade for 30 minutes after you apply sunscreen; it takes a while to be absorbed.) During the winter, people who live in the upper two-thirds of the country—roughly north of a line from Atlanta to Los Angeles—need to get the vitamin in other ways, because the sun never gets high enough in the sky to stimulate vitamin-D production.

Drink fortified milk—a lot of it. An 8-ounce glass contains only about 100 International Units (IUs). Cod liver oil is much richer in vitamin D (1,360 IUs per tablespoon), but it's tough to talk most people into a daily spoonful.

Take a supplement. Most multivitamins contain 400 IUs. And supplements with 1,000 IUs are beginning to show up at health-food stores. Is that too much? Probably not: The Institute of Medicine's suggested ceiling is 2,000 IUs.

deficiency to other autoimmune diseases, including rheumatoid arthritis and inflammatory bowel disease.

But keep in mind that there is no proof of a link between these conditions and a lack of vitamin D. "All we've seen are associations between vitamin-D deficiency and higher risk," explains Pennsylvania State University researcher Margherita Cantorna, Ph.D., an expert on the ways vitamin D affects the immune system. "We need more studies to prove deficiency is the cause. And we need to learn whether giving people vitamin D reduces their symptoms."

In the meantime, it wouldn't hurt to make sure you get enough vitamin D. While your dermatologist won't endorse tanning without sunscreen—"It's too easy to go from a little sun to too much," says Henry W. Lim, M.D., chairman of the dermatology department at Henry Ford Hospital in Detroit and a spokesman for the American Academy of Dermatology—it's easy enough to apply sunscreen after getting 10 minutes of sun without protection.

Experts' disagreements about exactly how much vitamin D you need shouldn't stop you from upping your intake either. Official guidelines under review by the NIH call for between 200 and 600 IUs a day, depending on your age, sex, and certain medical conditions. Holick and Plotnikoff think most people need at least 1,000 IUs, perhaps more, for optimal health. But even 1,000 IUs is just half the recommended upper limit.

The way to know you're getting enough vitamin D is to have a blood test. Holick believes that everybody should be tested once a year. He argues, "We test for cholesterol. We should test for vitamin-D deficiency, which could have an even bigger public health benefit." Plotnikoff also contends that checking your levels can be worthwhile. Still, rushing out to get a test may be rash; federal guidelines don't recommend routine testing.

If you're concerned, ask about vitamin D when you have your annual battery of blood tests. ▪

Award-winning health writer Peter Jaret is a contributing editor.

New Version of an Old Drug Chips Away at Osteoporosis

An old drug may be the newest thing for reversing osteoporosis. Strontium was widely used throughout the 1950s to help build bones until it fell out of favor over concerns that high doses interfered with production of vitamin D. But French researchers recently found that a low dose of strontium ranelate, a new version of the drug, along with vitamin-D and calcium supplements, cut spinal fractures by 41 percent over three years in women with osteoporosis. It also increased bone density by 14 percent.

The results are similar to those of the common drugs Evista and Fosamax. But those medications only harden existing bone; strontium ranelate, on the other hand, seems to make new bone tissue grow. Clinical trials are ongoing.

High Cholesterol and Weak Bones

High cholesterol could put you at risk for osteoporosis. In a recent study at Italy's University of Milan, postmenopausal women with LDL cholesterol above 160—the level experts consider high—were twice as likely to have weakened bones as women with lower LDL. Research from the University of California, Los Angeles, suggests that cholesterol accumulates near new bone cells and prevents them from growing. The good news: Cholesterol-lowering drugs seem to improve bone density.

Q + A

Swimming with Germs

Could germs in my neighborhood swimming pool make me sick? If so, how can I protect myself?

The chances that you'll pick up an infection in a public pool are pretty low, but it can happen. Chlorine is a potent disinfectant, but it doesn't instantly kill every single microbe carried into the water by your fellow swimmers. If one of those bugs survives long enough to sneak into your system, you might get sick. The most common poolborne ailment is diarrhea, usually triggered by germs from infected kids who aren't potty-trained (unfortunately, swim diapers aren't that effective). Keep yourself healthy by making sure that you don't swallow any water; even one accidental gulp could allow these germs to set up shop in your digestive system. Also, ask the pool manager how often the chlorine level is checked. Once a day just isn't enough; once an hour is ideal. Finally, find out how the pool scored at its last inspection, and try to find a swim facility that has a separate children's area complete with its own filtration system.

81

How You Can Lose the LASIK Woes

Dryness, distorted vision, and debilitating glare are not unusual after vision-correction surgery. Here's how to stare down the side effects.

BY WENDY LYONS SUNSHINE

After Cindy Brunett had LASIK surgery to improve her sight, she kept waking up every morning with her eyelids stuck shut. Forcing them open caused tiny rips in the surface of her eye, fogging her vision. And the 46-year-old mom from Canton, Michigan, suddenly became supersensitive to bright light. "It was extremely painful, just misery," she says. "I like to garden, and I couldn't tolerate being out there."

Fortunately, new remedies are helping people like Brunett get post-LASIK relief. Special drops have eliminated the stickiness in Brunett's eyes and improved her vision. "Prior to the drops," she remembers, "I spent a year in agony." Now she's enjoying her garden again.

More than four million people have chosen to get the surgery, and most seem satisfied. But in a recent university-backed study of about six hundred LASIK patients, published in the journal *Ophthalmology*, as many as 30 percent reported an irritating side effect, such as starbursts (spiked streaks radiating outward around a light), halos (glowing areas that encircle a light source), or uncomfortable glare. This finding was surprising because earlier eye-industry studies showed that only about 5 percent of patients usually report problems.

Why some LASIK patients suffer and others don't isn't always clear. It could be a shoddy laser or an unskilled doctor; people over age 40 or those who start out with very poor vision or dry eyes tend to have the worst luck. And even an otherwise-successful surgery may end up feeling like a failed one because healing, which differs from person to person, can trigger unpredictable changes on the surface of the eyes.

LASIK, or laser-assisted in situ keratomileusis, corrects both near- and farsightedness, so it's understandably popular. But it's not a walk in the park. After numbing your eye, the surgeon slices a round

> **Even a successful surgery may feel like a failed one because healing, which differs from person to person, can trigger unpredictable changes on the surface of the eyes.**

flap in your cornea's outer layer, folds it back, uses a laser to reshape your cornea, and then puts the flap back into place.

During the procedure, nerves that help keep your eyes lubricated are cut. That, in part, explains the post-surgery dryness. For most people, the nerves heal about six months later and the dryness goes away. But for up to 10 percent of patients—Brunett included—the dryness never quite disappears. Double vision is another potential problem, as is poor night vision.

How do you get relief if LASIK gives you fits? Here are four strategies to help you cope.

LUBRICATE, OVER AND OVER AND OVER

Gregg Russell, an optometrist and adviser to the Tampa, Florida–based Surgical Eyes Foundation, a nonprofit group for people with complications after surgery, sees 15 to 20 LASIK patients a month. Most have a number of complaints. "It's a challenge to sort out the puzzle," he says. Dryness, for instance, is often the culprit behind blurriness, and about 65 percent of his patients feel better after using one of several kinds of eyedrops.

Russell recommends over-the-counter artificial tears, such as Refresh Endura, Systane, or Theratears, along with a special kind invented by Frank J. Holly, Ph.D., a former professor of ophthalmology and biochemistry at Texas Tech University who has researched eye lubrication for years. Holly's drops (which go by such names as Dakrina, Dwelle, Freshkote, and Redkote) contain nutrients and other substances that lubricate eyes; he says they work better than traditional solutions, which often lose their effect when you blink.

Holly's drops have never been widely available (the business wasn't successful), but a company called Aqueous Pharma has licensed the formula and plans a national rollout in 2004. In the meantime, the drops are available by prescription through the ApothéCure pharmacy in Dallas,

which is affiliated with the Texas Institute of Functional Medicines, an alternative-medicine group. That may sound somewhat flaky, but Brunett got relief after trying Holly's drops for six weeks. Now she swears by them.

Contact ApothéCure at 800-969-6601 or www.apothecure.com.

REDISCOVER CONTACTS

It may seem like a crime to consider contact lenses after you've had your eyes zapped with a laser so you can get rid of them (or glasses) forever. But wearing contacts is an excellent way to reduce post-LASIK starbursts, glare, and double vision. Hard lenses (rigid gas-permeables) are usually the best choice, says James Saviola of the Ophthalmic Devices Division of the U.S. Food and Drug Administration (FDA). LASIK makes the eye surface flatter than normal; these contacts return a smooth, correctly shaped surface to compromised eyes, improving vision.

It may take several visits to an optometrist to get the right prescription, and "the fitting process is tedious," says David Hartzok, an optometrist in Chambersburg, Pennsylvania, who specializes in helping LASIK patients. "But when you've worked through the fitting process, we expect the lenses to work well."

Wanda Barreto, 48, a former accountant in Orlando, Florida, made several trips to optometrists before finding contacts that helped. "It's impossible to explain the distortions that we see," she says of herself and other LASIK patients. "It's like speaking Chinese to someone who doesn't speak Chinese." Barreto's hard contacts minimized the distortions, and now she's happy with her crisp 20/15 vision.

Don't like hard lenses? Two new types of soft lenses are currently being investigated. One is being tested by Marguerite McDonald, M.D., a researcher and clinical professor of ophthalmology at Tulane University who performed the first laser eye surgery in 1987.

GET LASIK A SECOND TIME

In 2002, the FDA approved a new LASIK procedure that may help people who've already had the surgery once, says James Salz, M.D., professor of ophthalmology at the University of Southern California and an FDA clinical investigator on lasers. The procedure, called wavefront, employs special software that carefully maps eyes, allowing for more precise use of the laser. It's thought to be beneficial for people who have trouble seeing at night.

"There's a chance this won't be helpful, and there's a slim chance it could make your eyes worse,"

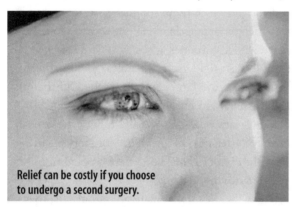

Relief can be costly if you choose to undergo a second surgery.

explains Salz, an attending surgeon at Cedars-Sinai Medical Center in Los Angeles who has performed over two thousand LASIK surgeries. "But on the whole it's working well." (First-time patients can now choose to have either wavefront or conventional LASIK. So far, results seem to be comparable.)

TRY ANOTHER PROCEDURE

Some doctors recommend other surgical techniques to fix LASIK troubles, such as PRK (photorefractive keratectomy) and LASEK (laser subepithelial keratomileusis). Unlike LASIK, neither of these procedures requires cutting a flap in the cornea before the eye is zapped with the laser. This can be useful if the cutting caused your problems, according to William Trattler, M.D., at the Center for Excellence in Eye Care in Miami. But even if a second surgery brings relief, it won't be a perfect solution. Nothing is. So if you have LASIK complaints, expect to do a bit of costly detective work. Says Barreto, "I spent $5,000 for surgery—and double that to find a solution." ■

Q + A Opening Eyes to Clearer Vision

I've heard about new contact lenses that you wear at night, helping you see clearly all day without them. Are they worth switching to?

The word from both wearers and doctors is that corneal refractive therapy (CRT) lenses, which were approved by the U.S. Food and Drug Administration in June 2002, are an overnight success. Here's how they work: These special rigid, gas-permeable lenses reshape the cornea (the front layer of the eye) while you sleep. After wearing them every night for one to two months, you should be able to get through a whole day without fumbling for your glasses or resorting to putting in contacts. Doctors recommend the treatment for people who are mildly to moderately near-sighted. (People who wear bifocals could use CRT lenses to correct distance vision but would still need reading glasses.) More studies are needed to determine the long-term effects on the cornea; complaints so far include blurriness and dry eyes, the same problems associated with other kinds of lenses. Daytime freedom from vision aids doesn't come cheap: CRT lenses, which need to be replaced yearly, cost around $1,000—about 10 times the price of regular hard contacts—and are not covered by most insurance plans.

Why Reading Glasses May Become a Thing of the Past

A simple 15-minute surgery could consign your reading glasses to the junk drawer forever. There's no timetable for it yet, but tests on animals and donated human eyes have been, well, eye-opening.

The procedure fixes a natural eye flaw. You see objects at different distances through a process called accommodation. Look at something far away, and your eye muscles stretch your lenses so you can focus on it. Look at something closer, such as this page, and your muscles return the lenses to their normal shape. As you age, lenses begin to stiffen. By age 40, they've lost 75 percent of their ability to relax, producing the presbyopia that makes up close vision so frustrating. But maybe not forever.

Accommodation restoration, pioneered by Arthur Ho, Ph.D., director of the Vision Cooperative Research Centre at the University of New South Wales in Australia, attacks the problem at its source. A doctor cuts a hole in the lens and suctions out the contents, mostly water and protein. Then a thick silicone-based liquid is injected into the lens to refill it. A quick burst of light solidifies the liquid into a stretchy gel, such as that found in a young, healthy lens. It's essentially a lens-replacement procedure—and that's the only real cure available, explains I. Howard Fine, M.D., clinical professor of ophthalmology at Oregon Health & Science University in Portland.

The treatment appears to allow for easy reading at about 4 inches, even better than the 12 inches made possible by most reading glasses. How long the improvement might last isn't clear yet, but the procedure is repeatable. It could also be useful for fixing cataracts, or clouding in the lens. Human trials began in 2004 in Australia.

Q + A

What Organ Donors Need to Know

I want to be an organ donor. Do I need to do anything besides check yes when I have my driver's license renewed?

Your desire to help others is good karma, since the waiting list for transplantable organs far exceeds the amount currently available. But after you get a donor card or indicate your intentions on your driver's license, you still need to make your plans clear to your family. One recent report showed that in hospitals nationwide, organ donators' wishes were actually carried out less than half the time. That's because this arrangement could be trumped at the last minute if your significant other or an immediate family member refuses to give consent, even if you've gone on record as wanting to be a donor. So cover your bases by having a chat now with your spouse, parents, or siblings about your decision.

Not Just a HEADACHE

You may be coping with migraines and not even know it. Fortunately doctors are discovering new ways to treat them.

BY EMILY SOHN

I used to blame my headaches on stress. Or drinking too many cocktails. Or not getting enough sleep. Or staring at the computer monitor for too long. When I woke up with a doozy not too long ago, I immediately regretted drinking that glass of red wine with dinner the night before.

Even for a supposed hangover, it wasn't pretty. There was throbbing pain deep inside my left eyeball. It hurt to look at my computer screen. It hurt to look outside. I even felt too queasy to eat. All I wanted to do was crawl back into my bed—but I had an important phone call to make. It's a crazy coincidence, I know, but I just happened to be researching migraines for a magazine article, and I had scheduled an interview with neurologist Seymour Diamond, M.D., founder of the Diamond Headache Clinic in Chicago.

As Diamond described the symptoms of a typical migraine, which include throbbing pain on one side of the head, nausea, and sensitivity to light, my own diagnosis seemed to hit me over the head. "That's exactly how I feel right now," I said. He didn't miss a beat, saying, "You have a migraine."

My symptoms are classic—how could I have missed the signals? It turns out, I'm not the only one who has. Some twenty-eight million Americans, most of them women, get migraines each year. More than half never receive a proper diagnosis. "Migraines are probably one of the most misdiagnosed and mistreated diseases," says Diamond, who is also the executive chairman of the National Headache Foundation.

In fact, the situation may be even worse than those appalling numbers suggest, if a recent study, published in November 2003 in the journal *Neurology*, is any indication. It showed that 58 percent of female neurologists and 35 percent of male neurologists had suffered migraines in the previous year. Among headache specialists, the numbers climb even higher, to 74 percent of females and 59 percent of males. Sure, it's possible that people with headaches might be more likely to become neurologists, but these physicians are also more likely to recognize the symptoms in themselves, says Houston neurologist Randolph W. Evans, M.D., an author of the study.

"I give lectures to doctors and nurses all the time," says Evans, who started getting migraines when he was in high school. "When I ask them to describe their headaches, almost invariably, they have migraines. These are doctors and nurses, and they don't know these are migraines they're having."

If your head hurts, it's worth the effort to figure out why. Untreated migraines take a heavier toll than previously realized on the spirits, pocketbooks, and bodies of sufferers. If you have migraines, you may well feel like a slacker—one recent study estimated that headaches cost $20 million a year in lost productivity. You almost certainly sometimes feel like an invalid, because improperly treating migraines (by throwing the wrong medicine at them, for instance) can breed more pain.

Naming your problem can make it easier to cope. But more importantly, it can also reduce the pain because recent research has produced an arsenal of new treatment and prevention strategies that are more effective than ever.

Elizabeth Pirsch knows too well what can happen when migraines go unrecognized. The 48-year-old lawyer from Alexandria, Virginia, has endured headaches nearly every day of her life since at least age 6. "I remember lying in bed and crying," she says, "and wishing someone would cut off my head because it hurt so much." By the time she was in high school, Pirsch was gobbling Dristan and Sinutab by the bottle. By the time she was diagnosed in her 30s, her migraines had spun so out of control that she was spending much of her time in bed. A lifetime of tensing against pain has left her with chronic shoulder problems and permanent knots in her muscles. "I think, 'My God, if I hadn't had migraines, life would have been so easy,'" Pirsch says.

It's easy to fall into the painkiller trap: Many people take over-the-counter pain medications more than two or three times a week and set themselves up for a lifetime of rebound headaches and escalating misery. "The pain mechanisms in the body adapt to having pain medicines on board," says neurologist

Untreated migraines take a heavier toll than previously realized on the spirits, pocketbooks, and bodies of sufferers.

Richard Lipton, M.D., of Albert Einstein College of Medicine in New York. Although experts don't fully understand the process, that seems to make the body's own pain-relieving chemicals partially shut down. Some 4 percent of people worldwide have daily or near-daily headaches, says neurologist Stephen D. Silberstein, M.D., president-elect of the American Headache Society, and most of the time rebound is to blame. "It's an epidemic," he says.

The agony of a migraine—which does not necessarily include a headache—can be hard for nonsufferers to understand. Telltale symptoms are many: In addition to the nausea and pulsing pain on one side of the head I experience, they include vomiting; pain that grows worse with physical exercise; and hypersensitivity to lights, sounds, smells, and touch. About 20 percent of migraine sufferers have visual auras, meaning they see zigzags or flashes of light, or lose their vision temporarily. Untreated, migraines can last days.

But for all the misery they cause, headaches are not always a socially acceptable excuse for missing work. Indeed, patients tend to blame themselves. Neurologist Stuart Stark, M.D., had finished medical school when he realized he had been getting migraines a few times a year for most of his life. "When I was a kid, I was told they were due to stress," says Stark, who lives in Alexandria, Virginia. "I was told that I couldn't handle stress so well. I thought it was my fault."

It's clear, however, that migraines are in the head—physically—not in the psyche. What happens in the brain is not fully understood, but imaging studies suggest that migraines start when an area of the brain near the base of the skull becomes overactive. This causes blood vessels around the brain to constrict and then dilate, in a cycle of pulses. Neurons in the brain start to fire aggressively, and the overamped firing spreads throughout the nervous system. (For some people, this hyperexcitability of nerves produces excruciatingly sensitive skin.) At the same time, inflammatory chemicals are released in the brain, along with the neurotransmitter serotonin.

All these things explain why some people live with migraines. But they could live without them. Some of the most important recent changes in treatment have grown out of a better understanding of a well-known class of prescription drugs called triptans. A variety of these medications (Amerge, Imitrex, and Zomig, for example) are available in a number of forms (pills, injections, nasal sprays). But they all work in pretty much the same way: by blocking the action of brain chemicals, thus interrupting pain signals.

Patients frequently take triptans 2 to 4 hours after a migraine starts. At that point, though, the drugs relieve pain in only about 40 percent of patients, says Harvard neurophysiologist Rami Burstein, Ph.D. Taking a triptan pill in the first 20 minutes of an attack aborts the headache in 93 percent of patients, Burstein reported in the *Annals of Neurology* in January 2004. The key is stopping the migraine before the overexcitement of nerve cells becomes too widespread.

Even better than treating migraines is preventing them—and there is a big push among experts to get patients to do just that. At its simplest, prevention means helping a sufferer avoid his or her headache triggers. These vary from person to person, and even from migraine to migraine, but they commonly include red wine, stress, over- or undersleeping, cigarette smoke, bright lights, and changes in weather or altitude. Changes in hormone levels can set things off, too, which might explain why more women than men have migraines and why women tend to get them at the start of puberty or menopause, or at the beginning of their periods.

Certain types of foods, such as chocolate, soft cheeses, and the artificial sweetener aspartame, can also cause problems. "Migraine patients need to be like a

DO YOU HAVE MIGRAINES?

Three simple questions are all that's needed to identify most migraine sufferers, reported neurologist Richard Lipton, M.D., in 2003 in the journal *Neurology*. He and his colleagues at Albert Einstein College of Medicine in New York intercepted 500 people who were seeing doctors for various reasons and found that 93 percent of patients who answered yes to at least two of the following questions were subsequently diagnosed with migraines.
1. Has a headache limited your activities for a day or more in the past three months?
2. Are you nauseated when you have a headache?
3. Does light bother you when you have a headache?

diabetic and read labels," says Michael John Coleman, the executive director of Magnum, a migraine-awareness group in Alexandria, Virginia.

But many people should do even more in the name of prevention. According to neurologist Silberstein, of Thomas Jefferson University in Philadelphia, more than half of people with migraines get them so frequently and so severely that they should be taking drugs daily to ward them off, yet only 5 percent do. Most migraine sufferers try to alleviate their pain instead of preventing it in the first place. "It's the difference between getting a vaccine and treating a disease after the fact," Silberstein says.

A number of prevention options are available, including drugs known as beta-blockers, as well as antidepressants—which are prescribed not because of their effect on mood but because of the chemical changes they produce in the brain. A drug called Topamax (topiramate), used for epilepsy, is also being studied as a migraine preventive. It seems to calm an overactive brain in two ways, Lipton says: by lowering levels of chemicals that excite the brain and by raising levels of chemicals that quiet it. "If migraine is a car," he says, "topiramate may simultaneously take the foot off the gas pedal and apply the brake."

Injections of Botox may help, too. More commonly known for its age-defying effects, the drug paralyzes muscles in the forehead, making wrinkles go away. But more than a decade ago, doctors began noticing that migraine sufferers who received the treatment were having fewer headaches. The connection has not been proven yet, and Botox is not officially approved for treating migraines (studies are ongoing). Still, many doctors are using the injections, which may prevent headaches in as many as 40 percent of chronic-migraine patients, Diamond says, perhaps by blocking the transmission of pain signals from muscles in the forehead.

Some alternative strategies look promising as well, Lipton says. In a recent study, the herb butterbur

root was as good as prescription drugs at preventing migraines, he says. The root occasionally causes stomach upset but it is basically low-risk, Lipton adds. Other alternative treatments that might be worth a try include the B vitamin riboflavin, the herb feverfew, and co-enzyme Q10. Chiropractic treatments, cognitive-behavior therapy, acupuncture, and biofeedback also may help prevent and treat migraines.

People with migraines might find relief from such treatments as Botox.

Ultimately, most migraine sufferers find that a combination of strategies offers the best chance at success. Susan Dyer, a customer-service representative from Seattle, has come a long way since her first migraine at age 23, when she spent the day on the floor with her newborn daughter because she was afraid she would drop the baby if she stood up. She was finally diagnosed more than two decades later.

Now 53, Dyer turns to the triptan Imitrex a dozen times a month, even though the drug saps her energy. She takes it when she has a steady headache or when the warning signals (auras and a feeling that her teeth are too tight) last more than a few minutes. Dyer has also learned to avoid her triggers, which include long naps. "I've had to give up one of my guilty pleasures," she says. The sacrifice has been worth it. "There is life after migraines," Dyer says. "See your doctor."

I plan to take Dyer's advice. I'm keeping a headache diary to help me spot any patterns in what I eat, how much I sleep, or how much stress I'm under. Next time I feel a migraine coming on, I'll go straight to my doctor to discuss my options. Only after that will I let myself crawl back into bed. Better yet, maybe I won't have to. ■

Emily Sohn writes for U.S. News & World Report *and* New Scientist, *among other magazines.*

A New Twist on

ACHING BACKS

A raft of research suggests that a hard workout may be the best therapy for back pain that won't go away.

BY LINDA MARSA

Kim Chester couldn't sit down—or stand up. It was the summer of 1999, and Chester had just finished tidying up her family's vacation cottage on Cape Cod. Suddenly she was hit by excruciating back spasms. "I was frozen in this crouching position for about 4 hours," the 46-year-old mother of two remembers. Her excruciating journey had just begun.

For the next several months, physical therapists treated Chester with heat packs, electrical stimulation, and light exercise—special stretches, nonimpact water aerobics, easy walking. But the pain never went away completely. And

Chester feared it might get worse, so she constantly babied her back. She even quit her software-sales job because the travel was too hard on her. "I couldn't take long car trips because I couldn't sit or go to social events where I'd be standing, and putting away the groceries was agonizing," she says. "My life was completely circumscribed by back pain."

Americans spend billions of dollars each year on surgery, pain pills, injections, chiropractic adjustments, massages, heat wraps, and outlandish fringe therapies to treat back pain.

She lived this way for three years. Then, out of desperation, Chester enrolled in a special back-pain program at New England Baptist Hospital's Spine Center in Boston. At first she couldn't believe it when the doctors told her to do everything the physical therapists had cautioned her not to, such as running on a treadmill or riding a stationary bike. But three months later, Chester felt better than she had in years.

Every year, 65 million experience back pain that limits their activities. It's the second most common reason for doctor visits, behind colds and flu. An astounding four out of five adults are stricken sometime in their lives, and a new Duke University study suggests that women suffer more often than men.

It's not unusual for a back-pain sufferer like Chester to seek out something—anything—that might help. Indeed, in an often-futile quest for relief, Americans spend billions of dollars each year on surgery, pain pills, injections, chiropractic adjustments, massages, heat wraps, even outlandish fringe therapies.

Yet a growing body of research suggests that a good workout designed by a doctor is better than anything else. Even for people who feel paralyzed by back pain, it may be the wisest alternative.

The dividends can be substantial. Several studies indicate that people who complete boot camps for aching backs feel much better: They experience less pain, don't require more treatment, and are more likely to return to work than back-pain sufferers who use conventional therapy. "There's more and more evidence that strenuous exercise makes a difference," says Richard Deyo, M.D., a back-pain expert at the University of Washington in Seattle, "especially for people with chronic back pain." How many people fit the profile? Roughly 15 percent of patients who see a doctor for back pain experience discomfort that lasts more than two months—the chronic kind.

FAREWELL, FEAR; HELLO, SWEAT

Boot camps like the one Chester attended aren't considered mainstream medicine—yet. According to Vert Mooney, M.D., clinical professor of orthopedic surgery at the University of California, San Diego, and one of the pioneers of this approach, only about 10 percent of back doctors across the country are on board. But the idea is

---

Stop Backaches Where They Start

At the office ...
- Make sure your chair is comfortable and provides good lower back support. There should be 2 inches between the front edge of the seat and the backs of your legs. Sit with your feet flat on the floor and your knees at 90-degree angles.
- Don't sit cross-legged; this cuts off blood circulation and puts your back out of alignment.
- Walk around every hour or so to prevent muscle stiffness.
- Take breaks to stretch.
- Put a rolled-up towel or pillow between your lower back and chair when sitting for long periods.
- Hold the telephone with your hand, or use the speakerphone or headset. Don't cradle the phone between your ear and shoulder; this can lock up the spinal joints in your neck and upper back.
- Wear soft-soled shoes with low heels. High heels cause the pelvis to tip forward, which upsets the spine's natural equilibrium.

At home ...
- Bend at your knees (not at your waist) when lifting heavy objects, letting your thighs do most of the work.
- Don't tote heavy purses or backpacks (equaling more than 10 percent of your body weight); they can lead to chronic neck and back problems.
- Sleep on a supportive mattress.

catching on. Clinics that use the boot-camp method are open in nearly all states.

Increasing disenchantment with standard treatments is fueling the programs' popularity. "The trend now is toward not just physical therapy but aggressive rehabilitation," says Richard Guyer, M.D., an orthopedic surgeon at the Texas Back Institute in Plano.

Boot campers, who may have trouble simply walking or carrying a bag of groceries, are encouraged to overcome their fear of activity and follow punishing exercise regimens using Nautilus-like machines that help them strengthen and stretch back muscles, making them stronger and more limber.

> Clinics that operate boot camps for aching backs are open in nearly all states. But this kind of aggressive therapy isn't considered mainstream medicine—yet.

Initially, participants go through an extensive diagnostic workup to determine their range of motion and levels of strength, flexibility, and ability to perform such ordinary functions as sitting in a chair or carrying a laundry basket. Then patients commonly participate in intensive 1- to 2-hour therapy sessions two or three times a week for up to two months.

In a typical workout, after about 20 minutes of stretching and cardio exercise, such as walking on a treadmill, campers hop on a series of weight-training machines that isolate back, abdominal, hamstring, and butt muscles—the ones that support the spine. In some clinics, participants even lift milk crates filled with steel bricks to strengthen muscles used in everyday tasks, such as unloading the dishwasher. Such exercises help patients get over fears that lifting will cause pain. "We concentrate on restoring real-life activity," explains Carol Hartigan, M.D., a rehabilitation physician at New England Baptist Hospital Spine Center and a professor of psychiatry at Harvard Medical School in Boston.

Patients' progress is carefully monitored: The amount of weight they have to push on each machine and the number of repetitions are gradually increased. Women typically start out with 40- to 50-pound weights and build up to 90 to 100 pounds. This may seem like a lot more weight than most women are accustomed to. But the extra weight helps exhaust muscles, and that leads to strength gains. "We want to challenge those muscles each time to the point of failure, where patients can barely do the repetition. That's how we build muscles," says Joseph Wegner, M.D., a specialist in rehabilitative medicine at Physicians Neck and Back Clinic near Minneapolis, which has treated more than twenty-five thousand people.

Patients are also encouraged to do a follow-up maintenance program on their own (for details, see "Boot-Camp Basics," page 94).

When Chester began her boot camp, she was in such pain that she almost felt disabled. The agony came from working muscles atrophied by disuse. But waking up those muscles is what counts. "I just sucked it up and got through it," Chester says. "Their philosophy of strengthening the muscles around the injury to compensate intuitively made sense."

WHERE DID ALL THE PAIN GO?

The handful of studies on the boot-camp approach supports Chester's intuition and experience. In a 1995 study, over six hundred thirty people with back pain for over two years completed an intensive exercise program at the Physicians Neck and Back Clinic. They had tried an average of six different treatments: 89 percent had already failed to get relief from less-aggressive exercise, 47 percent had tried chiropractic without success, and 14 percent had undergone at least one previous surgery. Three-quarters of the patients saw their pain disappear or subside substantially. A year after treatment, 94 percent of them were still feeling good.

A 1999 study at the same clinic, published in the *Archives of Physical Medicine and Rehabilitation*, showed that vigorous exercise may help sufferers avoid invasive treatment. Sixty patients were enrolled in a 10-week boot camp after their doctors had recommended surgery. Of the 46 who completed the program, only three ended up going under the knife. "Not only did people get better," Wegner says, "but also they stayed better."

Roughly fifteen thousand have tried a camp affiliated with New England Baptist Hospital's Spine Center over the past six years. Hartigan says most participants, like Chester, have improved. "In general, people who undergo the rehab demonstrate significant objective, measurable improvement in strength, flexibility, and cardiovascular endurance," Hartigan notes. "They also report less pain."

Researchers aren't sure why this taxing regimen works. They think it strengthens and limbers the dense network of muscles and ligaments that encases the bony vertebrae and rubbery disks of the spinal column and spinal cord. Heavy-duty workouts may also ease muscle cramps that often cause back pain.

Exercise seems to help people with chronic back pain get over their fears of such everyday activities as lifting grocery bags or emptying the dishwasher.

In addition, doctors speculate that exercise desensitizes people to pain messages sent out by the brain.

You might be surprised to learn that belief in the value of hard-core exercise to combat chronic back pain has a long history. A Swedish physician pioneered the use of strengthening exercises involving mechanical devices back in the 1850s, although the approach never became popular. Then, in the 1940s, two U.S. doctors resurrected it and built on it by developing specific moves to strengthen the back. But as modern medicine advanced, these concepts were abandoned in favor of passive strategies designed simply to treat symptoms.

Over the past 15 years, strenuous exercise therapy has regained legitimacy, thanks to people like Mooney, the orthopedic-surgery expert at the University of California, San Diego. Where doctors routinely prescribed traction and bed rest for acute and chronic pain—as well as painkillers, steroid injections, electrical stimulation, and other passive treatments—now some are turning to the polar opposite.

It's understandable. Research shows that muscles start to atrophy as soon as you stop moving, which makes back problems worse, not better. More than two days of inactivity can make muscles weak, stiff, and more prone to reinjury (it also weakens healthy muscles, making them more vulnerable, too). This unfortunate process is called deconditioning. Exercise, on the other hand, builds strength; enhances blood flow to disks, joints, and muscles; calms painful spasms; speeds healing; and boosts bone density.

THE RISK OF GOING ALL OUT

Despite the research and the testimonials of dramatic transformations from people like Chester, some experts remain cautious. Most doctors fall short of recommending the heavy-duty exercise that's the hallmark of boot-camp programs. More common are physical-therapy regimens that emphasize gentle exercise, such as the type Chester tried initially: stretching and low- or nonimpact activities, such as leisurely walking and water workouts.

While there is a growing consensus that exercise is helpful, and although several studies indicate that light exercise can bring relief, some doctors fear the hard-core approach because they worry that patients won't do it correctly—and that could lead to injury.

Light exercise, along with over-the-counter (OTC) painkillers, is still the way to go for people with sporadic bouts of back pain—periodic flare-ups triggered by poor posture, heavy lifting, endless hours of sitting immobilized at a computer, or straining little-used back muscles while breaking ground for your spring garden or hitting a few volleys with your dusty old tennis racket. The exercise/OTC combination helps most people feel better within

---

Boot-Camp Basics

Intensive rehabilitation programs use specially designed exercise equipment, such as products made by MedX or Cybex, as well as weight machines found in some health clubs. Using the machines targets muscles weakened from disuse, builds them up to compensate for injuries, and gives the spinal column more support.

Here is a typical doctor-supervised routine that involves hard-core exercise two days per week. You should perform one set of each exercise to the point of muscle failure—where you're too tired to do any more repetitions.

1. Lumbar extension. You sit in a padded chair, with your thighs anchored by straps so that your butt muscles and hamstrings won't do the work. You push your back against a bar weighted to a resistance of anywhere from 40 to 160 pounds, leaning back until your upper body is at roughly a 45-degree angle to the floor. The weight and the angle vary depending on the extent of the injury, gender, and progress. Repetitions: 20 to 30

2. Torso rotation. With your upper and lower body anchored, you work your abdominal area by pushing against a shoulder-high bar attached to weights. You work both sides of your torso by switching positions. The exercise stretches and builds muscles in the waist and restores joint motion in a stiff spine. Repetitions: 20 to 30

3. Ab isolation. With your hips anchored, you push forward against a chest-height pad attached to weights. How far forward depends on the severity of the injury, gender, and progress. Repetitions: 20 to 30

Do-it-yourself Maintenance
Physicians also recommend a routine that patients can do at the gym or at home. The regimen includes:
- Stretching seven days a week
- Strength exercises two days a week (to the point of muscle failure—usually 10 to 20 reps) on a Roman chair, also known as a back-extension machine. Three simple moves performed while using the machine will give your lower back muscles a solid workout. (The chair costs $125 to $250; ask your orthopedist or a back-clinic doctor about where to buy one. Your insurance may cover it.) You can also use an inflatable fitness ball to do comparable exercises.
- Motion exercises during the other five days of the week, using the chair or the ball. These are similar to the strength exercises but are performed with much less intensity. Improving range of motion is the goal; adding strength is not.
- Aerobic exercise three days a week (not on strength-training days) for 20 to 30 minutes. Low-impact options include brisk walking or stair climbing. High-impact types include jogging and aerobics classes.

Safety First
Don't be a do-it-yourself casualty: Consult with a doctor before you start using a Roman chair or a fitness ball.

a week or two. (For easy ways to avoid short-lived episodes of pain completely, see "Stop Backaches Where They Start," page 91.)

Critics of the boot-camp regimen also complain that it has never been put to a broad head-to-head test against conventional remedies, such as pain relievers, hot packs, or massage. They argue that the supporting evidence is largely circumstantial.

Besides, most people eventually recover even without treatment. "It could be just the natural history of their back pain—even people with herniated or degenerating disks will get better with time," says Jeffrey Wang, M.D., an orthopedic surgeon at the Geffen School of Medicine at the University of California, Los Angeles (UCLA).

The mystery behind most backaches is as good a reason as any to be cautious about taking aggressive measures. Most chronic pain results from disk cartilage that has degenerated or ruptured so that it's bulging painfully against tissue or nerves. But muscles can also become cramped from tension and stresses, such as heavy lifting or poor posture. And the back may simply degenerate as a natural part of the aging process, causing disks to deteriorate and the spinal column to narrow.

It's difficult to determine which treatment will work because X-rays or such imaging techniques as MRIs or CT scans, which can capture snapshots of soft tissue, may not yield an accurate picture of what's going on. So if someone who is seriously injured tries boot camp, a misdiagnosis could lead to trouble.

"People think that if they do these exercises, they're cured," Wang says. "While they may have gotten rid of their symptoms, if they have a huge amount of pressure on the nerves or there are serious structural problems in the spine, you're never going to be able to fix them without surgery."

In rare instances, back pain can be a red flag that something else is seriously wrong. You could have a spinal infection or a tumor, a ruptured disk, or a bone spur pressing against the spinal cord or the nerves. If you're feeling weakness in your leg that's causing you to stumble or trip, or you're losing bowel and bladder control, your spinal cord or nerves could be in danger (see your doctor as soon as possible if you have any of these symptoms).

But experts—even Wang at UCLA—agree that surgery is rarely the answer. Estimates suggest that only about 2 to 3 percent of patients can benefit. Plus, such side effects as infections, limited mobility, and persistent pain are not uncommon following invasive treatment.

The mystery behind back pain is a good reason to be cautious with any aggressive treatment.

To rule out the rare ailment requiring surgery, you should go to a back clinic staffed by M.D.s. You'll be tested extensively before being referred to a boot camp. No reputable doctor will refer a patient unless she's undergone a thorough checkup.

Of course, even if surgery or some other scary procedure is the last thing you're ready for, boot camp may not be the first. After people in crippling pain start the grueling workouts, getting them to stick with the regimen is often difficult; as many as one-third drop out. "The trick here is that these programs require compliance," the University of Washington's Deyo says. "It's very hard to get people engaged and keep them engaged in an exercise program."

Still, for pain that won't go away, aggressive rehab may be worth looking into before trying anything else. Kim Chester is convinced. While she still avoids activities that jar her back, such as running, she's felt good enough to go horseback riding and mountain climbing. She brags now about toting around a 50-pound water jug and comfortably pushing 90 pounds on a back-exercise machine. "I only wish someone had told me about this program sooner," Chester says. "I wasted years being in pain and inactive." ▪

Freelancer Linda Marsa writes a regular column about medical research for the Los Angeles Times.

Physical vs. Emotional Trauma: Why the Pain Is the Same

Picked last for dodgeball? Ouch! Passed over for a promotion at work? Ugh! Left at the altar? Argh! Everyone knows rejection hurts, but now science is helping to explain why.

Researchers at the University of California, Los Angeles, have shown that some of the same brain centers that are activated by physical pain also get busy when you experience a social loss or rebuff.

In the study, 13 volunteers played a computerized ball-tossing game while psychologists monitored blood flow to their brains. At some point during the session, each participant was excluded by two other players (in reality, the colleagues were virtual, created by the computer program). When the subjects became social pariahs, blood flow increased to areas of the brain known to register physical discomfort.

"We seem hardwired to be hurt by rejection," explains Naomi Eisenberger, a social-psychology graduate student and the lead author of the study. Having a social-attachment system piggybacked onto the pain system is probably an evolutionary safeguard to keep people

closely connected, she says. After all, it would have been hard for an early human to survive alone on the African savanna with just a weapon in hand.

The connection between emotional and physical pain is even demonstrated in language, explains Mark Leary, Ph.D., professor and chairman of psychology at Wake Forest University. In many languages (he has looked at 16), the same words are used to describe both physical and emotional wounds, he says—consider phrases such as "you cut me to the core" or "that hurt me deeply."

But there's good news, too: Once the part of the brain that responds to emotional distress is turned on, another area appears to step in and soothe the sting. Because this damping-down region is involved with emotional language, Eisenberger suggests that writing down your feelings can help you deal with your pain.

Another step may help as well, Leary says: accepting that the hurt of social situations is very real. "The saying that our parents taught us about 'sticks and stones will break bones, but words will never hurt us' is a complete lie," he says.

Q + A

When Meds Are Too Hard to Stomach

I take ibuprofen several times a month for back pain. Sometimes it upsets my stomach. Am I setting myself up for an ulcer?

The bottle of Advil in your purse probably won't do your stomach any serious harm. There's a lot of research linking regular ibuprofen use to gastrointestinal (GI) troubles, but those studies have looked only at people who continually take high doses—one or more tablets a day for months or years. Researchers at Stanford University School of Medicine recently completed the first study examining the occasional use of ibuprofen and other nonprescription pain relievers; the scientists found that taking as many as 10 pills a month doesn't raise the risk of ulcers or other GI bleeding problems. Your queasiness is probably just indigestion from the extra stomach acid the meds kick up. (Vomiting blood or passing black stools, which may signal blood, is more serious and warrants a visit to your doctor.) Taking the pills with food or switching medicines should prevent stomachaches.

How to Build a Better Memory

If you play your cards right, you can stay sharp as the years go by.

BY M.A. WOODBURY

J eez, I must be losing my mind!" You say it when you find yourself in your kitchen without a clue as to why. You say it when you can't find your keys—again—or when your neighbor's name escapes you. Those moments when memory fails are frustrating, and sometimes mildly frightening, but are they really a signal of things to come as you travel down the not-so-rosy-path to dotage?

In short: No. That's the encouraging message from neuroscientists who are delving into minds and memories at a furious pace. "Don't automatically expect that your memory will go to pot as you age," says James L. McGaugh, Ph.D., director of the Center for the Neurobiology of Learning and Memory at the University of California, Irvine. Just as staying out of the sun can prevent wrinkles, researchers say, taking action now to protect your memory can help ensure tack-sharp alertness in years to come.

That doesn't mean your mind won't undergo changes as you age, says Ruth O'Hara, Ph.D., assistant professor of psychiatry and behavioral sciences at Stanford University. Indeed, the memory center of the brain—the hippocampus—actually decreases in size as a person gets older, says O'Hara, who studies memory decline in aging.

But that's not as ominous as it sounds because for most people the most noticeable change is in the speed at which they process information. Starting in midlife, people take longer to learn new things. They also begin to notice something called the "tip of the tongue" phenomenon, says Molly V. Wagster, Ph.D., program director for neuropsychology of aging research at the National Institute on Aging. That's the feeling you get when you can't dredge up the name of the movie you saw last week. Then there's that pesky decrease in your ability to multitask—to divide your attention among your kids

> Just as staying out of the sun can prevent wrinkles, taking action now to protect your memory can help ensure tack-sharp alertness in the years to come.

in the backseat, your husband on the passenger side, and the car on your left trying to squeeze into your lane. (Memory comes into play here if you're distracted and forget that the car on the left is there.)

Despite all these nicks and scuffs, though, accuracy seems to remain intact, says Barry Gordon, M.D., Ph.D., founder of the Memory Clinic at Johns Hopkins Medical Institutions. What's more, there's mounting evidence that you can actually sharpen other aspects of memory as you age. In 2002, a major study showed that training in reasoning, memory, and speed of processing information bumped up mental function in healthy older adults—and it provided more than a temporary boost. Benefits were still evident two years later, most notably in participants who attended brief refresher sessions.

But the best news of all is that you can work on your mental fitness without signing up for the next memory study at a local university. The following are some of the most effective ways to hone your wits and keep them sharp.

USE IT OR LOSE IT
One of the most important steps you can take is to continue to learn, researchers say. You need something that's challenging but not stressful to figure out, says Janine Jennings, Ph.D., who studies memory at Wake Forest University in North Carolina. She suggests taking up Tai Chi, for instance (lots of moves to learn, all with exotic names), or chess if you've never played.

This strategy helps you stockpile mental reserves, says Edward Zamrini, M.D., a researcher at the Memory Disorders Clinic of the University of Alabama at Birmingham. How? Even if your brain cells decrease in number over the years, the connections between them can increase—if you stay mentally active. Memories seem to be stored as patterns of connections between nerve cells, so the more connections, the greater the odds that you'll be able to call up a memory.

GET PHYSICALLY FIT
Keeping your body in shape seems to be just as important as using your mind. That means that your diet should be full of antioxidant-rich fruits and vegetables, and that you should get plenty of exercise.

A study conducted at the University of Illinois at Urbana-Champaign shows the importance of fitness. Researchers looked at two groups of older adults: One group walked briskly three times a week for six months, and the other did stretching and toning exercises; everyone underwent cognitive tests at the beginning and the end of the study. Scores for the stretch-and-tone group remained stable, while those for the walkers improved.

MANAGE STRESS
Memory seems particularly vulnerable to long periods of extreme stress. When a person is subjected to it, a steroid hormone called cortisol is released into the bloodstream. Especially in high levels, this substance can disrupt connections between nerve cells, says Robert Sapolsky, Ph.D., a professor of biological science and neurology at Stanford University who has conducted research into the effects of stress in animals. In short, here's another reason to find a stress-busting routine that works for you.

CATCH YOUR Z'S
Until recently, there was no strong evidence of a link between sleep and memory, but that's changed. Memories are created in three discrete stages, the second of which requires sleep, says Harvard University psychiatry researcher Matt Walker, Ph.D. "If you learn something during the day and are tested on it that same day, there is no improvement in the memory," he says. "But after a night of sleep, that memory is improved." The bad news is that if you miss some sleep the first night, you've lost your chance; extra rest later won't help. So if you really want to remember something you've learned during the day, be sure to hit the hay on time that night.

WATCH THE SUGAR
Blood sugar (aka glucose) is the only fuel used by the brain. If you can't regulate it well, you may not be able to recall memories efficiently, a new study has found. There's growing evidence that people with diabetes have memory problems, but they're not the only people at risk. Antonio Convit, M.D., assistant professor of medicine at New York University School of Medicine, recently studied 30 nondiabetics, testing their thinking and memory, as well as how efficiently their bodies metabolized blood sugar.

The people who didn't regulate sugar well scored lower on the memory and cognitive tests and had smaller memory centers in their brains than those with good glucose control. The keys to avoiding problems with blood sugar, says Convit: Watch your calorie intake, control your weight, and exercise.

GO SLOW WITH SUPPLEMENTS

Ginkgo biloba is often touted as a memory enhancer and is intriguing enough to have prompted the National Institutes of Health to start a large study. But most experts remain skeptical. It's important to note that the supplement has potentially dangerous side effects (it can cause bleeding and blood clots, for instance). And ginkgo is not regulated by the U.S. Food and Drug Administration, says Gary Small, M.D., director of the UCLA Center on Aging, so you can't always count on getting exactly what the label promises. ◼

Mental First Aid

Have you lost your marbles—or just temporarily misplaced them? Chances are, recall strategies can help with the memory misfires you find irritating.

TEST YOUR MEMORY: Study this list* for up to 1 minute, then put it away. After 20 minutes, see how many items you recall.

Plank	Banker	Sauce	Umbrella	Abdomen
Reptile	Lobster	Orchestra	Forehead	Jury

8 or more items: Excellent.
Fewer than 5: This may indicate a problem with delayed recall. But don't panic: The problem may not be serious. To see how memory exercises can help, try the next test.

* Source: *The Memory Bible,* by Gary Small, M.D.

THEN IMPROVE IT: Study this list** for 1 minute. As you try to memorize these items, group words into similar categories (winter activities, things you do at the gym, or sports that use a ball). After 10 minutes, see how many you recall.

Snow skiing	Basketball	Tennis	Aerobic dancing	Bobsledding
Stairstepping	Hockey	Baseball	Ice skating	Spinning
Weight lifting	Golf	Volleyball	Kickboxing	Soccer
Yoga	Snowboarding	Cricket	Treadmill walking	Elliptical training

More than 10 items: You're on track to improving your memory.

** Source: University of Texas Learning Center

RESOURCES: For more memory information, visit www.agenet.com (look for "Ask the Experts" on the right-hand side of the page, click on the pull-down menu, and go to "Mental Fitness," where you'll find "Aerobics of the Mind"). Additional strategies for improving your memory are available at www.memoryfitnessinstitute.org.

vital *stats*

128

Millions of federal dollars spent on an antismoking campaign between 1991 and 1999

47

Billions of dollars the tobacco industry spent to market its products during the same period

17

Percent increase in sales of antidepressants in 2003

26

Percentage of people in a nutrition study who said they ate five servings of fruits or vegetables a day

---

13

Percentage of people who said they did after they were told the size of a serving

26

Number of hours the average commuter spends stuck in traffic each year

---

90

Number of hours the average Los Angeles commuter spends stuck in traffic each year

---

40-50

Percentage of American women who will have at least one suspicious mammogram that requires a follow-up

---

15

Percentage of British women who will

480

Number of mammograms a U.S. physician must read annually to fulfill quality-standard requirements

---

5,000

Number of mammograms a U.K. physician must read annually to fulfill quality-standard requirements

37

Percentage of Americans who prefer dark chocolate to white or milk chocolate

---

32

Percentage of people who earn less than $25,000 who prefer dark chocolate

---

43

Percentage of people who earn more than $75,000 who do

52

Percent more likely a supervisor is to fall asleep on the job than a lower level employee

---

71

Percentage of corporate pilots who have fallen asleep on the job

---

66

Percentage of hospital workers who have

16

Percentage of people who say their companies allow naps

1

Rank of students among people in 40 types of professions most likely to get a speeding ticket

---

38

Rank of cops

30

Number of chiropractors per 100,000 people nationwide

39

Number of chiropractors per 100,000 people in California

1

Rank of Atlanta among 18 cities where men are most likely to give their dates flowers

18

Rank of Boston

1

Boston's rank among cities whose single men say they're great catches

63.7

Average height, in inches, of the American woman

$789

Average increase in a woman's salary per year for every inch taller than average she is

---

Sources: National Cancer Institute; American Cancer Society; Gallup poll; National Data Corp. Pharmaceutical Audit Suite; *Journal of the American Dietetic Association*; Texas Transportation Institute; Chirobase; University of California, San Francisco; Quality Planning Corp.; University of Florida; Karolinska Institute; NASA; National Sleep Foundation; Mintel Reports; Match.com
—Reported by Laura Gilbert

female body

what you should know about
women-specific issues

How a Simple Test Saves Women's Lives

A stress test can predict if your heart's headed for trouble.

BY PETER JARET

If you have none of the usual risk factors for a heart attack—high blood pressure, elevated cholesterol, or history of smoking—that doesn't mean you're in the clear. But doctors now believe they can better predict whether you'll fall victim to the number-one killer of women merely by watching you move at full speed on a treadmill.

The elegantly simple standard stress test measures how hard you can push yourself while exercising and how quickly your heart rate returns to normal afterward. New research suggests these gauges—exercise capacity and heart-rate recovery—are remarkably powerful predictors of who will develop heart disease, even as many as 20 years following a stress test, says Samia Mora, M.D., a researcher at the Ciccarone Preventive Cardiology Center at The Johns Hopkins Medical Institutions in Baltimore. The finding comes from a recent analysis of almost three thousand women (some with known risk factors, some without) who took treadmill stress tests as part of a large 1972–76 study.

For years, cardiologists have given men these tests to determine whether their heart muscles are getting enough blood. The tests are also used to detect abnormal heart rhythms. But stress testing hasn't proved as useful in women, although the reason isn't clear (estrogen might be a factor). The upshot: Women are tested far less often than men.

That's a mistake, Mora says. In her study, women who scored low on stress tests were three times as likely as high scorers to develop heart disease. The test proved particularly useful for spotting women whose risk was high even though they didn't have conventional danger signs, such as a history of smoking, diabetes, elevated blood pressure, or high cholesterol. When these women scored low, they were 13 times as likely to develop heart disease as otherwise healthy women with high scores.

Another study, involving more than five thousand women, backs up Mora's research. Participants who performed well on treadmill tests were less likely to die from any cause during the next eight years.

"These are remarkable studies," says Michael Lauer, M.D., director of clinical research in cardiology at the Cleveland Clinic. "They prove that we have a simple way to predict risk in women that has long been overlooked." Lauer got hints of this discovery from a 1999 study that included both men and women; it showed that exercise capacity was a better predictor than even invasive imaging tests that examine cholesterol buildup in arteries. The latest research confirms this is true specifically for women.

It's not surprising that fit women have healthy hearts. But simply asking patients how much they exercise isn't a precise way of gauging cardiovascular fitness. A stress test solves that problem. "Exercise capacity is a more objective way of measuring fitness," says exercise epidemiologist Steven Blair, Ph.D., who directs research at the Cooper Institute in Dallas.

Doctors aren't yet recommending that every woman have a stress test, but plenty of women may be good candidates. According to a recent *Journal of the American Medical Association* report analyzing studies on hundreds of thousands of people, roughly 85 percent of men and women who develop heart disease have at least one major risk factor. That still leaves many who don't, and a stress test could help save their lives. But even for women with one or more risk factors, the test could help doctors more accurately assess their odds of developing heart disease.

Despite this promise, one problem is that cardiologists haven't known what to tell patients who score poorly. The simple answer? Get moving. Studies show that sedentary people who become more active can improve their exercise capacity by 15 to 30 percent, and Mora says new research shows exercise can boost heart-rate recovery, too. But the next step—proving that upping capacity or recovery leads to a healthier or longer life—won't be easy.

Doctors will have to follow people over a lifetime and make sure they exercise regularly, even though health experts have been famously unsuccessful at encouraging Americans to do it. Still, the new findings could change some minds about exercise.

A low stress-test score should also encourage doctors to more actively treat other heart disease factors, Mora says. "If a woman's cholesterol is moderately elevated but her treadmill tests look great, then we might tell her not to worry about the cholesterol," she explains. "But if her treadmill test results aren't so great, we might be more aggressive about lowering cholesterol."

In rare cases, people who are already active may score poorly on stress tests, a tip-off for doctors to look for heart defects or other threatening conditions.

A stress test costs about $150, and many doctors can perform them in their offices. But if you're curious—and frugal—you can try it on your own (see "Do-it-yourself Stress Test," at right).

Be prepared for disappointing results. In Mora's study, there were more low scorers than high ones. If your own numbers aren't up to snuff, it's time to schedule a doctor's appointment. You might pencil in more time on the stair-climber, too. ■

Longtime contributing editor Peter Jaret lives in Petaluma, California.

Do-it-yourself Stress Test

The safest and most reliable way to measure exercise capacity and heart-rate recovery is by taking a stress test in your doctor's office. But if you work out and aren't taking medication to control your blood pressure or heart rate, you can try a quick-and-easy check on your own.

1. To measure exercise capacity: Push yourself as hard as you can on an exercise machine that calculates METs, or metabolic equivalents (a measure of how much energy your body uses while you exercise). In a recent Johns Hopkins study, 7.5 METs was the average for women; top scorers hit up to 14.6 (the higher the score, the lower the risk of heart disease). If you score below 7.5 and don't get to the gym as often as you should, now's the time to start.

2. To measure heart-rate recovery: Push yourself as hard as you can doing any aerobic exercise (bicycling or using a treadmill, for instance, until you reach your maximum heart rate); without stopping quickly, count your pulse for 15 seconds. Multiply that number by 4 to calculate your per-minute heart rate. Stop exercising, wait 2 minutes, and calculate your heart rate again. Subtract the second number from the first to see how far your heart rate has dropped. In the Johns Hopkins study, the average drop was 55 beats—from 180 to 125, for instance. Top scorers saw their numbers fall by 66 beats or more. The more your heart rate falls, the lower your risk of heart disease.

What Every Woman Needs to Know About
Surgical Consent

Will students use your body as a practice dummy if you schedule surgery at a teaching hospital?

BY SUZ REDFEARN

Imagine you're about to undergo surgery and you're under general anesthesia. Did you know that at hundreds of hospitals, medical students might give you an unnecessary pelvic exam without your knowledge or explicit consent? In the United States alone, there are more than one thousand hospitals where this might happen.

It's not clear how often students do these exams. But they're performed strictly for education—there's nothing in it for you.

Ari Silver-Isenstadt, M.D., a pediatrician in the Baltimore area who has studied the issue, calls the exams a clear violation of patients' privacy. "Women should control access to their bodies," he says.

Silver-Isenstadt co-authored a 2000 study showing that half of patients would actually agree to such exams if only they were asked for permission. But another study he helped run in 2003 found that the

further along med students are in their education, the less concerned they are about asking permission.

The American College of Obstetricians and Gynecologists' Committee on Ethics says that patients must give "specific informed consent" prior to having practice pelvic exams done by students. But teaching hospitals usually have patients sign a vague consent form that makes no mention of such exams, says Michael Greger, M.D., a general practitioner who lectures at medical schools about what he sees as the inappropriateness of the procedure. The forms state only that students may be "involved in your care" or that your doctor might assign "designees" to assist. Greger says the students he encounters tell him these exams are still common.

The Association of American Medical Colleges (AAMC), a membership group for med schools, says performing pelvic exams without a woman's approval is unethical. But the group says it's not practical to list every procedure a woman may have on a consent form. The organization also believes that doing practice pelvic exams is necessary because med students learn best by working with real patients.

Experts disagree on whether the exams are done only during gynecological surgeries. Most of the time, that seems to be true: The attending surgeon is already working on that part of the body, perhaps removing an ovarian cyst or cervical cancer cells. In rarer cases, says Robin Wilson, J.D., a medical ethicist and University of South Carolina law professor, a woman may be having wholly unrelated surgery—say, a breast biopsy—and will still undergo practice pelvic exams.

California became the first state to ban non-consensual pelvic exams in the fall of 2003. And 14 nursing organizations asked the AAMC in 2003 to ban the practice at its member schools. Unfortunately, the group doesn't have the power to do so.

Wilson says many teaching hospitals won't confirm whether they allow the procedure. Several calls placed to teaching hospitals by *Health* were not returned.

How can you arm yourself against having a practice pelvic exam you didn't agree to? Tell your physician ahead of time that you don't want one performed while you're unconscious. Also, write explicit notes on everything you sign during your hospital stay. Wilson suggests that you voice your nonconsent to every doctor, nurse, or student you come in contact with. Don't be afraid, Greger adds, to write this message on your body, near the bikini line: "Do not perform practice pelvic exams on me." ∎

Suz Redfearn's work has also appeared in The Washington Post.

Be sure you can trust that the doctors will do only what you give them permission to do.

Teaching hospitals usually have patients sign a vague consent form stating that students may be involved with their care, but there is no mention of unnecessary pelvic exams.

New Report Reveals Painful Stats for Women Worldwide

Warning: Simply being a female in this world is hazardous. A disturbing new report from the United Nations Development Fund for Women finds that one in three women globally is likely to be raped, beaten, or otherwise abused in her lifetime. To combat this epidemic, U.N. Secretary-General Kofi Annan has called for a global policy of zero tolerance toward gender-based violence.

Beyond Morning
SICKNESS

Each year thousands of pregnant women deal with a frightening condition that leaves them unable to eat or drink anything.

BY DIANE MAPES

My sister Peggy is hooked up to an IV when I get to the hospital, tubes snaking out of her arm as if she were plugged into a modem. I settle a bundle of books and magazines onto her bedside tray and prop up a picture of her 21-month-old son, Charlie. "Hey, Peg, what's going on?" I ask, trying not to sound worried. I am terrified, of course. Peggy looks pale and flat, her face melding into the hospital pillow like an ornate piece of embroidery.

"The doctor wants to keep me overnight," she says. "I haven't been able to eat for a while. Food makes me sick. The smell of it, even." She pauses, a sour look flickering across her face.

At 38 years old and two months pregnant, Peggy has been in the throes of morning sickness for two weeks. Only it isn't like any kind of morning sickness I've ever heard of. She is constantly nauseated, throwing up 10, 11, 12 times a day. She has even missed work at the local

TV station where she's a news producer, and Peggy—whose strong work ethic rivals that of Henry Ford—never misses work. I've been worried for days. It's my official job as a big sister.

"So what did the doctor say?" I ask.

"That I'm dehydrated," she says.

Peggy's husband, Doug, is by her side. "She's not just dehydrated," he offers, "she's starving. She's lost 7 pounds in a week. The doctor took one look at her this morning and called the hospital."

"Did the doctor say why you're so sick?" I ask, looking from one to the other. "Did she say what's making you throw up so much?"

"Hyperemesis something or other," Peggy says.

Back from the hospital, I read everything I can find about a condition called hyperemesis

Women with extreme morning sickness are often depressed and isolated. Partners may think the disorder is all in their heads.

gravidarum (HG). I've never heard of it, but I learn it's been documented for hundreds, if not thousands, of years. As far as I can tell, the one established cause is pregnancy. Other than that, there are only theories about its origin: hormonal changes, abnormal thyroid levels, even psychological postulations about guilt and immaturity. It usually begins in the first trimester and ends in the second. But an unlucky few have it the whole nine months. And there is no cure.

Every year thousands of women suffer from HG. "It's not really that rare," Gideon Koren, M.D., a professor and senior scientist at the University of Toronto, tells me. "About 1 percent of all women will have it, and since there are 4 million births a year in the United States, this means 40,000 women a year have hyperemesis."

There's more to it, too. "Women with HG are depressed, isolated, and often not taken seriously," explains Koren, director of Motherisk, a counseling and research organization for pregnant and lactating women. "Many women tell us their partners and physicians think that it's all in their heads. That's a terrible accusation."

It gets worse: About a quarter of women with HG terminate their pregnancies out of desperation, inadequate care, or both, according to a survey by the Hyperemesis Education and Research Foundation (HER). A few develop complications and die.

My sister stays in the hospital for one night. But five days later she's back, surrounded by monitors, IV tubes, and the sounds and smells of sickness. I can tell she's crying, only her body is too dehydrated to produce tears. "I don't understand this," she says, her voice shaking. "I'm not a wimp. I've had morning sickness before." Most women do—80 percent, in fact.

But not like this.

Peggy has dropped another 5 pounds. She now weighs less than she did before the pregnancy. Her OB-GYN bumps up her dosage of Zofran, an antivomiting medication given to cancer patients undergoing chemotherapy, and decides to insert a peripherally inserted central catheter (PICC) line in her arm—it's a long, thin tube threaded along a vein until it hovers near her heart. Essentially, it's an open gateway into Peggy's body, a 24-hour delivery system for fluids, nutrition, drugs. My sister has gone from expectant mother to invalid.

What kind of disease is this? "It's an absolutely miserable one," says Kimber MacGibbon, R.N., a two-time HG victim who founded HER in 2000. "Your sister's lucky she has a doctor who caught it early. A lot of women don't."

Peggy's second hospital stay lasts two days. She returns two days later. Unable to tolerate so much as a sip of water, she relies on the PICC line for everything her body—and the baby—needs. A concoction of Zofran, Pepcid, and an antihistamine keeps her vomiting under control; the nausea, excessive salivation, and heightened sense of smell are constants.

"I'm worried about the baby," she says every time her nurse plunges a syringe into a port on the IV pole. "All these drugs. What if something happens?" Possible birth defects versus death by starvation. It isn't much of a choice. "The baby's going to be fine," I say, praying this will be true. "You're going to be fine."

I've done two weeks of research, and my head is spinning with horror stories about women who have suffered permanent damage, or even died, because of hyperemesis—author Charlotte Brontë among them. Then there's all the claptrap about women with HG not really being sick. The illness seems to be a lodestone for all kinds of psychological theories: It's caused by frigidity. No, it's stress. No, it's hysteria. No, it's an unconscious attempt at abortion.

Shari Munch, Ph.D., an assistant professor at Rutgers University School of Social Work, assures me that those theories are decades old. Munch is the author of several papers on HG, including a 2002 study in *Social Science and Medicine* showing that a great deal of HG research is based on outmoded claims about women's psychology and the female reproductive system. "We don't have any research proving it is psychogenic," Munch points out. "It's just become this medical folklore."

Why? The University of Toronto's Koren throws some blame at a male-driven medical establishment. "If it were happening to men," he says, "there would have been a solution long ago."

Peggy's third hospital tour lasts five days. Ten days later, her husband calls to tell me she has been admitted again. When I get to her room, Peggy looks as though she's been flattened by a rolling pin. The whites of her eyes are grayish yellow. She can't take a breath without feeling sharp, stabbing pains.

The next day, a pulmonary specialist diagnoses her with anaerobic pneumonia. Apparently, she had inhaled some vomit. Antibiotics and anti-inflammatories are added to her laundry list of medications.

I fume at the unfairness of it all. Like some fairy-tale imp, HG has stolen my sister's pregnancy, carried away her hope. Instead of shopping for baby clothes and indulging in late-night cravings for peanut butter and peaches, Peggy is trapped in a miasma of snaking tubes, twisting wires, blinking lights, and despair. The only glow in the room comes from the buttons on her IV port. She looks more like an earthquake victim than a mother-to-be. The illness forces her to stay in the hospital another five days.

When the next month goes by and Peggy goes back to work without another return to the hospital, I finally start to relax. Then the phone rings. I see it's my brother-in-law's cell, and my heart begins to pound. "Where are you?" I ask. "What's going on? Is everything all right?"

Peggy laughs. "Everything's fine, worrywart," she says. "We're just driving home from the restaurant." It takes a minute for her words to sink in. I know she's feeling better, even though she's still on anti-nausea medication, still carrying a PICC line in her arm. I know she's been able to eat a few meals here and there. But a restaurant seems too much to hope for. "You went out to dinner?" I ask. "You ate?"

"Yes, it's our anniversary," she says. "And then we stopped by a store."

I realize the nightmare is over.

"I bought a new dress," she adds. "A pink dress."

Her voice is filled with hope. "Size 0 to 3 months."

FIND AN EXPERT
For more information about hyperemesis gravidarum or to find a professional who is experienced at treating it, go to www.hyperemesis.org.

Nora Ruth, a healthy 6-pound, 11-ounce girl, was born in February 2004. Her aunt Diane Mapes is a freelance writer based in Seattle.

Q + A Good News for Pregnant Women: You Can Have Your Cheese and Eat It, Too

Is it true that I shouldn't eat soft cheese while I'm pregnant? I'm in need of a Brie fix.

Good news: You can indulge your craving as long as the cheese is pasteurized. In the past, the U.S. Food and Drug Administration (FDA) advised pregnant women to abstain because of listeria, a foodborne, soft cheese–loving bacterium that can be deadly to an unborn child. But new data shows that pasteurization wipes out listeria, persuading the FDA to green-light cheese made from pasteurized milk, which includes most varieties—soft, hard, or in between. Before you buy, check the label to make sure that the cheese you've chosen is pasteurized. You should still avoid other potential listeria sources, such as lunch meats and hot dogs (unless they're steaming hot), meat spreads, refrigerated pâtés, and refrigerated smoked seafood.

Why OB-GYNs Say Choosing a C-section Is OK

Some women want Cesarean sections so they can have their babies when it's convenient (or so they can avoid pain and other complications associated with vaginal deliveries).

The ethics committee of the American College of Obstetricians and Gynecologists now says elective C-sections are OK—sort of. Surgery is "ethically justified," the committee says, if it "promotes the overall health and welfare of the woman and her fetus" more so than natural birth, and if the patient is well-informed. A lack of evidence makes it impossible to know if C-sections are more dangerous, the committee notes. However, new evidence suggests that the surgery may boost the risk of stillbirth if you get pregnant again. Before you decide, do some research.

Expecting? Improve Your Genes with the Right Diet

If you make nutrition a priority when you're pregnant, scientists suspect that you may lower your child's inherited cancer risks. Simply by eating healthy, adults might be able to mend their own genes, too.

The emerging field of epigenetics is behind these surprises. It's showing that environmental influences can modify how genes function without actually altering DNA. The evidence? Duke University scientists recently reprogrammed the color of mice offspring and left them with diminished appetite, lower body weight, and less diabetes and cancer by enhancing the mothers' prenatal diet with B vitamins and related nutrients.

The nutritional enhancements seem to generate chemical signals that act as genetic stop signs. And studies of human twins and babies conceived through in vitro fertilization suggest that people are subject to similar outcomes.

Experts believe diet can alter your own genes as well. But they caution against gulping down supplements. "All nutrients have multiple genomic effects. So one has to be very careful," says Patrick J. Stover, Ph.D., associate nutritional biochemistry professor at Cornell University. "You may regulate one gene that is not beneficial while silencing another gene that is."

Trying to Get Pregnant? Drink Wine!

Women who have trouble getting pregnant may want to uncork a bottle of wine. Government, commercial, and academic researchers in Denmark recently discovered, after following almost thirty thousand women for nearly 2^1/$_2$ years, that those who drank anywhere from half a glass to seven glasses of wine a week were 30-percent less likely to go a year without conceiving than those who didn't drink wine. (Beer and liquor had a weaker effect.) Moderate wine consumption does seem to reduce heart-disease risk, and the researchers suspect wine-drinkers (and their partners) may be healthier overall than people who abstain.

ASPIRIN

The Answer to Keeping Moms and Babies Healthy?

BY JACQUELINE STENSON

Every year, about 7 percent of women who get pregnant develop a dangerous form of high blood pressure known as pre-eclampsia. It puts the fetus at risk and can create painful problems for the woman, such as headaches, abdominal pain, and swelling in the face, hands, and feet. The best prescription for this condition is not getting it in the first place. But how?

Researchers now think they have an answer: low-dose aspirin. It's widely used to prevent heart attacks, and it may help protect women from pregnancy-induced high blood pressure, according to an analysis in the journal *Obstetrics & Gynecology*. Previous studies had yielded conflicting results, so British researchers in search of a better answer combined data from more than a dozen major studies involving over twelve thousand women. They found that daily aspirin use was associated with a 14-percent lower risk of pre-eclampsia, reductions in premature delivery and stillbirth, and higher birth weights. "In women with risk factors, such as a history of pre-eclampsia or chronic high blood pressure, aspirin therapy should be considered," says study author Aravinthan Coomarasamy, M.D., of Birmingham Women's Hospital in the United Kingdom. (According to the American College of Obstetricians and Gynecologists, a pregnant woman is also at risk if she is having her first child, is age 40 or over, is carrying multiple babies, or is African-American.)

Still, aspirin remains controversial, because some of the largest studies in the new analysis found no overall benefit. "There is really no one conclusive clinical trial that settles this issue," says John Repke, M.D., chairman of obstetrics and gynecology at Pennsylvania State University's Hershey Medical Center. Plus, taking aspirin around the time of conception may increase the risk of miscarriage, according to a recent study in the *British Medical Journal*. But women in most major studies of aspirin and pre-eclampsia took the drug after their first trimesters, as the authors of the *Obstetrics & Gynecology* analysis recommend. "There doesn't seem to be a downside to this approach," Repke says, "and there are no other proven preventive methods." ■

> **In one study, daily aspirin use was associated with a 14-percent lower risk of pre-eclampsia, reductions in premature delivery and stillbirth, and higher birth weights.**

110

WALK OFF
Your Baby Weight

The average woman gains 25 to 35 pounds during pregnancy, and whatever is left after the baby is born can be tough to lose. You need a plan, and we've got a good one: *Walking Through Pregnancy and Beyond: How Expectant and New Moms Can Walk Their Way Through a Happy and Healthy Pregnancy and First Year* by frequent *Health* contributors Mark and Lisa Fenton.

Experts say it's OK to begin taking short walks after your baby's birth as soon as you feel up to it (unless, of course, your doctor has advised otherwise). That's where the Fentons come in. The chart below is for the Moderate Program (see their book for the Low-Key Program if you've never exercised before or the Challenging Program if you're already very active). It covers the first year post-baby and gives you goals for each three-month period. Feel free to switch the schedule around to fit your needs; just try not to plan too many brisk or fast workouts back-to-back. And if you need to, you can split each day's session into two or more parts. If you stick to this regimen, the Fentons say you should be back to your pre-baby weight within a year. ■

Post-Baby Exercise Plan

Follow this schedule to help you shed those extra pounds. (The Fentons also recommend strength and stretch workouts several times a week.)

	MONTHS 1–3	MONTHS 4–6	MONTHS 7–9	MONTHS 10–12
	INTENSITY: 1–2 (OF 5)	INTENSITY: 2–3 (OF 5)	INTENSITY: 3–4 (OF 5)	INTENSITY: 3–5 (OF 5)
M	25 minutes	35 minutes	35 minutes (brisk, 3.5–4 mph)	35 minutes (brisk, 3.5–4 mph)
T	30 minutes	30 minutes	45 minutes	50 minutes
W	25 minutes	35 minutes	35 minutes (brisk, 3.5–4 mph)	25 minutes (fast, 4+ mph)
Th	25 minutes	35 minutes	40 minutes	45 minutes
F	15 minutes	20 minutes	20 minutes	35 minutes (brisk, 3.5–4 mph)
Sat	35 minutes	45 minutes	50 minutes	60+ minutes
Sun	Off	Off	Off	Off

Put Your Mind Over Bladder

Always gotta go? Teach yourself to conquer incontinence.

BY WENDY LICHTMAN

It turns out there's a real name—a medical label—for the annoying thing that happens to me whenever I arrive at my front door. It's called "latchkey syndrome," and it goes like this: As soon as I get my key in my hand, I realize I have to pee immediately. Ignoring my mailbox filled with letters, I tighten my pelvic muscles, throw open the door, and drop my groceries, books, and papers on the hall table. Then, unzipping my pants on the way, I race to the toilet.

I do this every time I get home; it makes no difference whether or not I've recently used the bathroom. Which is why, after a few months, I begin to suspect this is no ordinary medical problem. When my gynecologist assures me that I don't have a urinary-tract infection, prolapsed bladder, or any easily recognizable ailment, I know I've somehow developed a conditioned response: Like Pavlov's dog salivating at the sound of a bell, I need to pee when I put my key in the door. It's a mind-body problem.

Naturally, I'm embarrassed to tell anyone about my experience, even a doctor. This is exactly how most people feel when they're incontinent. They don't talk about it with their partners or friends, and they don't discuss it with their physicians. This is unfortunate, because it keeps 13 million Americans—85 percent of them women—unnecessarily uncomfortable.

My doctor doesn't seem all that shocked by my symptoms. In fact, she seems glad that I've discussed the problem with her. After labeling it for me, she refers me to a specialist.

"You really can take more control of your bladder," Wendy Katzman, a physical therapist and assistant clinical professor at the University of California, San Francisco, assures me. "Approaching your doorway is a common trigger for the sudden, strong desire to urinate that's called urge incontinence. It's different from stress incontinence, where activities like coughing, sneezing, or laughing cause you to leak urine."

Katzman, who works at UCSF's Women's Continence Center (www.ucsf.edu/wcc), tells me that I can retrain my body and strengthen my pelvic muscles by practicing urge-suppression techniques, which sound like something I'd do if I were trying to give birth and quit smoking at the same time.

When I walk into my home, the first step is to sit still and take deep breaths while reminding myself that this is no emergency, that I can, in fact, postpone going to the bathroom. Next, I'm to do Kegel exercises, contracting and releasing my pelvic-floor muscles to strengthen them. Only when the urge to urinate passes should I stand up and walk—calmly—to the bathroom.

I can do all of that. I know how to breathe, and I can contract my pelvic floor; I remember doing Kegels when I was pregnant. And I'm old enough to have had real emergencies, so I know the difference between those and what happens at my front door.

But when I get home the next day and feel like I'm going to wet my pants, I do not want to breathe or Kegel. I'll try the urge-suppression-blah-blah stuff tomorrow, I think, as, bouncing up and down, I try to find the damn door key. Racing to the bathroom, I feel envious of Pavlov's dog, who, I am certain, never had to tell himself, "OK, it's a bell; it's just a silly bell. I don't need to salivate."

On the way home the following afternoon, I plan my attack. I can't have a full bladder, I tell myself, since I used the bathroom 20 minutes ago. I'll look at my mail first, I decide—just sit on my couch and do my behavior modification while I read.

I Kegel as I pretend to study the photo on a letter announcing a friend's art show. Breathing deeply, I remind myself that this is not an emergency. Walking into my own house is, in fact, the most normal of everyday activities. And then I reach into my purse, take out a pen, and write a note in my date book about the art show.

I feel so cool as I stand up and walk—walk!—to the bathroom.

For the next few weeks I am pleased with how well this works. As I sit on my couch, focusing on my breathing and my pelvic contractions, using mail as a distraction, the urge to pee really does subside.

There is no mail to distract me on Sundays. But when I come home after a bike ride and sit down in the living room with the newspaper, I'm halfway through the travel section before I realize I've been reading for 20 minutes. "This is amazing!" I announce to my husband. "I don't have to pee."

He is not quite as jubilant as I would like. But, then again, I never mentioned the problem to him in the first place. ■

Wendy Lichtman is a freelance writer in Northern California.

Alternative Relief

Here are some simple strategies to help you pacify a problem that plagues millions of women.

1. Keep a diary. Your doctor needs help to properly diagnose incontinence. Keep track of how often you urinate, the events surrounding any leakage, and what and how much you're drinking. Cutting back on coffee and fizzy drinks may help. (Don't stop drinking water! That's dangerous.)

2. Work your pelvics. By performing Kegel exercises—contracting and relaxing those isolated muscles in the floor of your pelvis that control the emptying of the bladder—you can curtail incontinence and prevent it from getting worse. Squeeze the muscles for a slow count of three, and then relax for a slow count of three. A set of 10 to 15, three times a day, will build strength.

3. Try biofeedback. Not sure if you're doing Kegels correctly? Biofeedback, a mind-body technique that relies on sensors connected to the pelvic-floor muscles, may help. Computer graphics and audible tones provide the feedback as you exercise your pelvics, while also allowing a therapist to measure your strength and individualize your workout. A typical regimen is three to four visits over eight weeks. Insurance plans frequently (but not always) pay for it.

4. Suppress the urge. Based on both physical and behavioral therapy, urge suppression helps control the sudden need to urinate typical of urge incontinence. (It's also helpful for curbing stress incontinence.) When you're in situations that trigger leakage, don't run to the bathroom; that teaches your bladder to be overactive. Instead, breathe deeply and distract yourself, which helps signal the bladder to relax.

Q + A

How to End Bladder Infections for Good

I follow my doctor's advice, but I keep getting bladder infections. What's the deal? And what can I do?

Until now, doctors couldn't explain why antibiotics sometimes fail to prevent bladder infections from coming back. According to conventional thinking, new bacteria invade the bladder, leading to an infection. But recent research has found that some recurring infections may be caused by bacteria that have stuck around—literally. In some instances, a podlike "biofilm" forms and clings to the bladder, shielding the germs from both antibiotics and your body's immune response. Randomly, the pod opens and releases the organisms, causing another infection. These findings could lead to more effective therapies, but for now your best strategy is to follow the standard advice: Take antibiotics preventively, practice good hygiene, and drink lots of fluids (64 ounces of water and 10 ounces of cranberry juice a day).

The Pill That Keeps Working?

Getting pregnant may not be easy once you stop taking the Pill. In a recent British study, women who took common estrogen-progesterone pills for more than four years failed to conceive for an average of nearly nine months, twice as long as women who had relied on condoms. But hormone-releasing IUDs (such as Mirena) and progesterone-only pills didn't delay pregnancy at all.

Researchers can't explain their findings, but U.S. experts refuse to blame the Pill. David Plourd, M.D., assistant professor of obstetrics and gynecology at the Naval Medical Center in San Diego, says the hormones that do the work are flushed from your system two days after your last dose—whether you've been using this method for 1 year or 10. Plourd notes that many women with irregular menstrual cycles take the Pill because it keeps them on schedule. Once they stop, it naturally takes them longer to get pregnant; that might have skewed the study's results.

What's certain is that injectables, such as Depo-Provera, will keep you out of the delivery room the longest. Your hormone levels remain high for several months after each shot, so it may take you up to 18 months to begin menstruating again.

More Estrogen = Meaner Women?

Are fertile women catty women? In a recent study, female volunteers rated the attractiveness of women's faces in photographs. The volunteers who were ovulating were harsher judges than those less flush with estrogen. Maryanne Fisher, M.A., professor of psychology at St. Mary's University in Halifax, Nova Scotia, thinks that fertility prods women to see their peers as rivals for the best mates. Do women act on their instincts? "I'd love to go to a dance club and listen to women talking in the washroom," Fisher says. "But getting permission might be tricky."

Fill Up His Coffee Cup to Improve Fertility

Brazilian researchers recently studied sperm samples from 750 men and found that the coffee-drinkers in the group had the best motility, meaning their sperm were the most active. "We argue that the caffeine in coffee acts as a stimulant for sperm," says Fabio Pasqualotto, M.D., Ph.D., who presented the research at a recent conference of the American Society for Reproductive Medicine.

Poor sperm motility is the culprit for 30 percent of America's 6 million couples who are unable to conceive. Although the men in Pasqualotto's study had normal sperm, he says the findings could point to a new infertility treatment. And he notes that other caffeine sources might be just as effective. Infertility researchers view the caffeine theory as plausible but preliminary. Pasqualotto plans more studies to see if more active sperm induce more pregnancies, as he expects.

Still, coffee isn't a cure-all. It doesn't appear to address other causes of male infertility, such as low sperm counts or imperfect hormone levels. And there's no sense in having your partner gulp down double espressos: In Pasqualotto's work, megadoses of caffeine made no difference.

Q + A

Getting to the Source of Yeast Infections

I keep getting yeast infections. Is it possible that my boyfriend is giving them to me? What can I do?

If you were thinking of spraying him with Lysol, don't. It's true that candida, the microscopic yeast responsible for the annoying itching and burning that signal an infection, can be passed between sexual partners. But new findings show that this is not what causes the problem to keep coming back. Researchers tested nearly one hundred and fifty women with recurring infections for candida, along with their partners. The scientists found the women got repeat infections whether or not the men were the source.

So the mystery continues: Candida lives harmlessly in the vaginas of some women but provokes regular flare-ups in others. Many women are able to get rid of infection symptoms for good by taking prescription antifungal pills for four to six weeks. (Make sure your doctor confirms that you have a yeast infection, because it's hard for you to be certain based on symptoms alone.)

OVARIAN CANCER

Why This Tough Fight May Get Easier

A new test could help women detect the disease early enough to cure it.

BY MARGIE PATLAK

Cancer is cruelly undemocratic: Some forms are relatively easy to beat, while others are just shy of a death sentence. For women, ovarian cancer lands in the killer category. Although experts already know how to conquer it—if they find it soon enough, it's treatable and beatable—early detection is all but impossible.

But that might change soon. A new test that shows promise in detecting ovarian cancer at a curable stage should be available by end of 2004.

The test looks for a telltale fingerprint, or protein pattern, in your blood. Find that fingerprint early enough, and it could save your life. Find out you don't have it, and you could receive some much-needed peace of mind. "Women at high risk for ovarian cancer have a tremendous amount of anxiety," says Emanuel Petricoin,

Ph.D., who works for the U.S. Food and Drug Administration's Center for Biologics Evaluation and Research and who helped develop the science behind the exam. "Just having a test that tells women they are OK would be a huge relief."

Who should be tested? Although a woman's risk of the disease is relatively small—only 1 in 57 women will eventually develop it—immediate

> The test may stop women from taking the severe step of having their ovaries removed simply to ensure that they won't get cancer.

family members of ovarian-cancer patients might want to get the test because their risk is three times as great as that of other women. Women over age 50 and those who have an immediate family member with breast cancer are also especially vulnerable to ovarian cancer.

The disease is the fifth most deadly cancer among women. More than 80 percent of the roughly twenty-five thousand women diagnosed with ovarian cancer in 2003 will have it in late stages, giving them a 35-percent chance of surviving for five years. The new test can't help them. But it may save women who wouldn't find the disease until it's too late. And it might stop women from having their ovaries removed merely to ensure they won't get the cancer—a procedure Petricoin calls a travesty. Premenopausal women who undergo this surgery not only become infertile, but also are more prone to osteoporosis, heart disease, and severe menopausal symptoms.

Health first told you about the test in 2003 when it was in development (it's a product of a new medical-science field called proteomics, or the study of human proteins). Since then, Petricoin; Lance Liotta, M.D., Ph.D., of the National Cancer Institute; and researchers at the biotech company Correlogic Systems have improved the test with better machinery. Correlogic has licensed two commercial labs to use it: Laboratory Corporation of America (LabCorp) and Quest Diagnostics, both with facilities nationwide.

No forward-looking trials have been completed. But while analyzing 216 blood samples taken from women with and without ovarian cancer, the developers of the new test were able to spot every case of the disease. Using a smaller set of 109 samples, they were able to find all 20 early-stage cancers in the bunch. Just as important, they got no false positives: In the samples believed to be cancer-free based on five years of observation using other available tests, there were no phony fingerprints suggesting cancer. In earlier testing with less effective machinery, the false-positive rate was 5 percent—small, for sure, but still worrisome. A test with a rate even this low could lead to unnecessary surgeries and overwhelming anxiety. So eliminating these false alarms was a major step.

Of course, there are caveats. First, clinical trials on roughly one thousand blood samples are ongoing, and the test might not look so invincible once results are in. Second, the exam hasn't been approved by the Federal Drug Administration (FDA), and it'll be more than a year before there might be enough results for the government to endorse it. Last, but hardly least, just because you can have the test doesn't mean you should.

Are You at Risk?

Only 1 in 57 American women will develop ovarian cancer, but your odds jump if you:

- **Have a mother, sister, or daughter with ovarian cancer.**
- **Have a mother, sister, or daughter with breast cancer, or you've had the cancer.** The relationship between ovarian and breast cancers is not well-understood, but it may be hormone-based.
- **Test positive on the BRCA 1 or BRCA 2 genetic tests for breast cancer.** This raises your risk, although it's not clear by how much. Studies suggest that between 16 and 60 percent of women who test positive for either genetic mutation will eventually develop ovarian cancer.
- **Have elevated levels of the cancer-associated protein CA 125.** That makes you about 36 times as likely to develop ovarian cancer within a year. But CA 125 isn't a reliable marker. Many women with higher-than-normal levels have benign conditions, such as pregnancy, or other cancers. Plus, tests for this protein detect fewer than two-thirds of ovarian cancers in women who actually have the disease.
- **Are over age 50.** Most ovarian cancers occur in women over 50 and half occur in women over 65.

Critics aren't convinced that it works. Although he labels Liotta and Petricoin's results "very encouraging," Robert Bast, M.D., an ovarian-cancer expert at the University of Texas M.D. Anderson Cancer Center, worries that no one can be sure yet about the test's accuracy rate. Experts also have no idea how often a woman who tests negative would need to be retested. Nicole Urban, Sc.D., head of the gynecologic cancer research program at the Fred Hutchinson Cancer Research Center in Seattle, says she wouldn't have the test now if she were at high risk for ovarian cancer. She adds, "It would be misleading high-risk women to make them think this test is ready."

But if the test is so preliminary, how can it be available at all? A wrinkle in government rules allows labs to offer the test without FDA approval. It's the organization's "home brew" rule, which lets commercial or academic outfits perform such tests (and issue results to doctors and patients) as long as they don't sell them to other facilities.

> Getting pregnant, breast-feeding, and taking the Pill all reduce your chances of getting ovarian cancer. Why? Researchers aren't certain, but cutting back on how often you ovulate may cut your risk.

What's more, because there's no real competition, commercial labs are eager to roll it out. "There is nothing comparable for detecting ovarian cancer, which speaks to its medical necessity," says Marcia Eisenberg, Ph.D., who supervises the research and development of molecular diagnostic tests at LabCorp.

Pelvic exams, X-rays, ultrasounds, and MRIs rarely spot ovarian tumors before they spread to a woman's abdomen; at that point, treatment tends to be ineffective. The one blood test currently available, which screens for a substance called CA 125, is good only for finding more cancer in women who've already had it and been treated. That test doesn't work for early detection; indeed, the National Cancer Institute says using it for screening leads to unnecessary surgeries.

The lack of FDA approval doesn't mean the new test is dangerous or second-rate. Companies that offer home-brew tests must comply with federal standards designed to ensure accuracy and reliability.

Any woman who wants to be tested would have her doctor or local lab mail her blood sample to either LabCorp or Quest Diagnostics, or she could visit one of the companies' patient centers. "We're assuming that most women would get it during their annual visit to their doctor," Eisenberg says. "It requires a tube of blood, and they'll get the results via the doctor." A LabCorp spokesperson says it will probably cost $100 to $125. (Your insurance company might not cover the test now but likely will if the FDA approves it.)

A positive test, though potentially a lifesaver, would not prevent invasive treatment. Biopsies would come next, and if those were positive, doctors probably would remove one or both ovaries and possibly nearby tissue. That's standard, as is chemotherapy for many patients. (If a single, small tumor is found on an ovary, just that ovary or a portion of it could be removed, perhaps preserving a woman's ability to have children.)

Without question, the test is so new that any woman who chooses to have it will be something of a guinea pig. But the payoff could be big. "We're looking at the toughest, hardest Holy Grail of diagnostics, which is detection of early-stage ovarian cancer," Petricoin points out. "If we can actually diagnose that, we can cure this disease."

That's not all. The promise of the test has researchers optimistic that they can develop copycats for early detection of breast, lung, and prostate cancers—and soon. Says Petricoin, "The sky's the limit." ■

Margie Patlak is a freelance writer whose work has appeared in the Washington Post *and* Los Angeles Times; *she has also written for the National Institutes of Health and the National Academy of Sciences.*

Q + A

Monthly Mishaps: Are They Caused by Head or Hormones?

When I have my period, I get extremely clumsy. Am I normal?

We can't say for sure whether you're normal or not since we've never met you. But we can tell you that you're not the only woman who experiences monthly butterfingers. They are a fairly uncommon symptom, though—rare enough to stay under the radar of medical science. (Nobody's getting research grants to study the connection between premenstrual syndrome [PMS] and minor run-ins with the coffee table.) So the exact link remains unknown. Some doctors suspect that this clumsiness is related to sleep disturbances, which are a significant part of PMS. An extra bit of drowsiness can leave you more prone to dropping the ball, literally. Be especially vigilant about getting 8 hours of sleep a night in the week before your period, and you might regain your usual grace.

Treat UTIs—Exam-Free

David Vinson, M.D., a clinical researcher at the Permanente Medical Group in Sacramento, California, followed more than four thousand women with urinary-tract infections who received advice and prescriptions from their doctors by phone. Vinson found the outcomes were similar to those of women who dragged themselves into the office for exams. (If your symptoms last more than 10 days, check with your doctor in person.)

Why It's OK to Skip Your Period

Seasonale, a new oral contraceptive, offers women an option for a menstrual cycle that's, well, seasonal. The pill contains hormones found in conventional oral contraceptives but is taken in a 91-day sequence—rather than the typical 28-day cycle—so you get your period only about every three months. Approved by the Federal Drug Administration in late 2003, Seasonale has contraindications and warnings similar to those of other birth control pills.

Sexism 101: Women Are Not Alone

Back in the 1960s, women's-studies courses seemed radical, yet they helped shed light on the female experience in a sexist society. Coming soon to classrooms near you: men's-studies courses, which focus on male friendships and body issues, and the costs of machismo (such as lack of time with the kids or ridicule for staying home with them). In the late 1980s, only about 40 men's-studies courses were taught in the United States. Now there are 500 and counting, according to the American Men's Studies Association, a nonprofit research group based in Albuquerque, New Mexico.

Jean's Journey with Cancer

We all know life doesn't last forever—we just act as if it does. Discover what one woman gains by no longer pretending.

BY DOROTHY FOLTZ-GRAY • PHOTOGRAPHY BY PAUL ELLEDGE

Almost two years ago, my 85-year-old father-in-law, Achie, totaled his car, and his life changed forever. My husband, Dan, drove to Pittsburgh the next day, packed up his father's belongings, and brought Achie to Knoxville, Tennessee, where we live. We found him an apartment around the corner from our house, and every day he would walk over for coffee or dinner.

His growing dementia worried us. Some days we'd pass him in the car, and he'd be standing still, turning his head as if he'd forgotten where he was. Despite our pleasure at having him closer, seeing daily how much age had eaten into his body and mind wore at us. The more fragile Dan's dad became, the more fragile we felt. We saw our own future. We upped our exercise, we cleaned up our diet, we arranged physicals.

Death is always far off for all of us—until it's not.

In January 2003, Achie fell and broke his hip. By February, he was in a nursing home. In his room, we hung pictures of Achie as a 4-year-old Buster Brown, as a high school football player, and as a soldier on Iwo Jima. He looks at the pictures and asks who the boy is. I look at them, too, and wonder how this soldier could now be sealed in a wheelchair, barely able to guide a spoon to his lips. Surely, I think, this won't happen to me. Yet in Danny's father I see a truer story.

Most of the time I'm blind about death, or at least about its inevitability. Despite the news of carnage and disease before me every day in the paper, I can keep its effect flat and on the page. I finish my orange juice, and I'm out the door for a run along the Tennessee River. It's my long life that's inevitable on days like this, days when my feet forget how many decades we've been pounding along together.

Still, when my close friend is diagnosed with breast cancer, Dan and I sit at the dinner table that night without much to say. I want to push back my fear by focusing on my friend. But what cancer opens to her she wants to face alone. She sends the news in an e-mail and asks us not to call. (I do call.) She keeps her condition secret. During chemotherapy, she is determined her wig will reveal nothing. I puzzle over her reaction. But what could be more private than touching the hand of mortality? The story my friend planned is perhaps not the one she'll get.

Death is always far off for all of us—until it's not. Five years ago, my family and I traveled to Norway to live for a year. Shortly before we left the States, I began having worrisome digestive problems. In short, no outing was safe unless I knew exactly where the bathroom was. I thought it was the result of jitters, but when the difficulty persisted, I hustled to a Norwegian doctor. Trying to explain such a fix in a foreign country wasn't easy, and the doctor looked grim as I described my symptoms. He ran through a list of possible diagnoses, including colon cancer, and instructed me on how to set up a series of exams. As he spoke, I began to cry.

A week later came the tests; then another week, and again I sat with my doctor while he phoned the lab. I felt my heart accelerate as he spoke, but in a moment he began to smile. "You are fine," he said. "It's probably nerves. Take fiber, drink wine, eat at McDonald's."

That afternoon, a crisp September day bright with sun and turning leaves, I walked down a broad avenue. I sat in a restaurant (not McDonald's) and had salmon, a glass of wine. I wandered in and out of food shops, fingering the fruits, and all I could feel was each breath I took.

I thought about this as I flew into the St. Louis airport. Since September 2002, I have been in touch with Jean Miller, a 45-year-old secretary, wife, and mother who has fought ovarian cancer for three years. She has undergone two surgeries and three rounds of chemo (and three bouts of baldness); when we met face-to-face, she was in radiation treatment. She'd invited me to walk, if not in her shoes, then beside them for several days, meeting her family, her co-workers, and her doctors, as well as the women in the St. Louis chapter of the National Ovarian Cancer Coalition, which she founded shortly after she was diagnosed. She'd offered to stand at the door of her disease, saying, "Let me show you."

In the summer of 1999, Jean, an athlete who power-walked four miles a day, found herself flagging. She began to have urinary-tract infections and chronic constipation, and her flat stomach began to swell. Her family physician diagnosed her complaints as a cocktail of irritable bowel syndrome, aging, and depression. But Jean wasn't comfortable with his answer. "I knew something was wrong," she says. A year after she began to drag, she felt lumps on her lower abdomen and asked a close friend to look. "Oh my God, Jean," her friend said, "Get to a doctor immediately."

Even though I didn't know why I got this cancer, this was something I was supposed to do, to be a vehicle to help other people understand this disease.

—Jean Miller

Her friend's urging came on July 4, 2000. Ten days later, she had surgery to remove large masses from her abdomen, cantaloupe-size tumors that Jean asked the doctor to photograph. "They've become a part of my body," she said, "and I want to see them." She had stage 2C ovarian cancer.

One of the many cruelties of this type of cancer is that initially it whispers, its symptoms hushed until it is well-advanced. Even when they speak up, those symptoms—such as gas, constipation, abdominal swelling, a feeling of fullness—are so easily read as indicators of less serious problems that only 10 percent of ovarian cancer is found in its earliest stages.

The disease will take the lives of more than fourteen thousand women in the United States in 2003, more than half of those diagnosed, a rate that would drop dramatically with early detection. Had Jean's initial doctor recognized her symptoms, for example, she likely would have had her ovaries removed and become a long-term survivor; for 95 percent of the women whose illness is caught in its early stages, the prognosis is excellent. The five-year survival rate for those whose cancer falls between stages 2 and 3, as Jean's does, is between 30 and 50 percent. And because her cancer has recurred repeatedly, her chances of surviving five years past diagnosis are "not that good," says her surgeon, Chotchai Srisuro, M.D., his round, kind face a comforting vessel for bad news. "She knows that," he adds quietly.

I meet Jean at her office—the volunteer office of St. Joseph Hospital of Kirkwood in St. Louis, where she is also being treated. She is slender, uncommonly pretty, with deep-set blue eyes, delicate features, and a warm smile. And she looks remarkably healthy, the only signs of illness and fatigue are the dark circles beneath her eyes.

As I watch Jean handle the details of her job, I see what has not come across on the telephone: She likes to have things under control. But for the last three years, she has had to surrender control to cancer. Since her diagnosis, she's had intermittent neuropathy (a loss of feeling), nausea, constipation, diarrhea, and "chemo-brain," the name she gives her occasional loss of short-term memory. Countless people have had their hands on her body and their say about her care. She says simply, "I have to trust those who help me."

And yet, as each treatment fails and the cancer refuses to budge, she's become intimate with a fact most of us work at denying: Control is not ours to have. The revelation comes in the daily surrender of moments that make us feel most alive, of intimacy, of appetite, of energy, of workouts. "I really miss a good sweat," she says. With each of these moments,

One of the many cruelties of ovarian cancer is that initially it whispers, its symptoms hushed until it is well-advanced.

Jean is forced to shed the denial that keeps most of us getting up in the morning.

She doesn't do it halfway. On the day she knew her hair would fall out (you can tell by a painful tension in your scalp, she says, like a too-tight rubber band on a ponytail), she called her husband, Glenn, and told him to bring home some film. On separate sheets of paper, she wrote the "Top 10 Reasons to Shave Your Head," David Letterman-style, posing with each page below her chin, her hair a little thinner in each photo. (One reason: bad hair day.) Her son, Scott, then 16, was appalled. "Nothing about this is funny," he said. Jean followed him into his room. "I can make this bad, or I can make it good," she said. "I'm choosing to make it good."

When Jean tells me this story, I think again of my friend with breast cancer and how she mourned the loss of her hair. She asked me to go with her to try on wigs, and soon we were giggling, trying out platinum, purple. She auditioned as a redhead and brunet, with a pageboy and a bob. An actress, she knows a lot about costumes and role-playing. And it was in groping for a disguise that she found a way to look illness in the eye. Soon she learned to go wigless, to find chic in her fuzz—and, maybe, to find a different sort of beauty in who she is and in the journey she'd taken.

For Jean, too, the journey had to mean something. The first step to meaning is finding a way past anger and terror. Jean's anger is no small detail. There's the fury she felt at the time wasted before the cancer was removed, and at its return nine months later. She says, "You fight like crazy that first time, and you do everything you're supposed to do, and then…."

There's the frustration she feels when medical professionals question her symptoms, saying, "No, you shouldn't be feeling that." There's the anger she felt at a friend who killed himself when she was working so hard to stay alive. There's anger toward friends who drop her because cancer's eye is too hard to look into and toward those who want details that don't belong to them. Says Jean, "You learn who you need to have close and who it's not healthy to have close."

I see this as I pass the day with Jean. She is unfailingly polite, but she is no false chirper. The number of times someone asks Jean how she is, how she's doing, becomes painful even to me. And each time, Jean seems to reach further for an answer that isn't a lie but that won't stop the conversation, either.

Anger and social dodges are not where Jean puts her efforts. She directs them at the cancer, primarily through the National Ovarian Cancer Coalition chapter she heads. For Jean, the equation is simple: Information can save women as she was not saved. "I realized that even though I didn't know why I got this cancer, this was something I was supposed to do, to be a vehicle to help other people understand this disease," says Jean.

This evening, I accompany Jean and Glenn to one of the monthly coalition meetings held at St. Joseph. We run into the building through torrential rain, and we are soaked when we enter the meeting room, as are the 15 or so women and men who have already arrived. Someone says, without irony, "But it always rains for us."

For the first few minutes, I focus on drying my short hair, glad to have a paper towel to hide behind. I am afraid of the scene I anticipate: depressed, dying women. How can I greet them? My mission seems so shallow. But to my surprise, except for one woman

in a wheelchair, no one seems ill or fragile or so very different from me.

Even more striking is the energy in the room. One woman reports on a new theory that harp music can boost immunity, suppressing cancer. The room fills with laughter as one woman answers, "I sure wish I'd known about that before I had chemo."

Jean's son says to me later, "They're all happy—not about their situation, but that they can do something, that they're not letting cancer run their lives."

But there's more. It's as if they've been released from the nagging details that keep healthy people tense. I ask Jean later how she handles stress. "I don't feel stress like I used to," she says. Of course, it's there, in her job, family, daily radiation treatments, nausea, fatigue, uncertainty, fear. But illness has freed her from the inconsequential. For Jean and women like her, worrying about when the plumber arrives or whether the dry cleaner can erase a spot is a luxury of good health. Theirs is not a TV-movie sanctimony; it's simply that they know, in a way most people never will, that this moment's pleasure is certain as nothing else is. As Jean puts it, "When we feel things, we *feel* things. And it's a huge blessing to really feel."

Jean's parents, Herman and Bernadette Pacini, live next door.

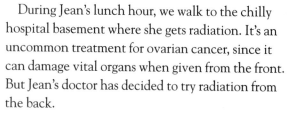

As I ask her how illness has changed her, how she faces the possibility of her own death, her answers make one thing clear: She has decided to turn cancer into a kind of power. "I have so much passion for things that I didn't have before—for what we do in the coalition and for every day and for the people I talk to. I hate having cancer and feeling sick all the time. But I wake up every morning and make a choice like everyone else to have a great day."

Still, moments of fear and frustration can overwhelm her. That's when she turns to her husband. "He's there to hold me when I sit on his lap and cry," she says. "He lets me show my anger. By the time I've done all that, we're laughing again."

> I don't feel stressed like I used to; it's there, but I wake up every morning and make a choice to have a great day. I have so much passion for things that I didn't have before.
>
> —Jean Miller

During Jean's lunch hour, we walk to the chilly hospital basement where she gets radiation. It's an uncommon treatment for ovarian cancer, since it can damage vital organs when given from the front. But Jean's doctor has decided to try radiation from the back.

Two therapists greet Jean as old friends would, and she climbs up on their table and lies down, pulling her pants below her hip bones. The toes of Jean's shoes are held together by a huge rubber band, and she holds a 6-inch rubber ring to keep her hands still. A laser bisects her horizontally and vertically, and its translucent red light forms a jewel-like cross over her body. When I ask her later if she is aware of the laser cross, its beauty on her body, her eyes fill with tears. "No," she says. "Thank you for telling me."

Jean's focus on healing is not blinkered. She knows her odds. "Sometimes I look around, and I take myself out of the picture," she says. "I watch Glenn and Scott, and think they'll do fine. I get a lot of comfort knowing they are there for each other, if it comes to that." She's also asked her oncology nurse to tell her what will happen to her body if she dies, how it will stop functioning.

"I know my body can only do this for so long," she says. "But I've come to accept that death isn't the end-all. In my mind, the journey continues. So I'm preparing myself for the next part. I know there will be a point when I say, 'Enough.'"

Sooner or later, Jean's story is everyone's story. Perhaps she has a better view, or more than most, she has learned to share what she can of it.

Like Jean, we all live with dying, but most of us notice that truth only intermittently. I see my friend's terror, I watch the decline of my 85-year-old father-in-law, and then I return to the daily. But for Jean, the daily is something else. She no longer marks her treatments on a calendar; when they stop

Jean calls her husband, Glenn, her "towering tree."

124

and start has become irrelevant, and attention to such things is another luxury she doesn't have. What she looks forward to is more basic: another 24 hours. In her case—and perhaps this is her gift—intensity is what she gets to have.

Some nights, Jean tells me, she lies awake and worries about what will become of her. "It's not the end that's hard," she says. "It's all the choices I have to make between now and then." But on other nights, she dreams she is a floating spirit, completely well, completely happy.

Contributing Editor Dorothy Foltz-Gray is writing With and Without Her, *a book about being and losing a twin.*

Q + A

Passing on Paps

Do I still need a Pap smear if I've had a total hysterectomy?

If you've had your uterus and cervix removed to treat such conditions as benign fibroids or irregular bleeding, it's perfectly logical to think that you wouldn't need to get a Pap smear. But this exam, the best check for abnormal cells in the cervix, can also detect vaginal cancer. If you're at high risk for this disease, then your doctor will likely still recommend that you get the test. You are considered to be at high risk if you are over age 50, have human papillomavirus, have had cervical cancer, or are a smoker, among other factors.

Otherwise, it's probably OK to skip the Pap, but you won't be able to avoid the stirrups completely. You should still have a yearly pelvic exam to detect signs of infection or other problems.

Exercise (at Any Age) to Beat Breast-Cancer Risks

Go for a walk to lower your risk of breast cancer. Researchers examining data on more than seventy-four thousand women in the Women's Health Initiative study recently found that exercise reduced risk regardless of age. It's known that young women who exercise regularly have lower rates of breast cancer. But until now, nobody was certain whether working up a sweat after menopause would cut your risk. Experts say all you need is 30 minutes per day of brisk walking, five days a week.

How Women *Really* Feel About Their Breasts

Six women open up about the impact their breasts have had on their lives.

BY DOROTHY FOLTZ-GRAY • PHOTOGRAPHY BY JOYCE TENNESON

I love my breasts. They are round and soft, just like the rest of me, complete but not showy, minimalist but declarative. In a world that adores big breasts, my understated pair has always seemed plenty to me, a public-enough announcement of my femininity.

As I've grown older, my breasts have also provided an odd comfort that feet, thumbs, and elbows just do not. Breasts connect me—and all women—to no less than everything: to my role as mother, to my children, to my lover, to sexuality, to beauty, to nourishment.

"The way a woman feels about her breasts is such a rich story because it covers so many aspects of being a woman," says Meema Spadola, producer and director of *Breasts: A Documentary*, shown on HBO, and author of the book *Breasts: Our Most Public Private Parts*. "Talking about our breasts is also a way of talking about sex, about power."

Every woman has her breast story. As that story shifts throughout her life, so does her relationship with her breasts. Breasts are, in short, at the heart of our richest links, as confirmed by the women whose tales follow. Their experiences demonstrate the unique connections that all women have with

their breasts, and how they learn to accept (or not) the bodies they're given.

ᖇᖇ

I could either wear a back brace or have a reduction. I chose the surgery. —Laryssa Zalisko, 23, art administrator and graduate student, Hoboken, New Jersey

Laryssa Zalisko

By the eighth grade, I had awkwardly large breasts. I didn't get upset until high school, when I couldn't wear the same clothes my friends did—tight tops and bikini bathing suits—without feeling like I was flashing my breasts. But in a sweatshirt, I felt

I was hiding them. So I alternated between both styles, unhappy either way.

By 19 I was wearing "grandma" bras with shoulder padding so the straps wouldn't cut into my skin. I was 5 feet 2 and weighed 120 pounds, wearing 34DDD bras; 34s don't come any larger. I was an intern at an art gallery, and I had to dress professionally. But even in a suit, I felt my clothes looked provocative. I decided to speak to a plastic surgeon about breast reduction. The doctor said I was a perfect candidate, but he also told me that to avoid surgery I could wear a back brace to prevent the strain caused by my breasts. I opted for the surgery.

Now I'm a 34C, a good handful. The fronts of my shirts touch my stomach—something I haven't felt in years. At first I had pangs of regret: Did I go too small? But four years later, I'm convinced that this is the size my breasts were meant to be.

෧෧

I'd rather have great skin than bigger breasts any day. —Portia Chery, 27, model, Brooklyn, New York

When I started getting breasts, I wanted big ones—not like Pamela Anderson's, but big enough for the boys to pay attention. I definitely didn't want the 32A breasts I got.

Back in St. Lucia, where I grew up, my friends and I thought one girl had big breasts because she slathered crayfish on them. So we'd grab crayfish out of the river and rub. On windy days I'd walk backward so my T-shirt wouldn't make an imprint of my breasts. Everyone said, "Yeah, Portia, she's so skinny. No booty, no tits, no nothing."

I started becoming more comfortable with my breasts when I was 17. I wore a skintight catsuit in a high school show, and people remarked, "Portia, I didn't know you had such a great body." It was around this time that I began modeling. I credit modeling with making me at ease with my breast size. Girls with big breasts can't do the runway modeling I do.

Portia Chery

Today, my breasts aren't even on the list of things I'd change. I'd rather have flawless skin. Men have never complained that my breasts are too small. They're sensual: You don't get smacked with them; they won't suffocate you. They make me happy.

෧෧

I hated the feeling that everyone was looking at me. —Melisa Frick, 33, personal trainer, Simi Valley, California

I was a late bloomer. In high school I was petite, a 32B. But during my first year of college, I gained 25 pounds and stopped working out regularly. By

Melisa Frick

the end of my freshman year, my breasts were enormous—34Ds. They became the first things everyone noticed. My friends even nicknamed me Missiles, Moogers, Chesty. I felt like one big breast.

By the time I graduated, I was a 34DD. Exercise was difficult because my breasts had become an obstruction. I had to go through great pains to keep them in place, wearing my regular bra and a sports bra under a tank top with a built-in bra. And this was before I even put on a T-shirt! I also hated the feeling that everyone in the gym was looking at me.

I looked into breast reduction, but my insurance wouldn't cover it. One doctor said, "I see women every day who want breasts like yours." But those women don't know about the bra straps digging into my shoulders. Or the problems I have finding a bathing suit that fits: If the top fits, the bottom's too big. Or how hard it is to find a comfortable sleep position.

Finally, one surgeon said, "Lose weight and strength-train, and you can solve this on your own." So I started working out six times a week, went from 140 to 117 pounds, and dropped to a 34D. Sure, my breasts are still a lot to handle, but I'm happier with them because of the shape I'm in.

༄

I grieved for my breasts. —June Donahoo, 55, former gym teacher, Knoxville, Tennessee

When you're going through breast cancer, you just want to live. I had my first breast removed in 1992. A year and a half later, they found a lump in the other breast, and I had a second mastectomy.

June Donahoo

I grieved for my breasts. They were part of me and my sexuality. I considered them perfect, a 36C. I asked my husband to take a picture of my breasts before the surgery in case I wanted to look at them. But I've never felt the need to do so. I guess it's just not that important.

At first it was hard to get out of the shower and see myself in the mirror. It took a while to look and say, "Well, it's not so bad," because even after the scars faded, my breasts were still gone.

I didn't want reconstruction; I'd had infections with the mastectomies, and they took a long time to heal. So I had myself fitted for a prosthesis to wear to work. But the first thing I did each day when I got home was to take the prosthesis off—it's very hot and cumbersome. Now I just don't wear it. I find going flat-chested a lot more comfortable, and, funnily enough, it really helps my golf game. I don't have to swing around my breasts. I'm just like one of the guys!

༄

I wanted to be more comfortable in clothing that shows my body. 5
—Laura Cozik, 36, fitness instructor and competitive dancer, Brooklyn, New York

In my teens I wore a C cup, and my breasts attracted a lot of unwanted stares. At first I wore a tank top over my bathing suit on the beach to cover them up. But eventually I liked the attention. Then, in my early 20s, when I began teaching fitness classes full-time and working for a dance company, I lost a lot of weight in my chest, and my cup size dropped to a B. What I didn't like was that the weight wasn't distributed evenly; most of my breast tissue fell below the nipple, leaving the top halves of my breasts flat.

The way they looked, especially when I was nude, really bothered me. They were very loose and moved around a lot. My boyfriend and I do competitive dancing—hustle and West Coast swing—and we wear flamboyant costumes. It's not a demure profession, and I like wearing clothes that show off my body.

So about two years ago I began thinking about having my breasts augmented. I didn't really like the idea of going under the knife, but I wanted more confidence about my breasts. I believed augmentation was safe, and I trusted my doctor. I received implants in September 2003.

Now my breasts are a full C again, with permanent cleavage. I no longer have to wear a restrictive bra to look good. And I definitely feel more comfortable

Laura Cozik

showing them off when I'm in dance competitions. I believe this is the way my breasts were always meant to look.

◎◎

My breasts aren't perfect, but they're part of who I am. —Ellen Joseph, 55, yoga instructor and Thai-massage therapist, Kingston, New Jersey

I grew up in a demure, intellectual household in New Jersey, but I was the one who was always a little naughty. At 20 I paid my way through college by dancing topless. But it wasn't always easy. Most of the dancers had bigger boobs than I did—my breasts are petite, 34AA. And one of my breasts is smaller than the other. But I'm a trained dancer,

Ellen Joseph

and I came to believe that people were looking at me as a performer, not as a pair of boobs. The first time I took off my top, it felt freeing, and I enjoyed the attention.

As a yoga instructor, I work in a profession where clothing is more body-conscious, athletic, and unique to the individual, as opposed to the clothing that is typically accepted in corporate settings. I believe I gravitated to my work because I can be myself—and my breasts are part of who I am. I'm proud of them. They've been good friends. ∎

Beware: Breast Implants Can Fool Mammograms

The evidence is clear: Implants make mammograms harder to read, according to a large-scale study in *The Journal of the American Medical Association*. The analysis found that the screens missed cancer in 55 percent of patients with implants, versus just 33 percent without them. If you've had augmentation surgery (or reconstruction that left original tissue in place), choose an imaging center that specializes in mammograms; you'll undergo a test that pushes the implants aside.

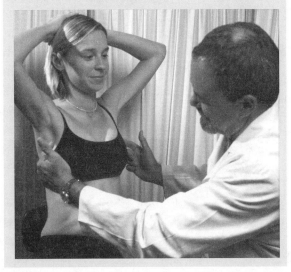

Why a Breast-Cancer Diagnosis Needs a Second Opinion

Are you confident that you'll receive the right treatment for a suspicious lump in your breast? If you get a second opinion after a mammogram, you should be.

University of Michigan radiologist Amy Rochester Guest, M.D., and colleagues recently found that second opinions netted different interpretations for a surprisingly high 45 percent of women who came to the school's clinic after being diagnosed with breast cancer elsewhere. In more than half of those cases, the second opinion led to a change in treatment, such as chemotherapy or lumpectomy rather than breast removal. Seven percent of all the women had more cancer than first thought, and a few discovered that they didn't have cancer at all.

Doctors often don't tell women that second opinions are available, so you have to seek one out for yourself, Guest says. A breast-cancer clinic is best. Check your insurance plan; most will pay for the extra certainty.

Surrogate Moms Seem Satisfied

Ever since the fierce custody battle in 1988 known as the Baby M case, people have asked whether a woman can really conceive and carry a baby for someone else without suffering emotional

trauma. In the largest study of its kind so far, the answer appears to be yes. British psychologists interviewed 34 surrogate mothers who had recently given birth and found that the majority suffered no adverse emotional consequences during the pregnancy or after. About a third of the women said they felt somewhat upset just after giving birth, but only two continued to be sad about a year after delivering. Still needed, researchers say, are studies on surrogates' reactions years down the line.

Why You May Not Need a Biopsy

A new technology may cut down on needless breast biopsies among women who have high cancer risks, dense breasts, or implants. Mammograms can miss cancer in these women, but the alternative—magnetic resonance imaging (MRI)—is known for mistakenly red-flagging benign spots. That often leads to a biopsy, an invasive, anxiety-producing test. But new software is improving the ability of MRI scans to determine if a suspicious spot is harmless. The program highlights potential malignancies by measuring how breast tissue absorbs dye over time. (The dye is injected beforehand.)

In an early trial, a version of the software called CADstream (CAD means "computer-aided detection") didn't miss any cancers and ruled it out in 12 of 24 benign cases. Among women with high risks, dense breast tissue, or implants, that means at least half whose lumps are considered benign may be able to skip a biopsy, says study director Connie Lehman, M.D., who supervises breast imaging at the University of Washington School of Medicine. Further studies may show that MRIs are useful for even more women.

The CADstream program is in use at 50 centers nationwide. Visit www.confirma.com for more information.

Why Women Take Pain More Seriously Than Men

It looks like men's and women's brains respond in fundamentally different ways to pain that comes from down under. In a study recently published in *Gastroenterology,* men and women were given painful stimuli in their lower colons and rectums (a small balloon was inflated in both areas). Men showed greater activation in brain regions involved with cognitive processing and pain modulation: The pain signal took a sort of express elevator to an area that allowed them to quickly identify the pain as nonthreatening and then damp it down. But in women, what lit up most strongly were areas of the brain, such as the amygdala, that process such emotions as fear. That kind of brain response to gastrointestinal pain may prevent women from quickly dismissing discomfort, the researchers speculate, and allow them to assess just how serious the threat may be.

Coming Soon: Candy Contraceptives

If swallowing a pill makes birth control a hassle, a chewable, spearmint-flavored version may be to your liking. The new option—a variation of an existing contraceptive, Ovcon-35—is now available from Warner Chilcott. The pill contains estrogen and progesterone (like the traditional kind) and is as effective as other pills on the market. It costs about $35 for a 4-week cycle, about the same as regular contraceptive pills.

Q + A   How the Pill Affects Menopause

I'm in my 40s, and I'm currently on birth control pills. How will I know when I'm entering menopause?

Chances are that you won't. The only way to know for sure is to go off the Pill and see if your period comes back (which could take a few months). In this case, though, ignorance might truly be bliss. For most women, the hormones in oral contraceptives curb hot flashes, irregular bleeding, and other symptoms that surface as menopause approaches. "The experience of menopause is going to be very different for a woman on the Pill than for other women," says Andrew Kaunitz, M.D., professor and assistant chair in the Department of Obstetrics and Gynecology at the University of Florida Health Science Center. So you might sail blissfully through the change without even realizing it. In fact, some women in their 40s start taking the Pill for just that reason, Kaunitz says. If curiosity gets the better of you and you decide to stop taking the Pill, keep an alternate means of birth control handy until you are certain that conception is no longer an issue for you.

If you're on the Pill, you could simply sail through menopause without any symptoms.

The SKINNY FAT Syndrome

Here's why thin women aren't necessarily healthier women.

BY STACEY GRENROCK WOODS

I've been skinny all my life. A few years back, when people asked me how I stayed that way, I'd always tell them the unqualified truth: "I eat all the wrong things, and I don't exercise." Now, I know you're thinking that can't be true, but hear me out.

I thought I was just lucky. I had spent my childhood and teens cavorting from dance class to dance class. Throughout my 20s, I kept my 5-foot-5-inch frame hovering around 100 pounds, even though I'd given up regular exercise. I figured I could continue to put away milk shakes and forgo sweating with impunity. But eventually I had to eat my words.

In fact, I was suffering from a condition I'll call "skinny-fat": I looked thin, but I was carrying around too much body fat. It's a deceptive—and dangerous—ailment. Slender or not, a person with this profile is at risk for many of the same ailments that can befall obese people.

I was age 30 the first time I noticed that things might not be as they seemed. Sitting in a low beach chair, I became aware that, at some point, my body had developed pockets of flab. I probed for some evidence of muscle but found none. My thighs felt bumpy like—you guessed it—cottage cheese. Large curd.

The American Council on Exercise (ACE) recommends that, depending on her build, a fit woman have 14- to 24-percent body fat. That amount helps regulate body temperature, cushion organs, and act as a fuel reserve. But ACE sets the bar for obesity at 32 percent, meaning that at least 5 percent of the population is obese even though these folks are not obviously overweight. Part of the reason may be Americans' obsession with thinness, not fitness, as the end result of dieting.

I could have stuck with denial; after all, I was still wearing size-2 pants. Instead, I joined a gym and hired a trainer, who suggested I take a body-composition test. Neither one of us could believe the results: Though I was underweight according to standard measures, I had 29-percent body fat—placing me on the brink of obesity.

> I was still a size 2, but my body had developed pockets of flab. My thighs felt like cottage cheese.

In the medical world, skinny-fat is known as sarcopenia, a condition marked by muscle and strength loss in people of otherwise-normal weight. A person of my size should have only about 15-percent body fat, says Steven B. Heymsfield, M.D., deputy director of the New York Obesity Research Center at St. Luke's–Roosevelt Hospital. My high fat percentage raised my risks of diabetes, high blood pressure, osteoporosis, and other illnesses. I would actually have been better off slightly overweight but more muscular, Heymsfield says.

Suddenly, looking good in clothes wasn't enough. I had to think about my health, which meant accepting that I wasn't exempt from eating sensibly and exercising. I started lifting weights and running several times a week. Before long, things got harder—that is, my thighs, back, and abs. After a few years of regular exercise, I still wear the skinny pants in the family, but now I've earned the right. ■

Stacey Grenrock Woods writes Esquire *magazine's sex column.*

How to Get Skinny-Strong

Face reality. There are several ways to determine your body-fat percentage, including underwater weighing (hydrodensitometry), measuring skin-fold thickness with calipers, and bioelectrical impedance, in which a small electrical current is passed through your body. Ask about these tests at your gym or doctor's office.

Watch what you eat. If you're cutting back on calories, make sure you're getting enough protein, calcium, potassium, and vitamins, all of which are necessary for building muscle.

Get active. Exercising is by far the most effective way to gain muscle and lose fat.

Check your medicine chest. Some medications actually cause muscle loss and weakness. Talk with your doctor about alternatives.

Exercise is the best way to gain muscle and lose fat.

Middle-Aged
and Loving It

Today 40- and 50-something women are discovering that growing older is much different (and better!) than expected.

BY MARION WINIK

People my age talk a lot about age. One of the things these 40- and 50-somethings sometimes say—after mourning the decline of their skin, hair, energy level, etc.—is, "Inside, I don't feel any different than I did when I was 12." Or 19. Or 25…. Wherever they pinpoint the archetypal moment of youth, the point is that the speaker feels like a young person in an aging body, an unchanging self in a changing vessel.

Well, I don't feel at all like I did at any of those ages—or at least I don't think so. My memory of my youth is not crystalline (you've probably seen the bumper sticker: If you remember the '70s, you weren't there). But based on what I can recall, I wouldn't want to feel the way I did in my younger years. Growing up was hard. To me, the idea that I might someday feel like a 12-year-old in an 80-year-old body sounds like the worst of both worlds.

I was actually pretty happy about turning 45 in May 2003. I had the sense that I was at the beginning of something—as if I had metamorphosed into a very young old person instead of becoming an older and older young person, as I'd felt for quite a while. In the same way that worldly eighth-graders turn into wide-eyed high school freshmen, on my 45th birthday I seemed to have crossed the boundary into a new demographic. I thought: Someday, I'll go to my son's graduation; someday, my husband and I will leave our empty nest for a tour of Thailand; someday, I'll hold my grandchild. Not only will my AARP card get me a discount at the movies, but also I'll actually be able to go on a whim—without three weeks of arranging babysitting, rides, and sleepovers for our five kids.

I was happy about turning 45. I had the sense that I was at the beginning of something … my enthusiasm for aging is a luxury. I know how lucky I am.

It's not that I don't realize there are challenges in midlife for women. After spending decades wrestling with our reproductive cycles, physical attractiveness, and roles as caretakers of children, we face dramatic redefinition in those areas. But is this such a bad thing?

Not according to Sandra Sundel, MSSW, Ph.D., co-author of *Women at Midlife: Life Experiences and Implications for the Helping Professions,* which summarizes the results of 232 studies conducted with women ages 40 to 60. The biggest surprise in the book is the pleasure that many women feel at midlife. The National Center on Women and Aging at Brandeis University found the same thing: In a poll of 1,000 women over age 50, more than half reported that getting older is much better than they had expected.

It may be that many problems affecting older women are overrated, Sundel says. Empty-nest syndrome, for one. "Most women work now," says the clinical social worker, "so once their kids leave home, they can put more energy into their careers or perhaps start a career they've been postponing." The result: more money, more opportunity, more freedom. Plus, marriages tend to improve when children leave, Sundel says.

Of course, many women in midlife are dealing not with college-age kids but preschoolers. According to the National Center for Health Statistics, the number of women in their early 40s who had babies more than doubled between 1980 and 2001; for 45- to 49-year-olds, the rate of increase is even sharper, tripling since 1990.

I am part of these statistics. I have two teenage sons, two teenage stepchildren, and a little girl who was born three years ago—when I was 42. My empty nest is a long way off. The thought of all those Chuck E. Cheese's birthday parties still to come is exhausting. But as another older mom I know points

Exercise, eat well, live moderately, and try not to get too bent out of shape about your hormones and your crow's-feet.

out, having a full nest can make you feel young or at least leave you with little time to contemplate your age. Having the energy of a young child in the house makes it feel like perpetual springtime. When I see my daughter growing, changing, learning, I think of a line from Dylan Thomas: "the force that through the green fuse drives the flower." Or as Jane said this morning while she practiced writing her lowercase *i,* a wobbly stem with a big spirally dot on top, "I is a flower." And I is a gardener; she blooms in me, too.

My little flower will be 10 or so when I reach menopause, if everything goes according to average. I'm nervous about that, I admit. I've had a rough time with PMS since I turned 30, and I wonder what will come next on the hormonal roller coaster.

"You shouldn't assume it will be awful," says Nancy Avis, Ph.D., professor of public health sciences at Wake Forest University School of Medicine and a co-investigator for the Study of Women's Health Across the Nation (SWAN). "Many women have no problems with menopause; some do. We don't know yet what factors make the difference."

SWAN is following a multiethnic group of 3,300 women from the prelude to menopause through its aftermath, tracking emotional and physical changes. But some things already seem clear, from SWAN and other studies. Menopause doesn't trigger depression for the majority of women, Avis says. Japanese women don't experience hot flashes as a rule, but 75 percent of Caucasian women do (the SWAN researchers hope to figure out why, among other things). Studies indicate that by the time a woman is on the other side of menopause, her interest in sex decreases somewhat, though this may be a result of aging rather than menopause itself.

Again, I wonder if that's such a bad thing. Sex, and questions about my own sexual attractiveness, stormed into my awareness more than 30 years ago, and those issues haven't been far from center stage since. I'm actually kind of intrigued to see them move to the side. What's going to happen in the available space?

My enthusiasm for aging is a luxury. The Brandeis study makes it clear that there are women who don't share this perspective, particularly if they're poor or have health or money problems. I know how lucky I am. In fact, one of the ways I differ from the younger me is now I have a sense of gratitude. I have already outlived many of my peers and loved ones. Instead of thinking "that will never happen to me" when I hear of a car accident or a person dying two months after

some sudden diagnosis, I have exactly the opposite reaction. Very sad things happen to people my age all the time, and I could be next.

I was self-destructive when I was young, but now I'm trying really hard to live. I have a little girl who will turn 30 when I'm in my 70s, and I don't want to miss any of the steps from here to there, not the soccer games or the algebra homework or the mother-daughter trip to the spa—not to mention my long-awaited, hard-earned empty nest. I exercise, eat well, and live moderately. And I try not to get too bent out of shape about my hormones and crow's-feet, because the long-term outlook is good. According to the Brandeis researchers, women over age 80 gave the most positive report of all on their emotional and mental health.

Which is good, because I know when I'm 80, I'm going to feel exactly like I'm 80.

Marion Winik is a commentator on National Public Radio and the author of First Comes Love.

Dating Again? Watch Out for This STD

If you're back on the singles scene, it's time to learn about trichomoniasis, a sexually transmitted disease (STD) that strikes 5 million American women every year. Studies show the number of people infected appears to be holding steady, yet half the women who have trichomoniasis are symptomless. That's a problem because if it's not treated, this disease can leave you infertile, cause premature birth, and make it easier to get HIV. (Women who do show symptoms often have a yellow or green vaginal discharge and pain when urinating.) The good news: In early 2004, the U.S. Food and Drug Administration approved an antibiotic called tinidazole. This new drug appears to be more effective than current remedies.

Over 50? Stand Tall with Soy

Plant chemicals can pack a punch. And the ones known as isoflavones may help your bones after menopause. In a recent British study, 77 postmenopausal women who took daily supplements of Promensil, an isoflavone extract made from red clover (which may help curb hot flashes), lost half as much bone mass in their spines after a year as those who took placebos.

Isoflavones probably mimic the effects of estrogen, which also can slow bone breakdown. Lorraine Fitzpatrick, M.D., an osteoporosis expert and former director of the Women's Health Fellowship at the Mayo Clinic, believes the study adds to a load of evidence suggesting isoflavones can help postmenopausal women. Remember, though, that hormone therapy or bone-building drugs can do more for women with osteoporosis, and isoflavones don't seem to strengthen younger women's bones. They may actually do the opposite by competing with estrogen's effects.

Study author Sheila A. Bingham, Ph.D., says she wants more evidence before recommending isoflavone supplements to postmenopausal women. Fitzpatrick's advice: Skip the supplements for now (the study was funded in part by the company that makes Promensil), and eat isoflavone-rich foods like soy and flaxseed, along with those high in bone-friendly calcium and vitamin D.

Why Your Bones Are Not Big Cola Fans

Drinking too many colas may seriously weaken your bones. Tufts University researchers recently found that women who drank at least one 12-ounce cola daily over four years had up to 5-percent lower bone-mineral density than women who drank fewer than one a week. Some experts had thought that cola guzzlers seemed to have lower bone density because they consumed the fizzy stuff in place of milk. But everyone in this latest study drank the same amount of milk, so the scientists now think the phosphoric acid added to colas (but not other soft drinks) for tartness interferes with your body's absorption of calcium in food.

Q + A   Be Good to Your Bones *Now*

My bone density–test results came back slightly below average. My doctor wants to wait and see how I test in a year, but I'm really worried about osteoporosis. Is there anything I can do in the meantime?

Because you fall into the gray area between having a skeleton of steel and bones as brittle as kindling, ask your doctor about an NTx test. While bone mineral–density tests reveal how much bone you currently have, the NTx test, which is particularly useful for women at high risk for osteoporosis, shows the rate at which you're losing bone mass. The procedure, which is covered by many insurance plans, measures the presence of N-telopeptide of collagen, a substance that is released in your urine when bone breaks down. Based on the results, your doctor may decide you need to take action right away, which could mean putting you on bone-protecting medication.

Five Women, One Age

Discover What Turning 40 Really Means

BY ANNE UNDERWOOD • PHOTOGRAPHY BY MELANIE DUNEA

Whether anyone dared to say it or not, turning 40 used to mark the beginning of the end. It was the age when you began noticing gray hairs, fine wrinkles, and memory lapses—and started letting go of your dreams. Today, the idea of a 40-year-old resigning herself to old age seems laughable. Women in their 40s and beyond are running marathons, taking on powerful jobs, traveling the globe, and having babies.

To uncover what the number means now, we put five very different 40-year-olds through a series of tests. We assessed their cardiovascular fitness, upper-body strength, skin, hair, bone density, and memory skills. The results showed that 40, if anything, is the new 30—a milestone, yes, but by no means the end. Sure, some of these women had to face the effects of choices they made more than 20 years ago (SPF was a little-known acronym then), while others discovered areas they are neglecting right now. To counter such inevitable imperfections, we asked experts to outline proven antiaging strategies. Despite a few kinks, these women show just how good 40 can look *and* feel.

CATHERINE LINDSEY

I'm very happy with where I am in life, but I'm surprised I'm still single.

Cardio: ★★★
Strength: ★★★★
Skin: ★★★
Hair: ★★
Bones: ★★★★
Memory: ★★★★

On a recent vacation, Catherine went to Spain, where her boyfriend ran with the bulls in Pamplona. We're betting that if she'd wanted to, Catherine could easily have made the run, too. She's been an athlete since age 12, when she started running on the lakeside paths of the island in Washington State where she grew up. Although a knee injury sidelined her for a while not long ago—and put a crimp in her tennis, skiing, and inline skating—physical therapy has helped her get back in shape. In fall 2003 she completed her third triathlon, even though she was unable to train for it properly. "I had to set a goal for myself," says the driven sports-and-entertainment lawyer.

Catherine's Achilles' heel: her hair. Under a microscope, the effects of 15 years of highlighting are evident. (Treatments that lighten, most of which require bleaching, tend to be more damaging than those that darken.) She recently began to notice more split ends but had no idea how extensive the damage was.

When hair is healthy, densely packed, shingle-like cuticles protect it from damage and keep it looking shiny. Coloring, blow-drying, and even brushing can break the cuticles—think of a storm that blows shingles off a home—leaving hair

exposed. Unfortunately, while you can reshingle your home, you can't call a construction crew to recuticle your hair. But taking better care of it assures that hair will be healthier when it grows back in.

KIMBERLY KONG
I'm learning to take care of myself both emotionally and physically.

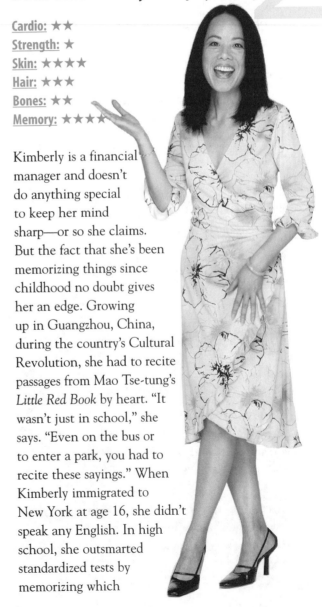

Cardio: ★★
Strength: ★
Skin: ★★★★
Hair: ★★★
Bones: ★★
Memory: ★★★★

Kimberly is a financial manager and doesn't do anything special to keep her mind sharp—or so she claims. But the fact that she's been memorizing things since childhood no doubt gives her an edge. Growing up in Guangzhou, China, during the country's Cultural Revolution, she had to recite passages from Mao Tse-tung's *Little Red Book* by heart. "It wasn't just in school," she says. "Even on the bus or to enter a park, you had to recite these sayings." When Kimberly immigrated to New York at age 16, she didn't speak any English. In high school, she outsmarted standardized tests by memorizing which

HAIR TIPS
Let your roots show. Allowing natural color to emerge between treatments will give your hair a chance to recover, says Laurie Polis, M.D., director of Soho Skin & Laser Dermatology in New York City.

Give your blow-dryer a rest. Air-dry hair, if possible; otherwise, turn the heat to a low setting, and hold the dryer at least 6 inches away from your hair to minimize damage.

Condition every time you wash. This is especially important for color-treated tresses. If you have oily hair, sometimes a coating of conditioner at the ends is all you need.

words belonged together, even when she didn't know what they meant. Go figure; she aced our memory test.

As a divorced mother, Kimberly strives to show her 11-year-old daughter, Marlena, how to live a balanced life. "It took me almost half my life to learn and confirm that emotions affect my physical well-being," she says. "I want my daughter to know that it's OK to be expressive—to laugh, to cry, or to be embarrassed."

For someone who had never set foot in a gym before participating in our tests, Kimberly is in remarkably good shape, thanks to urban living. "If the weather is good, I'll walk instead of take the bus," she says. Even so, she could benefit from more-regular weight-bearing exercise. This fact, coupled with a diet low in calcium, may have contributed to her low bone-density scores.

BONE-BUILDING TIPS

Eat calcium-rich foods. The best sources are dairy products, but you can also find this nutrient in such foods as fortified orange juice and cereal. A 40-year-old woman needs 1,000 milligrams of calcium a day, along with 400 International Units of vitamin D, which ensures your body will absorb the mineral. (Animal foods, such as eggs and fish, are rich in vitamin D.)

Supplement your diet. Because supplements differ according to how much and how often you should take them, follow the label to ensure maximum benefit.

Exercise regularly. For optimal bone density, combine jogging or walking with weight-training sessions (using free weights or machines).

DEIDRE TERZIAN

It's a time of evaluation. I'm still figuring out what I would like to be doing.

Cardio: ★★
Strength: ★★
Skin: ★★★
Hair: ★★★★
Bones: ★★★★
Memory: ★★

With her strong bones, great skin, and gorgeous hair, Deirdre embodies an enviable picture of life at age 40. Her hair is fine and therefore susceptible to breakage, but it is actually in excellent condition, thanks to her no-fuss routine (she's never colored it and rarely blow-dries it).

Less may be more when it comes to hair, but the same cannot be said for exercise. The cardio and strength test results were eye-opening, says Deirdre, who works for an interior-architecture firm. "I work out three times a week, but I guess I'm not pushing myself as hard as I think," she says.

She found the results of her memory test even more disquieting. "You wonder how I function in the world," she said afterward. But the fact is, although she scored below average, she's nowhere near losing her faculties. Odd memory lapses, especially trouble recalling names and words, are just part of being 40. Deirdre, who has never been married, already follows a major scientific recommendation for strengthening memory: She challenges her brain with new tasks. As her 40th birthday approached, she signed up for an acting class and began to study flamenco dancing, which she had grown to love when she taught English in Spain after college.

MEMORY TIPS

Stay mentally active. "Think of the brain as a muscle. The more you stimulate it, the stronger it gets," says our memory tester, Sergio Marini, Ph.D. Studies show that people with mentally demanding jobs experience less memory decline as they age, compared with those in less-challenging positions.

Get physical. "Aerobic exercise improves circulation and oxygen delivery to the brain," says psychiatrist Gary Small, M.D., director of the UCLA Center on Aging. Animal research also shows that exercise increases levels of a substance called brain-derived neurotrophic factor, which protects brain cells.

Relax. "Stress interferes with concentration, which is crucial for learning and memory," Small says. Chronically high levels of stress hormones shrink the hippocampus, the part of the brain that is critical for forming memories.

PATTY McGROGAN-FOST

I may not remember everything I learned in college, but I feel wise.

Cardio: ★★★
Strength: ★★★★
Skin: ★
Hair: ★★
Bones: ★★★
Memory: ★★★

Don't let Patty's petite frame fool you; she's a powerhouse. After she knocked out 30 full-body push-ups, even personal trainer Taylor was impressed. "We have a lot of guys who can't do that," he says. In addition to the workout she gets from running after two children, ages 5 and 8, Patty takes ballet once a week and kickboxing three times weekly. "Ballet is like yoga in motion," she says. "It requires a lot of stretching, which is helpful at an age when you can start to lose flexibility."

Of all Patty's excellent test results, the bone-scan findings pleased her the most. Her small build and a family history of osteoporosis put her at risk for developing the disease. But her commitment to a healthy diet and exercise has kept her bones strong.

A self-professed sun worshipper, Patty knew she'd flunk the skin test, though. Her penchant for puffing cigarettes in college also put her at a disadvantage. The skin analysis showed spots caused by the sun, and the UV test revealed damage below the surface that will show up as splotches within the next decade or so. "From now on I'm going to wear sunscreen all year round," Patty vows.

SKIN TIPS

Reduce sun exposure. More than 80 percent of sun damage occurs by age 21, and there is no way to reverse it. "But it's not a done deal," says dermatologist Arielle Kauvar, M.D., director of New York Laser & Skin Care. To minimize any future damage, seek out the shade and use your sunscreen.

Exfoliate. In-office treatments, such as chemical peels and microdermbrasion, can help remove sun-damaged cells, improving skin tone while stimulating the growth of new cells to reduce fine wrinkles, age spots, and acne scars.

Moisturize after showering. Applying cream when your skin is still damp will seal in water already on the surface.

SALLY AMICK-RUSSO
I feel so good about where I am.

Cardio: ★★★
Strength: ★★
Skin: ★★★★
Hair: ★★★★
Bones: ★★★
Memory: ★★★

Sally's complexion looks so smooth she could pass for a 26-year-old, according to her skin-test results. Sure, as a senior copywriter at Estée Lauder, she has access to beauty products galore, but most likely she has her sensitive skin to thank for staying virtually wrinkle-free. "I get sun poisoning easily, so I've tended to stay out of the sun most of my life," says this 40-year-old woman who has also never smoked.

Sally scored high marks on the cardio test, too. Given her disciplined workout routine, that's no surprise. This mother of two toddlers says that as her 40th birthday approached, she got serious about exercising again; marriage and kids had made it nearly impossible to squeeze in fitness regularly. Her husband, Rich, would work out in their basement gym, and eventually she grew tired of hearing him brag about his hour-long exercise sessions. "I'd be like, 'Great, I made dinner,' " she says. So Sally decided to cut back on the time she spent reading, watching TV, or just lounging around, and started running at least 45 minutes on the treadmill three times a week. As she puts it, "I wanted people on my 40th birthday to say, 'Damn, she looks good.' "

OK, we'll say it: She looks good, *really* good.

Her one weakness? A monotonous workout.
To make sure she challenges her whole body and to prevent boredom from sabotaging her motivation, Sally could benefit from more variety in her exercise regimen, including weight training.

FITNESS TIPS
Lift weights. It's good for bone health, self-esteem, and mood. "The physical confidence you develop translates into confidence in other areas," says Lisa Callahan, M.D., medical director of the Women's Sports Medicine Center at the Hospital for Special Surgery in New York City.

Vary your workout. Every few weeks, pick up heavier weights or add a hill to your walk—anything to challenge your muscles in new ways, Callahan says.

Stretch during and after exercise. Flexibility plays a crucial role in helping you stay agile. Avoid stretching before your workout, though; you may tear cold muscles.

Anne Underwood is a health and medicine writer for Newsweek *and co-author of* The Color Code: A Revolutionary Eating Program for Optimum Health.

The Tests of Time
We evaluated each woman in six areas that reveal the undeniable, if gentle, signs of aging by the time you reach age 40.

Cardio: Chase Taylor, personal-training manager at Equinox Fitness Clubs in New York, administered a standard treadmill test. Each woman strapped a heart-rate monitor around her chest and started walking; every 3 minutes, the speed and slope of the treadmill increased until each participant reached her target heart rate (roughly 85 percent of maximum).
★ 1.7 mph, 10-percent incline for 3 minutes
★★ 2.5 mph, 12-percent incline for 6 minutes
★★★ 3.4 mph, 14-percent incline for 9 minutes
★★★★ 4.5 mph, 15-percent incline for 12 minutes

Strength: Because women generally have strong legs, upper-body strength is the most revealing test of muscle mass. Taylor required each participant to do as many push-ups (full-body or bent-knee) as she could possibly muster. He also recorded the maximum weight each woman could manage for 10 reps on a Cybex chest-press machine.
★ Fewer than 10 bent-knee push-ups, 20 pounds pressed
★★ 10 to 30 bent-knee push-ups, 40 pounds pressed
★★★ 10 to 20 full-body push-ups, 50 pounds pressed
★★★★ 20 to 30 full-body push-ups, 55 to 60 pounds pressed

Skin: We used Procter & Gamble's Olay-Visia Complexion Analysis machine to take digital photographs of each woman's face under both fluorescent and ultraviolet light. The device analyzed the pictures pixel by pixel, measuring such characteristics as pore size, wrinkles, and evenness of texture. For a glimpse of changes to come, the UV reading evaluated sun damage in the dermis (below the top layer) that is not yet visible to the naked eye. Finally, based on a comparison with 1,200 other women ages 15 to 75, Proctor & Gamble (P&G) assigned each of our subjects a "skin age."
★ Skin age over 45
★★ Skin age 40 to 45
★★★ Skin age 30 to 40
★★★★ Skin age below 30

Hair: P&G's hair-analysis laboratory viewed strands of each woman's hair under a scanning electron microscope to detect evidence of damage.
★ Badly split
★★ Shows some damage
★★★ Healthy
★★★★ Very healthy

Bone density: Park Avenue Radiologists in New York City used dual-energy X-ray absorptiometry (DXA) scans to measure each participant's bone density. The typical 40-year-old woman should not expect to see significant bone loss, but the test is useful as a baseline to gauge future loss and to alert at-risk women about the preventive measures they should take now.
★ DXA score of −2.5 to −1 (osteopenia, a precursor to osteoporosis)
★★ DXA score of −1 to −0.5 (low end of normal range)
★★★ DXA score of −0.5 to 0.5 (middle of normal range)
★★★★ DXA score of 0.5 to 1 (upper end of normal range)

Memory: Psychologist Sergio Marini, Ph.D., of New York University's William and Sylvia Silberstein Institute for Aging and Dementia, administered standard tests that detect memory loss. Each participant had to recite a brief story verbatim, recall pairs of unrelated words, remember a number for each of a series of abstract designs, and—after those distractions—recite the story from memory again.
★ Below average
★★ Slightly below average
★★★ Average
★★★★ Above average

vital *stats*

32
Percentage of women who say doctors trivialize menopause symptoms

65
Percentage of women who say they treat menopause symptoms without consulting their doctors

20
Percentage of doctors who think hospitals should have smoking areas

1
Rank of smoking in causes of preventable deaths among U.S. women

5 MILLION
Number of deaths worldwide from smoking-related causes in 2000

37
Percentage of traffic deaths on New Year's Eve that were alcohol-related

47
Percentage of traffic deaths on Christmas that were

29
Percentage of women in the Northeast who say they feel successful at balancing work and family

50
Percentage of women in the West who say they do

3.3
Percent increase in American paychecks in 2003 (the smallest increase since the early '80s)

0.7
Percent increase in American paychecks in 2003 after inflation

50
Percentage of people who say they'd rather face a full e-mail in-box at work than the scale when they return home from holiday vacations

27
Percentage of Americans who now say they always finish their entire meal, no matter the size, when they eat out

20
Percentage of Americans who said they did in 2000

56
Percentage of extra calories people typically eat when served larger portions

23
Percentage of Americans who believe fast food is good for them

50
Percentage of adults who think being physically fit is a sign of success

36
Percentage of adults who exercise less than once a month or never

50
Percentage of American adults with elevated blood-cholesterol levels

37
Percent increase in sales of cholesterol-lowering supplements at natural-foods stores in 2003

50
Percentage of over-the-counter cholesterol-lowering supplements that do not contain the listed ingredients and/or do not effectively deliver those ingredients

33
Percentage of flowers bought for Christmas or Hanukkah

16
Percentage bought for Valentine's Day

American Institute for Cancer Research; National Consumers League; National Heart, Lung, and Blood Institute; ConsumerLab.com; SPINS; American Floral Endowment's Consumer Tracking Study/Society of American Florists; Susan G. Komen Breast Cancer Foundation; Jenny Craig Inc.; Slim-Fast; Yankelovich; Guinness World Records; Medscape poll; American Legacy Foundation; *The Lancet;* National Highway Traffic Safety Administration; Mercer Human Resources Consulting; Royal Caribbean; Gallup Poll; Carefree—Reported by Lisa Lee Freeman

chapter 4

nutrition

**how to eat right and
lose weight**

Live Better (and Longer)

with Antiaging Foods

New research suggests that eating right really can slow the aging process.

BY JOEL N. SHURKIN

Scientists used to sneer at the notion that what you eat could influence how you age. But the discovery of little things called antioxidants decades ago changed all that. Now the investigation into diet's role in preventing age-related diseases rages on in labs around the world. Entire conferences are addressing the topic: Witness the recent meeting of the American Aging Association and the American College of Clinical Gerontology in Baltimore, where the biggest names in aging and nutrition brought the most promising longevity-enhancing foods to the table. It was quite a feast.

The highlights of the menu were the foods most potent in antioxidants, nutrients that protect you from the wear and tear of everyday life. Researchers now recognize that although eating and breathing are clearly essential processes, they are also problematic ones. They produce free radicals: dangerous substances in your body, crammed with extra oxygen that eats away at your cells. More and more experts are convinced that loading your plate with antioxidant-rich foods can counter this damage. Scientists are also closer to understanding how specific food components, such as lutein in spinach and sulfur in garlic, may prevent such age-related problems as vision loss and heart disease.

While the concept of eating to slow the aging process is still controversial, the idea is gaining momentum. "It is clear that up to 70 percent of strokes and 80 percent of heart disease can be prevented by changes in diet and lifestyle," explains Balz Frei, Ph.D., the director of Oregon State University's Linus Pauling Institute, which researches the role of diet on disease.

> It is clear that up to 70 percent of strokes and 80 percent of heart disease can be prevented by changes in diet and lifestyle.
>
> —Balz Frei, Ph.D.

146

No one's found the Vegetable of Youth yet, but the recent conference confirmed that experts are taking the search seriously. We asked the researchers to hand over a coveted shopping list—the foods that show the strongest scientific potential for helping you forestall common age-related issues and live better longer. Can a handful of blueberries today help you remember the birthdays of everyone in your address book when you're 90? Read on to find out.

PROTECT YOUR **HEART**

Health-food stores don't have a lock on good-for-you foods. Hops, plants used to flavor most beers and ales, contain bioflavonoids that are six times as potent as the ones found in citrus fruits. You'd have to chug 450 liters of beer a day—more than two hundred six-packs—to obtain the maximum benefit, but even moderate drinking seems to offer some protection. A more realistic way to guard your heart is to eat a handful of nuts a day, according to research by Joan Sabaté, M.D., professor and chairman of nutrition at Loma Linda University School of Public Health in California. He suspects that a variety of compounds in nuts work together to reduce LDL (bad) cholesterol.

FOODS FOR YOUR TICKER

- Garlic: It helps lower cholesterol. If popping cloves daily is driving your family and friends away, there's research suggesting that supplements could be a good option (look for odor-free varieties).
- Onions: The bulbs contain sulfur compounds, which preliminary studies suggest can keep blood clots from forming.
- Oats: The bioflavonoids in this grain seem to prevent plaque buildup and control inflammation.
- Cold-water fish, such as salmon, tuna, and sardines
- Grape juice and red wine
- Beers and ales: The darker they are, the more potent they are.
- Nuts
- Fruits and vegetables
- Green tea

KEEP YOUR **MENTAL** EDGE

To raise your odds of taking home the Scrabble trophy long into old age, top your cereal with blueberries. In one study presented at the aging and nutrition conference, researchers asked a group of older adults to eat about 1 cup blueberries every day. After a month, the berry-eaters performed better on tests measuring mental skills and reported feeling sharper and more energetic than a group of seniors who went berry-free.

Scientists are also becoming sold on the idea that the bioflavonoids found in most fruits and vegetables could keep free radicals from harming the brain and possibly causing such mind-numbing illnesses as Alzheimer's. Experts suspect that since bioflavonoids shield plant cells, they may also protect human cells.

FOODS FOR THOUGHT

- Blueberries, raspberries, and blackberries: Wild blueberries tend to contain more brain-saving bioflavonoids than the domestic ones do.

- Black, green, and orange pekoe teas: These all contain bioflavonoids called catechins. But green tea may be the most beneficial. It contains the most epigallocatechin-3 gallate, an antioxidant that is particularly effective at preventing degenerative brain diseases.
- Green, leafy vegetables, such as spinach and kale
- Dark-skinned fruits, such as nectarines and red apples: The skin of such fruits contains the beneficial bioflavonoids, so be sure to leave it on.

LOWER YOUR CANCER RISK

The most intriguing cancer and diet research involves green tea—not only in your mug but also applied to your skin. Preliminary lab studies suggest that an experimental lotion made with green-tea leaves blocks the formation of skin tumors. And studies investigating the benefits of drinking tea show that substances in green tea may help repair sun damage. (Decaffeinated teas don't seem to work.)

Because the processes that lead to cancer remain largely a mystery, the search for preventive foods is tricky. Scientists hope that once they figure out what makes cells turn malignant, they will be better able to isolate specific protective nutrients. Until then, loading up on antioxidant-rich foods is your best strategy.

FOODS TO FIGHT CANCER

- Garlic: In laboratory tests, allyl sulfur, a chemical found in garlic, seems to help block the spread of cancer.
- Fruits, berries, and vegetables: Cabbage and broccoli in particular
- Soybeans
- Green tea

Joel N. Shurkin is a freelance writer in Baltimore and the author of nine books, mostly on the history of medicine and science.

The Ultimate Antiaging Meal

If the leading gerontologists and nutrition scientists were to assemble a menu show-casing some of the most promising foods that slow the aging process, it might look something like this.

First course: Roasted butternut squash soup with toasted almonds and pomegranate molasses

Main course: Grilled marinated bluefin tuna steaks with asparagus, oregano, and tomato confit; roasted-garlic mashed potatoes

Salad: Spinach, mushrooms, beets, goat cheese, and pecans

Wine: Chianti, Pinot Noir (Oregon or California), or Côtes du Rhône

Dessert: Three scoops of sorbet—blueberry, peach, and blackberry—served with cranberry-and-pistachio biscotti

After-dinner drink: Green tea

One More Reason to Eat Your Greens

It's no secret that salads made with mixed leafy greens are good for you. But preliminary research on a class of flavonoids called flavones may provide yet one more compelling reason to eat your greens (and other veggies, too). A collaborative study from Tufts University's Friedman School of Nutrition Science and Policy, Harvard School of Public Health, the University of Athens in Greece, and the U.S. Department of Agriculture shows that these substances may decrease breast-cancer risk.

Researchers looked at the diets of 2,000 Greek women and noted that for every 0.5 milligram of flavones—the amount in 1½ cups raw spinach or about 2 cups shredded iceberg lettuce—consumed per day, their risk of breast cancer dropped by 13 percent. You can also up your flavone intake by munching on a celery stick or sweet red or green peppers.

Further studies are being conducted to see if the results stand up. Even if they don't, you can't go wrong: Eat a bowl of leafy greens, and you'll still get a healthy dose of calcium, cancer-fighting antioxidants, and vitamin K.

Why Your Heart Aches for You to Eat More Tomatoes

Lycopene, the antioxidant in tomatoes that seems to lower men's risk of prostate cancer, may help you avoid heart disease.

Harvard University researchers found that middle-aged women who consumed high levels of lycopene —the equivalent of a ¼ cup tomato sauce or three medium-size tomatoes per day—for an average of five years were about 30-percent less likely to develop heart disease than women who got far less of the antioxidant. Why? It's not clear, but lycopene might slow production of LDL, or bad, cholesterol. Researchers found that tomato sauce packed the most preventive punch in the study; its oils probably boost lycopene absorption.

Add Beans to Your Grocery List

Turns out beans are chock-full of more than just protein, vitamins, calcium, and fiber. U.S. Department of Agriculture researchers, trying to figure out which beans are best for you, discovered that legumes pack more antioxidants than previously thought. Black beans, for instance, have the same amount of cancer- and heart disease–fighting phytochemicals as grapes and cranberries. As a rule, darker beans contain more of the good stuff. The researchers say eating one half-cup serving two to three times per week is as beneficial as drinking a glass of red wine each day.

ENERGY FOOD

What Your Body Could Be Missing

Say good-bye to blood-sugar highs and lows. Learn the right way to welcome carbs back into your diet.

BY CHRIS WOOLSTON

Wendy Tage, a 35-year-old interior designer in Bozeman, Montana, talks fast, thinks fast, and lives fast. "I'm running from 6 in the morning until 9 at night," she says cheerfully. She's the prototypical high-energy woman, but not long ago she felt as if someone had pulled the plug. She barely had enough strength to get through the daily routine of her full-time work, the household chores, and her part-time gig as a chauffeur for her two young children. She knew she needed help when she started envying her kids' 8:30 bedtime. Tired of being tired, she scheduled an appointment with her doctor, who gave her

a complete physical, measured her iron levels, checked her thyroid, and sent her home with a clean bill of health. "She said, 'You're fine, Wendy. You're just getting older,' " Tage recalls. "I couldn't accept that."

Without a diagnosis, Tage took a suspicious look at her life: Should she cut back on work hours? Pull

Researchers understand a great deal about the complicated interplay between diet and energy, but many people are still eating like it's the Dark Ages.

her daughter out of gymnastics? Or was there a less drastic solution, one that would allow her to do what she wanted and feel good, too? Although her doctor never said a word about diet, Tage wondered if her food choices could be part of the problem. So she started keeping a food journal. "I kept track of everything: what I ate, what I drank, and how many sticks of gum I chewed," Tage says. "You'd be amazed how much you can find out about yourself."

Her records told a grim story. Here was a woman who never missed her morning coffee but sometimes went all day without a glass of water. She would sometimes go from her bed to her lunch break without a bite to eat, and when she did sit down to a midday meal, it often came with a side of fries.

Food means energy, and Americans aren't exactly starving themselves. So why are so many people running on fumes? Just about everyone knows the afternoon crash that follows "forgetting" lunch, and they surely are familiar with the post-Thanksgiving-feast couch coma. And now all of America is discovering modern ways to bottom out, with diets that don't provide what the body needs. The fact is that researchers understand a great deal about the complicated interplay between diet and energy, but many people are still eating like it's the Dark Ages. Whether they're stuck in a bad habit or caught in the thrall of a new diet, they don't treat carbohydrates, the body's preferred source of energy, with the necessary respect. They eat carbs at the wrong times, in the wrong amounts—and then they wonder why they're dragging through another day.

So if your energy is flagging, there may be a simple solution: Rethink your fuel.

AVOID THE LOW-CARB CRASH

The late Robert Atkins often claimed that his diet would increase energy by burning fat cells, but for many people it doesn't work that way. "People on low-carbohydrate diets tend to feel sluggish," says James W. Anderson, M.D., a professor of medicine and clinical nutrition at the University of Kentucky and a fellow of the American College of Nutrition. "They lose weight, but at what cost?"

In a balanced diet, carbohydrates are the body's chief source of fuel. When you eat an apple or a bagel, you effortlessly break down the carbs into glucose (sugar), the basic currency of energy. Your brain and muscles can't function without glucose. In fact, as far as your body is concerned, a steady supply of blood sugar is just as vital as a pulse. "The body works very hard to maintain blood-glucose levels, come hell or high water," Anderson says.

The average woman requires approximately 50 grams of carbohydrates a day; if she falls short, her system must go to extraordinary lengths to keep

To avoid the energy crashes caused by a sudden drop in blood sugar, eat plenty of fruits and veggies, stay hydrated, and snack on only moderate amounts of fat, protein, and sugar.

her blood-sugar levels from crashing. Yet the "induction phase" of the Atkins diet allows her no more than 20 grams of carbs. That forces her liver to start breaking down fat to save on glucose. It sounds like what every dieter wants, but it's actually not clear whether the process leads to more weight loss. And using fat for energy involves a labor-intensive alchemy. In essence, the body burns energy to make energy, leaving a dieter stuck at the starting line.

The high-fat, burger-without-the-bun approach has another energy drawback, Anderson says. Studies show that much of the fat from that burger ends up floating in the bloodstream in the minutes and hours following the meal. Inevitably, small clumps of fat will gum up the narrow capillaries that feed the muscles and the brain, not unlike sludge in a fuel line.

Avoid the temptation to revive yourself with a can of Coke or a big slice of cake. Your blood sugar could climb too high, then fall too quickly—leaving you where you started.

That's probably why many people feel tired after a fatty meal, he says. The engine still runs, but it doesn't rev like it should.

The jury's still out on the long-term health effects of low-carb diets, but the short-term consequences for mood and energy are starting to come into focus. Research in the mid-1990s showed that high-fat, low-carb meals often make people feel drowsy and feeble. And a 2003 study from Southern Illinois University at Edwardsville offered a glimpse of what can happen if you combine a low-carb diet with exercise. Seventeen men and women exercised regularly while spending three weeks on a normal diet and three weeks on the Atkins diet. After each workout, the subjects filled out questionnaires on attitude and energy levels. A pattern quickly emerged: Volunteers felt more rundown physically and mentally when their bodies were starving for carbs.

"Most people feel energized after exercise, but [subjects on the Atkins diet] weren't energized at all," says sports psychologist Brian Butki, Ph.D., the lead author of the study. (He's now at Colorado State University.) "Every single person noted a downturn."

Not all the participants were bothered by their decline in energy—some barely noticed it, while others felt wiped out. The same variability probably exists outside the research lab, but if Atkins has left your engines sputtering and stalling out, then you might want to modify your approach. The South Beach diet is one option. Although it's low in carbs, it won't overload your system with saturated fat.

If you're still feeling sluggish, it may be time for an old-fashioned low-cal, well-balanced diet. "Many people actually feel very energized on a low-calorie diet," Anderson says. When you're constantly packing away food, the body becomes a digestion machine. Consuming fewer calories frees up energy for more important things, such as chasing kids or staying awake during an afternoon meeting.

YOU DON'T HAVE TO HIT THE WALL

People suffering from a low-carb letdown may fantasize about piles of pancakes swimming in syrup, but carb-loaded treats won't catapult them through their day. Quite the contrary: Many people crash a few hours after a high-carb meal. Their energy wanes, their hands tremble, their minds wander, and they feel an inexorable pull toward the refrigerator. People who get this sinking feeling often assume that their blood sugar has dropped dangerously low. But that assumption is almost certainly wrong.

Remember: Your body wants to keep blood sugar on an even keel. When you eat a large load of carbs, your system responds by producing extra insulin, which takes glucose out of your bloodstream and transports it to your muscle cells to be used. As long as you produce the right amount of insulin at the right time, you'll feel fine.

Unfortunately, a huge dose of carbs has a tendency to expose any quirks in the way a person handles them, says Richard Hellman, M.D., a noted diabetes expert at the University of Missouri–Kansas City and secretary of the American Association of Clinical Endocrinologists. For example, many Americans (between 25 and 40 percent) have some degree of insulin resistance, meaning they have lost some sensitivity to the hormone. The body compensates by pumping out more insulin than usual, but the reinforcements tend to be late in coming. Often when a person with insulin resistance has a high-sugar repast, such as a cinnamon roll with an orange-juice chaser, the large burst of insulin arrives long after her glucose levels have already started to fall. It's like turning on an industrial vacuum when all you need is a dust rag; for an instant, your blood sugar will plummet.

That sets off alarms throughout the body. The main warning bell is adrenaline, the hormone that surges through your veins whenever you sense danger. In this case the peril isn't real; your body will prop up blood-sugar levels before they fall too far. But the combination of the slight dip in blood sugar and the jolt of adrenaline can make you feel weak and trembly.

Insulin resistance is particularly common among people who are overweight. But you don't have to be overweight—or even insulin-resistant—to hit bottom after a high-carb meal. Some very thin people, those who have recently lost large amounts of weight, and women with pear-shaped bodies are also prone to crashing, possibly because they are overly sensitive to insulin. Again, their blood sugar falls too quickly, setting off alarms. Lean, muscular people are at a disadvantage, too, Anderson says. In this case, it's because their muscles devour glucose so rapidly, leaving few reserves when a rush of insulin hits.

Whether you're overweight, muscular, or thin, you can avoid the jitters by watching your diet. The most crash-resistant one, Anderson says, is heavy on high-fiber sources of carbohydrates (fruits, vegetables,

whole grains), along with moderate amounts of fat and protein and very little added sugar.

If you still get that sinking feeling, you can quickly raise your blood sugar with a graham cracker or a piece of fruit, but you'll have to put up with a little shakiness until the adrenaline clears. Avoid the temptation to revive yourself with a can of Coke or a big slice of cake. Your blood sugar might climb too high again and then fall too quickly, leaving you right where you started.

EAT SMALL, EAT OFTEN, EAT GREEN

Wendy Tage is no expert in nutrition, but she knew enough to be alarmed by what she saw in her food journal: She knew she couldn't last half a day without eating, and she realized that a Big Mac and fries usually made her groggy. So she committed herself to a more sensible diet—and, as it turns out, a more energetic one as well.

Over the course of a typical day, Tage has a bowl of Cream of Wheat at 6 a.m., a bagel at 8 a.m., a piece of fruit in the midmorning, a sandwich for lunch, a dinner of meat and vegetables, and plenty of water. "I don't diet," she says. "I eat what I want when I want." What she wants gives her plenty of pep. In fact, she's stumbled upon the nutritionist's prescription for energy: Have several small meals and snacks throughout the day; stay hydrated; and eat a healthy mixture of carbohydrates, fats, and proteins.

This balanced approach to eating can help anyone, says Lisa Dorfman, a Florida-based registered dietitian and a spokeswoman for the American Dietetic Association. Carbohydrates provide a near-instant lift, while fat and protein are digested more slowly. So spread a little hazelnut butter or peanut butter on that bagel, and you'll be off to a great start. A glass of skim milk and an apple make an excellent midmorning snack. Lunch might be a turkey-and-veggie sandwich on whole wheat bread; pasta primavera with Parmesan could help you end the day on an up note.

Tage has another, more idiosyncratic remedy for the blahs: Whenever she feels tapped out, she takes a cue from a certain nautical hero and pops open a can of spinach. Tage isn't anemic, but she swears the iron it provides gives her an extra boost within a few days.

She just might be on to something: In a 2003 study, researchers in Switzerland gave iron supplements to 136 women who were suffering from unexplained fatigue. None of the subjects had anemia, but many of these women had iron levels in the low-normal range—and they got a significant lift from the pills.

Many women could use a little extra iron. More than 10 percent of American women are iron-deficient, according to the National Center for Health Statistics: not necessarily anemic but definitely suffering a shortfall of this vital mineral. That doesn't mean loads of women should start popping iron pills. Even though your body needs it, too much iron can cause constipation, and a serious overload can be toxic. A safe way to raise your iron levels is to follow Tage's lead by getting your iron from food—spinach, of course, but also beans, dried fruits, or, best of all, lean red meats. (The mineral is not as easily absorbed from plant sources.) A recent Australian study found that iron-rich foods can improve energy just as much as supplements, but without the risks.

Today, Tage feels more energetic than ever. She manages to get through her days without hitting the wall, and she tucks her kids in at night without feeling the urge to join them. If her energy ever does waver and wane again, however, she'll be sure to start another food journal. She doesn't want to give her doctor another chance to remind her she's growing older. ▪

Chris Woolston is the co-author of a forthcoming book on childhood obesity.

Herbal Zingers

The leaves and seeds of some plants can give you a lift—think of tea and coffee. But do herbal energy drinks, tablets, and potions really help? According to Mark Blumenthal, executive director of the American Botanical Council, a few are worth a try.

Asian ginseng: A staple in China and Korea, Asian ginseng has an enthusiastic following in the United States, too. But several studies have tested its effect on athletic performance, and not one found an improvement.

Blumenthal notes that the study doses fell short of those used in herbal medicine. "A lot of people feel better after taking it," he says. "I've used it off and on for many years." He says people who don't feel a lift can try doubling the dose recommended on the label. "Unless you have high blood pressure, a double dose shouldn't be a problem," he says. "Hypertensive people shouldn't take large amounts." Keep in mind: You want Asian ginseng (*Panax ginseng*), not American ginseng (*Panax quinquefolius*).

Maté and guarana: Herbs often added to energy drinks, maté and guarana can give you a lift. But take note: While they supposedly stimulate the body without causing jitters, the herbs' active ingredient is chemically identical to caffeine.

Schizandra: This Chinese herb is less well-known than ginseng, but Blumenthal believes it has just as much potential to boost energy. Schizandra is very safe, and it has no known adverse side effects, he says.

Why More Foods Are Going "Gluten Free"

Found in wheat, rye, barley, and some oat products, gluten is a protein that causes problems for more than one million people in the United States who suffer from gluten intolerance or celiac disease. For them, traditional cereals, breads, and pastas are off-limits. And gluten is often hidden in foods where you wouldn't expect it, such as many canned soups or sauces, where it's sometimes used as a thickener. Gluten can do serious damage to the small intestines of people with celiac disease, causing abdominal pain, bloating, gas, diarrhea, or fatigue. Anecdotally, some people without celiac disease also report fewer bowel problems and say they feel more energetic when they go gluten free (GF), says Joseph Murray, M.D., director of the Celiac Disease Clinic at the Mayo Clinic in Rochester, Minnesota. But there's not much scientific evidence to connect gluten with general fatigue or other symptoms in the absence of celiac disease, he says.

Luckily for folks who are forced to go the gluten-free route or who choose it voluntarily, GF products are becoming more available in the natural- and specialty-foods sections of mainstream grocery stores. The number of new GF products released in 2003 jumped 88 percent from the number released in 2002, according to the market-research firm Products can Online in Naples, New York. "Not only has the prevalence of these products increased, but the flavor and nutrition of the products have improved, too," says Lola O'Rourke, R.D., a spokeswoman for the American Dietetic Association who specializes in gluten intolerance.

Many GF products use rice, corn, potato, or arrowroot flours, which are all safe for people who can't tolerate gluten. But more-nutritious alternative flours—made from amaranth, soy, or garbanzo beans, for example—are rising in popularity.

Nu-World Foods uses amaranth, a good source of fiber, protein, and iron, to make cereal and breadcrumbs (good for meat loaf or casserole toppings). And Bob's Red Mill Natural Foods sells a GF bread mix that uses garbanzo flour. The company also includes tapioca, corn, and sorghum flours in such products as a GF brownie mix that contains Ghirardelli cocoa and a GF pancake mix that creates a fluffy breakfast favorite. With so many delicious options available, there's no reason for gluten intolerance to get in the way of enjoying a good meal.

Q + A

The Grapefruit Diet: Healthy, but Not Magical

How come I keep hearing about the grapefruit diet? Does it really work?

Don't count on it. There has been some buzz about grapefruits and weight loss recently, mainly because of a 100-person study that found dieters who exercised and ate a grapefruit half with each meal lost an average of 3.6 pounds over 12 weeks. That's right, about a pound per month (please cover your mouth when you yawn). If that doesn't make you dismiss the diet outright, consider this: The research hasn't been published in a peer-reviewed scientific journal, and the results need to be replicated before they're considered more than a fluke by any reputable weight-loss authority. Don't get us wrong: We're not knocking grapefruits, which are low in calories and high in vitamin C. But they don't contain any magical substance proven to make the fat drip off your thighs. Stick to portion control and regular exercise for that.

The Choose the Best, Lose the Rest Diet

We hit the diet books to come up with the ultimate you-can-do-it plan. Here are five strategies that will help you take the weight off—and keep it off—for good.

BY PETER JARET

Despite the best-selling titles, product labels, and magazine covers that say otherwise, there's no real secret to losing weight. "We know exactly what it takes," says University of Pennsylvania researcher Gary Foster, Ph.D., one of the country's leading experts on the subject: In a nutshell, eat fewer calories than you burn. The maddeningly tricky part is finding a diet you can live with that will keep the pounds off once you've lost them.

For just a brief moment the Atkins-style high-protein, low-carbohydrate approach looked as if it could be the one. Major studies published in 2003 showed that the popular weight-loss regimen is safer than anyone expected—and that it works.

A refresher: In the longest running experiment, Foster and his colleagues compared two teams of overweight men and women. One group received copies of *Dr. Atkins' New Diet Revolution* and was asked to stick to its directions as closely as possible; the other participants were instructed to follow a conventional low-fat regimen. At the end of six months, the Atkins dieters had lost almost twice as many pounds as the people in the low-fat group, 15 versus 7. And most surprisingly, even after eating unlimited servings of such high-fat foods as bacon and burgers, their cholesterol levels looked fine.

Then the scales tipped.

The multitude of diet plans have left many women wondering exactly what they should eat.

Dieters on both plans regained their weight, the Atkins group gaining back the most. By the end of the year, average weight loss was similar in the two groups. And it wasn't that much: about 9 pounds among those on Atkins and 5 pounds among the low-fat dieters.

What happened? Blame it on boredom. As anyone who's been on a slash-and-burn diet, such as Atkins or a low-fat diet, knows all too well, you get tired of eating basically the same foods every day.

"Tell me about it," says Janet Gurry, 36, a sales-account manager in New York City. In January 2003, 30 pounds heavier than she wanted to be, Gurry went on Atkins. Within a month she'd lost about 12 pounds, but by Valentine's Day she was getting tired of meat. "I had my period around then, and I had this craving for pancakes. I was so sick of bacon and eggs that I thought, 'Why not?' " she says. "By the following Monday, I think I'd put on 7 pounds. Within a month I'd gained 15 pounds. It was very demoralizing."

Call it the dieters' dilemma. The reason many diet plans work is the same reason most fail—they make certain foods off-limits. "Americans are overweight in part because we live in a world with incredible abundance and an incredible variety of foods to choose from," says Hollie Raynor, Ph.D., a researcher at Brown University. And the more foods people have in front of them, the more they tend to eat. When researchers at Tufts University analyzed the diets of 71 men and women, they found that the greater the variety of sweets, snacks, condiments, entrées, and carbohydrates people ate, the fatter they were.

Atkins, the blockbuster South Beach diet, and other popular weight-loss plans systematically banish many of those temptations. They give dieters a rationale for saying no by blacklisting (or at least severely limiting) entire categories of foods, such as carbohydrates, fats, or anything processed. But when a diet is too restrictive, most people on it ultimately rebel. "That's the dilemma," Raynor says. "Too much variety motivates appetite and encourages people to overeat; too little makes it hard for people to stick with an eating plan for long."

Is there a happy medium between too little and too much variety? There is, and the message is simple: Choose the best, lose the rest. Instead of nixing entire food groups, it's smarter to help yourself to the very best in each category and reserve foods that contain calories (and not much else) for special occasions. You will have more choices—and less chance of boring your palate—than on either high-protein or low-fat plans but still enough structure to keep you from eating everything in sight.

> The harsh reality is, portion size *does* matter. But if you're choosy about what you eat, you don't have to measure every ounce.

"Ultimately, dieting is about being in control," says Megan McCrory, Ph.D., the Tufts University scientist who headed the study on variety and weight loss. "People want to blame their genes for making them overweight. They think they'll find the secret to weight loss in some fad-diet book. But in the end, it really comes down to making smart choices each time you sit down to a meal or grab a snack. It's up to you."

Most importantly, this commonsense approach to dieting works. For 10 years, the National Weight Control Registry (NWCR) has been gathering data from successful losers, people who've lost more than 30 pounds and kept the weight off for at least one year. "With few exceptions, people who manage to lose significant amounts of weight and keep it off don't follow extreme diets," says NWCR founder Rena Wing, Ph.D., a weight-loss expert and professor of psychiatry at Brown University. "They reduce fat, decrease calories, and increase their physical activity."

To help you create your own personal plan, one you can mold to your tastes and lifestyle, we've reviewed the latest studies of the concepts behind the most popular regimens; we've also ditched the potential pitfalls. The result: A diet you can live with for the rest of your life—at home, at work, and at restaurants. All you have to do is follow these five simple rules.

1 EAT A SERVING OF **PROTEIN** AT EVERY MEAL.

In every recent study pitting Atkins against low-fat diets, people on Atkins lost weight faster. Why? There are probably several explanations, but the most important reason, experts say, is that protein seems to be more filling than simple carbohydrates or fat. "Protein in the form of lean meat or fish is a real calorie bargain," says Linda Stern, M.D., an assistant professor of medicine at the University of Pennsylvania and co-author of another recent study that compared the Atkins diet with low-fat regimens. "It fills you up and provides a lot of nutrition on relatively few calories." In Stern's study, people in the high-protein/low-carb group ate about 460 fewer calories a day than they burned. Those following the low-fat plan had a calorie deficit of only about 270 calories a day, even though both groups could eat as much as they wanted.

There may also be a slight metabolic advantage to protein-rich meals. Carol Johnston, Ph.D., a scientist at Arizona State University, has found that body temperature climbs a little higher after a high-protein meal than it does following a high-carb

> Eating protein seems to give your metabolism a slight boost, while also filling you up; the overall effect is that fewer calories are consumed.

one, increasing the number of calories burned. Researchers at the Royal Veterinary and Agricultural University in Copenhagen reported that switching 18 percent of total calories from carbs

to protein causes the body to burn about 3-percent more calories over the following 24-hour period. For someone eating 1,400 calories a day, that would mean an extra 42 calories burned—not a lot, but enough to lose a few extra pounds every six months.

"The original Weight Watchers diet, which was very liberal with protein, recommended 2 ounces at breakfast, 4 at lunch, and 6 at dinner," Stern says. "Given the latest findings, that looks like pretty good advice."

CHOOSE Eggs (hard-boiled are portable) • Low-fat yogurt and cheese • Peanut butter, other nut butters, and nuts • Lean meat and poultry • Legumes • Soy products, such as tofu, tempeh, and edamame (raw or steamed soybeans) • Sunflower seeds

LOSE Hamburger and marbled meats, which are laden with saturated fat • High-fat dairy products • Processed meats, such as bologna, pepperoni, and bacon

2 EAT TWO SERVINGS OF **FRUITS** AND **VEGGIES** AT EVERY MEAL.

Protein may be key for weight loss, but carbohydrates, especially the ones in high-fiber fruits and vegetables, keep the weight off. In fact, recent findings show that the more carbs people eat, the less they're likely to weigh. In 2002, experts at the U.S. Department of Agriculture (USDA) reviewed data from nationwide surveys of what people eat and what they weigh. On average, adults who ate the most carbohydrates were slimmer than those who ate the least. Why? The analysis showed that high-carb diets tended to be lower in calories and energy density (the number of calories per ounce of food).

The USDA study didn't distinguish between types of carbohydrates, but you should. Most likely, the carb addicts in the study weren't feasting on sugary colas or candy or simple starches, such as white bread—they were eating high-fiber vegetables, whole grains, and fruits. These carbs take time to digest, preventing spikes in blood-sugar levels and making you feel full longer. That's not just a theory. Analyzing data from a variety of studies, Tufts University scientists found that when people add more fiber to their diets, they eat less—about 10-percent fewer calories for every 14 grams of fiber consumed.

High-fiber carbohydrates offer dieters another crucial edge: They're a low-calorie way to judiciously add variety to your menu. McCrory, whose 1999 study showed that too much variety encourages weight gain, uncovered an exception to the rule. The wider the range of vegetables, grains, and fruits on the menu, the more likely people are to maintain a healthy weight.

In addition, cutting back on simple carbs made with highly refined flours could be even more effective than following a low-fat diet, according to a 2003 study at Children's Hospital Boston. The researchers found that overweight and obese people who eliminated refined sugars and simple carbohydrates lost more weight and shed more body fat than volunteers on a low-fat plan.

CHOOSE Whole-grain cereals and breads • Whole wheat pasta • Brown rice • Leafy green vegetables • Cruciferous vegetables, such as broccoli, cauliflower, and Brussels sprouts • Legumes • Fruits, such as apples, pears, and berries • Sweet potatoes

LOSE French fries • Cookies, doughnuts, and pastries • Candy • Potato chips • Sugary soft drinks • White bread, pretzels, and crackers

POUR ON THE HEALTHY FAT.

Let's face it: Naked steamed vegetables get pretty old after a while. Fat makes foods satisfying, and it just plain tastes good. Some forms of it—fish oil and unsaturated oils, such as olive and canola—may even protect against heart disease and cancer. Amazingly, after years of recommending low-fat diets, leading nutrition scientists now say there's no evidence that people lose weight—or body fat—by eating less fat.

Walt Willett, Ph.D., an expert at Harvard School of Public Health, reviewed dozens of dietary studies, with fat ranging from a meager 17 percent of calories to a

> Don't be a fatphobe. Evidence shows you can lose weight on both low- and high-fat diets; it's the calorie count that matters.

whopping 40 percent. Dieters on the plans lost about the same amount of weight and flab. Even where there was a difference, it wasn't much. In one study, subjects replaced 45 full-fat foods with low-fat versions. The volunteers reduced their fat intake by 7 percent, but after six months they'd lost just over a pound.

The campaign to get Americans to cut back on fatty foods—the biggest nutrition experiment ever conducted—further proved the point. Fat consumption went down, and folks got fatter. Why? Many people decided that a low-fat label was a license to scarf down a whole bag of chips or cookies in one sitting, and they ended up consuming even more calories.

The message? Don't be a fatphobe. Evidence shows you can lose weight on both low- and high-fat diets; it's the calorie count that matters. Eat foods you love, whether they're high in fat or not. Just remember that gram for gram, fat contains twice the calories of carbohydrates; treat yourself to the best and savor small portions. Once you've reached your goal (think positively!), you'll need to modify this strategy a bit. Watching fat intake is important in preventing the pounds from creeping back. The most convincing evidence comes from the NWCR: On average, people who have lost a significant amount of weight and kept it off for a year or more eat only about 24 percent of calories from fat, about 10 percent less than the average American eats.

Regardless of the mode you're in, losing or maintaining, look for ways to trim bad fats (saturated and hydrogenated, or trans, fats) from your menu. Both are notorious for clogging your arteries, so you're better off without them.

High-fiber fruits and vegetables can help you keep weight off.

CHOOSE Nuts • Popcorn made with canola or olive oil • Lean cuts of beef and pork (look for the words *loin* and *round)* • Broiled or grilled dishes • Bread with olive oil

LOSE Processed foods (chips or crackers, for example—unless they're made without trans fats) • Fried foods • Bread soaked with butter (a little bit goes a long way) • Cream soups and sauces

Add a Dash of Common Sense

There are many reasons diets backfire, but one often-overlooked pitfall is unrealistic expectations, says University of Pennsylvania weight-loss expert Gary Foster, Ph.D. When he and his colleagues asked a group of overweight and obese women how much weight they needed to lose over the next six months to consider their diet a success, the volunteers said they'd be "happy" losing 63 pounds and would consider dropping 55 pounds "acceptable." They lost an average of 35 pounds, a "stunning success," according to the researchers, but far below what the women expected. "Dieters begin with unrealistic expectations. When they don't achieve them, they get discouraged and stop dieting," Foster says.

Here's where some common sense comes in. No one gains or loses 10 pounds in a week.

If you're seeing progress on the scale—even slow progress—you're on the right track. Losing an average of 1 to 2 pounds a week is a realistic goal, but keep in mind that you may not be able to sustain that rate. Blame it on what researchers call the plateau effect, a variety of factors that may slow your progress.

Remember, too, that a splurge now and then doesn't spell the end of any diet. It could even be crucial to long-term success, says Megan McCrory, Ph.D., a nutrition scientist at Tufts University. "If you're starting to feel bored, it's OK to treat yourself to something special, but think of it as a treat," she says. The next day, go back to a sensible eating plan, throw in an extra 15 minutes of exercise, and you'll be on your way again.

LEAVE HALF YOUR DINNER ON YOUR PLATE.

The latest diet studies provide new evidence of an old truth: To lose weight, you've got to eat less. But in today's supersize world, it's hard for dieters to have a realistic sense of what a healthy portion should be—and even harder to stop there. Studies have shown that people tend to do as their mothers told them and clean their plates, no matter how big. In one study presented in 2003, Pennsylvania State University researchers varied the portion size of baked ziti over several months in a public cafeteria. Even when the serving had grown by 50 percent, people who bought the ziti still polished off the dish, eating an average of 172 extra calories. Yet when they were later asked about the different amounts, the group rated both the small and large portions as appropriate servings. The challenge is figuring out how much is reasonable to consume during one sitting and learning to leave food on your plate.

CHOOSE A piece of your favorite chocolate instead of a subpar variety—make your calories worth it. • Smaller servings. Still hungry? You can always have more or something else. • The 5-minute pause. Give your flatware a rest every 5 minutes. It can take up to 20 minutes for you to feel full, so this offers your body a chance to say, "Hey, enough already!"

LOSE All-you-can-eat buffets • Restaurant-hopping or the take-out habit. Most restaurant portions are double the reasonable serving size, so share or order two appetizers instead of an entrée. • Snack foods in bulk (put them in zip-top bags, and eat only one portion) • Oversize plates and bowls—the bigger the surface, the larger the serving

KEEP A TELL-ALL FOOD DIARY.

There's more to weight loss than what's on the menu. Dieting is as much a mental hurdle as a physical one, and people use all kinds of motivation strategies. One proven way to stay on track is to keep a food diary and record everything you eat. It may sound like a hassle, but it works.

Keeping a food diary not only keeps you accountable, but also helps reveal the sources of trouble that have snuck into your diet.

In one study, researchers found that keeping a food diary was an even better predictor of weight loss than exercising regularly. For many people, food journals function like gut checks. If you know that you're going to have to account for that bag of potato chips later on, then you might think twice about how hungry you really are.

Food diaries can also help reveal the sources of trouble: simple carbs that have sneaked back into your cabinets, for instance, or a few too many high-fat foods. If the scale saboteur isn't obvious, look over your diary, and identify a couple of high-calorie, low-nutrient foods that you can easily live without during the following week. ■

CHOOSE A stylish journal (or a PDA, if you're the techie type) • A supportive friend • A supercool scale • A night out or a ski weekend to celebrate victories

LOSE Obsessive scale-hopping. Weigh yourself only once a week, at the same time, wearing the same clothing. • Unrealistic expectations • Situations or people that tend to trigger binges • All-or-nothing thinking. If you slip up, don't beat yourself up. You can't be perfect all the time. Just get back on track.

When Weight-Loss Surgery Doesn't Work

More and more Americans are turning to bariatrics to slim down—but not all are getting the results they expected.

BY JOHN T. WARD • PHOTOGRAPHY BY LISA SPINDLER

For more than an hour, Peg Vaccaro bided her time, lost in the crowded ballroom of a downtown New Brunswick, New Jersey, hotel, an obese 54-year-old retiree packed in among hundreds of women built a lot like her. Vaccaro focused anxiously on the front of the room, where speakers were delivering ecstatic reports from the front lines of the war on fat, raving about a medical procedure that had transformed their lives.

It would be fair to assume that Vaccaro had been drawn to this meeting for new and prospective patients by the same mix of curiosity and desperation that attracted so many of those around her. She looked like just one more morbidly obese American deciding whether to become part of the juggernaut that put more than one hundred thousand people on operating tables in 2003, quadruple the number of just five years earlier. And given the electric mood at the Hyatt Regency that night, it wouldn't have been surprising if she had gotten swept up in the fervor s the parade of postoperative speakers—like the onlookers, nearly all female—talked about their energetic new lives, showed off their now-unflabby upper arms, and applauded the handsome young surgeon who'd made it all possible.

But the moment Vaccaro rose from her chair and opened her mouth during the Q&A, it was clear that she was no surgical naïf and that she hadn't come to praise a modern-day Dr. Kildare. "I had a less-than-ideal result," she said, capturing the whole room's attention without a microphone.

As many as 25 percent of gastric-bypass patients regain most of their lost weight after five years.

Yes, Vaccaro continued, everything had gone as expected in the first 12 weeks after her operation. If she overloaded her new stomach, which had been surgically reduced to the size of an egg, she suffered "pain beyond excruciating"; if she ate the kinds of food known to trigger abdominal distress, such as sweets, she felt shaky and sick. But that was OK, because that's how it was supposed to work. Fifty-three pounds melted off her frame in three months, bringing her down to 250 pounds, a number she hadn't seen on the scale in 15 years. Expecting to mirror the experience of typical patients, Vaccaro looked forward to losing dozens more pounds over the next 15 to 21 months before her weight would plateau.

Instead, on the first day of the fourth month, Vaccaro said, she woke up with "a raging appetite and the capacity to indulge it." Trying to stay within the 1,000-calorie-per-day limit her surgeon recommended, she ate 2 ounces chicken with some lettuce for dinner, but she was still starving, she said. When more chicken failed to sate her, she broke the rules and gobbled down some cookies. To her amazement, her body did not rebel. Without pain, she began to gain. She went on a tear. Within just a few days, she put on 7 pounds. Her surgeon examined her, assured her that her re-engineered digestive system was working as intended, and urged her to stick to the diet, she said. But back at her town house near the Jersey shore, Vaccaro, a divorcée who lives alone, found herself losing the battle with the kitchen cabinet.

Now, just nine months after her surgery, she was back to fighting flab the low-tech way, through diet and exercise, Vaccaro told the ballroom crowd. But she wasn't here to castigate anyone. Instead, her tale was intended as a warning about the dark side of bariatric, or weight-loss, surgery. "Look, this is their bread and butter," she said of the medical professionals on the dais with the postoperative patients. "You think they're going to tell you not to have it?"

So much for the notion—fueled by media coverage about slenderized weatherman Al Roker and Playboy-posing singer Carnie Wilson—that bariatric surgery is a surefire way for the fattest of the fat to quickly shed pounds. Here's a dirty little secret: For some people, the surgery simply doesn't work. Even in the most effective and widely used procedure, known as the gastric bypass, as many as one-quarter of patients regain most of their lost weight after about five years, says Robert E. Brolin, M.D., one of the field's leading surgeons and a past president of the American Society for Bariatric Surgery (ASBS). Similar procedures have failure rates (generally defined as a loss of less than half a patient's excess pounds) as high as 80 percent, he says.

A growing number of mental-health professionals blame these failures

on inadequate pre- and post-op attention to the psychological underpinnings of obesity. The problem could get worse: ASBS members, along with other health-care professionals, are considering new guidelines, the first since 1991, that could change the criteria for surgery and thus potentially expand the eligible U.S. patient population, which already numbers about 15 million by conservative estimates. Ironically, the push for looser requirements is coming to a head just as insurers in Florida and Nebraska are dropping coverage for weight-loss operations, citing safety concerns and pressure from cost-conscious employers.

Vaccaro experienced the downside of the phenomenon in more dramatic fashion than most other regainers. Many backsliders achieve the rapid weight loss that is typical of first-year post-ops and then find that the lifestyle changes necessary to keep the weight off are harder to make than anticipated. In a 2002 study of 99 patients who'd undergone gastric-bypass operations two to seven years earlier, nearly half reported that they regularly lost control of their eating. Significant weight regain was common.

The reasons some surgeries fail aren't fully understood, but part of the problem seems to be mechanical. The stomach, which is stapled down from the size of a football to little more than the size of a golf ball, stretches over time. Patients may learn to graze, training themselves to avoid the gastrointestinal pain and vomiting that come from eating forbidden foods.

Other regainers stumble on unresolved emotional issues surrounding food. Margo Maine, Ph.D., a Connecticut psychologist and eating-disorders expert, says surgical weight-reduction programs don't do enough to screen for psychological problems that might pinpoint potential backsliders. Instead, she says, the desperately overweight are allowed, even enticed, to submit to a procedure that is effective only when they are able to do post-op what they have never been able to do pre-op: stick to long-term diet and exercise regimens. "Patients think it's going to be a relatively easy change in their lives," says Maine, the author of *Body Wars: Making Peace with Women's Bodies*. "In fact, for many people food has always been their emotional touchstone, their way of coping, of comforting themselves. It's been many, many things to them that they haven't yet come to understand. There are lots of people who cannot successfully make that change."

> **Success means patients have to do post-op what they could never do pre-op: stick to diet and exercise plans.**

Bariatric surgeons do routinely caution patients that although the procedure jump-starts weight loss, major lifestyle changes must follow to keep the pounds off. Even so, many doctors admit to having a better handle on performing the operations than weeding out the people who should not have them. In part, the disconnect between surgical skill and the nuances of patient selection reflects the relative infancy of bariatrics, which in the 1990s came roaring out of the backwaters of medicine with new techniques and devices. Now, though, with the field booming amid an obesity epidemic, the demand for better screening tools is pressing.

Yet while a good deal of the research in recent years has focused on the psychological factors that influence weight gain, little attention has been paid

to identifying specific people who are likely to experience diet blunders after surgery. In its current guidelines, the ASBS tells members that before being approved for surgery, candidates should be free of significant psychological issues and drug and alcohol addiction, informed about what they're getting into, and motivated to lose weight. But at its Web site, the society contends that pre-op screening for potential failures "is of limited value." Scott Shikora, M.D., head of the bariatric program at Tufts–New England Medical Center in Boston, says he's had patients out-eat the surgery; some of those people, he acknowledges, may not have been good candidates for the procedure in the first place.

So what justifies the popularity of surgical weight loss? In the realm of bariatrics (a term derived from the Greek word for "heavy"), many surgeons argue that real success is not so much about reaching a desired clothing size as it is about losing enough weight to alleviate or even eliminate life-threatening health problems, such as high blood pressure, asthma, sleep apnea, and Type 2 diabetes. "We're treating disease; we're not treating a lifestyle," says Philip Schauer, M.D., director of bariatric surgery at the University of Pittsburgh.

Compared with dieting and exercise programs for the morbidly obese, which have long-term success rates in the low single digits, surgery is a smashing success, its proponents say. "I look at the 25-percent failure rate from the glass-half-full perspective," bariatric surgeon Brolin says. "They're 100-percent failures pre-op."

But the real wonder of bariatric surgery may be that something so seemingly makeshift works at all. The most dramatic and long-lasting results are associated with a type of gastric bypass called a Roux-en-Y (pronounced "roo-en-wye" and named after a 19th-century Swiss physician), in which the surgeon staples off part of the stomach, leaving a small pouch that restricts the volume of food that can be eaten at once; overfill it, and you may vomit. A section of the small intestine is connected to the pouch, allowing food to sidestep a large portion of the stomach. This hastens the movement of food to the lower bowel, causing a reduction in the

absorption of some nutrients and calories—and occasionally causing painful bouts known as "dumping," in which sugars, fats, and some dairy products pass through too quickly. Then there is the little-understood role of an appetite-regulating hormone by the name of ghrelin, which may be reduced by this surgery. Through some combination of these effects, Roux-en-Y patients typically drop about 60 percent of their excess weight within the first two years.

Even done laparoscopically (a minimally invasive approach), this is major surgery, and it isn't for the merely overweight. According to National Institutes of Health guidelines adopted by most insurers that cover bariatric procedures, patients must be morbidly obese, or roughly

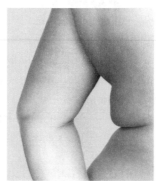

Surgery Saved My Life I didn't expect to be slim. I just wanted to be able to walk.

Before my laparoscopic Roux-en-Y surgery, I weighed 341 pounds and couldn't walk 100 steps without stopping to rest. I'm a 54-year-old mail carrier in Roscommon, Michigan. I'm on my feet much of the day, so you can imagine that my weight was a problem. After surgery I dropped 100 pounds, but I gained back 20 and settled at 260. I'm perfectly satisfied at this weight. I can walk, work, and do things around the house without discomfort. I even bought a kayak—a vessel not exactly designed with the obese in mind—and I love it.

Food? I love eating more than all other leisure activities. I love to prepare food, I love to think about preparing it, and most of all, I love to eat it. I can make saddle soap taste good. It's the worst addiction on the planet, simply because it's the one thing you can't quit. But I learned

not to keep things around the house that I would be tempted to overeat, such as ice cream. The one real weakness I allow myself is orange juice; I drink a lot of it, which could be what keeps my weight up. I'm just thankful that I can still eat foods I enjoy, even if it means having smaller portions.

The hype is that the surgery will make you slim and beautiful. The reality is that you will be slimmer, but probably not as slim as you would like. I think that's what makes some people fail: They start out with the wrong motivation and expectations. Frankly, I really didn't care how I looked. I just wanted to be able to walk and breathe and move around. If not for the surgery, I'm convinced I'd be dead or disabled by now.

—Jennifer Mann as told to John T. Ward

100 pounds over their ideal weight. Technically, this means having a body mass index (BMI)—a ratio of weight to height—of 40 or higher, or a BMI of at least 35 if weight-related health problems are present. (So a woman who is 5 feet 6 inches, weighs 248 pounds, and is otherwise healthy would be eligible.)

> **I look at the 25-percent failure rate from the glass-half-full perspective. They're 100-percent failures pre-op.**
> —Robert E. Brolin, M.D.

Because ever-increasing numbers of Americans fit the profile, the bariatric industry is hot. The ASBS expects the number of operations to swell to at least 140,000 in 2004—up from 16,200 a decade ago. And surgeons have waiting lists that now include teenagers.

There's ample evidence of small-time cheating to get borderline candidates into the operating room, too. Staci Woodruff, a Dallas insurance-company employee, was 100 pounds overweight according to standard charts, but she registered just shy of the minimum BMI (40) her insurer demanded. Her choice, as she saw it was to: "either gain 10 pounds to acquire a BMI of 40, have the surgery, and end life in a fat prison, or try again to lose 100 pounds on my own." She gained the weight and overshot her target, going into surgery with a BMI of 42. (She has since lost 100 pounds, from a starting weight of 270 pounds.) Perhaps more common are physicians who nod and wink at patients who get around the guidelines using such ruses as stuffing their pockets with rolls of quarters before they step on the scale.

Against the backdrop of this runaway phenomenon, it appears that surgeons are ignoring important warning signs of potential relapse, says Allen Lindsay, Ph.D., a clinical psychologist who has performed more than five hundred pre- and post-op evaluations of obese patients for surgeons in his St. Petersburg, Florida, practice. In a study he conducted involving 140 postoperative bypass patients, Lindsay found high levels of sexual-abuse history, depression, and psychological problems linked to food consumption, all red flags for people who are undergoing bariatric surgery. But according to Lindsay, doctors often dismiss those conditions as irrelevant to surgical outcomes. "The surgeon says, 'I can correct this problem; I can redo your interior architecture,' but he or she is not trained to look out for the factors—emotional, historical, psychological, behavioral—that may have influenced this problem and will still exist, post-surgery, in their entirety," Lindsay says.

Cathy S. Reto, Ph.D., a registered nurse and clinical psychologist who works with bariatric patients in San Diego, says the psychological aspect is also given short shrift post-op. With the intense new expectations thrust on them, many patients need one-on-one counseling, she says. But too often, she notes, follow-up care is left to enthusiastic amateurs—patients themselves—who form support groups, usually with informal ties to their surgeons or the hospitals where their procedures were performed. Dangerous mixed messages can follow, as illustrated by the experience of Holly Zoba, who lives in the Finger Lakes region of New York state. Zoba says her doctor was adamant before her surgery about which foods she had to avoid afterward: "no soda ever, diet or otherwise; no sugar, no bread, nothing high in fat," she says. "He really drilled those things into my head. I walked into this support group, and everyone there had a soda sitting in front of her. And the talk was all about what they could

> **A history of sexual abuse, depression, and psychological problems are linked to food consumption. If these issues are ignored, there is a higher chance for postsurgery relapse.**

get away with: 'I can eat a whole candy bar if I eat it in small pieces throughout the day.' 'I can eat a sandwich now.' I ran from the meeting. I thought, 'This is the last thing I need: ways to cheat this surgery.' "

In light of this kind of criticism,

weight-loss-surgery programs are increasingly employing teams of psychologists, social workers, nutritionists, and physical therapists to prepare patients for the world after bypass surgery, as well as to filter out those candidates who are not ready to undergo the procedure. "This is truly an example of a multidisciplinary approach to obesity and not treating it like an appendectomy," explains Paul J. Friday, Ph.D., chief of clinical psychology at the University of Pittsburgh Medical Center (UPMC) Shadyside.

Pittsburgh's program, for example, starts with a 35-page medical and diet history that patients must complete before meeting with a mental-health professional for an interview and psychological testing. A workshop with a nutritionist and a 4-hour seminar on risks and expectations—dubbed "Bariatrics 101"—are mandatory. Following surgery, patients are strongly encouraged to keep their follow-up appointments and can avail themselves of home-nursing visits, post-op counseling, and physical therapy.

The upshot, according to Juanita Warman, M.S.N., a nurse practitioner in the Surgical Weight Loss Center at UPMC's Magee-Womens Hospital, is that few patients who complete these types of programs encounter problems following their operations. True bariatric failures, though, tend to "vanish into the woods," Friday says, noting that morbidly obese people are often prone to developing agoraphobia and other aversions to social interaction, especially if their BMIs exceed 50.

Peg Vaccaro was not one of those who vanished into the woods. By her reckoning, she would have benefited from better preoperative screening and postoperative guidance. An alcoholic in recovery for nearly 21 years and an ex-smoker for 15, Vaccaro says she disclosed both addictions to her surgeon, who was satisfied that she'd conquered them. But Vaccaro now believes that she replaced her old dependencies with a food addiction that might have been detected by better medical scrutiny. As for post-op care, she says that aside from receiving advice on what and how much to eat, she gets little in the way of constructive help from medical professionals. "They throw it back on the patient and say, 'You're not following directions,' " she says. "But what they don't realize is that we can't, just as we couldn't *before* the surgery."

> **Even though the surgery wasn't a total success, it has had some significant benefits. "I'm breathing better, walking more, and generally feel better than I did at 303 pounds."**
>
> —Peg Vaccaro

Despite her far-from-svelte outcome (Vaccaro estimates that she weighs about 250 pounds, but she's reluctant to get on a scale), she does not completely regret her decision to have the surgery. In fact, she is even considering having a second operation, one known as a distal bypass, which shortens the functional intestine even further, leading to a reduction in the absorption of food and increasing the patient's reliance on protein drinks and vitamin supplements.

Vaccaro's new surgeon has cautioned her that she will probably lose no more than 50 pounds, if that many. But Vaccaro says she may be up for the gamble because, in spite of all her gripes about the first operation, it did have some significant benefits. "I'm breathing better, I'm walking more, and I feel generally better than I did at 303 pounds," she says, citing her presurgery peak weight. She may not be a big loser—and that's OK with her. ■

John T. Ward is a New Jersey–based freelance writer who has previously written about weight-loss surgery.

Getting to the Root of Overeating

Maybe the problem isn't what you eat, but why you're eating it. The Solution, a popular weight-loss program, helps people focus on the emotional roots of overeating.

BY FRAN SMITH

The weight-loss program that changed Dawn Galbo's life involved no dieting, no drugs, no grueling exercise. She dropped 80 pounds by learning two basic coping skills that she, like many people, never quite mastered as a kid: She learned how to take care of herself emotionally, to lift herself from the depths of sadness and anger rather than seek refuge in a pint of Häagen-Dazs, and she learned how to set limits.

This may sound too easy to be effective, and maybe too New Agey. Indeed, the program, called The Solution, encourages participants to share their feelings *a lot*, often through lingo and rituals that baffle outsiders. But it has legions of enthusiastic supporters, and there's evidence that its simple approach can work. It also rests on a commonsense premise: Overeating is a response to emotional distress. Developed at the University of California, San Francisco (UCSF), The Solution helps people learn to manage that anguish differently, head-on, by asking themselves a few questions throughout the day, especially when the urge for a bag of cookies strikes: "How do I feel?" "What do I need from others and myself?" "Are my expectations reasonable?" "What is the essential pain in this situation?" "What's the reward if I comfort myself from within—and skip the Oreos?"

Over time, that internal dialogue is supposed to become second nature, and the craving for excess food should vanish. You will, quite naturally, eat only as much as your body needs, and the extra fat will melt away.

Simple enough—at least in theory.

When ceramics artist Galbo discovered The Solution in 1998, she was a wreck. She was in her early 30s. A couple of years earlier, the man she had recently broken up with came to her studio and threatened to kill himself. She begged him to call his therapist. Instead, he drove to a friend's house and shot himself in the head.

He survived, but Galbo sank into depression. She painted every room in her house blue. She moved her bed into the living room because she couldn't bear to sleep in the bedroom they'd shared. Days, she dragged herself to her studio, where she ran a pottery school; evenings, she flopped into bed, cried, and ate. A whole pizza at a sitting. A pint of Häagen-Dazs Dulce de Leche before sleep. Two six-packs of tofu pudding at 3 a.m.

Galbo, who is 5 feet, 5 inches tall, had been 10 to 25 pounds overweight since age 11. Now she ballooned to 198. Her breasts chafed her stomach. Her thighs rubbed themselves raw. She barely had the energy to walk, let alone teach 8-year-olds how to make a beautiful pot or bowl. "My God," she thought. "I cannot live like this."

Then she heard about Laurel Mellin, M.A., R.D. An associate clinical professor of family and community medicine and pediatrics at UCSF and creator of The Solution, Mellin said people could simply shut off the drive to stuff themselves. Galbo bought Mellin's book The Solution: For Safe, Healthy, and Permanent Weight Loss. When she finished reading, she called Mellin and asked for help.

At age 55, Mellin has spent half her life showing people how to slim down, not by counting calories or demonizing foods but by satisfying the emotional hunger that she believes propels overeating. The Solution is all about training yourself to recognize and express the anger, sadness, and guilt that are part of life, along with happiness, gratitude, and love. It is about finding and living in balance.

Mellin is not the only obesity expert to focus on the emotional roots of overeating: Phil McGraw, Ph.D., better known as Oprah sidekick Dr. Phil, famously exhorts dieters to change "from the inside out." And two recent studies suggest strong links between psychological distress and obesity.

In a 2003 study of 336 midlife women, researchers at the University of Pennsylvania found that mood was the strongest predictor of significant weight gain in women—even stronger than what the participants reported about their eating or exercise habits. A few years earlier, a Finnish study of 2,359 men and 2,791 women found that stress-driven eaters had the highest average body mass index of all the subjects. The researchers concluded that "programs aimed at preventing and treating obesity should cover the way in which people deal with emotions, ways of achieving greater emotional support, and strategies for handling stress caused by unemployment or work."

But in America's current obsession with obesity, the role of emotions receives scant attention. Instead, the finger is pointed at carbohydrates, killer fats, and giant portions. "People are eating and drinking to excess," Mellin says. "Having every McDonald's stop supersizing is not a solution. The solution is within people themselves."

Mellin developed her ideas while working with overweight children and teens 25 years ago. The program she created then, called Shapedown, was one of the first intensive weight-management systems for kids, and it used a novel approach. For one thing, parents were required to participate. For another, Shapedown didn't push calorie counting; it focused on emotional development. The plan taught kids to communicate what they felt, and it showed parents how to listen, respect their children's needs, and set and stick to reasonable limits.

But the longer Mellin worked with families, the more she understood that parents often lacked the inner resources Shapedown nourished in their children. "The kids changed really quickly, but their parents didn't," she says. "The kids stopped overeating. But their parents would say to me, 'I can't set limits with myself. How do I do it for my kids?' "

In 1991, Mellin launched The Solution—basically, Shapedown for grown-ups. She quickly realized that these older participants would need longer to make changes than the 10 weeks Shapedown required. Adults were more likely to have well-worn strategies for avoiding painful feelings. They tended to think through their problems instead of experiencing the underlying fear, anger, or sadness. Or they used food (or alcohol, work, television, or sex) as a distraction. Some of The Solution's initial clients said they felt terrified that if they probed deep hurts or even daily letdowns, they would find it impossible to function.

That very first group of 11 adults held together for 12 weeks, then for 12 weeks more, and for nearly a year after that. (Mellin now says that it takes a year or more for grown-ups to master the necessary skills.) But almost everyone lost weight and felt happier with their lives, she says. Soon there was a waiting list for The Solution.

Now Mellin presides over a mini-industry, with Web chats, online bulletin boards, and more than one hundred groups meeting weekly, in person or by phone. Although most people join to lose weight, Mellin says the program works for all sorts of excessive behaviors, including heavy drinking, overwork, overspending, smoking, and drug abuse.

The Solution has legions of enthusiastic supporters who have learned how to manage emotional distress to lose weight.

Almost all of those who want to lose weight do, she says—and they keep it off. But only three small studies, two by Mellin and her colleagues and one by a Solution participant, have tested her claims.

Mellin tracked 26 Solution members through 18 weeks of treatment and followed up on them after two years, then again after six. At 18 weeks, the average weight loss was 12 pounds. At the end of two years, the 22 people she was able to check in on had lost even more: 17 pounds on average. Those findings were published in 1997 in the *Journal of the American Dietetic Association*. The six-year follow-up, presented in 1999 at the annual meeting of the American Dietetic Association (ADA), analyzed data on 16 participants and found even more improvement: an average 22-pound weight loss. Symptoms of depression decreased during that time, too.

In the other study, Nancy Bates, R.D., D.P.H., a research associate at the University of Illinois, surveyed 134 people in advanced Solution courses. She had more than a professional interest: She's lost weight on the plan, and she feels happier. In Bates's unpublished analysis, 91 percent of participants said their moods had improved after completing the program; 83 percent reported better relationships. About 75 percent said that they nearly always overate before trying The Solution. Almost none said they frequently ate too much after they became involved with it.

As Mellin acknowledges, these studies lack the scientific merit of controlled clinical trials. Still, The Solution has received endorsements from some prominent obesity researchers, including John P. Foreyt, Ph.D., director of the Behavioral Medicine Research Center at Baylor University. "I was very impressed," he says of Mellin's findings. "This is the only study I'm aware of in which people continued to lose weight after the intervention ended." And Molly Gee, R.D., M.Ed., chair of the ADA's weight-management practice group, says, "I think the approach is right on."

The Solution also has a fiercely loyal following among women who have battled weight problems for most of their lives. "The whole-life approach was what I needed," says Diane Merlino, an actress in San Francisco. The experience transformed her life. She dumped a boyfriend who made her miserable, began singing in dinner theaters—and, yes, lost 30 pounds.

"Learning to understand how I'm feeling, learning to develop more-reasonable expectations, those were the breakthroughs," Merlino says. "The weight loss was the result."

Galbo was 11 when divorce broke her family apart. Her mother moved across the country, leaving Galbo with her father. She found her balm in eating. "I just turned to food for everything," she recalls. "I soothed myself with food. I rewarded myself with food." Her increasing bulk also provided a safe way to lash out at her mother. By Christmas, Galbo had gained 30 pounds. When she stepped off the plane, her mother began to sob.

Galbo joined Weight Watchers in high school and even worked there part-time. But no diet, then or over the next 20 years, shaved more than 5 pounds off her figure. And the weight always returned.

Still, by most outward measures, Galbo's life seemed enviable. By her 20s she was living near her mother. She had a growing reputation for her sculptural ceramics, and her pottery school got enthusiastic write-ups in such journals as *Clay Times*. She had a boyfriend she was crazy about.

But in 1995 he and Galbo had a tumultuous falling-out. A week later came his suicide attempt. For the next two years, eating—her reflexive source of comfort—became a brutal self-punishment.

From the moment she heard about The Solution, Galbo saw it as salvation. The message of balance resonated—balance, after all, lies at the heart of a potter's work. In 1998, Galbo joined Mellin's first telegroup. Every Monday at 1 p.m., the artist dialed Mellin's office along with a dozen other people from around the country. For two hours, participants spilled their feelings about work, family, taxes, friends, traffic tickets—everything that can knock someone out of kilter, or "below the line."

How to Find Balance

The Solution is a tool kit that enables you to cope with the challenges of life, from a pile of bills to divorce or the death of a loved one. The program's founder, Laurel Mellin, M.A., R.D., describes how to "pop" yourself into balance in her 2003 book *The Pathway,* currently in paperback. Here's a taste.

Let's say you want some ice cream—now. You're trying to lose 5 pounds, but you feel you can't resist. OK, stop a minute. Notice your thoughts: You want that ice cream. You can almost see it in the bowl.

Ask yourself how you feel. Perhaps you're stressed; you've been glued to your computer, trying to catch up on work. And, yes, you feel overwhelmed—the deadline's looming. Now go deeper, beyond "smoke screen" feelings, such as restlessness and anxiety, to "natural" feelings, such as anger, sadness, fear, guilt.

Maybe you're angry because you have so much work and sad that life is so difficult. Guilty because you've been distracted and tense with your family. And afraid that you'll blow the deadline and that your boss will yell at you, hate you, fire you.

Really experiencing these feelings allows you to comfort yourself without the ice cream. But nurturing isn't enough. You must set limits to assure yourself that you have control and that you're safe, as the following internal dialogue illustrates.

Are my expectations reasonable? Hmmm, not exactly. In order to meet the deadline, I expect myself to work around the clock at the expense of my health and family.

Is my thinking positive and powerful? No again. I'm telling myself that I don't matter; the only thing that matters is the deadline.

What are the encouraging words I need to hear? All I can do is my best. My work is not my life.

What is the essential pain I must face so I won't be in this tailspin? I am not perfect. My boss may be mad. I have needs other than work.

What's the earned reward? I don't have to be perfect to be wonderful. By admitting that I need more time, I can do a good job, and more of my needs will be met, so I'll be healthier and happier. I will be proud of myself for doing my best at work but also in achieving some balance in my life.

And that ice cream just might remain in the freezer.

Then group members practiced skills for bringing themselves into balance, or popping "above the line." This involved doing what Mellin calls a cycle. First, you ask a set of questions that helps you nurture yourself—in effect, as if you were talking with a responsive internal mother: "How do I feel?" "What do I need?" Next, you ask questions that help you set limits, conversing, if you like, with a protective inner father: "Are my expectations reasonable?" "Is my thinking positive and powerful?"

The nurturing questions help you connect with your deepest feelings, the 5-year-old within. The limit questions help you act on your feelings as a grown-up, an adult who finds that cravings have faded away.

The drill is chanted often—to retrain the limbic brain, Mellin says. Thought to be the seat of emotions and drives, this area is shaped early in life. When parents effectively nurture and set limits, Mellin says, the brain develops to favor a life of balance. But when parents, however loving, do not nurture well or provide adequate boundaries, the wiring favors imbalance.

In Mellin's view, most weight-loss programs ultimately fail because they take only a rational approach to diet or exercise, an approach that utterly ignores the primitive urge to overeat. That's why people almost always regain weight after dieting or substitute other self-destructive indulgences, such as smoking or reckless spending. The Solution works long-term, Mellin says, because it fixes the faulty wiring that produces insatiable cravings.

When Galbo started the program, she told the group about the puddings, the pizzas, the fact that when she got angry with her mother, she would head to the drive-through for burgers and fries, then gleefully list every fattening morsel for her mom.

But Mellin didn't nudge Galbo about her binges. She rarely discussed food at all, in fact, beyond the healthy eating plan in *The Solution* book and such nuggets as "If you're not waking up hungry, you're probably eating too much." Instead, she encouraged Galbo to visit and vent her hurts.

At first Galbo found this hard to do. Then, one week, Mellin was late for the group meeting, which infuriated the artist. "Go ahead," Galbo remembers Mellin saying. "Give it to me. What are you feeling?"

"I'm feeling angry that you're late," Galbo said.

"You don't sound angry," Mellin answered.

Galbo yelled, "I'm feeling angry! I'm angry that you don't care!"

"What do these feelings remind you of," Mellin asked, "from before you were 5?"

Galbo said tearfully, "On the first day of kindergarten, my mother took me to the wrong class. Instead of paying attention to me, she was focused on herself."

"What do you need?"

"I need the focus to be on me. I need to pay attention to myself."

After that exchange, Galbo discovered she had plenty of anger to go around. She was enraged by the old boyfriend who'd shot himself, by the demands of running her ceramics school. If eating didn't kill her, she might work herself to death.

The Solution practically ignores the topics of food, diet, and exercise. Instead it focuses on fixing the faulty wiring inside our heads that produces the insatiable cravings for food.

Galbo can't say exactly how she lost weight. One morning she realized she hadn't binged on pudding in six months. Another time, she opened the freezer, noticed the ice cream, and simply didn't want it, just as Mellin had promised. Late in her training, in what Mellin calls "lifestyle surgery," Galbo closed the school to concentrate on her art, and she started dating again.

One day she stepped on the scale. It read 118.

Galbo has grown closer to her mother. They still argue from time to time, but now Galbo hangs in for the fight instead of slamming the door and driving off for a cheeseburger. Recently, when her mom snapped at her, Galbo said, "If you don't start acting nice, I'm going to Jack in the Box." Her mother's face sagged. Galbo hugged her. "Mom," she said, "I don't do that anymore."

When Galbo started The Solution, a change like this seemed like a prize beyond reach. Now, she says it wasn't so hard. All she had to do was grow up.

That's the answer—and the challenge—Mellin holds out to millions of people: Grow up. Listen to your feelings, express them directly, set reasonable expectations for getting your needs met. Don't blame yourself, but take responsibility.

Growing up, of course, takes time. But the process can be joyful, and the payoff tremendous. "I've blossomed into the person I would have been if I hadn't been stunted emotionally when I was 11," Galbo says. "I'm just happier now." ■

Fran Smith's work has appeared in Salon, San Jose Mercury News, USA Today, *and other publications.*

Yo-yo Dieters Face Another Hurdle

Two out of three American women are currently trying to lose weight. Here's hoping they succeed. But here's the real battle: keeping the weight off. Among the millions who put pounds back on after dieting, fewer than 5 percent of them are able to lose them again. Why? Your body's chemistry may be to blame. The remedy? Unfortunately, you've got to work harder to keep flab from coming back.

In recent research conducted at Osaka University in Japan, Kazuko Masuo, M.D., Ph.D., found that obese male dieters who regained weight had a few things in common: blood pressure high enough to be labeled hypertension; raised levels of norepinephrine, a stimulant hormone; and too much insulin in the blood. The findings, which Masuo says also apply to women, suggest that insulin resistance and a nervous system in overdrive could be as guilty of making you regain weight as french fries.

Another explanation for relapse is resistance to leptin, a hormone produced by fat cells that is thought to decrease hunger and increase metabolism. The relapsers in Masuo's study were all found to have high levels of the chemical, suggesting that their bodies were producing extra amounts to cope with their resistance, explains William S. Cook, M.D., a researcher in the Department of Surgery at the University of Texas Southwestern Medical Center in Dallas. Cook and colleagues recently found a way to overcome leptin resistance in rats. Masuo says controlling leptin could become a mainstay of weight management in the near future.

Until then, here's how to avoid diet sabotage: Find out if your insulin and blood pressure are high. Keep them in check with exercise, healthier meals, and medication if needed. Use them as motivation to steer you away from the drive-through.

How Comfort Foods Really Do Battle Stress

Reaching for junk food whenever the stress monster strikes is not a personal weakness: It's an evolutionary instinct. Furthermore, it actually works—judging, at least, from a recent study in rats. Scientists at the University of California, San Francisco, found that when chronically anxious rats ate sweet and fatty foods, the resulting increase in their abdominal fat lowered levels of stress-producing brain chemicals. High-energy foods help rats flee hungry cats, and they may have helped our cave-dwelling ancestors, too. But these days fatty foods result in belly bulge and the risk of assorted ailments. So if stress makes you reach for comfort food, the researchers say, you should at least jog to get it.

How You Can Manage Your Metabolism with This High-tech Weight-Loss Device

Why can some women eat whatever they want without gaining any weight while others pack on pounds faster than you can say chocolate-cherry cheesecake? Experts chalk it up to puzzling differences in how fast humans can burn calories. But now high-tech tools are solving that metabolism mystery and helping to trim waistlines.

Thousands of weight-loss centers and health clubs are using portable devices that precisely determine your resting metabolic rate (RMR), the number of calories you burn while your body is at rest. If you're trying to lose weight, knowing your RMR helps you calculate how many calories to consume and how many to burn through exercise.

The process is simple: You breathe into a mouthpiece or face mask, and the device measures how much oxygen you take in and how much carbon dioxide you breathe out. The results are far more accurate than traditional estimates based on your age, weight, and height. Those can be off by hundreds of calories, says Richard Gordon, an exercise physiologist at Cedars-Sinai Medical Center in Los Angeles.

Once you know your RMR, you're well on your way toward getting an individualized eating and exercise plan from a dietitian or fitness counselor.

Fees for a metabolic workup range from $40 to upwards of $200. Experts say the tools, which go by the names BodyGem and New Leaf, are especially useful for anyone who needs a little extra motivation. (To find a fitness center that uses these devices, go to www.newleaf-online.com.)

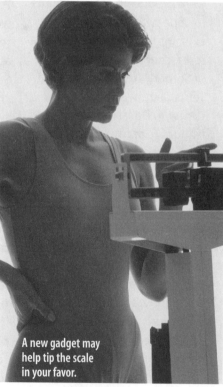

A new gadget may help tip the scale in your favor.

A Slimmer Glass, a Slimmer You?

A recent study suggests that if you want to cut calories, you may be better off ordering a highball than a double old-fashioned. Researchers at the University of Illinois at Urbana-Champaign found that regardless of the drink, people pour more into short, wide glasses than into tall, skinny ones, and they end up drinking more as a result.

Eighty-nine men and women were randomly given either short or tall glasses with the same capacity and were instructed to help themselves to juice in a self-serve cafeteria line. The people with the short, wide glasses poured 19-percent more (6.8 ounces versus 5.7 ounces)—even though they thought they were pouring less—than those with the highballs. That's a difference of 15 calories, if the subjects chose orange juice.

"We tend to undercompensate for the width of a glass," says Brian Wansink, Ph.D., professor of consumer psychology and author of the study. Because people believe a tall, slender glass holds more, he says, they're less likely to fill it to the brim.

The solution? Choose your barware wisely. "If you want to be short and wide, drink out of short, wide glasses. If you want to be tall and thin, drink out of tall, thin glasses," Wansink says.

Nutrition on the Go **Grocers provide on-demand help.**

In a perfect world, people could have their questions about how to eat healthfully answered when and where they buy their food. So it comes as a pleasant surprise that supermarkets—both natural-foods and mainstream—are granting that wish by expanding their nutritional programs to educate customers. Now, many shoppers can receive dietary counseling from their favorite grocery stores by Web, over the phone, or in person.

"People are more health-conscious and more confused than ever," says Ellen Speare, nutrition coordinator for Wild Oats Natural Marketplace, whose program has been leading the way for the last nine years. The demonizing of carbs in popular culture is a repeat subject. "There's a lot of misinformation out there that I try to correct with scientific facts," she says.

Wild Oats' program covers 102 markets in 24 states. In the six Denver stores, Speare evaluates customers' current diets. (The service costs $25, a fact that Speare says weeds out those "who want to sit and talk about football.") She also answers about 20 calls a day, a number that has continued to significantly increase, she notes.

Mainstream grocers are embracing the concept as well. Kroger, which operates two thousand–odd stores nationwide, maintains a toll-free number (866-632-6900) staffed by registered dietitians (R.D.s); they answer questions about product labels and offer guidelines for callers interested in, for example, low-fat diets. Albertsons, which has more than two thousand grocery stores in 31 states, including California, Texas, and Florida, has received positive customer feedback for its nutrition program. The company is presently expanding the staff of R.D.s at its hotline and Web site (888-746-7252, www.albertsons.com).

"For customers who have specific questions about dietary restrictions or product ingredients, our dietitians can assist them with understanding labels and planning meals," says Stacia Levenfeld, a spokeswoman for Albertsons.

Back at Wild Oats, Speare most commonly prescribes menu ideas that are convenient

Getting the answers to your nutritional questions is only a phone call away.

and easy to prepare. "A lot of eating well is just planning meals and buying food for the week," she says.

Nelda Mercer, R.D., a spokeswoman for the American Dietetic Association, applauds the convenience of hotlines and in-store counseling. "Getting good advice on demand is the Cadillac of customer service," she says. But consider the source. "Make sure the person is credentialed as a registered dietitian and is giving science-based information."

fast FOOD

The New Generation

The fast-food industry is becoming more health conscious. New options are changing the way you eat on the go.

BY KERRI CONAN • PHOTOGRAPHY BY JEANNE DOZIER CLAYTON

Pop into one of the four O'Naturals across New England, and you immediately whiff the difference between it and traditional fast-food joints. Instead of hamburgers, steak sizzles on the grill, ready to slip between slices of flatbread still warm from the oven. Salads might come topped with Asian-marinated wild salmon, a few walnuts, or smoked tofu. Potatoes and chicken nuggets are baked, not fried. And for Sunday brunch, you're greeted by the aromas of such home-cooked breakfast foods as applewood-smoked bacon and eggs.

O'Naturals is one of the new generation of restaurants that are changing the way America eats on the go. Dubbed "quick-casual," these eateries are serving up innovative meals—many of them healthy—for about $5 to $10, and in less than 10 minutes. Baja Fresh and Chipotle Mexican Grill are among the latest national chains that offer speedy counter service with fresh food in mind. Others, such as O'Naturals, are neighborhood restaurants (for now) with big ideas.

Fresh ingredients are only the starting point. Many new fast-food pioneers try to offer as much organic, naturally raised, or locally grown food as possible.

"Almost every meal eaten in a fast-casual restaurant is one less meal eaten at a traditional fast-food chain," says Bob Goldin, executive vice president of Technomic, Inc., a Chicago research firm that tracks the food industry. "People are tired of burgers, pizza, and chicken." So more and more places are figuring out how to make fresh, wholesome food convenient on your terms—whether you want to grab it and go, eat a nourishing family meal on the way home from a big game, or have a low-key bite with a date.

Technomic estimates that at least 5,000 of these forward-thinking restaurants have sprung up across the country, out of a total of 241,600 fast-food places. The combined annual sales of these restaurants is about $6 billion, a small but rapidly growing portion of the $140 billion fast-food category.

For O'Naturals founder Gary Hirshberg, the idea to create a fast-food alternative with an organic theme came from running Stonyfield Farm, a New Hampshire dairy that produces naturally sweetened organic yogurt. "O'Naturals is a lot like eating in your own kitchen," Hirshberg says. "We give people the chance to have everything their way, only you don't have to prepare it."

For the new fast-food pioneers, fresh ingredients are only the starting point. Many try to offer as much organic, naturally raised, or locally grown food as possible to put even more distance between them and the drive-throughs. But there's a twist: You're always in the driver's seat when it comes to choices, whether you eat in or take out. This makes ordering a meal a lot like cruising through a cafeteria line, only someone else serves up the chicken, holds the mayo, or stuffs the burrito. All you have to do is choose what you want, answer a couple of questions, and point.

A few quick-casual restaurants, such as O'Naturals and Chipotle, also serve wine, beer, and even margaritas. That may help explain why customers are coming back for dinner, something conventional fast-food restaurants have been trying to get them to do for years with little success. Dinner sales average about 50 percent at O'Naturals and 40 to 45 percent

for Chipotle, for example, compared with 25 to 30 percent for mainstream chains.

Watch for more healthy fast-food alternatives coming soon. One of the most unusual is Cereality, an all-cereal, all-day-long café in Tempe, Arizona. Here, cereal takes all forms: hot and cold, with lots of toppings, in snack bars and trail-mix treats, or blended into fruit-and-yogurt smoothies called Slurrealities. You can even concoct your own cereal mix to take home. "We wanted to provide a totally unique experience with a very familiar and comforting food," says Cereality president David Roth, who hopes to bring the concept to airports, college campuses, and offices.

In Boca Raton, Florida, Healthy Bites Grill lives up to its name, serving lean buffalo burgers on whole-grain buns, Philly-style "cheesesteak" with thin slices of portobello mushrooms instead of beef, low-sugar smoothies, and pie made from organic apples. And several other small chains—such as Crazy Bowls and Wraps, of St. Louis, and Noodles, with locations in nine states—are working to give you a quick bowl of fresh veggies, starch, and protein.

French fries aren't the only side you'll find at today's fast-food restaurants. Healthier alternatives are popping up in many establishments.

The *Health* Under-500

Make a run for our favorite new speedy lunches.

O'Naturals

Spicy Peanut Salad
Mesclun greens, lots of veggies and cilantro, special dressing, topped with optional Asian-marinated Alaskan wild salmon
Calories: 290 • Fat: 14g

Healthy Bites Grill

Colorado Burger
Lean buffalo meat on a multigrain bun with chipotle sauce, lettuce, and tomato
Calories: 385 • Fat: 8g

Chipotle

Two Soft Carnitas Tacos
Made with naturally raised pork in flour tortillas; topped with lettuce and tomatillo salsa
Calories: 463 • Fat: 17g

Panera Bread

Low-Fat Garden Vegetarian Soup
Packed with such veggies as corn, spinach, and red peppers; simmered with navy and lima beans
Calories: 90 • Fat: 0.5g

Good Times Burgers

Mighty Deluxe
The familiar burger, only better; made with naturally raised beef and fresh toppings
Calories: 476 • Fat: 21g

Such classics as burgers, tacos, and fries are now getting makeovers, too. At Topz, a chain with seven Southern California locations, the handmade beef patties and fries are much lower in fat and calories than the industry standard (10 grams of fat per burger, compared with 33 grams in a Big Mac). Good Times Burgers & Frozen Custard, with 35 restaurants in Colorado, recently started using Coleman Natural Meats, from cattle raised without growth hormones or antibiotics. And Chipotle, a bigger chain owned largely by McDonald's, fills Carnitas Burritos with Niman Ranch brand pork (another meat raised naturally on small farms) at all 275 locations nationwide. Chipotle is also moving toward cooking with antibiotic-free chicken and serving organic black beans where supplies are available. Those moves come as activists and the media are spotlighting how restaurant suppliers treat animals. People for the Ethical Treatment of Animals has sued KFC over the way its farmers treat chickens, and McDonald's has said it is giving its beef suppliers two years to phase out the use of growth-promoting antibiotics—a step highly lauded by the health community.

Add the menu changes at traditional fast-food giants, such as Burger King, McDonald's, Wendy's, and others, and health-conscious folks have more choices than ever when they're eating out. Here are some examples:

- Chilled lettuce, grape tomatoes, and slices of sweet onion are joining the ketchup and pickles that once passed for vegetables.
- Dressed-up salad options include lighter dressings and even ethnic touches.
- Burger King now sells baguette sandwiches made with grilled chicken breasts.
- Subway continues to lead the low-fat pack, with 10 sandwiches weighing in at less than 6 grams of fat.

Chains that serve fresh salad meals, such as Wendy's and McDonald's, are already seeing their recent sluggish sales start to turn around. Wendy's, for example, saw its sales growth increase from

2.1 percent in 2001 to 4.7 percent in 2002. (That's compared with an average 15 percent-per-year growth rate at quick-casual restaurants.)

Wherever you eat, remember that calories still count, no matter how healthy they are for you. And some of these newer restaurants' offerings are packed with them.

Wherever you choose to eat, just bear in mind that calories still count, no matter how healthy they are for you. And some of these newer restaurants' offerings are packed with them. Chipotle's Vegetarian Burrito, for instance, weighs in at 1,120 calories (federal guidelines suggest an average daily diet of about 2,000 calories). "Fresh-Mex chains cultivate an aura of healthfulness, and sometimes it's deserved," says Michael Jacobson of the Center for Science in the Public Interest. "But because Chipotle doesn't reveal calories or other nutrition information, most people wouldn't have a clue that their Vegetarian Burrito is the equivalent of an over-stuffed corned beef sandwich—plus 350 calories." At Panera Bread, another quick-casual chain, the Tuscan Chicken and Sierra Turkey sandwiches have 950 calories, 56 grams of fat, and more than 2,000 milligrams of sodium.

You can certainly find healthier alternatives there and at Chipotle. So if you want to hurry this freshening trend along, keep supporting the best of these new choices. Restaurants will take bigger strides toward better fast food as long as you keep beating a path to their doors. ◼

Additional reporting by Su Reid-St. John.

Go for the Guacamole

Feel free to make guacamole your dip of choice. Avocados are chock-full of magnesium, and recent studies suggest that eating magnesium-rich foods is well worth it.

The more magnesium in your diet, the less likely you are to develop Type 2 diabetes, Harvard University researchers say. And people living near water with high concentrations of magnesium and other elements have lower rates of heart attacks, according to the findings of Finnish researchers.

The mineral—which helps to control blood pressure, to regulate nerve impulses, to build strong bones, and to protect the heart from electrical abnormalities, such as arrhythmias—is also plentiful in green, leafy vegetables; nuts; whole grains; certain fruits; and shellfish. Eating at least five servings of those foods per day will help you meet the recommended daily allowances for people age 31 and up (420 milligrams for men and 320 milligrams for women).

Still, don't stress about having a dangerous deficiency. That's rare among Americans. The real goal should simply be to get more than you do now. "We're realizing that we can get enough magnesium to prevent deficiency," says Katherine Tucker, Ph.D., an associate professor of nutritional epidemiology at Tufts University in Boston. "The new evidence is showing that higher levels than those currently recommended are optimal."

More smart ways to up your intake: Eat a handful of almonds, 1 cup raw spinach, or 1/2 cup golden raisins. A multivitamin that contains magnesium may help, too.

Are Genetically

SAFE

GMO's are stirring up controversy in the food world. We answer six questions to help you figure out if they're really safe.

BY ALISA BLACKWOOD

If you're a label reader (and with all of the frightening food news lately, who isn't?), you may have seen the lingo "non-GMO" on more and more packages on grocery-store shelves. You might have even caught part of the debate among international health experts and politicians, who have fervent opinions about the value—and potential costs—of using genetically modified organisms, aka GMOs, in the breeding of crops destined for human consumption. The debate is so heated in some parts of the country that voters in California's Mendocino County approved a ballot measure in March 2004 that bans the growing of genetically engineered crops. Concerned citizens in Colorado, Hawaii, Maine, Ohio, Texas, Vermont, Wisconsin, and other states have also formed their own grassroots groups

About 80 percent of food on grocery-store shelves contains genetically altered ingredients, but you won't find any labels that say so.

to push for labeling laws (right now there are none) and more-rigorous safety testing, or to speak against GMOs altogether, says Ronnie Cummins, national director of the Organic Consumers Association.

But you may not be sure exactly what the fighting's about or why you should care. On the pages that follow, we answer six essential questions about GMOs to help you choose what to put on your table.

What are GMOs, and what are they used for? GMOs are created by injecting genetic materials from plants, animals, or bacteria into crops in hopes of creating some new and beneficial traits. For example, one of the most popular genetically modified (GM) crops is a corn

Modified Foods to EAT?

plant that's capable of producing its own pesticide, called Bt, which is also used in spray form by some organic farmers. The idea is to make the plant resistant to insect damage and to limit the amount of harmful pesticides farmers have to spray. Other GM plants, such as Roundup Ready corn, were created to survive the spraying of the herbicide Roundup, which kills weeds and would normally kill the plant, too, says Stephen H. Howell, Ph.D., director of the Plant Sciences Institute at Iowa State University.

Researchers are also using the technology experimentally as a way to nutritionally enhance fruits and vegetables.

Some GMO supporters say that both applications are necessary to help feed a growing world population, especially in poor countries where both drought and famine are common. But there is very little agreement on whether biotechnology offers a uniform way to address world hunger. "We have plenty of food for the world right now. It's not the deficiency of technology that's a problem for developing countries," explains Jane Rissler, Ph.D., a senior staff scientist with the Union of Concerned Scientists, a nonprofit watchdog group that partners with 80,000 researchers. The international hunger problem, she says, stems from "poverty, corruption, and poor distribution."

What kinds of foods contain GMOs?

About 80 percent of the food on grocery-store shelves already contains at least some ingredients made from altered genes. This means that almost any processed food, from salad dressing to snack crackers, could contain GMOs, unless it has been certified organic (federal regulations explicitly restrict food manufacturers from using the organic seal on products made with GMOs). That's because corn, soy, and canola are the top three GM food crops in the United States, so anything that is produced with corn syrup, high-fructose corn syrup, or soybean or corn oil might include GMOs.

Very little fresh produce on the market, though, is genetically engineered, with the exceptions of most papaya, some squash, and a few strains of sweet corn. Meanwhile, we're not the only ones consuming GMOs—animals do, too. GM corn and soybeans are often used in livestock feed, though there's no evidence that GMOs show up in your steak or chops.

Should I be concerned about the safety of GM foods?
Federal agencies, such as the U.S. Food and Drug Administration (FDA) and the U.S. Department of Agriculture (USDA), say that they are safe, and there have been no

181

documented cases of illness due to consumption of GMOs. The American Medical Association agrees at this point and has encouraged ongoing research in the field.

But critics are worried that a loophole in federal law could lead to problems: The FDA does not currently require that makers of GM foods submit their products for review or approval before marketing them to the public. However, the organization does encourage companies to submit their data, says James Maryanski, Ph.D., the FDA's biotechnology coordinator. "As far as we know, all the products [on the market] made by bioengineering have been reviewed by the FDA," he says. "We do expect the companies to provide us with enough data to show they've done the right tests. We stand behind the products that we have looked at and believe those foods are as safe as other foods in the marketplace."

The FDA is attempting to tighten the process by drafting a proposal that would require all biotech crops to be reviewed before going public. The USDA announced in January 2004 that it also intends to update and strengthen its biotechnology rules regarding GMOs, though any possible changes are still in the research phase.

Critics also say that because there is no system in place for tracking products that contain GM ingredients and no labeling that lets consumers know which products contain them, there isn't a good way to monitor the health effects of eating GM foods over the long term. "This is a continuing bone of contention," Rissler says. "The proponents say there is no evidence of harm. And the skeptics say, 'How would you know? The food is not labeled.'"

What do GM crops mean for the environment? "I think a lot of scientists agree that there are no known environmental problems with the crops that are out there now," says Allison Snow, Ph.D., who studies environmental risk and genetically modified crops as a professor of ecology at Ohio State University. But organic farmers are becoming increasingly concerned about maintaining the integrity of their crops. For example, if Bt corn is planted too close to a neighboring organic-corn crop, cross-pollination could occur and contaminate the latter.

Scientists on both sides of the debate also widely agree that insects will eventually become resistant to the Bt crops, Snow says. "It could happen any year now. Then we would be back where we started, and we would have lost a valuable tool for managing insects," Snow says.

Rissler says she is also concerned about the possible effects of GM Atlantic salmon currently under review by the FDA. The fish, developed by Aqua Bounty Technologies Inc., have been engineered to grow twice as fast as traditionally farmed salmon, likely making this new breed more economical to raise, says Joseph McGonigle, the company's vice president. If such salmon are raised in ocean pens instead of on land-based farms, the chance of escape is higher. This could lead to the decimation of the wild population if the re-engineered and native salmon mate, Rissler says. As a precaution against this, McGonigle says that only sterile female GM fish would be used for commercial farming. However, sterility is not 100-percent assured.

Is it possible to live completely GMO-free? Probably not. A study commissioned by the Union of Concerned Scientists and released in February 2004 already suggests that seeds that are supposedly non-GMO may be unintentionally tainted. Genetically engineered DNA was found in at least half of the small sample of tested corn and soybean seeds, and about 83 percent of the canola seeds. Even if you buy only certified-organic products, you probably can't avoid GMOs completely. That's because it is also possible for organic food crops to become inadvertently contaminated.

As for non-GMO labels, be aware that the claim is not regulated. A USDA certified–organic label is currently the best indicator that a product did not (to the best of the producer's knowledge) use ingredients made from genetically engineered seeds, says Holly Givens, a spokeswoman for the Organic Trade Association.

Some grocers are trying to make it easier for consumers to get their hands on GMO-free (or nearly GMO-free) foods. Three national chains—Trader Joe's, Wild Oats, and Whole Foods Market—have chosen to use only ingredients not developed through genetic engineering for their private-label products, in part because of customer requests. "We want to stay true to our core values by selling food that is as close as possible to the way nature intended," says Whole Foods spokeswoman Kate Lowery.

What will we see next from the biotech-food market? Here are some
GM foods that might end up on store shelves:

- The FDA and USDA are currently reviewing safety data on a variety of genetically engineered wheat that would tolerate the herbicide Roundup.
- Researchers are also working on wheat varieties that would resist drought, be less allergenic to those with gluten intolerance, and be more nutritious.

Consumers may also start seeing major nutritional benefits in the future:

- In 2003, scientists at the University of California, Riverside, announced that they genetically engineered a corn plant to produce up to four times the normal amount of vitamin C by inserting a gene from wheat plants. Researchers have filed a patent application and are soliciting companies that might be interested in commercializing the product.
- Harvard scientists say it may be possible to one day insert a gene into cattle and poultry that would result in beef, milk, and eggs containing the omega-3 fatty acids found in salmon, says Jing X. Kang, M.D., Ph.D, a cell biologist at Massachusetts General Hospital. Kang's research team recently bred genetically engineered mice that make their own omega-3s, a breakthrough he sees as a useful model for developing edible animals to do the same.
- Other biotech foods that are currently in development include a vitamin A–enhanced rice and a tomato with increased amounts of the cancer-fighting antioxidant lycopene.
- Monsanto Co., which is the largest producer of GM seeds, is continuing to tinker with soybeans in hopes of developing a variety that could produce an oil containing few or no saturated and trans fats. ■

Alisa Blackwood is Health's *associate food and nutrition editor.*

Caution: Food Allergies Are Often Mistreated

The emergency room may be a dangerous place for people with allergies to foods, such as nuts, eggs, and shellfish. Experts at Massachusetts General Hospital found in a recent study of 21 hospitals that only 16 percent of those patients admitted for allergic reactions receive epinephrine, which allergists recommend for halting a potentially life-threatening reaction known as anaphylaxis. (That's when your throat can swell and blood pressure can plunge.) ER doctors usually prescribe antihistamines or steroids. If you have food allergies, ask your physician about getting a prescription for epinephrine (it's administered by an injection), as well as a referral to an allergist.

How a Special Kind of Coffee Gives Farmers a Fair Shake

The benefits of these beans may change the way you order your morning cup of joe.

BY ALISA BLACKWOOD

A revolution is brewing across the country. A growing number of mainstream coffee companies and cafés are paying premium prices for "Fair Trade Certified" beans to guarantee that the farmers who produce them are paid a living wage.

Because coffee prices have hit all-time lows, many farmers don't make enough money to cover their costs or to take care of their families. But when importers agree to buy Fair Trade coffee, they pay a minimum of $1.26 per pound—more if it's also certified organic—and agree to buy directly from Fair Trade Certified producers. This eliminates middlemen who frequently take most of the profits, sometimes giving only 10 cents per pound to the farmer. (Makes you wonder what happens to the rest of the $10 you pay for a pound of coffee.)

But Fair Trade java is good for you, too. More than 80 percent of it is certified organic. Another bonus: Most of it is shade-grown, meaning no forests were clear-cut to make room for planting.

Imports of these beans have grown from about 2 million pounds a year to 12 million pounds a year since 1999. Starbucks and Seattle's Best have been selling Fair Trade coffee since 2000 and 2001, respectively, although you have to ask for it (neither chain brews it regularly). Also, Sara Lee Coffee & Tea has been supplying Fair Trade coffee to restaurants and cafeterias across the country for more than two years. Little by little, other major companies, as well as your favorite independent cafés, are following suit.

In fall 2003, Procter & Gamble introduced Millstone Mountain Moonlight Fair Trade Certified coffee, which is available by mail order or online (800-729-5282, www.millstone.com). And Dunkin' Donuts became one of the movement's largest supporters in spring 2004, when it rolled out a new line of espresso-based beverages using only Fair Trade Certified coffee. Check Wild Oats Markets, Trader Joe's, most Albertsons stores, or an independent coffee shop if you're buying beans to take home. You can also find a retailer in your area by logging on to www.transfairusa.org.

The beans may cost an extra dollar or two, but when you consider all the perks of Fair Trade, you might just decide the cost is worth it.

Pour Another Cup of Decaf

It's tough to pass over sinfully sweet pastries by the office coffeepot. But you may have fewer regrets if you wash 'em down with a cup of decaf. A recent British study found that people experienced less-intense sugar rushes from decaffeinated coffee than from regular coffee or water.

What's wrong with a sugar rush? Sure, the burst of energy feels good at first, but then your pancreas pumps out insulin to move that sugar from your blood to your muscles. And when the sugar's gone, you may feel sluggish or dizzy. You might even wind up having a nasty headache.

Chemicals called polyphenols in regular and decaffeinated coffee seem to suppress the sugar surge by slowing the rate at which your intestines absorb the sweet stuff, explains study author Linda Morgan, Ph.D., a biochemist at the University of Surrey. But regular joe counteracts some of that effect; after sugar hits your bloodstream, the caffeine delays its arrival in your muscles, ensuring a bigger and longer rush. Researchers think that explains why decaffeinated coffee came out on top in the study.

Maybe you're not brave enough to go caffeine-free in the morning. But now you've got another reason to mix some decaf with your high-octane brew.

Get an Extra Jolt from Your Morning Java

That no-foam grande latte could protect you from Type 2 diabetes. Finnish researchers found that women who drank three or four cups of coffee daily cut their odds of developing the disease by 29 percent. Caffeine may be the key: It's known to heighten the production and efficiency of insulin, the hormone that stops working properly in diabetics. Worried about what all that caffeine may do to your sleep schedule? Good news: Decaf contains diabetes-fighting magnesium and chlorogenic acid, which may help lower blood sugar.

The Link Between Alcohol and Belly Fat

No respectable doctor will tell you to start drinking if you don't like it. But new evidence linking alcohol and body shape might make you thirsty for a glass of Cabernet. Researchers at the University of Buffalo recently found that people who drink tend to have less belly fat than those who don't and that people who drink a little every day tend to be thinner around the middle than those who drink only on weekends.

No one's sure why. But your drinking patterns may have some biological effect on the way you store fat, explains Joan Dorn, Ph.D., a preventive-medicine expert. Dorn and other researchers measured the belly fat carried by 2,300 women and men, and asked participants whether they had ever drunk alcohol, and if so, how much in the past 30 days. Those who had four drinks on a Friday and none for the next six days, for instance, were fatter than people who had one drink everyday. "You can't just look at how much people drink," Dorn says. "You have to look at when they're drinking it." What you drink seems to be a factor, too: Liquor-drinkers were the fattest.

There's no getting around the significance of belly fat. It's not just about how you look or how much you weigh. The more fat around your middle, the higher your risk of heart disease. Not surprisingly, Dorn and Ronald Krauss, M.D., an American Heart Association spokesman, say abstainers concerned about their hearts shouldn't take up drinking simply because of one piece of research. But Dorn says her study adds to a persuasive body of evidence suggesting up to a drink a day for women and two for men may keep the cardiologist away.

How to Get Five-a-Day in the Freshest Way

Discover why so many families get their vegetables delivered straight from the farm.

BY BRIAN LAVENDEL

Siri Carpenter grew up eating what she calls Midwestern meat-and-potato dinners served with soggy sides of frozen peas or corn. But since her family became one of thousands nationwide to take part in a movement called community-supported agriculture (CSA), her dinner table boasts fresh local vegetables as the main course.

In summer 2004, an estimated sixty to ninety thousand families like Carpenter's received weekly deliveries of produce from farms in their area. The arrangement is a win-win one for health-conscious diners and local farmers, experts say. Not only does it help consumers meet their five-servings-a-day quota of fruits and vegetables, but also guarantees that participating farmers—who often struggle to survive financially—will have a group of buyers each season.

Since the program's start in 1986, the number of CSA farms has grown to about one thousand nationwide. Members sign up at the beginning of the harvest and pay a membership fee of between $300 and $650, depending on the amount of produce they want. (That works out to only about $15 to $30 per week.) As a member, you're entitled to a family-size share of the total harvest, which is usually delivered once a week for five to seven months.

Before Carpenter, 32, joined the CSA movement through Harmony Valley Farm in Viroqua, Wisconsin, she "never felt very excited about vegetables," she confesses. But being a farm member made Carpenter more conscious and thoughtful about what she puts on the table for her family, she says. With an abundance of flavorful, just-picked produce in the house, she's less likely to stop and pick up a pizza after work or rely on processed foods.

Because CSA produce comes directly from nearby farm fields, it tends to be among the freshest food you can buy. That means its nutritional value is at its peak: The quality of vitamins and other nutrients in most vegetables is at its highest at harvest, says Marita Cantwell, Ph.D., a vegetable-crop specialist at the University of California, Davis. As a bonus, many CSA farms grow their food organically.

And if Carpenter's 2-year-old daughter, Grace, is any indication, CSA might even provide a solution to that age-old parental problem of getting kids to eat their vegetables—and actually like them. Grace's surprising new favorite is that quintessential kids-hate-it vegetable: Brussels sprouts. ▪

Search for a CSA farm near you at www.csacenter.org.

Say YES to Yogurt

As yogurt crosses the line into dessert territory, here's how to keep a nutritious snack on this side of healthy.

BY KERRI CONAN

Even true-blue fans admit that plain yogurt is downright tangy. But with its potential benefits—calming a turbulent stomach and providing a calcium boost—who wants to miss a bite? To make the taste of yogurt more appealing, choices have multiplied into such syrupy sweet treats as candy-topped sundaes and puddinglike desserts. So how do you keep your waistline from expanding as fast as the yogurt selections in the dairy case?

Even plain yogurt contains naturally occurring milk sugar, or lactose. Each cup averages about 19 grams. Factor in sweeteners (such as sugar, corn syrup, or pureed fruit), and the sugar content can climb to more than 30 grams in a 6-ounce serving—almost as much as in a can of soda. In fact, some of the yogurt smoothies now available pack as much as 46 grams of sugar per serving. And the calorie counts can vary widely, ranging from about 100 to 300 in a serving.

But don't let that keep you from sampling the goodness of yogurt. Researchers have recently found that the calcium in dairy products can actually help you maintain muscle and promote weight loss by making fat cells break down more efficiently.

If you're trying to reach (or stay at) a healthy weight and minimize your sugar or carbohydrate intake, read the label. When the total calories of a particular yogurt are closer to 300, you're better off thinking of it as an occasional indulgence than an anytime snack. Or try our five easy ways to enjoy yogurt more often—without putting on pounds.

1. Custom-blend. Buy plain yogurt, add your favorite fruit, and sweeten to taste. A teaspoon of honey adds flavor and 24 calories. Two tablespoons of unsweetened applesauce has only about 12 calories, not to mention trace amounts of vitamins and minerals.

2. Go halfsies. Combine your favorite fruit-flavored yogurt with an equal amount of plain yogurt to lighten the calorie (and sugar) load.

3. Create "grate" tastes. Capture the fiber and flavor of fresh fruit in every bite. Start with 1 cup plain fat-free or low-fat yogurt. Using the large holes of a box grater, shred fresh peaches, pears, or apples into the yogurt, making sure to catch the juices. Drizzle with maple syrup for an extra hit of flavor.

4. Make a blender-free smoothie. Got a reusable water bottle or glass jar? Scoop in 8 ounces plain nonfat yogurt, and top with 2 ounces ice-cold fruit, tomato, or carrot juice. Shake and go.

5. Try savory. Plain yogurt complements the flavor of veggies, especially cucumbers, tomatoes, greens, and beets. Dollop a big spoonful on your next salad or plate of steamed vegetables. Or fill a blender with 1 cup yogurt and 1 cup raw vegetables (such as red bell peppers and cucumbers) for a quick serving of chilled soup. ■

Go <u>Nuts</u> for Butters

A wide variety of new nut spreads may give your metabolism a lift.

BY WAYNE KALYN

If you're one of the millions who are cutting back on carbs and pumping up the protein, you may have already put peanut butter back on your grocery list (sans jelly, of course). This childhood staple supplies as much as 8 grams of protein in a 2-tablespoon serving and only 6 to 8 grams of carbohydrates—making it an ideal food for anyone who's living a lower carb lifestyle.

It's not just peanut butter that deserves a spot in your pantry. Spreads made from almonds, cashews, soy nuts (roasted soybeans), and sesame seeds can help people seeking healthy sources of protein add a little diversity to their diets. "Nuts and nut butters are unique packages of nutrients that work together in very beneficial ways," says Richard Mattes, Ph.D., professor of food and nutrition at Purdue University and author of several studies on nuts.

Peanut butter is rich in monounsaturated and polyunsaturated fats; it also contains vitamin E, the phytochemical resveratrol (the same compound found in red wine), the amino acid arginine, and fiber, among other nutrients. Experts believe the synergy of these nutritional all-stars provides the health benefits documented in many studies, from contributing to weight loss to lowering the risks of Type 2

diabetes and heart disease. Although the research to date has focused on peanuts, such nuts as almonds and pecans may confer similar benefits. In fact, the U.S. Food and Drug Administration has made the heart disease connection official by now allowing purveyors of almonds, hazelnuts, pistachios, walnuts, and pecans, as well as spreads made from them, to claim on their labels that eating 1½ ounces per day of most nuts may reduce the risk of heart disease.

The heart-health bonus, the theory goes, stems from the good monounsaturated and polyunsaturated fats in nuts, Mattes says. But other substances also contribute, helping lower triglycerides and LDL cholesterol without decreasing healthy HDL.

And while it may seem contradictory that high-fat nut butters can help you stay trim (they contain between 7 and 9 grams of total fat per tablespoon), studies suggest they can do just that. People who eat nuts or nut spreads on most days consume less during the day, Mattes says. There's also evidence that regular nut consumption elevates your resting metabolic rate, increasing the number of calories you burn.

Despite the health benefits of nut butters, many people who reject the low-carb trend are hesitant to add such fatty items to their shopping lists. As a result, manufacturers have churned out a few lower fat, lower sugar versions of peanut butter in particular, although these aren't necessarily better. Reduced-Fat Skippy, for instance, contains 5 fewer grams total fat than regular Skippy but 2 grams more

sugar and 8 grams more carbs. Simply Jif has 1 gram less sugar and half the sodium of its regular counterpart but doesn't lose any of the fat.

No matter which product you choose, look for a spread with few ingredients on the label, says

How the Spreads Stack Up

All nut butters contain about the same amount of calories and fat, but each has different levels of other key nutrients and a unique nutritional portfolio. This nut-by-nut profile compares five popular butters, their health benefits, and ways you can incorporate them into your diet. (Nutritional values based on a 2-tablespoon [1-ounce] serving.)

BUTTER/NUTRITIONAL PROFILE	WHAT'S GOOD ABOUT IT	HOW TO CHOOSE AND USE
PEANUT 7 grams of protein (only soy-nut butter is higher), 16 grams of total fat, 3 grams of saturated fat	Contains the most niacin, a B vitamin that may help reduce cholesterol and blood pressure. Is a good source of heart-healthy folate and magnesium, which helps you maintain strong bones and regulates blood pressure.	Natural brands tend to be darkest and have the richest flavor. Mix with chili powder, Cajun seasoning, tomato paste, milk, and water to make a sauce for grilled chicken; blend into salad dressings; or add to quick breads.
ALMOND 5 grams of protein, 20 grams of total fat, 1.8 grams of saturated fat	Has more vitamin E, which is good for the heart, and bone-strengthening calcium than any other nut. A study published in summer 2003 in *The Journal of the American Medical Association* showed that a diet rich in soluble fiber, including almonds, reduced cholesterol as effectively as statin drugs.	Varieties made from unblanched almonds (with skins) are darker and contain more health-promoting flavonoids than butters made from blanched nuts. Spread 1 tablespoon on a toasted raisin bagel, and top with apple slices; or substitute for peanut butter in cookie recipes.
CASHEW 5.6 grams of protein, 16 grams of total fat, 3 grams of saturated fat	Is a good source of iron—great news for vegetarians and premenopausal women, who often run low. Also is high in zinc, which promotes immune function, and in copper, which plays a role in iron metabolism.	Is creamier and slightly sweeter than peanut and almond butters. Combine cashew butter with coconut milk and chile-garlic sauce to make a tasty dip for chicken kebabs.
SOY NUT 8 grams of protein, 11 grams of total fat, 1.5 grams of saturated fat	Soy isoflavones may lower cholesterol; they also reduce the risk of bone loss and lower blood pressure in postmenopausal women. New research suggests that young women who eat soy may reduce their breast-cancer risk.	Made from dry-roasted soybeans, soy-nut butter has a slightly gritty texture. Look for unsweetened brands. Mix a small amount with orange juice, banana, and yogurt for a protein smoothie.
SESAME SEED 5 grams of protein, 16 grams of total fat, 2 grams of saturated fat	Sesame-seed butter (made with unhulled seeds) and tahini (made with hulled seeds) are rich in phosphorus, calcium, and magnesium, which are all critical to bone health. Provides more than 15 percent of your recommended daily iron.	Is best used in cooking instead of as a spread. To make hummus, mash tahini with chickpeas, lemon juice, garlic, and olive oil. Blend sesame-seed butter with vegetable oil and soy sauce for a tangy salad dressing.

Melissa Stevens Ohlson, M.S., R.D., a nutrition consultant at the Cleveland Clinic Foundation. Natural varieties, in which the oil separates from the butter, usually contain just the nut and a little salt, and are a bit healthier than types with added sugars and oils. Organic butters are perhaps the best choices because they contain minimal levels of pesticides as well. If the layer of oil on top is unappealing to you, pouring off a little won't compromise the flavor or texture.

Smooth, creamy brands—such as Skippy, Jif, and Peter Pan—stay that way because unhealthy hydrogenated fats have been added to keep butter and oil blended. Still, two studies indicate that the amounts of these trans fats are negligible, Ohlson says. If Skippy is your favorite, the benefits of eating it far outweigh those of avoiding nut butter altogether.

A wide range of natural nut butters populates supermarket shelves these days. So if you're in a peanut rut, pique your palate with cashew, almond, and sesame-seed varieties. And think beyond the PB&J sandwich. These creamy spreads can add flavor to muffins, sauces, marinades, salad dressings, even cookies and smoothies. ■

Wayne Kalyn's writing on health and nutrition has been nominated for a James Beard Award.

Q + A

Safety First for Peanut Allergies

I am allergic to peanuts, can I eat soy nuts?

Probably. Even though both of these crunchy snacks are known as "nuts," soy nuts are actually legumes, such as peas and beans. While people allergic to one nut are often also allergic to another, a recent study found that the same rule does not necessarily apply to legumes. Nonetheless, it's best to have an allergy test done; that should settle the question.

Nuts: The New Diet Food?

Do nuts make you fat? Not according to a mounting body of evidence. Scientists at Purdue University, building on earlier research, recently found that people who ate 500 calories' worth of peanuts daily for eight weeks (about 100 nuts per day) didn't gain weight. The researchers think that the nuts' protein and unsaturated fat may help burn calories and keep you full, making weight control easier.

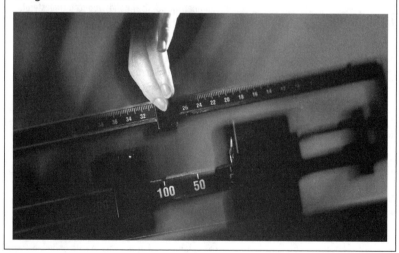

Why You Shouldn't Ban Butter from Your Child's Diet

Butter is no health food. Eat too much, and you increase your risk of obesity, which may lead to heart disease, diabetes, even cancer. But would you believe that butter may protect preschoolers from asthma? Dutch researchers recently analyzed the diets of nearly three thousand 2-year-olds and then checked to see how many had asthma at age 3. Only 1.5 percent of the kids who ate butter every day became asthmatic, compared with 5.1 percent of those who didn't eat it as frequently. Asthma was less common in those who regularly consumed whole milk, too. The authors of the study, which was published in the journal *Thorax,* speculate that the fatty acids, vitamins, and minerals in milk fat may help keep the immune system healthy.

Many pediatricians already recommend whole milk for kids under 2; tots need fat for their brains and central nervous systems. After that, lower fat milk is recommended so kids don't get doughy. Is it time to add butter to the recommended list? "It's going to take several more studies before we jump on board," says Kathleen Sheerin, M.D., a spokeswoman for the American Academy of Allergy, Asthma and Immunology. The study authors agree. But maybe now you'll feel better about making those delightfully buttery cookies.

Attention Fish-Lovers: Remember to Check Your Mercury Intake

If fish is a regular part of your diet, you may be concerned about how much mercury you're consuming. That's especially true in light of the latest warning from the U.S. Food and Drug Administration and Environmental Protection Agency (EPA) advising women in their childbearing years to eat no more than 12 ounces of seafood per week and to vary the type they eat. Log on to www.gotmercury.org, enter your weight and the amount and type of fish you ate over the previous week, and the calculator will tell you whether you're over the EPA's designated safe limit. If you are, cut back by eating fish lower in mercury, such as catfish or canned light tuna.

Drink Milk to Stop Travelers' Trots

Scientists in the Netherlands added 1,100 milligrams of calcium (that's about 4 cups of 1-percent milk) to the daily diets of 32 healthy volunteers and, 10 days later, infected them with a type of bacteria that commonly causes travelers' diarrhea. Members of that group recovered one day earlier than participants who didn't get the additional calcium. (Taking a supplement of the mineral may yield the same effect.) Of course, prevention is the ultimate way to keep sickness at bay: When you're in doubt, avoid eating suspicious foods in the first place.

Time to Change Your Cooking Oil

Discover why alternative oils—such as sesame, flax, and grapeseed—may be worth a drizzle.

BY KERRI CONAN

Olive oil has long enjoyed a place of honor at the dinner table, not only for its nutritional virtues, but also for the fruity flavor it adds to salads, marinades, and sautés. Lately, though, other oils seem to be stealing some of its thunder.

Take sesame oil, for instance. Early research by the American Heart Association (AHA) suggests that it's good for your heart, helps lower blood pressure to the point of reducing patients' dependence on medication, and can control diabetes. But using this toasty Asian oil in the kitchen isn't as simple as swapping it for your extra-virgin (as we heard one TV reporter suggest in her coverage of the AHA study). Sauté a chicken breast in it, and you'll end up with flavor so powerful that you'll be calling for Chinese takeout instead.

The sesame-oil study is just part of a growing body of research suggesting that olive oil isn't the only healthy choice on supermarket shelves. Oils made from grapeseeds, flaxseeds, peanuts, and tree nuts (such as almonds and walnuts) all have their own benefits. Is it time for you to change your oil, then?

While health experts aren't advising that you abandon the extra-virgin just yet, they say you'll get the biggest nutritional bang from consuming a variety of oils. The ultimate goal, then, both for your well-being and your palate? A combination of monounsaturated fats—offered by olive, canola, and peanut oils—and polyunsaturated fats, such as those in soybean, walnut, and grapeseed oils, according to Christine Pelkman, Ph.D., assistant professor of nutrition at the State University of New York at Buffalo.

We probably don't have to remind you why we've been dipping into the olive oil more frequently for the last decade or so. A quick summary: Research shows that it helps shore up the immune system and contains a wider range of cancer-fighting antioxidants than other oils. Its monounsaturated fat has also been shown to increase blood levels of

The vibrant flavors in these oils might lift you out of the valley of ho-hum vinaigrette salad dressings, giving you a tasty reason to keep up your vegetable consumption.

beneficial HDL cholesterol and decrease dangerous LDL. Then there's the practical side—a good extra-virgin oil from California or Greece adds a unique zest to fresh field greens or a bowl of pasta.

According to Pelkman, your body uses fatty acids from both mono- and polyunsaturated oils to maintain optimal health. "Different fats are metabolized in different ways," she adds, "and scientists are looking at how they affect all sorts of issues, from lowering cholesterol to their impact on blood clotting and inflammation in the body."

There are practical advantages to experimenting with these oils, too. Their vibrant, interesting flavors, for instance, might just lift you out of a vinaigrette valley of ho-hum salad dressings, giving you a tasty reason to keep up your vegetable consumption. That means you'll probably also use less of your favorite oil, a good thing no matter how healthy it is. After all, 1 tablespoon contains 120 calories.

So are you ready to get cooking with some of these newer, healthier oils? Before you do, keep in mind that it's not exactly foolproof—unless you have a cheat sheet. Here's a rundown of five of the most promising kinds, their taste profiles, and ways you can use them in everyday foods and recipes.

FLAXSEED OIL

While salmon and mackerel are the most abundant sources of omega-3s, flaxseed oil provides the highest concentration of these fats of any nonfish food. Omega-3s have been garnering plenty of attention recently for their potential roles in helping fight cancer and improve memory. Columbia University researchers, with backing from the National Institutes of Health, are even looking into flaxseed's potential to protect postmenopausal bone and heart health, as well as reduce breast-cancer risk.

Highly perishable, flaxseed oil is usually found in the refrigerated sections of health-food stores and is

syrupy in consistency, especially when chilled. It has a strong bitter-apple flavor that might take some getting used to. Use it only in salad dressings, chilled sauces, or other dishes that you don't have to put on the stove or in the oven, because heat destroys the omega-3s particular to this oil (heat does not affect the omega-3s in salmon, though).

> Use flaxseed oil in chilled recipes, such as salad dressings and refrigerated sauces; if you heat flaxseed oil, the omega-3s in it are destroyed.

Recipe idea: You can create a lively vinaigrette by whisking 1 teaspoon flaxseed oil with 2 tablespoons frozen apple-juice concentrate (the sweetness of the juice helps temper the bitterness of the oil). Stir in ½ teaspoon Dijon mustard and a few grinds of fresh black pepper. Toss with greens, or pour over grilled pork tenderloin.

SESAME OIL

A condiment and a cooking oil in one, sesame oil—available in raw, toasted, and even seasoned versions—delivers a characteristic tang to Asian dishes. While researchers study the benefits of its antioxidants, the oil's high levels of phytosterols may prove to be even more significant. These are the same plant compounds that the federal government's National Cholesterol Education Panel recommended in 2001 as a way to help lower cholesterol.

Generally, the darker the oil, the richer and nuttier its flavor. This versatile ingredient also works well as a component of dipping sauces; a dressing for slaws and salads; or a seasoning for just-cooked foods, such as soups, steamed fish, poultry, and stir-fries. Use it only with dishes requiring low heat, such as simmered sauces or slowly glazed vegetables.

Recipe idea: Steam some fish fillets with a sprinkling of fresh minced ginger and garlic. While it's cooking, whisk together a quick sauce of equal parts sesame oil, soy, rice-wine vinegar, honey, and water. (Use 1 teaspoon of each ingredient for every fillet.) Pour the sauce over the fish just before serving.

PEANUT OIL

Perhaps there's a good reason that Mr. Peanut has been smiling down from the cooking-oil shelf at your local supermarket all these years. Peanut oil is not only high in monounsaturated fat and vitamin E, but also it's low in saturated fat (2.5 grams per tablespoon). A recent study suggests that dieters on a moderate-fat regimen that includes peanuts and peanut oil maintain better blood-lipid levels than those who follow a low-fat diet.

Refined peanut oils like the type on most supermarket shelves can be used for popping popcorn, frying, roasting, grilling, and sautéing. Unrefined oils can be used in sauces that require low to medium heat or in salad dressings and marinades that require no cooking.

Recipe idea: Cut up carrots, green beans, peas, cabbage, or beets; place in skillet, and add a drizzle of oil. Dust with brown sugar, and cover; cook over low heat, shaking pan frequently. When vegetables are crisp-tender, remove cover and continue cooking 1 or 2 minutes more or until vegetables are shiny and golden.

NUT OILS

Just like their sources, nut oils have unique nutritional profiles. Almond oil, for example, is high in vitamin E, while walnut oil contains heart-healthy levels of omega-3 fatty acids. Both oils are also good sources of phytosterols; each lends a mild, nutty flavor to foods.

You can cook and even bake with refined nut oils, which can withstand temperatures of up to 350° without smoking or losing their nutritional benefits. (Substitute equal amounts of refined almond or walnut oil for all or part of the butter in your favorite cake and cookie recipes, or use them in baking recipes that call for vegetable oil.) Unrefined nut oils also make full-bodied vinaigrettes and rich seasonings for cooked vegetables. (Spectrum produces a range of these oils that is available at most natural-foods stores and some supermarkets.)

Recipe idea: Steam or boil potatoes, and toss in a couple of garlic cloves. Drain the mixture well, and mash over low heat with a splash of buttermilk and a drizzle of walnut, almond, or hazelnut oil. Season with salt and black pepper.

GRAPESEED OIL

Ranging in color from pale to bright green, not unlike the finest olive oil, grapeseed oil has its own portfolio of healthful qualities, along with a distinctive flavor. It's high in polyunsaturated fat and also contains phytosterols. And while some other highly polyunsaturated oils—such as corn, safflower, and canola—have gotten a bad rap for lowering HDL levels, grapeseed acts more like olive oil, raising HDL and lowering LDL.

Grapeseed oil acts like olive oil by raising HDL (good cholesterol) and lowering LDL (bad cholesterol).

The taste is pleasantly tart but not overly bitter. Use in marinades, sauces, dressings, and stir-fries, or for pan-frying or roasting.

Recipe idea: Make a rub for meat and poultry by starting with your favorite Southwestern or Cajun spice blend. For every 2 tablespoons of spices, stir in 1 teaspoon grapeseed oil and a squeeze of lime. Spread over chicken breasts, chops, steaks, or hamburgers. Cover and refrigerate for a few hours before grilling or broiling. ■

Kerri Conan is a contributing editor.

Be Choosy About Chocolate

The next time you're ready to yell "chocolate" when someone asks what you want for dessert, contain yourself and say "dark chocolate" instead. Scientists in Italy recently found that eating dark chocolate can raise levels of antioxidants in the blood by 18 percent. But munching on milk chocolate, or downing the dark stuff along with a glass of milk, seems to have zero impact (beyond immense pleasure). These findings appeared in the journal *Nature*.

Antioxidants reputedly help fight off infections and cancer.

They're generally found in fruits and vegetables, as well as in all forms of chocolate. But proteins in milk, the researchers think, may bind to the antioxidants in chocolate and prevent your body from getting at them.

Dark chocolate also appears to slightly raise good cholesterol, or HDL, and slow down the toxic effects of bad cholesterol, or LDL. But its perks are not a license to binge. To get the same antioxidant-boosting benefit achieved by the people in the study, you'd have to eat the equivalent of 2 1/2 regular-size

chocolate bars. That amounts to 25 percent of a typical day's calories and includes 33 grams of waist-ballooning fat and 50 grams of cavity-producing sugar, the upper limit for daily consumption suggested by the National Academy of Sciences.

"Chocolate cannot replace antioxidants from fruits and vegetables," says lead study author Mauro Serafini, Ph.D., a scientist at Italy's National Institute for Food and Nutrition Research in Rome. "Those are the real health foods."

Meat's Link to Colon Cancer: A Whopper or the Real Deal?

Don't you hate the pang of regret that comes with giving in to a craving for an artery-clogging burger? Here's a reason to dispense with some of that greasy guilt: Researchers at the National Cancer Institute recently found that women who ate the equivalent of one large burger a day were no more likely to get colon cancer than those who ate less than 1 ounce meat daily.

Andrew Flood, Ph.D., and his colleagues asked more than forty-five thousand women, most over age 50, how often they ate meat and then tracked them for an average of 8 1/2 years.

Neither red meat nor processed types, such as deli ham or hot dogs, increased colon-cancer risk. "There's not a large body of evidence about meat and colon cancer," Flood notes. "Most published studies have shown no significant link."

Still, the American Institute for Cancer Research recently declared that meat and fat are "probable" factors in colon-cancer risk. So who's right? It's not clear yet.

Maybe how you cook your burgers makes a difference. Lesley Butler, Ph.D., an assistant professor of epidemiology and preventive medicine at

the University of California, Davis, recently found that people who ate well-done and panfried red meats were more likely to get colon cancer than those who ate baked, broiled, and less-done meats. The reason? Cooking meat longer and at higher temperatures boosts the formation of compounds that may cause cancer, Butler says. Marinating meat and flipping it often while cooking lessens that effect by cutting back on charring.

How to Fix a Better
BURGER

A cowgirl shares five healthy recipes (beef and beyond) for a favorite food.

BY PAULA DISBROWE • PHOTOGRAPHY BY RAY KATCHATORIAN

As a chef at a working cattle ranch that doubles as a fitness retreat and spa, I'm not in a position to be beef-phobic. Thank goodness! To the contrary, I think a fat, juicy burger (ideally, the kind that requires two hands to hold) is one of life's great pleasures. For that reason, we fire up our grill several times a week. But a gal—along with our guests—cannot live by beef alone, and I'm crazy for other kinds of burgers, such as those made from turkey, buffalo, or tuna. The following recipes have universal appeal, but with a decidedly Texan flair. Time to head back to the fire—I've got burgers to flip.

Shopping Smarts

Don't go too lean. It's tempting to reach for the leanest ground meats—but resist that impulse. Superlean meats (95- to 99-percent fat-free) don't make for juicy burgers, and they're easily over-cooked. Choose sirloin or ground chuck; they are low in fat, but not too low. For ground turkey, I like the 85-percent lean variety (also labeled "15-percent fat") that's mostly dark meat, but 91- to 93-percent lean mixtures work well, too.

Buy it cold; keep it cold. Choose packages of pre-ground meat that are cold to the touch and tightly wrapped. Make meat (ground or otherwise, and seafood, too) the last thing you put in your grocery cart, and if it's going to take you more than an hour to get home, pack your purchase in an ice chest. Use uncooked ground meat, poultry, or seafood within one to two days.

Check the color. The surfaces of ground beef, buffalo, pork, and poultry should be red, and their interiors should be dark. If the meat is flecked with snowy white spots, it's going to be fatty.

BORDER BURGERS WITH CHIPOTLE KETCHUP

These buffalo burgers (shown at right) eat like beef but with a fraction of the fat. Buffalo is pretty easy to find at supermarket chains nationwide (for more info, see www.greatrangebison.com). If you can't find it, beef is fine; just leave out the cheese to keep the fat in check.

Prep: 10 to 15 minutes • **Cook:** 10 minutes

½ cup ketchup
1 tablespoon finely chopped drained canned chipotle chiles in adobo sauce
1¼ pounds ground buffalo
½ cup (2 ounces) grated Monterey Jack cheese
1 teaspoon dried thyme
½ teaspoon ancho or other chili powder
¼ teaspoon cinnamon
1 clove garlic, minced
¾ teaspoon kosher salt
½ teaspoon freshly ground pepper
Cooking spray
4 hamburger buns, toasted
1 medium red onion, thinly sliced

1. Combine ketchup and chipotle chiles in a small bowl, and mix until well-blended. Set aside.
2. Combine buffalo and next 7 ingredients (buffalo through pepper) in a bowl. Mix gently with a fork, and divide into 4 equal portions, shaping each into a ¾-inch-thick patty. Place patties on a plate lined with plastic wrap; cover and refrigerate until ready to cook.
3. Coat cold grill or skillet lightly with cooking spray; preheat to medium heat.
4. Place patties on grill rack or in skillet; cook 4 minutes. Turn and continue cooking an additional 4 to 5 minutes or until centers are slightly pink.
5. Place burgers on bottom halves of buns; top each with 2 tablespoons chipotle ketchup, onions, and top half of bun. Yield: 4 servings (serving size: 1 burger).

Calories 461 (41% from fat); Fat 20g (sat 8g, mono 7g, poly 2g); Protein 33g; Carbohydrate 34g; Fiber 2g; Cholesterol 76mg; Iron 2mg; Sodium 902 mg; Calcium 182mg

Border Burgers with Chipotle Ketchup

Prep Work

Clean up your act. Wash countertops, cutting boards, and your hands thoroughly with hot soapy water before preparing foods and after handling raw meat or poultry. Also wash any plates or utensils that have come in contact with raw meat before reusing them for cooked foods.

Don't overwork meat. The less you handle it, the more tender and juicy your burger will be.

Use a fork to mix in the seasonings. Don't squeeze the meat with your hands, or the patties will be too dense.

Chill before you grill. Once you've shaped the patties, keep them in the fridge until you're ready to cook. This will help protect you from foodborne illnesses. Plus, in the case of more-fragile seafood patties, such as our tuna burgers, chilling will keep them from falling apart.

TURKEY BURGERS WITH GRILLED TOMATOES

Using 85-percent lean ground turkey ensures that these burgers are satisfying yet still virtuous.

Prep: 15 to 20 minutes • **Cook:** 15 minutes

¼ cup low-fat mayonnaise
½ teaspoon grated lemon rind
1¼ pounds 85%-lean ground turkey
1½ tablespoons chopped fresh marjoram
1 tablespoon chopped Italian parsley
2 green onions, finely chopped
½ teaspoon crushed red pepper
1 garlic clove, finely minced
1 teaspoon kosher salt
½ teaspoon freshly ground black pepper
Cooking spray
4 (¼-inch-thick) slices tomato
8 slices ciabatta bread or 4 whole-wheat English muffins, toasted
8 thin slices avocado
4 lettuce leaves

1. Combine mayonnaise and lemon rind in a small bowl, stirring well with a whisk. Cover and refrigerate.
2. Combine turkey and next 7 ingredients (turkey through pepper) gently with a fork until well-blended. Divide into 4 equal portions, shaping each into a ¾-inch-thick patty. Place patties on plate lined with plastic wrap; cover and refrigerate until ready to cook.
3. Coat cold grill or skillet lightly with cooking spray; preheat to medium heat.
4. Place patties on grill rack or in skillet; cook 6 minutes. Turn and cook an additional 5 to 6 minutes. Remove from grill or skillet; keep warm.
5. Place tomato slices on grill rack or in skillet; cook 1 to 2 minutes until lightly charred. Remove from grill or skillet using a metal spatula.

6. Place burgers on 4 ciabatta slices. Top each with a grilled tomato slice, 1 tablespoon mayonnaise mixture, 2 avocado slices, lettuce, and a ciabatta slice. Yield: 4 servings (serving size: 1 burger).

Calories 475 (44% from fat); Fat 24g (sat 4g, mono 10g, poly 6g); Protein 35g; Carbohydrate 34g; Fiber 7g; Cholesterol 108mg; Iron 5mg; Sodium 942mg; Calcium 233mg

CHUCK WAGON BURGERS WITH GREEN CHILES

Our guests at the ranch eat light at breakfast and lunch so that they can splurge on these hearty burgers. A blend of sirloin and chuck creates the meatiest flavor around. Recent health scares about mad cow disease have many consumers reaching for organic or hormone-free beef; both work equally well in this recipe.

Prep: 5 to 10 minutes • **Cook:** 15 minutes

¾ pound ground sirloin
½ pound ground chuck
3 tablespoons canned chopped green chiles (such as Ortega)
½ teaspoon ground cumin
1 teaspoon kosher salt
½ teaspoon freshly ground black pepper
Cooking spray
1 large sweet onion, cut into ¼-inch-thick slices
4 hamburger buns
¼ cup barbecue sauce (such as Stubb's)

1. Combine first 6 ingredients in a large bowl. Mix meat mixture gently with a fork until well-blended. Divide into 4 equal portions, shaping each into a ¾-inch-thick patty. Place patties on a plate lined with plastic wrap; cover and refrigerate until ready to cook.
2. Coat cold grill or skillet lightly with cooking spray, and preheat to medium-high heat.

3. Place patties on grill rack or in skillet; cook 6 minutes. Turn and cook an additional 7 to 8 minutes.

4. Place onion slices on grill rack or in skillet, and cook 2 to 3 minutes over medium-high heat or until charred and softened, turning once halfway through cooking time.

5. Place burgers on bottom halves of buns; top each with 1 tablespoon barbecue sauce, onions, and top half of bun. Yield: 4 servings (serving size: 1 burger).

Calories 354 (33% from fat); Fat 13g (sat 5g, mono 5g, poly 1g); Protein 30g; Carbohydrate 28g; Fiber 2g; Cholesterol 76mg; Iron 5mg; Sodium 682mg; Calcium 83mg

TUNA BURGERS WITH CILANTRO MAYONNAISE

The best way to make this burger is to use fresh fish—canned won't cut it. Chill the tuna, cutting board, and knife for 30 minutes before chopping to keep the meat from becoming mushy.

Prep: 10 to 15 minutes • **Cook:** 15 minutes

¼ cup low-fat mayonnaise
1 tablespoon chopped fresh cilantro
1¼ pounds fresh tuna
½ jalapeño pepper, stemmed, seeded, and minced
1 teaspoon grated fresh ginger
1 teaspoon toasted sesame oil
2 tablespoons vegetable oil
1 teaspoon kosher salt
½ teaspoon freshly ground black pepper
Cooking spray
4 hamburger buns, toasted
1 cored and sliced yellow tomato
1 Kirby cucumber, thinly sliced

1. Combine mayonnaise and cilantro; cover and refrigerate.

2. Slice tuna into thin matchsticks. Cut the matchsticks into cubes, and continue chopping until the pieces are roughly ⅛-inch square.

3. Mix tuna, jalapeño, and next 5 ingredients (through black pepper) gently with a fork until well-blended. Divide into 4 portions, shaping each into a ¾-inch-thick patty. Place patties on plate lined with plastic wrap; cover and refrigerate for 1 to 3 hours.

4. Coat cold grill or skillet lightly with cooking spray; preheat to medium heat.

5. Cook patties 4 minutes. Turn and cook an additional 3 to 4 minutes until centers are slightly pink (do not overcook). Plate burgers; keep warm.

6. Place burgers on bottom halves of buns; top each with cilantro mayonnaise, tomato, cucumber, and top half of bun. Yield: 4 servings (serving size: 1 burger).

Calories 466 (43% from fat); Fat 22g (sat 3g, mono 9g, poly 8g); Protein 39g; Carbohydrate 28g; Fiber 2g; Cholesterol 59mg; Iron 4mg; Sodium 679mg; Calcium 96mg

Grilling Guidance

Preheat your grill. When it's good and hot, scrub it with a stiff wire brush; then turn off heat, let grill cool, coat the grate with cooking spray, and turn on heat again. The burgers will be less likely to stick, and they'll come out with those great-looking grill marks.

Cook meat completely. To protect yourself against foodborne illnesses, ground beef and game should be cooked to an internal temperature of 160 degrees (juices should run clear at this point); poultry should be cooked to 165 degrees. While the U.S. Food and Drug Administration suggests cooking fish patties, such as our tuna burgers (recipe at left), to 155 degrees, some chefs and restaurateurs say it's OK to undercook them slightly if the fish is top-grade and handled correctly.

Save it safely. Refrigerate leftovers immediately after cooking.

MEATY MUSHROOM BURGERS WITH NUTTY CHEESE SPREAD

These satisfying meatless burgers are put together like Oreos: Grilled portobello mushrooms sandwich a creamy filling. Chill the filling so it won't ooze out during baking.

Prep: 1 hour, 5 minutes • **Cook:** 15 minutes

3	ounces Neufchâtel cheese, softened
¼	cup freshly grated Parmesan cheese
2	green onions, finely chopped
2	tablespoons toasted sunflower seeds
1½	tablespoons chopped fresh basil
1½	tablespoons soy sauce
2	tablespoons sherry vinegar
½	teaspoon kosher salt
¼	teaspoon freshly ground black pepper
8	medium portobello mushroom caps

Cooking spray

6 cups mixed salad greens

1. Mix first 5 ingredients well with a fork; cover and chill 1 hour.
2. Combine soy sauce, vinegar, salt, and pepper. Place mushrooms, gill sides up, on a baking sheet; drizzle evenly with soy sauce mixture. Marinate 1 hour.
3. Coat cold grill lightly with cooking spray; preheat grill to medium-high heat (or oven to "broil").
4. Place mushrooms, gill sides down, on grill rack or broiler pan; cook 5 minutes. Remove mushrooms from grill rack or broiler pan; top each with 1 tablespoon of cheese mixture. Press 2 mushrooms together gently, filled sides touching. Repeat procedure with remaining mushrooms.
5. Preheat oven (or reduce heat if oven used for broiling) to 350°.
6. Bake mushroom "sandwiches" on a nonstick baking sheet at 350° for 8 to 10 minutes or until cheese mixture begins to melt.
7. Divide salad greens evenly among 4 plates; top

with mushroom "sandwiches." Yield: 4 servings (serving size: 1 burger with greens).

Calories 177 (43% from fat); Fat 9g (sat 4g, mono 2g, poly 2g); Protein 11g; Carbohydrate 15g; Fiber 5g; Cholesterol 21mg; Iron 3mg; Sodium 807mg; Calcium 142mg

Roast potato wedges drizzled with olive oil, kosher salt, freshly ground pepper, and dried thyme at 400° for 20 to 25 minutes (turn once at the halfway point). Yum!

About the Ranch

Sprawled over 5,250 acres, Hart & Hind Fitness Ranch boasts 16 miles of hiking trails that wind through canyons and creeks in Rio Frio, Texas (about 170 miles east of Austin and 95 miles from San Antonio). Guests begin their week-long retreats by meeting with the ranch's fitness director, who helps them set personalized goals and physical challenges for their stay; options include yoga, horseback riding, and, of course, hiking. Guests can also sign up for cooking classes with cowgirl chef Paula Disbrowe or a bread-making class with David Norman, the ranch's manager and an acclaimed baker (as well as Paula's fiancé). For details, call 866-868-1264 or log on to www.hartandhind.com.

Get the Inside Scoop on
Faux Sugar

Are sugar substitutes sweet deals for carb cutters, or are they diet saboteurs?

BY AMY YOUNG

No matter how dedicated or enthusiastic she might be at the outset, nearly every dieter ends up looking for that loophole—a way out, a foolproof plan for having her cake (literally) and eating it, too. When calorie counting was all the rage, we mobilized our "just a sliver" strategy. When fat was demonized, we learned to tolerate the gumminess of fat-free fare. But as weight-loss gurus and doctors alike have turned an extracritical eye toward carbohydrates—low or no-fiber starches and sugary snacks in particular—well, we were stumped. What good was getting the green light on fatty foods, such as nuts, olive oil, cheeses, even the occasional steak, when we couldn't indulge in dessert?

The answer, some carb counters think, may be artificial sweeteners. They've been around, it seems, forever—in diet sodas, no-calorie juices, the ubiquitous pink-and-blue packets on restaurant tables. But with the surge of interest in carb cutting and the relatively recent introduction of Splenda, a sweetener that claims to be more versatile in the kitchen than its predecessors, these sugar subs have taken on new life. Could they be the loophole Atkins devotees are looking for?

Almost all the artificial sweeteners on the market are low-carb—they won't send your pancreas into overdrive and your blood sugar skyrocketing—but it's one of the newest products in the category, sucralose, that's generating the most excitement in the food world. First sold in the United States in 2000 as Splenda, the little yellow packets seemed like just another way to spike your coffee without paying the price. But in the last couple of years, the number of Splenda-sweetened products has exploded. Besides soda, you can find it in hot cocoa mix, syrup, pie filling, applesauce, and ice cream.

What sets Splenda apart, foodies say, is that it retains its sweetness under high heat better than other artificial sweeteners. Because you can buy Splenda in bulk, as you would regular sugar or flour, you can cook and bake with it—throwing open the doors to a delectable new world of culinary options that extends beyond the typical low-cal cold-dessert staples, such as pudding and cheesecake.

> In the last couple of years, the number of Splenda-sweetened products has exploded. Besides soda, you can find it in hot cocoa mix, syrup, pie filling, applesauce, and ice cream.

"It's a very stable ingredient," says John Iachetti, executive chef at New York's Regency hotel, which has been the hotbed for caffeine-infused power breakfasts since Sweet 'N Low was the only option. Iachetti became intrigued with Splenda when he noticed empty packets that had been left on tables by guests who had brought their own stashes. So he began experimenting. Now he serves it up himself in such treats as lemon meringues and *panna cotta*.

And the rest of America appears to be taking Iachetti's cue. In 2003, sales of low-calorie sweeteners soared an estimated 20 percent, according to independent research group Information Resources; Splenda accounted for 97 percent of the dollar growth in the category.

Are sugar substitutes the diet loophole of the day? To find out, we've zeroed in on the claims that seem too good to be true—and what they mean for your health.

claim #1
FAUX SUGARS ARE SAFE.

If *safe* means not causing disease or death, artificial sweeteners are safe for most people. The older sweeteners—aspartame and saccharin—have had a rocky past when it comes to safety rumors, though they now seem to be in the clear. It is widely recognized that the studies at the root of the cancer scares of the early '80s were poorly designed and that humans would have to consume outrageous amounts to reach levels that were toxic to laboratory rats. "Anything taken to the extreme could cause cancer," points out Jean Weese, Ph.D., associate professor of nutrition and food science at Auburn University in Alabama. According to the U.S. Food and Drug Administration, a 150-pound adult can drink as many as 20 (12-ounce) aspartame-infused sodas a day and still be within what officials deem the "acceptable daily intake." (For a 50-pound child, that's six sodas.)

That doesn't mean everyone is free to partake. Aspartame must be used sparingly by people with phenylketonuria, a rare disease that prevents a component of the artificial sweetener from being metabolized. And those who are prone to migraines might be well-advised to stay away, too. The link between food and the condition is controversial, but some doctors believe migraine sufferers may lack an enzyme to digest aspartame properly.

So far, sucralose, which still has a relatively young history compared with other sweeteners, has not been caught up in the swirl of any health-scare storm. But just because it's safe doesn't mean it's healthy. With sugar stand-ins popping up in more products on grocery-store shelves and restaurant menus, some nutritionists fear that people may be more tempted than ever before to replace healthy snacks with junk food. After all, part of the nation's obesity crisis stems not only from a diet that's laden with sugar (Americans are still eating on average 2½ times as much added sugar as the Food Pyramid calls for), but also from one that is bereft of such nutrient-rich foods as fruits and vegetables. "I think sweeteners are great for people who have to be careful, like diabetics," says Samantha Heller, M.S., R.D., senior clinical nutritionist at New York University Medical Center. "But for everyone else, I think it's a good idea to moderate intake of both artificial sweeteners and real sweeteners. People should be focusing on eating a more balanced diet."

claim #2
IT TASTES JUST LIKE SUGAR.

That depends on who's doing the tasting. Compared with the real thing, "artificial sweeteners appear to be simpler molecules with regard to the number of sites on them capable of stimulating sweet receptors, so they may stimulate only a subset of the receptors stimulated by sugar," explains Linda Bartoshuk, Ph.D., an experimental psychologist and taste-perception specialist at Yale University School of Medicine. Some people won't notice the difference, but others are genetically programmed to experience taste much more intensely—particularly bitter notes, including those associated with the aftertaste of faux sugars. Those people are referred to as supertasters, Bartoshuk says.

So if the flavor of a sweetener doesn't sit well on your tongue, you'll probably never fool yourself into thinking it's just as tasty as sugar. Some people with especially sensitive palates find man-made sweeteners metallic, cloying, or bitter, forcing those folks to reach for plain water when regular soda isn't an option.

Gourmands who use Splenda, though, say they work around those challenges by experimenting. "When sugar hits your tongue, it gives a flavor that pops," explains the Regency's Iachetti. "Artificial sweeteners don't percolate that way. The taste is more mellow." To achieve the lift Splenda desserts might be missing, he gives his pastries a bit of tartness with such fruits as lemon. Gale Gand, executive pastry chef and partner at the acclaimed Chicago restaurant Tru (and a developer of recipes as a paid consultant for Splenda), says she mixes the faux sweetener with brown sugar to get a moister batter for such soft baked goods as muffins and with white sugar for better flavor.

claim #3
SWEETENERS CAN HELP YOU LOSE WEIGHT.

If people existed in a vacuum, this would be true. But they live in a world filled with food options, temptations, excuses to eat whether they're hungry or not. As a result, like the low-carb diet itself, sweeteners are not a foolproof tool for weight loss.

The studies that explore the efficacy of sweeteners as a way to lose weight tend to be short-term and contradictory, their conclusions sketchy. When a group of Danish researchers compared overweight men and women taking sucrose (sugar) supplements with those taking artificial-sweetener supplements for 10 weeks, they found that the fake-sugar group did in fact lose weight, albeit only a small amount (no more than 2.2 pounds). Meanwhile, a study out of Edinburgh, Scotland, concluded that there is no

With sugar stand-ins popping up in more products and restaurant menus, some nutritionists fear that people may be tempted to replace healthy snacks with junk food.

difference between a weight-loss plan that reduces sugar and one that doesn't.

Why don't artificial sweeteners give dieters a clear-cut advantage? The issue isn't calories. There are none (OK, *almost* none—one packet contains less than 1 calorie).

Consider sucralose, for instance: Engineered from a sugar molecule that has had three of its hydroxyl components replaced with chlorine, it's not recognized by the body and, therefore, does not accumulate in it. Even if it did, the flavor is 600 times as intense as that of sugar—so only an infinitesimal amount is needed to sweeten food.

But this hardly gives you permission to indulge with abandon. Dieters learned that lesson from fat-free foods, which cut out the fat calories but loaded up on sugar calories. Even worse, people ate SnackWell's products by the boxful, thinking they were being "good"—only to take in more total calories than if they had just savored a few honest-to-goodness chocolate-chip cookies.

The same caveat goes for low-carb treats. "A low-carb snack is not a free pass to binge—or an excuse to order more dessert for dinner," says David Heber, M.D., Ph.D., director of the Center for Human Nutrition at the University of California at Los Angeles. For instance, if you drank three Snapple a Day Low Carb smoothies at snack time (with 90 calories and 7 grams of sugar each), you'd actually have been better off indulging in a single bottle of the meal-replacement version (210 calories, 36 grams of sugar).

These words of caution all sound elementary, but putting them into practice is not easy. Further, many critics of sugar-free products say that fake sugar can actually cause you to eat more. They say the body simply doesn't know what to do when the brain registers "sweet" but there are no sugar molecules to process. This physiological confusion, the theory goes, might push dieters to cave in to sweet treats (or binge on sugar-free ones). But, again, the proof is sketchy. In a study out of a hospital in Sheffield, England, that examined the habits of women who were described as "fairly diet-conscious," researchers found that consuming diet drinks instead of full-sugar versions did not help participants cut calories; to the contrary, these beverages caused the subjects to indulge in more carbohydrates the following day. In contrast, a recent Columbia University review of studies about the impact of artificial sweeteners on body weight found that sugar substitutes had no effect on cravings whatsoever and actually helped dieters to lose weight.

"So far there's no substantial data," points out Allen S. Levine, Ph.D., a researcher at the University of Minnesota who recently reported on the connection between sugar and cravings in rats in *The American Journal of Clinical Nutrition*. "The problem with the issue of craving is that it brings about the notion of drug addiction. But if you ask the question 'Are we motivated to eat sweets?' then the answer is yes. At the end of a big Thanksgiving meal, you may be satiated, but you still have something sweet. Clearly, you're not doing it for hunger or nutrients—you're doing it for pleasure. We don't have to say that you're craving it, but you're desiring it. We're hardwired to eat sweets."

Which perhaps explains why it can be so hard to eat just one cookie, whether it's baked with artificial sweeteners or not. Choose the one made with real sugar, and the guilt may be enough to fight your urge to overindulge; opt for the fake one, and you might not have it in you to stop at just one or two.

It seems, then, that artificial sweeteners are just like any other diet tool: Because they're not one-size-fits-all, they have to be customized to fit each individual's habits and lifestyle. "Try to learn about which high-carb foods are especially difficult triggers for you, such as cookies, cakes, or muffins," says Heber, whose latest book, *The L.A. Shape Diet*, discusses the role of lean protein sources, fruits, and vegetables in keeping appetites under control. Be vigilant with these foods, whether you are eating the sugar-free versions or not, and then you can indeed have your cake and eat it, too. ■

It seems that we're hardwired to eat sweets, which explains why it's hard to eat just one cookie. If you opt for the cookie made with an artificial sweetner, you still don't have the right to overindulge.

The New Taste of Sugar

Get the skinny on the latest sweet stuff.

BY ALISA BLACKWOOD

Indulging in your favorite cakes and cookies is part of what makes special occasions so sweet. And when you're baking these special treats, granulated white sugar is the only way to go ... or is it? From muscovado brown sugar to honey, there is a growing number of options on grocery-store shelves these days, including natural, organic, and gourmet sugars, as well as alternative sweeteners made from plants and grains. So with the choices moving far beyond what was in your old sugar bowl, how do you decide what's best for your recipes—and your health?

There's a whole new world of granulated sugars available today, with butterscotch and deep molasses flavors.

You might be surprised to learn there's little evidence that moderate amounts of sugar raise your risk of obesity or are more harmful than other foods within the context of a balanced diet, says David Ludwig, M.D., Ph.D., director of the obesity program at Children's Hospital Boston. (Most types of sugar contain about 15 calories per teaspoon.) But remember not to let your craving for sweet snacks replace whole foods, such as fruits, vegetables, nuts, and legumes, Ludwig cautions. Skimp on those, and you'll likely face health problems down the road.

Many health-food advocates prefer such natural sweeteners as raw sugar or honey over the refined white stuff because they contain more nutrients and are less processed. Nutritionists say these options (especially those with high molasses content) sometimes contain small amounts of calcium, potassium, or magnesium, but the amounts aren't that significant.

The desire for natural and organic sugars is part of the overall movement toward foods grown without chemical pesticides or herbicides, says Stephanie Childs, a spokeswoman for the Grocery Manufacturers of America. New products, such as organic powdered or cane sugars, are becoming more available in larger natural-foods chains. Even some mainstream retailers, such as SuperTarget, sell organic sugars. This is good news, but it's important to note that sugarcane and sugar beets, the two sources of all forms of sugar, are not grown with as many fertilizers or pesticides as vegetable crops.

Two primary reasons to choose a specific sugar are its flavor and texture. Nothing works as well as granulated sugar to add volume and help brown cookies and pastries. But there are all kinds of granulated sugars, and it helps to understand the subtle differences among each, says Maggie Powers, M.S., R.D., of the International Diabetes Center at Park Nicollet in Minneapolis. For example, if you're making gingerbread cookies, try replacing the refined brown sugar you normally use with unrefined light brown muscovado sugar; these crystals have a deeper molasses flavor and color. To give cakes, cookies, and fruit pies a different look, sprinkle them with larger turbinado sugar crystals, which will add a noticeable crunch.

Whether you're looking for natural or organic, light or dark, our sugar-shopping guide will give you the scoop on all the new products available, as well as how you can use them to add texture and wonderful flavor to your baking.

SUGARS COMPARED

Unrefined granulated varieties are made from extracted sugarcane or sugar-beet juice, which is evaporated until the sucrose crystallizes; the process helps these sugars retain some or all of their natural molasses coloring and taste, says Margaret Wittenberg, author of *Good Food: The Comprehensive Food and Nutrition Resource* and vice president of marketing and public affairs at Whole Foods Market. The darker the sugar, the more complex its flavor. In comparison, white sugar undergoes a refining process that strips it of its molasses color and flavor. (Regular brown sugar is usually refined white sugar that has been sprayed with molasses to restore these attributes superficially.)

Refined does not mean that a sugar has been bleached or chemically processed, but rather that the natural sucrose has been separated from the sugarcane's plant material, according to Evelyn Brewster, a spokeswoman for the Sugar Association, an industry trade organization. Wittenberg underscores that it's inaccurate to refer to any sugar on the market as "unrefined" or "raw," because the terms generally refer to a product that's not white and is simply less refined than conventional sugar.

The following sugars and sweeteners can be found at specialty stores or in the natural-foods sections of major supermarket chains, such as Wild Oats and Whole Foods Market.

BARLEY-MALT SYRUP
What it is: This product is made from sprouted barley that is dried, soaked in water, and then cooked into a thick liquid. Because it is slowly digested, it won't raise your blood glucose as quickly as table sugar.
Uses: Barley-malt syrup has a strong malt-and-molasses flavor that pairs nicely with ginger, carob, and chocolate; it works well in cookies, too. It can be substituted for sugar cup for cup, as long as the other liquids in the recipe are reduced by ¼ cup.

BROWN-RICE SYRUP
What it is: This unrefined sweetener has a caramel flavor and golden color. It's made by adding a small amount of sprouted barley to cooked brown rice. Naturally occurring enzymes then break down the starches into maltose, glucose, and complex carbohydrates. What's left is strained and then cooked into a syrup. It tastes less sweet and more mellow than honey, corn syrup, or maple syrup. Like barley-malt syrup, brown-rice syrup is absorbed slowly into the bloodstream, making it easily digestible.
Uses: It works best as an ingredient in baked cookies, since they don't need to rise, but not as well in muffins, cakes, and other baked goods. To substitute brown-rice syrup for granular sugar in cookies, follow the same cooking directions as those for barley-malt syrup. You can also use this sweetener in marinades or salad dressings.

DEMERARA
What it is: A coarse, golden sugar made up of sticky crystals that are a bit smaller than turbinado's crystals.
Uses: Demerara dissolves slowly and makes a subtle sweetener for tea, coffee, and hot cereals, or a crunchy topping for cakes and cookies.

GRANULATED CANE JUICE

What it is: Also called whole-cane sugar, this sweetener comes from whole sugarcane that is crushed to extract the juice. The liquid is then rapidly evaporated by heat; fanning it while it's hot removes the moisture quickly and helps transform the juice into granules instead of crystals. This sugar is dark brown, with a buttery natural molasses flavor. It's coarser than refined white sugar, but the granules are small. It is also highly porous (so it dissolves quickly) and adds bulk in baking.

Uses: Try it in recipes calling for brown sugar; you might need to adjust the liquid measurements, though, because this sweetener is not as moist as other brown sugars. Granulated cane juice is particularly good in recipes using chocolate, as well as in barbecue sauces.

HONEY

What it is: This popular sweetener is a mixture of fructose and glucose formed from nectar by an enzyme called invertase, present in the bodies of bees. It has a distinct taste, often with hints of clover, orange, or sage, depending on the source of the nectar. It is 25 to 30 times as sweet as white table sugar. It's also filtered to remove debris; because there is no uniform filtering process, however, honey from a local producer may contain more wax or pollen. While some people are allergic to honey, a pollen allergy shouldn't affect your tolerance for it, says the National Honey Board. Note, though, that children younger than 1 year old should not consume honey, because it may harbor *Clostridium botulinum* spores that can cause infant botulism, a rare but serious disease that attacks a baby's nervous system.

Uses: To incorporate honey into recipes for baked goods, substitute ¾ cup honey for 1 cup white sugar and reduce the other liquids by ¼ cup. Honey can also be used in glazes for meat and fish, or as an emulsifier (in place of oil) in salad dressings. It has 64 calories per tablespoon.

MUSCOVADO

What it is: Muscovado can be either light or very dark brown. The light kind has a butterscotch flavor, while the dark version tastes more like caramelized molasses.

Uses: Substitute light brown muscovado for regular brown sugar in pecan pie or in a baked-ham glaze; or use it to make butterscotch pudding or icings for cakes and cookies. Dark brown muscovado gives a special flavor to many sweets, from mincemeat and plum pudding to gingerbread and chocolate-based recipes, such as fudge.

STEVIA

What it is: Available in both powder and liquid forms, stevia is a natural no-calorie sweetener that's becoming increasingly popular with people who desire (or need) to go sugar-free. It's extracted from the leaves of the stevia plant, which is native to Paraguay; after processing, the extract is 300 times as sweet as white table sugar. To some palates, the sweetener tastes slightly of licorice and leaves a bitter aftertaste.

Uses: Add stevia to drinks and recipes instead of sugar, but you'll probably have to experiment if you want to use it for baking, since it lacks the bulk of sugar and is much sweeter. Stevia has not been approved by the Federal Drug Administration for specific use as a sweetener, but it is sold as a dietary supplement in natural-foods stores.

TURBINADO

What it is: A chunky, light tan sugar that is formed after the first crystallization of sugarcane juice. It has been partially washed to remove some surface molasses and reduce stickiness.

Uses: The larger crystals take longer to dissolve in liquids than fine sugar, but some people enjoy the brown-sugar taste in coffee or tea. It works best as a sweet, decorative topping for muffins or cookies. ■

Alisa Blackwood is Health's *assistant food editor.*

SOUPS
That Soothe

These dishes are true comfort foods that nourish your body, one spoonful at a time.

RECIPES BY CAROL PRAGER • PHOTOGRAPHY BY LEIGH BEISCH

These recipes, geared to those who have little time to stir a pot, may make those chilly days of the winter a bit more tolerable. Except for the chicken noodle, all of these soups can be made vegetarian by substituting an ingredient or two. Serve them as first courses or as one-dish meals with hunks of crusty bread.

Gingery Lentil Soup

GINGERY LENTIL SOUP

Prep: 10 minutes • **Cook:** 35 minutes

2   teaspoons olive oil
3   medium carrots, chopped
1   medium onion, chopped
2   teaspoons grated peeled fresh ginger
1   teaspoon minced garlic
1½ teaspoons curry powder
¼   teaspoon salt
¼   teaspoon freshly ground black pepper
2   (14-ounce) cans fat-free, less-sodium chicken broth, plus enough water to equal 4 cups
1   cup brown lentils, rinsed and drained
1   (14.5-ounce) can diced tomatoes, drained

1. Heat oil in a large saucepan over medium heat. Add carrot and onion; cover and cook 3 minutes or until softened. Stir in ginger and garlic; cook 1 minute. Add curry, salt, and pepper; cook 30 seconds.
2. Stir in diluted broth and lentils; bring to a boil. Reduce heat; simmer, covered, 20 to 25 minutes or until lentils are tender. Stir in tomatoes; cover and simmer 5 minutes. Divide soup evenly among 4 bowls. Yield: 4 servings (serving size: 1½ cups).

Calories 253 (11% from fat); Fat 3g (sat 0g, mono 2g, poly 1g); Cholesterol 0mg; Protein 17g; Carbohydrate 42g; Fiber 15g; Iron 5mg; Sodium 615mg; Calcium 66mg

WILD MUSHROOM–BARLEY SOUP

Prep: 20 minutes • **Cook:** 25 minutes

¼ ounce dried porcini or shiitake mushrooms
1 cup boiling water
1 tablespoon olive oil
1 medium onion, finely chopped
½ cup finely chopped fennel or celery
½ pound cremini or white mushrooms, sliced
1 teaspoon minced garlic
2 teaspoons chopped oregano or thyme
½ teaspoon salt
¼ teaspoon freshly ground black pepper
1 (14-ounce) cans fat-free, less-sodium chicken broth
1 cup chopped seeded tomato
1 tablespoon dry sherry
½ cup uncooked quick-cooking barley

1. Combine porcinis and 1 cup boiling water in a bowl; cover and let stand 20 minutes or until tender. Drain porcinis in a colander over a bowl, reserving liquid. Line a strainer with a paper towel, and pour porcini liquid through strainer; reserve liquid. Rinse porcinis thoroughly; finely chop.
2. Heat oil in a large saucepan over medium heat. Add onion and fennel; cover and cook 5 minutes or until softened. Add creminis, garlic, oregano, salt, and pepper; cook 3 minutes or until creminis release moisture.
3. Stir broth, tomato, sherry, barley, chopped porcinis, and reserved porcini liquid into cremini mixture; bring to a boil. Reduce heat; simmer 10 to 12 minutes or until barley is tender. Divide soup evenly among 4 bowls. Yield: 4 servings (serving size: 1½ cups).

Calories 175 (21% from fat); Fat 4g (sat 1g, mono 3g, poly 1g); Cholesterol 0mg; Protein 8g; Carbohydrate 27g; Fiber 6g; Iron 2mg; Sodium 553mg; Calcium 38mg

GOLDEN POTATO–CAULIFLOWER SOUP

Prep: 15 minutes • **Cook:** 32 minutes

Croutons:
1 teaspoon ground cumin
1 teaspoon olive oil
1 cup cubed French or Italian bread
Soup:
2 teaspoons olive oil
⅓ cup finely chopped shallots
⅓ cup finely chopped celery
2½ cups sliced cauliflower (about ½ small cauliflower)
¾ pound sliced peeled Yukon gold potato
2 (14-ounce) cans fat-free, less-sodium chicken broth
½ teaspoon salt
¼ teaspoon ground red pepper
1 teaspoon lemon juice
2 teaspoons chopped chives (optional)

1. Preheat oven to 350°.
2. To prepare croutons, combine cumin and 1 teaspoon oil in a bowl; add bread cubes, and toss to coat. Spread bread cubes on a baking sheet. Bake at 350° for 10 minutes or until golden. Cool croutons slightly; set aside.
3. To prepare soup, heat 2 teaspoons oil in a large saucepan over medium heat. Add shallots and celery; cover and cook 2 minutes. Stir in cauliflower, potato, broth, salt, and pepper; bring to a boil. Reduce heat, cover, and simmer 15 to 20 minutes or until vegetables are tender. Add lemon juice. Place vegetable mixture, in batches, in a food processor; process until smooth. Divide soup evenly among 4 bowls; serve with croutons, and top with chives, if desired. Yield: 4 servings (serving size: 1½ cups).

Calories 171 (22% from fat); Fat 4g (sat 1g, mono 3g, poly 1g); Cholesterol 0mg; Protein 7g; Carbohydrate 28g; Fiber 4g; Iron 1mg; Sodium 629mg; Calcium 43mg

SMOKY BLACK-BEAN SOUP

Chipotle chili powder is made from
smoked jalapeño peppers.

Prep: 15 minutes • **Cook:** 11 minutes

2 teaspoons olive oil
1 (4-ounce) piece baked ham, diced
1 medium onion, diced
1 medium zucchini, diced
1 teaspoon minced garlic
¼ to ½ teaspoon chipotle chili powder
1 (14-ounce) can fat-free, less-sodium chicken
   broth
2 (15-ounce) cans black beans, rinsed, drained,
   and divided
¼ teaspoon kosher salt
½ cup water
2 tablespoons low-fat sour cream (optional)
2 teaspoons chopped fresh cilantro (optional)

1. Heat olive oil in a large saucepan over medium-
high heat. Add diced ham, and cook 2 minutes or
until lightly browned. Add onion and zucchini;
cover and cook 4 minutes, stirring occasionally. Stir
in minced garlic and chipotle chili powder; cook
30 seconds. Add chicken broth, ½ cup black beans,
and salt.
2. Puree remaining beans with ½ cup water in a
blender until smooth; stir into soup, and bring to
a boil. Reduce heat, and simmer 2 minutes. Divide
soup evenly among 4 bowls. Garnish with sour
cream and cilantro, if desired. Yield: 4 servings
(serving size: 1¼ cups).

Calories 268 (19% from fat); Fat 6g (sat 1g, mono 2g, poly 2g);
Cholesterol 20mg; Protein 19g; Carbohydrate 34g; Fiber 13g;
Iron 5mg; Sodium 1,252mg; Calcium 93mg

CHICKEN-NOODLE SOUP
WITH SPINACH

For the best flavor, use freshly grated nutmeg.

Prep: 10 minutes • **Cook:** 20 minutes

2 teaspoons olive oil
1 teaspoon minced garlic
3 (14-ounce) cans fat-free, less-sodium chicken
   broth
2 skinless, boneless chicken-breast halves
1 (1-inch) cube Parmesan cheese, preferably
   with rind
¼ teaspoon salt
¼ teaspoon freshly ground black pepper
¼ teaspoon grated whole nutmeg
½ cup uncooked tubetti (tiny tube-shaped pasta)
   or other small pasta
1 (5-ounce) package baby spinach
¼ cup shaved fresh Parmesan cheese

1. Heat oil in a large stockpot over medium-low
heat. Add garlic; cook 10 seconds or until fragrant.
Add broth, chicken, Parmesan cube, salt, pepper,
and nutmeg. Bring to a boil; reduce heat to medium,
and simmer 10 minutes. Remove chicken; set aside.
Remove Parmesan cube; discard.
2. Return broth mixture to a boil. Add pasta; simmer 9 minutes or until pasta is tender.
3. Cut chicken-breast halves into thin strips; return
to soup. Stir in spinach, and simmer 1 minute or
until wilted. Divide soup evenly among 4 bowls;
sprinkle with ¼ cup shaved Parmesan cheese. Yield:
4 servings (serving size: 1 cup).

Calories 252 (18% from fat); Fat 5g (sat 2g, mono 2g, poly 0g);
Cholesterol 38mg; Protein 24g; Carbohydrate 27g; Fiber 3g;
Iron 3mg; Sodium 842mg; Calcium 101mg

Spicy Chili-Garlic Sauce

RECIPE BY LORI LONGBOTHAM

What it is: When red chilies reached China about a hundred years ago, cooks almost immediately began using them to make sauces. That idea caught fire across Southeast Asia, setting palates aflame in such places as Indonesia, Korea, Thailand, and Vietnam. The ingredients in chili-garlic sauce tend to vary from country to country and can range from salt or vinegar to ginger or fermented soybeans.

What's so good about it: Red chilies are rich in capsaicin, an antioxidant that gives the pepper its heat; the sauce contains a more concentrated amount than the peppers alone. Plus, there's all that beneficial garlic.

Where to find it: There are usually dozens of pastes and sauces available at Asian markets. You will also find that most grocery stores carry one or two types. There's no need to worry about spoilage—although it may lose some of its heat with age, a jar of chili-garlic sauce will last almost indefinitely in the fridge.

Some ideas: Experiment with chili-garlic sauce in dishes to which you'd normally add crushed red pepper. Or you can try one of these tasty suggestions.
- Spread a small amount thinly and evenly atop grilled eggplant.
- Spice up sautéed vegetables, such as green beans or squash.
- Mix with a little vinegar or lemon juice to marinate chicken or lamb.

CHINESE CHICKEN-NOODLE SOUP

Prep: 10 minutes • **Cook:** 15 minutes

2 (3-ounce) packages ramen noodles, broken into 3-inch lengths
2 teaspoons canola oil
1 tablespoon grated fresh ginger
2 garlic cloves, minced
3 (15.75-ounce) cans low-sodium, fat-free chicken broth
1 tablespoon low-sodium soy sauce
1 teaspoon chili-garlic sauce
2 boneless, skinless chicken-breast halves, thinly sliced
Freshly ground white or black pepper
4 scallions, thinly sliced
2 cups prewashed baby spinach

1. Place noodles (discard seasoning packages) in a bowl; cover with boiling water. Soak 3 minutes; drain under running water. Divide among 4 soup bowls.
2. Heat oil in a saucepan over medium heat. Stir-fry ginger and garlic about 30 seconds. Add broth, soy sauce, chili-garlic sauce, chicken, and pepper to taste; bring to a boil. Reduce heat to low; simmer 5 minutes, or until chicken is done. Remove from heat; stir in scallions. Ladle soup over noodles. Top with ½ cup spinach and chili-garlic sauce to taste. Yield: 4 servings (serving size: 2 cups broth, ½ cup spinach, and ½ cup noodles).

Calories 293; Fat 4g (sat 0g, mono 2g, poly 1g); Cholesterol 34 mg; Protein 28g; Carbohydrate 35g; Fiber 4g; Iron 4mg; Sodium 650mg; Calcium 59mg

Get Extra Zing with Fresh Ginger

What it is: Likely originated in Southeast Asia, ginger has been prized as a remedy for queasy stomachs, colds, and as an appetite stimulant. Eastern cultures pair it with seafood. Young ginger, which is usually 3 to 4 months old, has thin, pale skin and tender, juicy flesh. The mature (7- to 10-month-old) kind has a dull, yellowish beige skin; a slightly more fibrous pulp; and a sharper, spicier flavor.

Where to find it: Mature ginger is available year-round at most supermarkets; young ginger is typically sold only at Asian markets during the summer. Find firm bulbs that have taut, thin skin. Refrigerate it wrapped in a paper towel in an unsealed plastic bag. It should last several weeks if you change the towel when it gets moist. Ginger is past its prime when the skin becomes wrinkled or the flesh gets dried out.

Some ideas:

- Steep thin peeled slices in rice vinegar, and add to dressings or sauces.
- Combine grated ginger with garlic and green onions, and add to stir-fries, poached fish, chicken, or steamed vegetables.
- Perk up hot and cold beverages, broths, sauces, and dressings with our Ginger Extract.

GINGER EXTRACT

1 pound coarsely chopped peeled fresh ginger

1. Place one-fourth of the ginger in a blender or food processor. Process until a fine paste forms; remove from blender. Repeat the procedure with remaining ginger. Place ginger paste in a fine sieve over a bowl, pressing with the back of a spoon to extract juice. Discard paste. Cover juice, and refrigerate.

CABBAGE SALAD WITH GINGER-SOY DRESSING

You can store the remaining dressing for up to two weeks by covering and refrigerating it.

⅓ cup rice vinegar
¼ cup mirin (sweet rice wine)
¼ cup low-sodium soy sauce
2 tablespoons Ginger Extract
2 tablespoons canola oil
1 teaspoon dark sesame oil
2 cups thinly sliced napa (Chinese) or Savoy cabbage
2 cups grated carrot
2 green onions, chopped
10 large mint leaves, thinly sliced
¼ teaspoon freshly ground black pepper

1. Whisk together first 6 ingredients in a small bowl.
2. Combine ¼ cup dressing with napa cabbage and remaining ingredients, tossing well to coat. Cover salad mixture, and refrigerate at least 3 hours. Yield: 4 servings (serving size: 1 cup salad and 1 tablespoon dressing).
Note: Ginger Extract contains few calories and no fat or cholesterol, so these values are not included in the salad's nutritional analysis.

Calories 156 (46% from fat); Fat 8g (sat 1g, mono 2g, poly 5g); Cholesterol 0mg; Protein 2g; Carbohydrate 16g; Fiber 3g; Iron 1mg; Sodium 560mg; Calcium 36mg

Recipes adapted from Essentials of Asian Cuisine: Fundamentals and Favorite Recipes, *by Corinne Trang.*

SALADS
Fit for Winter

That's right—salads aren't just good for warmer
months. Fill up on the cooler season's "good"
carbs with these one-dish suppers.

RECIPES BY TRACY SEAMAN • PHOTOGRAPHY BY LEIGH BEISCH

Winter's fresh produce has much more to
offer than the standard bowl of lettuces
with a slab of grilled chicken. Each of
these recipes offers deep flavors, and a host of vitamins, minerals, and antioxidants, making it easy to
be good during the cold season.

BROCCOLI SALAD WITH SESAME DRESSING AND CASHEWS

Prep: 10 minutes • **Cook:** 10 minutes

1 large bunch broccoli rabe, woody ends trimmed
2 heads broccoli
1 tablespoon sultana (golden) raisins, chopped
¼ cup coarsely chopped salted cashews
1 tablespoon toasted sesame oil
1 tablespoon vegetable oil
3 tablespoons seasoned rice-wine vinegar
2 large garlic cloves, finely minced or pressed
   through a garlic press
Large pinch cayenne pepper
2 teaspoons sesame seeds, lightly toasted

1. Rinse broccoli rabe well, and steam just until
tender but still bright green, about 3 to 4 minutes.
Rinse broccoli rabe in a colander beneath cold
running water. Drain well, and then wrap in a
clean tea towel to absorb any excess water. Chop
broccoli rabe into small pieces.
2. Cut broccoli florets from stems, and cut into
small (½-inch) pieces. Steam just until tender
but still bright green, about 3 to 4 minutes. Rinse
in a colander beneath cold running water. Drain
well, and wrap in a clean tea towel to absorb
excess water.
3. Place rabe and broccoli florets in a large bowl
with raisins and cashews. Whisk together the
oils, vinegar, garlic, and cayenne. Drizzle over
salad, and lightly toss. Sprinkle with toasted
sesame seeds. Serve salad at room temperature or
chilled. Yield: 6 to 8 servings (serving size: about
1¼ cups).

Calories 101; Fat 6g (sat 1g, mono 2g, poly 2g); Cholesterol 0mg;
Protein 4g; Carbohydrate 10g; Fiber 1g; Iron 1mg; Sodium 44mg;
Calcium 56mg

SHRIMP, GRAPEFRUIT, AND AVOCADO SALAD

Prep: 15 minutes

1½ cups red grapefruit sections (about 2 grapefruits)
¾ pound large shrimp, cooked, peeled, and deveined
1 tablespoon fresh grapefruit juice
2 teaspoons extra-virgin olive oil
½ teaspoon kosher salt
⅛ teaspoon ground white pepper
1 teaspoon sugar
4 cups slivered romaine lettuce hearts
1 avocado, peeled and cubed (about 1 cup)
1 tablespoon minced fresh chives

1. Combine grapefruit sections and shrimp in a medium bowl, and set aside. In a small bowl, whisk together grapefruit juice, oil, salt, pepper, and sugar.
2. Place the lettuce in a large bowl, and drizzle with dressing, tossing gently to coat; divide among 4 plates. Divide shrimp mixture, avocado, and chives among salads. Yield: 4 servings (serving size: 2 cups).

Calories 224; Fat 11g (sat 2g, mono 6g, poly 2g); Cholesterol 166mg; Protein 20g; Carbohydrate 14g; Fiber 5g; Iron 4mg; Sodium 341mg; Calcium 71mg

Shrimp, Grapefruit, and Avocado Salad

MUSTARD GREENS SALAD WITH PORK AND ASIAN PEAR

The mustard greens have a peppery flavor you'll enjoy. They are also more fibrous than other types of green.

Prep: 10 minutes • **Cook:** 7 minutes

1 (5-ounce) piece pork tenderloin, trimmed
¼ teaspoon freshly ground black pepper
Cooking spray
¼ cup finely chopped scallions
2 tablespoons fresh lime juice
2 tablespoons extra-virgin olive oil
1 tablespoon honey
½ teaspoon kosher salt
6 cups de-ribbed and chopped mustard greens
¼ cup sliced pitted dates
1 Asian or Bosc pear, cored and cut into julienne strips

1. Sprinkle pork with ground black pepper. Coat a nonstick skillet with cooking spray. Heat coated skillet over medium-high heat. Add pork, and cook 2 minutes, or until browned, turning occasionally. Cook pork 5 additional minutes, or to desired degree of doneness; remove pork from heat. Set aside, and keep warm.
2. Combine scallions, lime juice, olive oil, honey, and salt in a small bowl; stir well with a whisk. Place greens, dates, and pear in a large bowl; drizzle with dressing, and toss gently to coat.
3. Cut pork diagonally across the grain into thin slices. Divide salad evenly among each of 4 plates; top salad with pork. Yield: 4 servings (serving size: about 2 cups).

Calories 199; Fat 9g (sat 1g, mono 6g, poly 1g); Cholesterol 23mg; Protein 10g; Carbohydrate 23g; Fiber 5g; Iron 2mg; Sodium 181mg; Calcium 97mg

COLLARD SALAD WITH ROASTED TOMATOES, BACON, AND MUSHROOMS

Prep: 5 minutes • **Cook:** 30 minutes

1 pint cherry tomatoes
Cooking spray
8 teaspoons extra-virgin olive oil, divided
Kosher salt
Freshly ground black pepper
1 pint sliced cremini (baby bella) mushrooms (about 2 cups)
2 large garlic cloves, minced
3 turkey-bacon slices, cut into slivers
10 cups de-ribbed and chopped collard greens, rinsed and drained
1 tablespoon balsamic vinegar

1. Preheat oven to 400°.
2. Place tomatoes in a medium glass baking dish lightly coated with cooking spray. Drizzle with 2 teaspoons oil and a pinch each salt and pepper. Bake at 400° for 15 minutes, until tomatoes are hot and skins are wrinkled. Cover with foil; set aside.
3. Place 2 teaspoons oil in a large nonstick skillet over medium-high heat. Add mushrooms, and sprinkle with a pinch each salt and pepper. Sauté just until mushrooms are tender and golden brown, about 5 to 8 minutes. Transfer to a plate, and keep warm.
4. Add 2 teaspoons oil to the same skillet over medium-high heat, along with half of garlic and half of bacon; sauté 30 seconds. Add half of collard greens, and stir-fry just until greens are wilted; transfer to a large metal bowl. Repeat with remaining 2 teaspoons oil, garlic, and bacon; sauté briefly before adding remaining greens. Stir-fry just until greens are wilted; add to bowl.
5. Add tomatoes and mushrooms to the bowl with greens. Pour vinegar into skillet (be careful of fumes); simmer 30 seconds. Drizzle over salad,

and lightly toss along with salt and pepper to taste. Serve warm. Yield: 4 servings (serving size: 1 cup).

Calories 150; Fat 10g (sat 2g, mono 6g, poly 1g); Cholesterol 9mg; Protein 6g; Carbohydrate 13g; Fiber 5g; Iron 1mg; Sodium 156mg; Calcium 147mg

ROASTED ROOT VEGETABLES WITH GOAT CHEESE

Prep: 15 minutes • **Cook:** 35 to 40 minutes

1 pound parsnips, peeled
2 large fennel bulbs, trimmed
1 pound peeled sweet potatoes, cut into 2-inch pieces
1 large red onion, peeled and quartered
2 tablespoons extra-virgin olive oil
2 tablespoons white balsamic vinegar
¾ teaspoon kosher salt
½ teaspoon minced fresh rosemary
½ teaspoon minced fresh thyme
¼ teaspoon freshly ground black pepper
1 cup (4 ounces) crumbled goat cheese

1. Preheat oven to 450°.
2. Cut parsnips crosswise into thirds, then lengthwise into quarters. Cut fennel bulbs in half vertically. Cut each half lengthwise into ½-inch-thick slices.
3. Place parsnips, fennel, sweet potato, and onion in a large roasting pan; drizzle with oil and vinegar. Sprinkle with salt, rosemary, thyme, and pepper; toss well to coat. Add ¼ cup water to pan. Roast for 35 to 40 minutes, or just until vegetables are tender and beginning to brown (stir once halfway through cook time). Top with goat cheese before serving. Yield: 8 servings (serving size: about 1½ cups).

Calories 189; Fat 8g (sat 3g, mono 4g, poly 0g); Cholesterol 11mg; Protein 5g; Carbohydrate 25g; Fiber 4g; Iron 1mg; Sodium 219mg; Calcium 107mg

COOKING ESSENTIALS

Ready to bump your kitchen abilities up a notch? Then stock your pantry with these six special items.

BY SUSIE QUICK

Nose around the kitchen of a gourmet chef, and you're sure to find staples worthy of a true food snob: oils and vinegars pricier than most folks' best bottle of wine, cheeses with tongue-twisting names, herbs you'd need a botany degree to identify. But for the home cook who cares more about her health than holding her own at Le Cordon Bleu, how important is it to have a pantry outfitted with the best? We say it's crucial. Using the highest quality ingredients—such as a fruity, cold-pressed extra-virgin olive oil instead of one with the consistency of motor oil—means a small amount will provide a full-flavor payoff. That's an obvious advantage for anyone who wants to get the most out of the calories she's eating, both flavor- and healthwise. But you don't need the palate of a gourmet to distinguish the good from the great. This guide to the six essentials that we keep on hand in the

Use high-quality ingredients—such as a fruity, cold-pressed extra-virgin olive oil—so that a small amount provides full-flavor payoff.

Health Test Kitchens gives you inside info on ingredients that can transform dishes from just OK fare to four-star cuisine.

BALSAMIC VINEGAR

We're just smitten with vinegars on the whole—white balsamic, red wine, sherry, rice wine, and Champagne, in particular. But if we could have only one vinegar, it would be a good imported red balsamic.

Why it's good for you: The real benefit is that a little balsamic vinegar goes a long way. A few drops can greatly enhance the flavor of your food and cut down on the need for lots of salt and fat.
How to choose: Traditional aged balsamic from Italy

is the ultimate. Like a fine wine, it is aged any-where from 12 to 25 years and can be pricey, cost-ing from $80 to $200 a bottle. You can find decent younger versions for around $20 at higher end grocers, as well as at some online retailers. But even a $5 to $10 supermarket brand will work well for dressings or sauces that require reducing a large amount of vinegar.

Uses: The expensive stuff has a strong flavor, so use a light touch. A small amount is enough to flavor such foods as steamed asparagus or other vegetables, without adding oil or salt. Cheaper brands are more versatile: Add 1 teaspoon to homemade or prepared tomato sauce for extra zing, or blend with an equal amount of olive oil for a quick vinaigrette. For your next get-together, try this simple appetizer: shards of Parmigiano-Reggiano lightly drizzled with aged balsamic and served with crusty bread.

GOURMET SALT

A pinch of kosher or sea salt can improve your meals from the ground up, bringing out the natural flavors in most foods, even sweets. But there's a big difference in flavor and sodium levels among the array of choices beyond table salt.

Why it's good for you: Kosher salt contains about half the sodium per teaspoon of table salt and has none of the additives (anticaking agents, whiten-ers, and iodine). Sea salt is extracted from ocean water through evaporation by sunlight or heat. Its flavor comes from trace minerals, mostly magnesium, calcium, and potassium. Less-salty varieties contain more of these minerals than they do sodium chloride.

How to choose: A salt's origin and processing method directly affect its flavor, texture, and cost. For kosher salt, our choice is Diamond Crystal because it doesn't taste as bitter as some other brands. Among sea salts, we prefer *fleur de sel*, a premium type derived from pools along France's northern Atlantic coast. If you want to experiment,

try Maldon sea salt, which comes in delicate flakes, or a gray Celtic variety. Most supermarkets carry at least one kind of sea salt (Hain is a good all-purpose brand). You can find more at gourmet or online retailers.

Uses: We prefer the milder kosher salt for baking and cooking. Save the more intense, earthy sea salt for seasoning at the table—a touch usually provides enough flavor to enhance your meals.

FLAT-LEAF PARSLEY

We could go on and on about how much better fresh herbs are than their dried-up cousins. While we do cook with a few dried herbs—thyme, oregano, bay leaf, and marjoram—fresh is our first choice in all other cases. The true essential for any health-conscious cook, though, is flat-leaf Italian parsley, which is much more tender and toothsome than the curly kind.

Why it's good for you: Parsley, along with such fresh herbs as chives and basil, contains folate, fiber, and vitamin C. It adds intense flavor without a lot of calories.

How to choose: Look for bright green leaves with no signs of wilting. Bunches that have their root ends usually stay fresh the longest. Place the roots in a jar with a small amount of water, cover loosely with a plastic bag, and refrigerate. For parsley without intact roots, wrap unwashed leaves in damp paper towels and place in sealed plastic bags in the crisper. Rinse and spin-dry before chopping or mincing.

Uses: It's usually best to add parsley and other fresh herbs near the end of cooking to maintain their fla-vors. You can coarsely chop parsley with chives or mint and toss with Boston or romaine lettuces. To give sauces, salad dressings, or soups a quick hit of green, add parsley pureed with a small amount of olive oil, salt, lemon zest, garlic, and minced scal-lion greens. This mixture will keep for up to two weeks in the refrigerator; just place it in a jar with a little oil. (If you like, substitute basil or cilantro for the parsley.)

GARLIC

A true cook's house isn't a home without the aroma of sautéed garlic enveloping the kitchen. The distinct scent comes from a compound called allicin, which is formed when fresh garlic is crushed or cut. But it's not just the smell that's appetizing; the unique flavor makes garlic an essential ingredient in such savory dishes as Italian *pasta all'olio*, Asian stir-fries, and a wide variety of stews and soups.

Why it's good for you: Historically, garlic has been used worldwide to treat a host of ailments. Research suggests that allicin and other sulfur-containing phytochemicals in garlic may help lower LDL cholesterol and prevent stroke, cancer, and arthritis.

How to choose: Once garlic is chopped or crushed, the healthful compounds last only a few hours at room temperature or a few days in the

fridge. So toss the powdered or minced stuff (it tastes bitter anyway), and go for fresh bulbs. The giant bulbs, called elephant garlic, are actually a form of leek and have a milder flavor. Store whole garlic in a cool, dark place (think pantry, not refrigerator) to keep it from sprouting, since the flavor becomes less pungent as the bulbs age and dehydrate.

Uses: Heat inactivates allicin and destroys some of the flavor, so be sure to sauté or cook garlic only as long as necessary. Slowly baking the cloves gives them a nutty flavor and a buttery consistency that goes great on a slice of fresh bread. Take advantage of the compounds in raw garlic by finely mincing cloves for salad dressings and sauces.

UNSALTED BUTTER

A little dab of wholesome butter imparts richness to vegetables or baked goods. And when it comes to flavor, there are no comparisons.

Why it's good for you: As we've said before, butter is hardly a health food. But keep in mind that the saturated fat in butter doesn't drive down your HDL cholesterol levels as the trans fats in margarine do. And if you go with an organic brand, you get the extra benefits of butter made with milk that comes from hormone-free cows raised on organic pastures and feed.

How to choose: Organic butter may have just as much saturated fat as regular, but we think organic tastes better. Look for the certified-organic seal to make sure you get what you're paying for. Our current favorite: Organic Valley's European Style Cultured Butter, which has won awards from the American Cheese Society. Organic or not, we like unsalted butter better than salted. Unsalted has superior texture and flavor (salt is usually added to mask an inferior butter's flaws). Butter will keep on a shelf in your refrigerator—but not in the door, where the temperature is warmer—for up to four months.

Uses: Gently sauté vegetables, chicken, or fish in a blend of one part butter and two parts olive or canola oil. The oil prevents the butter from burning and increases the proportion of healthful fat while keeping the butter flavor intact. To make a better butter spread, mix equal parts butter and extra-virgin olive oil or cold-pressed canola oil. Keep refrigerated in a tightly sealed container or small tub; stir before using.

EXTRA-VIRGIN OLIVE OIL

The easiest way to turn your cooking into a paragon of virtue is to switch from industrial-grade vegetable oil to extra-virgin olive oil. It's milled soon after the olives are harvested using cold pressing, a mechanical process that extracts the oil naturally, without heat or chemicals (both of which are used in the manufacture of most cooking oils, including the majority of non-extra-virgin olive oils).

Why it's good for you: Several studies have shown that when olive oil is substituted for saturated fat in the diet, its antioxidants can help control high blood pressure, reduce cholesterol, and protect against heart disease and certain types of cancer.

How to choose: You used to have to spend at least $20 for a good bottle of oil, but that's no longer the case. Such brands as Bertolli and Colavita are available for around $5 at your local supermarket. Flavors vary widely; some oils are fruity, with an herbal or citrusy nuance, while others taste almost peppery. Try a few different types to explore their subtle variations. High-quality oil can be deep gold to bright green and can look cloudy (that means it's unfiltered) or clear. On the label, look for words like *cold-pressed*, in addition to *extra-virgin*, and either the date of bottling (which should be recent) or a "use by" date that is

more than six months away. Store your purchase tightly sealed in a cool, dark place (but not in the refrigerator) away from heat—in other words, as far away from the stove as possible.

Uses: Although many people think extra-virgin oil is only for dressing salads and drizzling over soups and such, most Italians wouldn't dream of cooking with anything else. It works best for low-heat sautéeing or braising—this type of cooking preserves both flavor and antioxidants. (We especially like to "poach" eggs for a couple of minutes in a small amount of extra-virgin oil in a covered non-stick pan.) ■

How This Sweet Treat Keeps Sickness at Bay

Sure, it makes oatmeal taste better, but cinnamon could have a higher calling. U.S. Department of Agriculture researchers found that daily cinnamon supplements reduced total cholesterol, bad cholesterol, and triglycerides 13 to 30 percent in a study of 60 men and women with Type 2 diabetes. That's comparable to benefits seen with statin drugs. Richard Anderson, Ph.D., the study's author, thinks cinnamon may be just as useful for healthy people.

In previous test-tube studies, Anderson found the spice contains a polyphenol similar to insulin, the hormone that clears sugar from the blood. Cinnamon seems to help the body use insulin more efficiently. "This reduces insulin resistance, which is the cause of Type 2 diabetes and a major risk factor for heart disease," Anderson says.

In the latest research, it was found that cinnamon also cut blood-sugar levels by 20 to 30 percent, which can help prevent the damage diabetes can inflict

on nerves and blood vessels. "Some people who were taking medications for diabetes have been able to get off them and use cinnamon alone," Anderson says.

The spice has no known risks and negligible calories. Study participants got a bang from just 1/2 teaspoon per day, which is easily added to your diet. If you go the supplement route, though, skip cinnamon oils because the polyphenols are removed in processing.

vital *stats*

67

Percentage of Americans on low-carb/no-carb diets who do not know that tomatoes contain carbs

47

Percentage who do not know that apples contain carbs

14

Percentage who mistakenly think steak is a high-carb food

49

Percentage of Americans who give flowers and plants to say "I'm sorry"

10

Percentage of Americans who give jewelry to say "I'm sorry"

3

Percentage of Americans who give alcohol to say "I'm sorry"

75

Percentage of American husbands who reach orgasm about 2 minutes after sex begins

15

Average number of workdays per year people with marital problems miss

10 to 40

Number of moles the average person has

50

Number of moles that puts you at risk for skin cancer

1

Rank of skin cancer among the most common cancers in America

100%

Potential cure rate of skin cancer if it is caught and treated before it spreads

95

Number of girls born per 100 boys in North America

86

Number born per 100 boys in China

44

Percentage of dads who say they don't want anything for Father's Day

$71

Average amount women say they plan to spend on a Father's Day gift

$33

Average amount men say they plan to spend on one

29

Percentage of Americans' favorite activities that involve exercise

38

Percentage of Americans' favorite activities that involved exercise in 1995

37

Percentage of overweight people who say they watch sports

31

Percentage of thinner people who say they watch sports

50

Percentage less likely a passenger in a silver car is to be seriously injured in an accident than someone in a white car

24

Percentage of new cars in the United States that are silver, the most popular color

66

Number of additional daily calories from soda or fruit juice that Americans consume now versus 27 years ago

1

Rank of summer among seasons in which the main allergy trigger is grass pollen

63

Percentage of allergy sufferers who don't know that rain can make allergy symptoms worse

4.48

Average number of workdays allergy sufferers miss each year because of flare-ups

1

Rank of Atlanta among the worst cities for allergy sufferers

10

Percentage of teens who want to be doctors, the top profession named by teens polled

$130,610

Median annual wage of a family practitioner

8

Percentage of teens who want to be actors

$23,470

Median annual wage of an actor

Sources: Shape Up America!; Society of American Florists; Circuit City; National Retail Federation; *British Medical Journal–University of Auckland;* PPG Industries; Obesity Research; National Cancer Institute; Harris Interactive; Porter Novelli; *British Medical Journal;* Allergy Action Plan; Harris Interactive–U.S. Bureau of Labor Statistics; Kinsey Institute; Journal of Marriage and the Family —Reported by Laura Gilbert

fitness

**the best exercises for
a healthy body**

12 Simple Ways to Burn More Calories

Use these tips from top experts to make the most of your exercise routine.

BY KIMBERLY WONG

1 JOG THROUGH WATER. "We call it 'surf 'n' turf,' " says Mary Sanders, an exercise physiologist at the University of Nevada, Reno. Running in water is one of the most strenuous activities you can perform because the wet stuff is about 12 to 15 times as resistant as air. Running at your hardest, you can burn about 17 calories per minute, twice as much or more than what a 143-pound woman would burn moving at a pace of 5.5 miles per hour on asphalt.

2 START FAST. Don't be fooled; slow and steady won't win the race. Researchers at the College of New Jersey found that after a short warm-up, cyclists who punched up the intensity during the first half of their workouts and then cruised for the second half burned about 10 percent more calories than those who started slow and finished fast. "By getting the high-intensity part of your workout over first, you'll mobilize stored-up fat and then efficiently burn it during the lighter part of the workout," says Jie Kang, Ph.D., lead researcher and associate professor of health and exercise science at the College of New Jersey. He says this strategy should work for any cardio activity: walking, running, swimming, whatever. To see these benefits, a 40-year-old jogger would need to work at an intensity of about 7 on a 10-point scale for the first half of her run, and then drop to about 5 for the second half.

3 WARM UP BEFORE YOU LIFT. A short spin on a bike or jog on a treadmill (enough to get your heart rate up) warms your muscles and tendons and gets fluids flowing in the joints; this increases your muscles' elasticity, allowing you to handle heavier weights and endure a longer workout. "It takes about 5 to 10 minutes to increase your heart rate," says Kelli Calabrese, a spokeswoman for the American Council on Exercise. "But if you do that before a strength-training session, you'll actually burn more calories."

4 SHUT UP, AND DANCE. Here's the perfect excuse to sign up for that hip-hop dance class you've been itching to try. Surprising your body with new activities—dance, a new sport, you name it—forces it to work harder because it's doing unfamiliar movements and using muscle groups in different ways. In the process, you'll burn more calories than you would by doing the same-old same-old, explains Dixie Stanforth, an exercise physiologist at the University of Texas at Austin. How much more? Each minute, a 150-pound woman will burn 7.1 calories with her fancy (and vigorous) footwork versus roughly 4.8 calories while walking 4 miles per hour.

5 WORK OUT IN THE A.M. We hesitate to push this idea for obvious reasons (sleep being the primary one). But research has shown that people who exercise in the morning keep their metabolism elevated for hours and thus get a jump on burning calories. "As the day goes on, fatigue sets in, and you're going against your body's natural circadian rhythm," Calabrese says. That's why it may be harder to motivate yourself to get to the gym after work—your body is ready to wind down and relax. Studies also show that people who start each day with a workout tend to stick with their exercise programs longer.

6 FUEL UP FIRST, AND THEN WORK OUT. Grab a banana before you hit the gym, and it may actually help you slice off more calories in the long run. "You will be able to exercise harder and for a longer period if you consume carbo-hydrates before exercise," Calabrese says. Shoot for 100 to 200 calories to nibble on: Yogurt, a piece of fruit, peanut butter and crackers, or half an energy bar are all excellent choices.

7 USE THE SURGE STRATEGY. A highly effective way to churn through more calories without having to work out for longer periods of time is to include in your cardio exercise spurts of speed followed by short breathers. After a warm-up, push yourself a bit harder than usual for a short surge, and then slow down to a more moderate pace to recover. Repeating this pattern several times in a single workout session will give you a higher calorie tally than you'd earn if you kept your pace steady the entire time.

8 DO A TRIATHLON AT THE GYM. It doesn't require the endurance of an Olympic athlete: Simply split your usual 30- or 45-minute workout into three segments: For example, pedal on a stationary bike, power-walk on a treadmill, and step onto an elliptical trainer for 10- or 15-minute bursts with no rest in between. This routine will help you keep up your heart rate and increase the burn. Swapping machines is just another easy way to work your muscles differently during a single session.

9 **TAKE TO THE SAND.** Here's some easy-to-remember advice for scorching calories: The softer the surface, the more you burn. By walking or running on the beach, you'll use 20 to 50 percent more calories than you would going at the same pace on a hard trail or asphalt. This isn't easy—if you've ever had to sprint through the dunes after a toddler, then you know what we mean. Just think of the additional calories you're burning as, well, the icing on the cake.

10 **DON'T SLOUCH.** We hate to channel your mother, but she did have a point. Not only is slouching unattractive, but also if you do it on the elliptical trainer, stair-climber, or treadmill, you risk cheating yourself out of the benefits these machines are supposed to provide. Most form flaws, Stanforth says, happen because you're trying to take the load off your leg muscles by propping yourself on your arms. That makes the routine feel a little easier, but a less-challenging workout probably won't help get you fitter, trimmer, or more toned anytime soon. Be sure to maintain a neutral spine to protect your back, keep your abs tight, and go easy on the handrails. On elliptical trainers, if you're not really pushing and pulling the hand

levers (and you don't have any balance issues), let go. That will zap any tendency you might have to lean on them.

11 **USE YOUR ARMS.** Getting both your upper and lower body involved can provide a big calorie-burning advantage. So if you're short on time or want to get everything you can out of your usual 45-minute workout, try total-body activities, such as rowing, swimming, or cross-country skiing. You can even gain a slight uptick by exaggerating your arm swing while you walk.

12 **TUNE IN TO YOUR MUSCLES.** People who sleepwalk through their programs are likely to get less out of them. "Really focus on your body while you exercise," Calabrese advises. For instance, you should concentrate on using your abdominal muscles, hips, and quadriceps to power up your walk. And when you come up during a crunch, instead of allowing your mind to wander, center your attention on contracting your abs and moving your ribs closer to your hip bones. ■

Freelance writer Kimberly Wong lives in San Francisco.

Let the Music Move You

If you've ever encountered an aerobics instructor with a Michael Bolton fetish, then you know that the wrong music can make a good workout go bad. But the opposite is also true: The right music can give you the extra juice to power through your fitness activity of choice, whether it's a class, a hike on the treadmill, or a session on the elliptical trainer.

There's even scientific proof to back up this theory. In one study, exercise physiologists at the University of Kansas had a group of 18 people do four sets of moves on stationary bikes, all at the same intensity. During the first three sets, the participants listened to music—the first was up-tempo, the next was classical, and the last were tunes they chose themselves. During the fourth set, they sweated in silence. Afterward, the group reported that the workouts with music felt easier to do than the one without.

Retro Workouts

The leg warmers and shiny spandex stashed in your attic aren't the only trends left over from the 1980s. Some workouts from the big-hair decade (and earlier) are still around and going strong—and for good reasons. Here's an update.

RICHARD SIMMONS: SWEATIN' TO THE OLDIES (1988)	JANE FONDA: COMPLETE WORKOUT (1988)	JAZZERCISE (1969)
HOW WE KNOW IT'S HOT: It recently ranked number 236 on Amazon.com's top-selling videos list (the blockbuster *Titanic* was 3,477).	HOW WE KNOW IT'S HOT: Amazon.com recently ranked it 196 on its list of top-selling videos.	HOW WE KNOW IT'S HOT: Instructors teach more than seventeen thousand classes per week in the United States. (You probably know a closet Jazzerciser.)
WHAT IT IS: A simple 43-minute low-intensity workout of aerobics and stretching, accompanied by live music from an oldies band	WHAT IT IS: A challenging 70-minute workout involving low- and high-intensity aerobics, along with weight training	WHAT IT IS: A 60-minute blend of jazz dance, aerobics, and resistance training set to a mixture of jazz, country, funk, and Top 40 music
WHY IT'S CHEESY: Richard's trademark skimpy striped shorts, a set that looks like a high school gym, and the "swim" dance. Need we say more?	WHY IT'S CHEESY: Jane's belted stretch leotard just can't be comfortable. (Also, her use of weights during the leg workout and shoulder rolls could be dangerous.)	WHY IT'S CHEESY: With a name like Jazzercise, this doesn't rank very high on the hip-and-cool scale. But if it gets you moving, go for it.
WHY IT'S WORTH ANOTHER LOOK: Richard's enthusiasm and cast of real people—both large and small—make this video accessible and enjoyable. One Amazon.com enthusiast says, "It's been two years now, and I still enjoy Richard's videos when I feel like giving my mood a push."	WHY IT'S WORTH ANOTHER LOOK: It's easy to follow at your own pace, and the workout can be divided into two parts if you're short on time. As one Jane lover says on Amazon.com, "Jane Fonda still rocks!"	WHY IT'S WORTH ANOTHER LOOK: Founder and CEO Judi Sheppard Missett keeps up with the latest exercise research and periodically changes the workout to keep it current. Fan Sheila Adams of Raleigh, North Carolina, says, "It's easy to just concentrate on the music and the steps and forget you're exercising."

"Most researchers agree that there are positive effects of music on endurance and exercise performance, allowing people to work out longer or at higher intensities than when no music is present," says Luis F. Aragón-Vargas, Ph.D., professor of exercise science at the University of Costa Rica, who has studied the subject.

"I believe music has a positive effect because it distracts people from the effort; it takes their minds off the strain and pain of exercise. The music, as long as people like it and it is played at a reasonable volume, adds an element of enjoyment."

Luckily, now it's easier than ever to match music to both your workout pace and your taste. Resources designed with fitness instructors in mind, like www.workoutmusic.com and www.mywalkingmusic.com, let you buy premixed compact discs and cassettes. You can also use your computer to download inexpensive (and legal) tunes from sites like www.buymusic.com.

Take the Fear Out of Fitness

Discover how to break through the barriers keeping you from a better body.

BY BEN BROWN

Somewhere between the season of forgotten New Year's resolutions and the onset of swimsuit despair is the peak time for exercise guilt. "Why can't I stick with a fitness plan?" you wonder. "What's wrong with me? Am I just a loser?"

No, you're not a loser. But you may be a scaredycat. Fear is one of the biggest reasons people give up on exercise, according to a growing number of sports-psychology and fitness authorities. But these same professionals have devised simple strategies for getting over your fear and getting on with your workout.

The fitness-attrition problem is big. Approximately half of the people who begin an exercise program quit within the first six months, according to Kathleen Martin Ginis, Ph.D., professor of kinesiology at McMaster University in Hamilton, Ontario.

Ginis and other experts say that two types of fear in particular are driving the dropouts. The first—anxiety about not being able to perform exercises correctly or looking stupid doing them—can curse anyone who is struggling through the learning curve for a particular activity, regardless of her fitness level. The apprehension may be more intense for someone who's new to exercise, but this fear could also keep a runner away from the lap pool, for instance, or a treadmill junkie from hopping on the elliptical trainer.

The other type of fear, known as social physique anxiety, "is connected with concern that others are negatively evaluating our physique," says kinesiologist David Conroy, Ph.D., of Pennsylvania State University. Women—no surprise here—are especially vulnerable.

In Ginis' studies, women who were new to exercise tended to feel more exhausted and were in a worse mood after exercising if they worked out in front of mirrors (everywhere in a typical health club) or if they used exercise videos that featured ultrafit women or supermodels. This, Ginis says, suggests that "maybe it's not the exerciser per se; maybe it's the environment."

One of the top reasons women avoid the gym is the fear that they won't see people who look like them.

If typical fitness experiences undermine their confidence and heighten their anxiety, Ginis says, "it's no wonder these women drop out."

But the change-the-atmosphere message has gotten through to the people who direct fitness programs for a living. "The intimidation issue is huge," says Jill Kinney, co-founder of San Francisco–based Club One, which owns 22 clubs and manages another 78 facilities in 10 states.

Research by Kinney's company and other experts in the fitness industry suggests that one of the top reasons people tend to avoid the gym is, as Kinney puts it, the "fear that you'll go into a club and there won't be people who look like you."

The power of the fitness-fear factor is among the driving forces behind the growth of women-only clubs, such as Curves. "We women are self-conscious just walking around in the world. We don't need to go into a fitness facility and feel even more self-conscious," says Donna Stauber, Ph.D., director of health and nutrition for Curves International Inc., which oversees some seven thousand franchises throughout the United States and Canada.

Here's how you can apply what the pros have learned to your own fitness ambitions.

Rethink your definition of exercise. Think of it as movement, any movement—not necessarily something that you have to do in a gym or at a track. Gardening is exercise; so are walking the dog, playing tag with your kids, and strolling through the woods picking blackberries.

If you've been unsuccessful at sticking with a traditional program before, focusing on simply moving more in these ways may not only help you burn calories now but also may prepare you mentally and physically for other activities in the future.

Be environmentally conscious. Shop around for fitness experiences that make you feel nurtured and accepted. That's pretty easy if you walk, say, in your neighborhood or on a trail—unless it's frequented by local college cross-country teams who

make you feel that you're moving at a snail's pace as they zoom past you.

Finding a comfort zone can be more challenging, though, in health-club situations. Consider women-only facilities.

Test the waters. If you're interested in trying a new class—Pilates or hip-hop, for example—borrow a video from a friend or the library, and try it at home first. That will show you what to expect and allow you to practice a little before you make your debut in a group situation.

> Learn to think of fitness as movement—any type of movement—not necessarily something you have to do in a gym or at a track.

Get one-on-one help. Almost all clubs now offer personal training to help you overcome your fear of incompetence, and often the first session is free.

Know your triggers. If groups freak you out, find a secluded (but safe) path or track where you can walk or run. If you like the anonymity of a fitness class or the cardio room, stay toward the back (away from the mirrors if they make you uncomfortable). If physique anxiety is your hang-up, start with an activity, such as yoga, that you can do on your own.

Call out the cavalry. If you're the social type, tackling a new activity in a supportive group environment can make the effort less intimidating; other members can help you through or distract you from your fears.

Focus on the positive. Think of the many things exercise can do for you: feeling less winded when you work in the yard or play with your kids; being more optimistic, more energetic, less stressed, and—oh, yeah—less of a scaredy-cat. ■

Learn to Love Your Workout

If you think of exercise as more drudgery than treat, then you may be pushing yourself harder than you have to. Researchers at the University of Illinois at Urbana-Champaign and Iowa State University put each of 60 physically fit men and women in their 20s through a treadmill test, gradually increasing the speed and incline until the participants felt too tired to continue. The scientists discovered that the point at which most of the subjects started to wish they were on the couch instead was when they were working so hard that they crossed over the threshold from aerobic exercise to *an*aerobic exercise. That's when lactate, an acid that triggers pain in your muscles, starts to build up. Study author Steven J. Petruzzello, Ph.D., associate professor of kinesiology and psychology at the University of Illinois, says previous studies have shown that exercising at or just below this threshold provides the same health benefits as going above it.

Preliminary results from an Iowa State follow-up study among previously sedentary middle-aged women suggest these findings may have broader applications. Whether or not that turns out to be the case, overdoing it can tax both your mind and your muscles, so don't be afraid to back off a little if that's what you need to do to keep moving.

Q + A

Sleep Better with the Right Fitness Routine

I thought exercise was supposed to help you sleep better. I started running after work, but I still struggle to fall asleep. Why is this?

It's not what you're doing so much as when you're doing it. If you switch to an a.m. exercise schedule, you'll probably nod off faster. That's just what happened to one group of women over the course of a year during which University of Seattle researchers had them walk, cycle, or stretch for an hour every morning. A second group of people who exercised every day at 6 p.m. reported that dozing off became harder. If you can't squeeze exercise into your morning routine, at least keep your evening workout short. In the study, exercising for 25 minutes or less after 6 p.m. didn't make it harder to fall asleep.

Rx for High Blood Pressure: Longer, Easier Workouts

If you or someone you know has hypertension, there's something you need to know: The American College of Sports Medicine (ACSM) recently revised its recommendations regarding how long, how often, and how hard you should work out—as well as which type of exercise you should do—if your blood pressure meets or exceeds 140 systolic (the upper number) and/or 90 diastolic (the bottom number).

The updated position suggests longer and more-frequent exercise sessions at a lower intensity than had been previously recommended, plus some resistance training. Here's what you need to know.

- Exercise at least four days a week (preferably daily) for at least 30 minutes a pop.
- Shoot for moderate intensity, about a 12 on the Borg Scale for Rating of Perceived Exertion (which ranges from an "I'm reaching for another handful of chips" score of 6 to an "I'm working so hard I'm about to collapse" 20). You should be panting—and sweating—a bit but still able to carry on a conversation.
- Make aerobic exercise a major part of your fitness routine, and supplement it by including some resistance training.
- As always, get your doctor's OK before beginning any workout program.

The rest is up to you. Any aerobic activity will fill the bill. Feel free to break up your exercise session into separate bouts, as long as they are each at least 10 minutes long.

The Back Row: Not So Bad for Beginners

Fitness experts have long urged folks to use the mirrors on weight-room and aerobic-studio walls to check their form—and get an ego boost at the sight of their metamorphosing muscles. But a new study says beginners might be better off exercising without the looking glass.

Researchers at McMaster University in Ontario put 58 previously sedentary women on exercise bikes, sometimes in front of a mirror, other times with the mirror covered. They found that women who could see their reflections tended to feel more tired and were more moody than those who couldn't. Lead author Kathleen Martin Ginis, Ph.D., says that the mirrors may have made the women self-conscious, since they weren't used to seeing their bodies sweating and working hard.

If you're a newbie who has just joined a gym or signed up for a fitness class, there's no need to ask for a refund. Just stake out a mirror-free corner of the workout room, or keep your eyes on the TV monitors while you're on the treadmill. But be sure to tell the weight-room trainer or your fitness instructor that you're new so he or she can watch for glitches in your form. When you feel more confident, give the mirror a try—you might like what you see.

How Exercise Can Ease Arthritic Joints

A recent study discovered that rheumatoid arthritis patients who participated in 1-hour workouts twice a week (combining cycling, strength training, and high-impact sports, such as volleyball or basketball) reported feeling less achy and more agile after two years, compared with patients who underwent standard physical therapy. This workout treatment is not recommended for everyone, so ask your doctor if you're a good candidate for it before you start.

Not Your Grandma's
Water Workout

The newest classes put everything from yoga to Spinning under water. So jump in!

BY SHARON EDRY

I didn't have high hopes as I entered the pool area of a popular New York gym to take a class called Water Works. I had heard it was the cool new way to get a good workout, but I just couldn't shake the image of senior citizens splashing to the oldies.

That picture, though, had nothing to do with reality. I got a no-holds-barred experience blending resistance training, cardio, and boxing moves, complete with a dance-club soundtrack and a sizzling-hot Brazilian instructor named Leandro. It was tough, the time flew, and by the end, my muscles felt like jelly. The next morning, they were as sore as they would have been after any land-locked class.

Water fitness is being touted as the latest exercise trend at health clubs, spas, and community centers across the country, but I had to see it to believe it. What I remembered from previous encounters (lap swimming not included) was that pool activities were OK if you were interested in rehabilitation or in protecting arthritic joints from stress. But now, with such classes as aqua yoga, kickboxing, Pilates, circuit training, and even cycling, the newest generation of water workouts is really worth getting your hair wet for, regardless of your fitness level.

"There's a lot more diversity in the types of classes, including high-intensity versions," says Julie See, president of the Aquatic Exercise Association in North Venice, Florida. "People are amazed at how hard the workout can be."

Research bears out one of the major benefits of water exercise: It's as effective as working out on terra firma but with lower injury risk. For example, a 2002 Finnish study found that after 10 weeks of resistance training, people who exercised in water were nearly as strong as those people who trained on land, with less impact on their joints.

> Water adds resistance that makes you work opposing muscle groups equally, using those you don't typically use while walking and exercising on land.
>
> —Alicia Armour

What's the secret? Water transforms virtually every movement—leg lifts, punches, squats, kicks, and jumps—into a new challenge for your muscles. "Water adds resistance that makes you work opposing muscle groups equally, using those you don't typically use while walking and exercising on land," says Alicia Armour, an exercise physiologist at the Duke Center for Living in Durham, North Carolina.

Working out in water also removes the gravity factor, so it helps you avoid the injuries that can accompany higher impact land exercise, such as running, walking, and some forms of aerobics.

"Water fitness is a great cross-training tool because it's almost no-impact, thanks to the buoyancy of the water," Armour says.

You may be thinking that water exercise is too difficult for the average person. But take it from me—and I'm as average as they come—you can adapt any water class to your own level. Here's how.

Work with (or against) the water. The more of your body's surface that moves against the water, the more effort you'll use. Adjust your hand positions as needed. For instance, slicing the water with your hand in karate-chop position is easier than pushing against it with your hand cupped.

Try pool tools, or leave them in dry dock. Such toys as aqua dumbbells, webbed gloves, and colorful foam "noodles" may look wimpy poolside. But submerged, they can become tools for a full-on workout that will get you in shape without leaving you drenched (at least in sweat). If the equipment makes the exercises too challenging, ditch it and ask your instructor to show you the proper way to do the moves without using any accessories.

Switch gears. If the class seems too easy, try increasing the speed and force of your arm and leg movements to increase drag; to ease up, switch to slow motion. ■

Freelancer Sharon Edry lives and writes in New York.

Think again if you're convinced water exercise would bore you.

Exercise for Your Independence

You know staying physically active can help keep your body young even though the calendar says you're getting older, but that's not the whole story. A new study from the University of Pittsburgh suggests that the more you move, the longer you'll be able to live independently—even if you don't start until you're eligible for senior-citizen movie discounts. Researchers followed 229 women between ages 50 and 65 for 17 years and found that those who were sedentary over the study period were $1^1/_2$ times as likely to have a hard time with daily activities (such as shopping, household chores, climbing stairs) as active women. Think of your workouts as a way to ensure something priceless: your ability to live on your own after you retire (although we wouldn't mind having some help around the house).

GET MOVING
to Live Longer

The latest research proves that women who exercise
live longer than those who don't.

BY SU REID-ST. JOHN

A new study says the key to a longer life isn't some murky herbal tonic (even if it does come with a 30-day money-back guarantee), but exercise. Of course, years of research have hinted at the idea that the more you move, the longer you'll live; it's been demonstrated that exercise helps improve such age-related markers as cholesterol levels, blood pressure, and even muscle strength and functionality. But the latest findings by Chicago-based researchers connected with the St. James Hospital and Health Centers' Women Take Heart Project go a step further.

In 1992, nearly six thousand healthy women over age 35 took treadmill tests to determine their exercise capacity (the greatest amount of oxygen they were able to consume per minute during an activity). Each woman pushed herself as long as she could, stopping when she could go no further. At that point, the scientists measured her exercise capacity in terms of metabolic equivalents, or METs (the higher this number is at the point of

exhaustion, the fitter you are). Ten years later, the researchers checked back in with these women. Those who had died during that period averaged about two METs lower in exercise capacity during the initial test than the women who were still alive. For every one-MET increase, the risk of death (from any cause) was 17-percent lower. Previous studies of men have found an 8- to 14-percent risk reduction per MET, so being physically fit may be even more important to a woman's health than to a man's.

So what does all this mean for you? If you're not exercising regularly, just moving around for 30 minutes five times per week—the standard recommendation—can lengthen your life. Folks who are already active should pick up their pace, suggests lead study author Martha Gulati, M.D., M.S., assistant professor of medicine at the Rush Heart Institute in Chicago. "If your workout feels easy," she says, "it's time to kick it up a notch." ■

Running Is Good Business

Small-business owners looking for success may want to consider spending less time in the office and more time at the gym. That's what researchers from Ball State University in Muncie, Indiana, discovered when they surveyed 336 Midwestern entrepreneurs. They found that businesses that were owned by runners who hit the trail at least four times per week had average sales two to three times as high as companies whose owners didn't run regularly.

The findings didn't surprise study author and assistant professor of management Michael Goldsby, Ph.D. Exercise of any kind, he says, affects the way you look and feel, which in turn shapes the impression you make on clients and investors. It might be a stretch to think that logging more miles on the treadmill will help your company make the Fortune 500—but given the many proven benefits of exercise, it sure couldn't hurt.

Why Its OK to Go for the Cheap Kicks

A recent survey conducted by the American Orthopaedic Foot & Ankle Society found that 79 percent of runners routinely pay at least $80 for their running shoes, while only 6 percent choose to spend $40 or less. The kicker? Expensive shoes cause just as many injuries as their cheaper cousins. So forget the price tag—buy what feels best on your feet.

Q + A   End Exercise Headaches

Sometimes when I get off the StairMaster, my head hurts so much it feels as if it's going to explode. Could I be allergic to exercise?

You're more likely experiencing effects of acid buildup. When you exercise, your muscles release acids into your bloodstream, says Merle Diamond, M.D., associate director of the Diamond Headache Clinic in Chicago. Headache experts think the acid can cause the blood vessels in your scalp to expand and press painfully against nearby nerves. To counter the pain, drink plenty of fluids before exercising and don't work out on an empty stomach. Also, be sure to warm up slowly and cool down when you're finished. Within a few weeks, these tactics should let you exercise without the pain. If they don't work—or if the headaches are accompanied by dizziness, weakness, or other symptoms—talk to your physician about what you're experiencing. "Your doctor may want to give you a CAT (computerized axial tomography) scan but will probably end up telling you everything's OK," Diamond says.

Step Up Your Stride

This no-sweat, no-hassle walking program can help you keep your weight in check.

BY MICHELLE DALLY

Like many other Americans, 44-year-old Carole Kacius, of Indianapolis, had no idea how little she actually moved during the day. Her job as director of the public-health program at Indiana University kept her busy nonstop from 9 to 5. On top of that, tending to three kids and her husband left her exhausted every evening. So Kacius was sure she was anything but sedentary. After she clipped a pedometer to her waistband as part of a program aimed at getting people to move around more, she discovered that busy doesn't necessarily mean active—and that she had a lot more in common with couch potatoes than she'd previously thought.

Soon Kacius began making small changes, such as starting a family ritual of after-dinner walks and taking longer routes for office routines. "I'd park farther away and take the stairs in the parking garage. And instead of eating lunch at my computer, I'd make myself get out for lunch, walk somewhere," she says. In a matter of months, Kacius increased her daily activity from fewer than 1,000 steps per day to about 8,000 steps, or approximately 4 miles. Now, six months later, she says she has more energy and has lost an impressive 10 pounds.

That outcome is exactly what the fledgling program America on the Move (AOM) was designed to bring about, says James O. Hill, Ph.D., chairman of the Partnership to Promote Healthy Eating and Active Living and director of the Center for Human Nutrition at the University of Colorado's Health Sciences Center. The initiative kicked off in July 2003 following pilot programs in Indiana, where Kacius was one of 500 people who participated, and Colorado, where more than one hundred and fifty thousand people joined. AOM wants people to increase their daily activity by 2,000 steps, or about a mile, and decrease daily food intake by 100 calories, a little more than what's in a slice of white bread.

It's an approach that works, according to experts. "Small, sustainable changes—move a little bit more, eat a little bit less—can make a big difference in your health and weight," Hill explains. Compared with the much more ambitious goal of 10,000 steps a day advocated by Shape Up America! (a program founded by former Surgeon General C. Everett Koop), AOM's recommendations are an easier sell because they don't force a lot of big lifestyle modifications at once, says Cedric Bryant, Ph.D., chief exercise physiologist for the American

Council on Exercise. AOM also helps to prepare its participants for one of the most challenging parts of weight loss: maintenance. "With this program, the changes are easier, and they can be maintained for a lifetime," Bryant says.

AOM was exactly what Kim Winkel, 43, had been looking for. "I've struggled with my weight and health all my life," says the Fishers, Indiana, middle-school social worker and single mother of two. "I'm not the gym-workout kind of girl, but this pedometer has made all the difference." Winkel discovered that just wearing the step counter gave her incentive to move more. "It keeps you mindful of where you are and what you should be doing," she says. Now, Winkel ignores the protests of her daughters, ages 11 and 15, and parks in the space farthest from the grocery store. When she has to copy something at work, she uses a machine on a different floor. Winkel has gone from an average of 3,000 steps a day to between 7,000 and 13,000, a progression she says has helped her lose 10 pounds over four months.

Simplicity is the secret to AOM's success, Hill and his colleagues say. Unlike a health club or a group exercise class, the program is cheap and accessible day or night, at work or at home. The only cost is the pedometer (about $10 to $30 depending on the model). You log on to www.americaonthemove.org, where you can sign up, record your progress, and get encouragement and helpful hints. No public weigh-ins, no complicated calorie-counting. You simply cut out a cookie, soda, or couple of chocolate kisses every day. It's that easy.

So what if you *are* a gym-workout kind of girl and think AOM is for babies? You'd better think again. "The step counters are tremendous eye-openers, even for those of us who have a scheduled, structured exercise routine," says Ruth Ann Carpenter, M.S., R.D., director of the Research Dissemination Center at the Cooper Institute in Dallas. "So we run for 3 miles and then sit on our butts for the rest of the day," she says. "But because we are getting more sedentary and because our environment entices us to eat, eat, eat, it's likely that this is not enough to

Unlike workouts at a health club, this program is cheap and accessible day or night, at work or at home.

stave off creeping obesity as we age. We need to look for as many opportunities throughout our day to move, or at least not sit."

American adults have been gaining an average of 1 to 3 pounds each year, every year, for the past generation, and they're passing the tradition on to their children. The need to reverse this trend is of national importance, Hill says.

That sense of urgency would make Carole Kacius something of a hero. Her three children—ages 6, 5, and 3½—each have their own pedometers and compete daily to be the first to reach 1,000 steps. (Running around the Ping-Pong table is a favorite means to that end.) Now, on family trips, Kacius and her husband look for trails full of runners, walkers, inline skaters, and bike riders. One of her sons actually graphs the number of steps he takes per week to chart his progress. "It's become part of their lives, part of their wiring," she says. "That's been such a great surprise—an added bonus."

Walk (or Run?) Off the Pounds

How hard should you work when you exercise? It depends on how fit you already are.

BY SU REID-ST. JOHN

The controversy over the importance of adding intensity to your workout continues. Some experts recommend short bursts of intense activity to jump-start your weight loss as well as to cut your exercise time. Now, though, a new study published in *The Journal of the American Medical Association* calls that concept into question. Researchers at the University of Pittsburgh, Brown Medical School, and Wake Forest University measured weight loss in 184 women, who were divided into four exercise groups of various intensity and duration combinations, and who were asked to cut down to from 1,200 to 1,500 calories per day. All the groups lost weight during the year-long study. Surprisingly, though, while women in the two groups that did the longer workouts lost an average of about 3 to 6 pounds more than those who exercised for shorter periods, the intensity of those workouts didn't seem to matter. So what gives?

The fact that the study participants were sedentary and overweight makes a difference, says I-Min Lee, M.D., associate professor of medicine at Harvard Medical School. When people who don't typically exercise get active, they'll lose weight no matter what intensity they're working at, as long as they burn more calories than they take in. But this doesn't mean that a stroll down the block is the energy-burning equivalent of sprinting or tackling hills. "Doing more-intense exercise for the same amount of time will burn more calories," Lee confirms.

Barry Franklin, Ph.D., director of cardiac rehabilitation and exercise laboratories at William Beaumont Hospital in Royal Oak, Michigan, agrees, adding that vigorous exercise will also increase your aerobic fitness, which will allow you to work out longer and harder. "If weight loss is your goal," he says, "it does pay, without question, to increase either the duration or the intensity—or both—of your exercise."

Simply put, if you are already active but your weight loss has leveled off over a couple of months, you need to either cut more calories or increase your energy output; adding intensity to your workout is an easy way to accomplish the latter.

If you've hit a fitness plateau, it may be time to push your routine up a notch.

Cross-Training the Smart Way

Doing the same workout all the time can be tough on your body, not to mention your motivation level. Cross training can prevent burnout and injury, and it can ensure a well-balanced exercise program that includes endurance (three to five times a week), strength, and flexibility training (both two to three times a week).

Finding moves that complement what you do is key, since the idea is to give overworked muscles a breather while you work on neglected ones. We turned to Carol Torgan, Ph.D., an exercise physiologist and a spokeswoman for the American College of Sports Medicine, for suggestions on which exercises to pair with seven popular activities.

IF YOU...	TRY	WHY	ALSO TRY
WALK OR RUN	Weight lifting, yoga, or Pilates	To prevent imbalances among the muscles in the fronts and backs of the thighs, as well as to stretch hamstrings and hips	Lower impact cardio alternatives, such as biking and swimming, to reduce the load on the legs
TAKE KICKBOXING OR STEP CLASSES	Weight lifting	To prevent muscle imbalances	Lower impact options, such as water aerobics or cycling, plus yoga or Pilates for flexibility, balance, and core strength
PLAY TENNIS	Hiking, walking, jogging, or inline skating	To balance tennis' stop-and-start action with sustained moderate-intensity cardio	Yoga or Pilates for shoulder, arm, back, and hip flexibility, and for core strength
BIKE OR SPIN	Weight lifting, walking, or jogging	To build upper-body muscle and to maintain and build bone with weight-bearing cardio	Yoga or Pilates for flexible hip, thigh, and back muscles (which can improve bike position) and for core strength
WEIGHT-TRAIN	Swimming and yoga or Pilates	To burn calories as well as strengthen your heart with cardio, to build core strength, and to keep muscles flexible	Walking or jogging for weight-bearing cardio
DO PILATES OR YOGA	Swimming, biking, or jogging	To burn calories and strengthen your heart; also to maintain bone density (jogging in particular helps here)	Weight lifting once or twice a week (some Pilates and yoga classes focus more on flexibility and balance than strength)
SWIM	Walking, jogging, or strength training	To build and maintain bone with weight-bearing cardio	Yoga or Pilates for shoulder, back, and hip flexibility, and for core strength

237

Knock Out Knee Problems

Knee injuries strike 10 million women every year. Here's how to avoid them.

BY KIMBERLY WONG

One look at my knees, and it's pretty obvious that I wasn't into Barbies or television as a kid—it was more like baseball and bike riding for me. The scars from sliding into third and wiping out on my Schwinn haven't completely faded; neither have my tomboyish tendencies. But over the years, I have become more careful about how I use my body—especially my knees—because I know it would probably take more than a Band-Aid to fix the injuries I face. I've seen it happen too many times to think I'm immune: In 2003, in the span of two weeks, three women on my weekend soccer team each blew out a knee. All of them needed surgery to repair damaged ligaments and have only recently been able to return to the field.

The fact that female athletes like my friends and I are particularly susceptible to knee injuries is old news in sports medicine and orthopedic circles. The most recent estimates from a University of Michigan study say that women who participate in sports that involve jumping, turning, and twisting—such as soccer, basketball, and tennis—are between two and nine times as likely to rupture a knee ligament as their male counterparts.

But you don't have to be a jock to end up with a bum knee. Overall, women are six to eight times as likely as men to sustain some kind of knee injury. Each year, approximately ten million women see their doctors for knee pain, often caused by such seemingly harmless activities as lifting heavy boxes, climbing stairs, or squatting too much in the garden. That's compared with the 5.5 million women who seek professional help for headaches annually.

> You don't have to be a jock to end up with a bum knee. Women are six to eight times as likely as men to sustain knee injuries.

What's making women go weak in the knees? Researchers blame everything from hormones that make us more susceptible to injury during ovulation to a lack of calcium that decreases bone density. But one of the most likely causes is the way women are built. Our thighbones tend to curve inward from hip to knee, putting added stress on the joints. Plus, our muscle strength tends to be out of balance. Women often use the quadriceps (the massive muscles on the fronts of the thighs) much more than we use the hamstrings on the backs of our legs, which leads to an imbalance between the two muscle groups.

You can't do much about your bone structure. But with a few smart moves, you can prevent some of the most common knee problems—or get the kinks out if they're already giving you trouble. Here's how.

GETTING OFF TRACK

The problem: Your kneecap aches.

The cause: Patella (aka kneecap) injuries are number one on the list of knee problems for women who exercise regularly. Your kneecap is supposed to glide up and down as you extend your leg, explains Edward Wojtys, M.D., professor of orthopedics at the University of Michigan. But the angle at which women's muscles pull makes it easy for the kneecap to slide off track and rub against surrounding bone, causing pain and swelling around the sides or back of the leg behind the kneecap. You may also hear or feel some cracking.

Who's at risk: No matter how old you are, doing too much of a new activity too soon—especially such activities as hiking, running up or down hills, or anything else that requires you to jump and land over and over again—can catch your knees off guard and overload them.

What you can do: Don't panic if your kneecaps are already on the sore side. "The good news about patella pain is that it's very treatable," explains Jo Hannafin, M.D., Ph.D., orthopedic director at the Women's Sports Medicine Center at the Hospital for Special

To help avoid knee pain, always increase the intensity of your workout gradually.

Surgery in New York City. "The vast majority of women respond very well to exercise and strengthening programs to improve the kneecap's alignment."

To help prevent pain, build up your endurance (never increase the length or intensity of your workout by more than 10 percent per week), and concentrate on strengthening the adductor muscles, the ones near the inside of the knee that keep the kneecap in line. You can work the adductors by copying a famous Jane Fonda move: Lie on your side, bend your top leg, and place your foot on the floor in front of your bottom leg; slowly raise and lower your bottom leg.

ALL WORN OUT

The problem: Your knee swells up like a balloon.

The cause: Something's got to protect your knee from all the pounding it takes, and that's where the crescent-shaped cartilage called the meniscus comes in. It's the shock absorber that cushions and distributes the force on your knee. When the meniscus breaks down, flaps can form, causing irritation that can eventually lead to pain and swelling. The pain typically starts on the inside of the knee at the point where it bends, but you may also feel it at the same spot on the outside of the knee. Take these signs seriously, since even small tears can eventually lead to arthritis.

Who's at risk: For women in their 30s or younger, it usually takes a traumatic event—a major wipeout on the ski slopes, perhaps, or an awkward landing after a layup—to tear the meniscus. As women hit their 40s and 50s, though, the cartilage starts showing signs of wear and begins to provide less protection from injury, to the point that simply squatting the wrong way could cause it to tear. Being overweight affects the meniscus as well, since extra pounds put a heavier burden on it.

What you can do: To minimize your symptoms, Hannafin recommends taking an anti-inflammatory, such as aspirin or ibuprofen; applying ice to decrease swelling; and beginning a leg-strengthening and flexibility program. If you have had pain for several weeks without having suffered an obvious injury to your knee, see your doctor, because some meniscus tears require surgery. (If the pain occurs right after intense activity, though, don't wait longer than two or three days to check in with your physician.) To guard your knees against a meniscus tear, try to concentrate on stretching and strengthening your hamstrings, quadriceps, hip flexors, and iliotibial band, the band of tissue that runs from your thigh down over your knee to your tibia. (For specific exercises, go to our Web site at Health.com and click on "Fitness.") If you are heavy, shedding those extra pounds also can help take the pressure off the meniscus.

Jumping and other high-impact activities are tough on knees, but you can protect them with stretching and regular exercise.

GOING OVERBOARD

The problem: You experience soreness above or below your knee that worsens over time.

The cause: Overdoing it on the length or intensity of an exercise session—such as running too far or too fast—could leave you with such nagging injuries as stress fractures in the bones around your knee, inflamed muscles surrounding your knee, or even tendinitis in your kneecap. In the beginning, soreness follows whatever activity you are doing. Soon the knee begins to hurt during the activity, and eventually you feel pain in the course of normal movement, or even at rest.

Who's at risk: According to Bert Mandelbaum, M.D., director of the Santa Monica Orthopaedic and Sports Medicine Group, this problem mainly

Three Moves for Healthy Knees

These exercises can keep your knees from aching (or worse) by shoring up the muscles around the joint. Do two sets of 15 reps two to three times a week for best results.

1. Hamstring curls (for hamstrings): Attach one end of an elastic exercise band to a pole or the leg of a heavy piece of furniture, and tie the other end around your ankle. Stand facing the pole so that the band is pulled tight. Keeping your hips stationary, slowly pull your leg back, bending your knee (you should feel a slight burn in the back of your thigh). Switch legs.
2. Straight leg raises (for quadriceps and hip flexors): Lying on your back, with your legs

straight, slowly raise one leg off the floor for a count of 15 or 20 seconds, then very gently lower it. Switch to the other leg. To challenge yourself further, add ankle weights for more resistance; start with 3 pounds, and gradually work your way up to 8.
3. Wall squats (for hamstrings, buttocks, and inner quadriceps): Stand with your back against a wall, with your heels just over a foot away from the wall and a medium-size ball (a soccer ball or basketball will do) between your knees. Squeeze the ball as you slowly slide down the wall until your knees are as close to a 90-degree angle as is comfortable. Count to 3, and then slide back up.

affects women in their 40s and 50s. That's when estrogen and bone-density levels start to plummet, making bones and tendons more vulnerable to injuries.

What you can do: To heal an overuse injury, allow your body to rest until your knee is no longer sore. To avoid an injury in the first place, be sure to increase your workouts gradually. If you're a runner, for instance, don't ramp up mileage and intensity all in one shot. "Really listen to your body," Hannafin says.

AN UNFORTUNATE TWIST

The problem: In the midst of an activity that involves sudden shifts in direction, your knee pops, buckles, and swells; you feel intense pain; and your knee gives way if you try to put any weight on it.

The cause: Chances are you've torn your anterior cruciate ligament (ACL). One of the four knee ligaments that connect the thighbone to the shin-bone, the ACL keeps the knee stable as it rotates. When it ruptures, it's like a cable snapping.

Who's at risk: A torn ACL is most common in high school and college athletes. But all active women need to be aware of the danger, especially those who participate in sports—such as basketball, skiing, and soccer—that involve quick changes in direction, pivoting, and twisting. ACL injuries can happen to anyone, however; you could tear yours during a fall, in a car accident, or even while playing fetch with your dog.

What you can do: This is a serious injury (most women who tear their ACLs need surgery), so you should see your doctor right away if it happens to you. To help keep your ACL healthy and intact, "maintain your conditioning," Hannafin advises. "You are more likely to get injured if you're fatigued and you don't exercise on a regular basis." You should also make an effort to strengthen the leg muscles—the hamstrings and inner quadriceps—that support your knee (see "Three Moves for Healthy Knees" at left). Agility and proper form when jumping and landing are important, too. Remember to always keep your knees bent when you land, whether you're pulling down a rebound or hopping off a ladder. ■

San Francisco–based writer Kimberly Wong has played soccer for 25 years without knee problems. But while Wong was reporting this story, her beagle, Maddie, was diagnosed with a torn ACL.

Good News for Shoes: They're Not to Blame for Knee Pain

Fans of legendary dress shoes made by Manolo Blahnik or Jimmy Choo (or even the cheap knockoffs) know that 4-inch heels can make your feet hurt if you wear them too long. But fashionistas might be surprised to learn that high heels aren't likely to cause knee pain. A recent British study compared 29 women who had osteoarthritis of the knee—in which joint cushioning wears down—with 82 who were problem-free. Shoe preference had no effect on arthritis risk. Researchers say that maintaining a healthy weight is the best way to prevent knee pain.

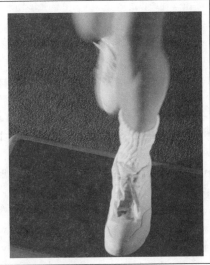

Nurture Your BODY IMAGE

A new form of yoga delves deep to give your self-perception a positive spin.

BY DOROTHY FOLTZ-GRAY

When I walked into Mark Stevens' yoga studio, I wasn't expecting much more than a good stretch and maybe some stress-releasing meditation, but I did feel a little performance anxiety. I was just sure this class was full of strangers who could twist themselves into pretzels at will.

I'd heard that Stevens' brand of yoga, called Anusara, was helping people feel better about their bodies, but I didn't expect a single hour to make much of a difference. After all, though I'm pretty comfortable with the frame I've got, it's taken years of running, weight lifting, and other activities for me to get over the body confusion that plagued me as a fat kid.

So I was grateful for the warmth and acceptance that Stevens and his students exhibited at his studio, Awakening Heart, in Asheville, North Carolina. In no time I felt perfectly comfortable hoisting my butt skyward in the downward-facing-dog pose, my body turning into an inverted V. During the session, we were cracking jokes and having fun as we joined in this common endeavor of poising our bodies and minds as close as we could to the edge of grace.

Anusara, created a mere six years ago, is an infant compared to other types of hatha yoga. But it's gradually gaining popularity because of its unique ability to help the devotee lift her body image and limber her muscles at the same time.

Anusara founder John Friend says, "In other systems of yoga, the body may be considered inferior to the spirit, but we look at the body—any type of body—as the miraculous expression of the supreme." In a culture where so many women and men are at war with their bodies, this type of approach has quite a market. There are more than one thousand instructors and two hundred and fifty thousand Anusara students worldwide, Friend says.

Much like other yoga variants, Anusara includes such poses as forward bends and the plank. But even as you focus on correct body position, Anusara cues your inner self as well. "We use heart-oriented language," says Suzie Hurley of Willow Street Yoga Center in Takoma Park, Maryland. "Instead of 'Take your arms up,' I say, 'Extend your arms from your heart, and reach for the very highest.'"

Anusara asks you to move in a way that expresses your spirit and attitude, a request I'm not sure I've ever encountered before in an exercise class. Nor has any yoga instructor ever cued my heart. But I thought that maybe if I learned to follow those gentle prompts, my body and spirit would become more connected.

It's the alignment of more than just muscle and bone that lies at the center of Anusara. To that end, the class vibe tends to be less about achieving the perfect pose and more about enjoying the journey. As I move into a forward bend, I consult Stevens on what my goal should be. He laughs and says, "There is no goal. Just do what you can do." On this particular day, my hamstrings are not ready to let me bend forward and place my palms flat on the floor, but my body is doing the best it can. Stevens encourages me to acknowledge this as a small victory.

> ## The principles of yoga help people become less preoccupied with their bodies and more appreciative of their spiritual side.
> —Robinson Welch, Ph.D.

That kind of positive perspective can help people change the troubled relationships they have with their bodies, explains Anusara instructor Christina Sell, author of *Yoga from the Inside Out: Making Peace with Your Body Through Yoga*. "If you believe the body is an expression of the divine, you begin to change the way you want to move your body, to stretch it, to respond to it," she says.

In just the span of an hour, I felt the power of accepting, even loving, what my body could do. This may sound sappy, but how often do any of us focus on the beauty our bodies are capable of? To do that, even briefly, felt like both a release and a lesson, an illustration of mind/body harmony that didn't seem like a lot of New Age hooey.

Still, Anusara isn't a body-image counseling session. "You won't get a rap about how you should feel better about your thighs," Sell says. "But if you know that body image is something you want to make peace with, then Anusara can help."

Even if you don't have hang-ups about your hips, Anusara could do you some good. When 27-year-old Heidi Andersen of Asheville signed up for Stevens' class, she simply wanted to try a new version of yoga. But in the year she has been practicing Anusara, she has noticed a new appreciation of her self-described big-boned body. She recalls a pivotal moment in her first session. "We were doing warrior pose, and I was tensing my hands. Mark came over and said, 'Hey, Heidi, let your fingers party.' That was very powerful. I thought, 'I've been taking yoga too seriously—like I take my life. I should open up.'"

But Anusara has not in any way cornered the market on body acceptance. Other forms of yoga have the potential to heal as well, explains Beth Hartman McGilley, Ph.D., a clinical psychologist who focuses on body image and eating disorders. "People with a distorted body image often turn exercise into a form of abuse, but that's hard to do with yoga," she says. "It's gentle and breath-centered, and it invites you back into your body in a welcoming, nonthreatening way."

In fact, some eating-disorder programs have begun to add yoga to their regimens. "The principles of yoga help people become less preoccupied with their bodies and more appreciative of their spiritual side," says Robinson Welch, Ph.D., co-director of the Weight Management and Eating Disorders Program at Washington University School of Medicine in St. Louis.

That's how I feel in Anusara class as I attempt my first handstand. Stunned at my own courage, I prop myself on my hands facing away from a wall and scuttle my feet halfway up. I look like an overturned L, but this is the closest I've ever come to doing a full handstand. And I have to admit that I feel grateful and triumphant, kind of like a little kid who has just ditched her training wheels—and, yes, like a grown-up who is learning to appreciate a body that is divine. ■

Yoga Faces Friendly COMPETITION

The ancient practice of *qigong* promises good health and renewed energy. Here's why many people are attracted to it.

BY CATHERINE DOLD

In a Boulder, Colorado, conference room in a nondescript office building, a dozen women of various ages and sizes swing their arms above their heads, left to right, their hands slowly streaming through the air on cue. Lurking in the back row, I try to follow everyone else's gentle, flowing movements, feeling less like the swaying willow I am supposed to be mimicking and more like a clumsy tumbleweed.

During a move that *qigong* instructor Steven Ridley calls "heart to sky," I squat and make a scooping motion to "gather chi." I then rise, bring my hands upward and out, arch my back, and open my arms. Repeating the motion several times, I try to concentrate on my breathing and watch my limbs with "soft eyes," as Ridley directs. One movement flows into another, and before I know it I've followed Ridley through 18 different moves of

> **Qigong is more forgiving than other fitness routines: If squatting is hard, a little bend at the knees will do just fine. Some who find yoga discouraging say they have no problem with qigong.**

qigong, all of which are designed to free my chi, my vital energy, my life force.

Free my chi? That's exactly what Ridley and other practitioners say is happening. Qigong (pronounced chee-KONG), an ancient Chinese practice, promises good health through the cultivation and balance of chi (chee). So move over, yoga. Those who practice qigong regularly say it can reduce stress, speed healing, and improve sleep, digestion, circulation, immunity, and longevity through its meditative approach to fitness. But does it deliver?

Western science hasn't proved it. Nonetheless, qigong is getting nods of approval and is popping up in mainstream medical centers, including some run by Kaiser Permanente (which sponsors Ridley's class), the largest HMO in the country, as well as spas and health clubs wanting to capitalize on the booming interest in fitness regimens that address both body and mind.

"We initially offered qigong classes to our chronic-pain patients," says Carol Mills, a health-education specialist at Kaiser Permanente Colorado. "Some of them are quite immobilized and can't do anything. But with qigong you can adapt the exercises to your physical ability—and if all you can do is lift your arm while seated, it's better than nothing." The patients told Mills and their doctors that the instruction was a big help, so the classes were opened to other Kaiser Permanente health-care-plan members.

Holly Gautier, R.N., director of cancer-patient services at Stanford University Medical Center, also cites positive patient feedback as a primary reason for offering qigong classes. But science is also beginning to support the use of such mind-body disciplines as qigong; researchers have found that these activities can ease the stress of living with cancer, Gautier says. And studies of the cancer patients at Stanford who have taken classes in qigong and other mind-body practices have shown that participants are more relaxed, feel less stressed and fatigued, and have an increased sense of well-being, she adds.

Qigong can help restore a sense of control over your life, a sense of self-empowerment—a big boon for anyone who has to deal with an ongoing illness and the many doctor visits that go along with it. "It's like an internal body scan. There are then specific exercises that can be done to alleviate lots of different issues," says Arnold Tayam, Stanford Medical Center qigong instructor and director of the Longevity Center in San Jose, California. Qigong gives people practical tools to alleviate such symptoms as chronic pain and low energy, he says.

Qigong is sort of the granddaddy of Tai Chi. It is one of the primary branches of traditional Chinese medicine, along with herbs, massage, acupuncture, and nutrition.

Like acupuncture, qigong makes use of a complex system of internal pathways called meridians, which are thought to run along the length of the body, a bit like longitude lines on a map. Western scientists have not identified this elusive network, but according to Chinese medicine, meridians carry chi throughout your body. Your chi can become stagnant or blocked within this system; some describe the obstruction as a feeling of sluggish-ness or powerlessness. Qigong can keep chi flowing and balanced. When chi is balanced, life is good.

"Qigong calmly centers us, but it also gives us energy to use," explains Ridley, who has studied the technique since 1975. "It's like getting a general acupuncture treatment every day."

The simple moves of qigong leave students feeling less stressed.

CHECK YOUR CHI

Some qigong classes focus on fitness or meditation; others are more suited to people who haven't exercised for a while. Try a few different methods, and choose the approach that you like the best.

- To find a teacher, contact the National Qigong Association (888-815-1893 or www.nqa.org).
- To read more, try *Qigong for Staying Young: A Simple 20-Minute Workout to Cultivate Your Vital Energy*, by Shoshanna Katzman.

But is it a workout? In class, Ridley leads us through six moves that he says will clear our organs of sluggish chi. These motions are accompanied by visualizing specific colors and making distinctive "healing sounds." Thinking green and chanting "shhhuuu" supposedly helps to cleanse my liver; filling my head with visions of whiteness and chanting "seeahhhh" is said to send good thoughts to my lungs.

It all seems a bit silly, but I end up feeling surprisingly invigorated. Even with such slow, deliberate movements and a meditative focus, I've worked up a light sweat. Plus, these very simple moves just feel really good. I'm not wiped out as I sometimes am after a strenuous workout. Instead, I'm clearheaded and energized. Another student of Ridley's, Helen Eisner, says she feels so relaxed after class that she practically drifts home.

For novices, qigong requires no more effort than a game of "follow the leader." Most of Ridley's students do nothing more than remove their shoes to prepare for class.

Qigong is also more forgiving than other fitness routines: If squatting is hard, a little bend at the knees will do just fine. Some who find yoga discouraging because they can't get into the positions say they have no problem with qigong, Tayam notes.

Ridley concentrates on one set of movements he has chosen for his classes, but there are thousands of routines and an endless number of ways to practice qigong. Some health clubs offer fusion classes, such as chi sculpt and chi dance.

At the Red Mountain Spa in St. George, Utah, such mind-body techniques as qigong are hot, says Ann Topalian, who is assistant fitness manager there. "Nobody here misses our old programs of strength training and cardio workouts," she says. "People are still getting many of the same fitness benefits with the mind-body programs, but they just don't realize it."

For me, qigong won't replace hiking, skiing, or inline skating. But after Ridley's class, I felt serene and relaxed, like I'd had a good, if gentle, workout. Maybe that's what freeing my chi feels like. ▪

Catherine Dold is a health and science writer in Boulder, Colorado.

Bringing Kids to the Club

Attention, moms: We know you need time to yourselves, but if a new movement continues, you may have to share the gym with your children. Across the country, independent fitness clubs and regional chains, such as New York Sports Club and The Sports Club/LA, have begun providing kid-specific classes—such as Spinning, weight training, yoga, and kickboxing—that children can attend while their parents work out.

The International Health, Racquet & Sportsclub Association now estimates that nearly a quarter of the nation's gyms offer active options for kids—and we're not talking traditional day care here—at the same times as the adult classes. Parents are obviously warming to the idea of a safe, secure exercise environment for their kids, too: Between 1999 and 2003, preteen and teen memberships at clubs increased by 65 percent.

To find a gym program for your kids, check with local fitness centers. Make sure your child receives an OK from the pediatrician before getting physical.

The percentage of overweight children has more than doubled since the early 1970s, and parents are often the best motivators for kids to start moving. So there's no better reason to lure your offspring off the couch and into the gym with you.

How to Get the Best Gym Deal

Planning to join a gym? Don't settle for just any club; educate yourself before you commit.

Visit the gym.
Or even better, take advantage of a free trial period. Go during your usual workout time, and pay particular attention to:
- Wait times for treadmills or other machines
- The condition of the fitness equipment
- The presence (or absence) of spotters in the weight room
- The cleanliness of the shower stalls and locker room
- The atmosphere: Do you feel comfortable working out here?

If you like what you see ...
Take the contract home, and look it over carefully with these questions in mind (courtesy of the International Health, Racquet & Sportsclub Association and the Federal Trade Commission):
- Does the contract contain what you were promised by the club representative?
- How long is the cooling-off period? Clubs are obligated to allow contract cancellations without penalty for a certain period after signing; lengths vary by state.
- Does the contract require you to cancel in writing, or can you do so by phone?
- If you had to cancel your agreement due to a move or injury/illness, would you get a refund?
- Does the club automatically renew contracts upon expiration?

Check with your attorney general.
- A state-by-state listing is available at www.it-pays -to-complain.com; click on "Attorneys General" to see if the club is mentioned.
- Or check out the Better Business Bureau's Web site (www.bbb.org) to see if any complaints have been lodged against the club. If not, grab your sneakers; this is the gym for you.

Sip to Keep Cool

Everyone knows that staying hydrated during your workout is important. But exactly how much fluid is enough? To find out, we turned to Bob Murray, Ph.D., director of the Gatorade Sports Science Institute (and a well-respected independent researcher in the hydration field). He offers the following suggestions.
- Drink 16 to 20 ounces of water, fruit juice, or sports drink about 2 hours before you exercise.
- Determine how much fluid you need during your workout, based on how sweat-soaked you are afterward. Here's a guide:
  - Light (your skin is moist and a little sweat is visible around your collar): 4 to 6 ounces every 15 minutes
  - Moderate (your skin and clothes are noticeably wet): 8 to 12 ounces every 15 minutes
  - Heavy (your skin, clothes, and hair are completely drenched): 12 to 16 ounces every 15 minutes

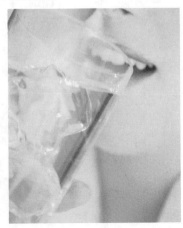

BODYWORK

Get a Better *Rear* View

Shape up your bottom with these three easy gravity-defying moves.

WORKOUT BY PETRA KOLBER • PHOTOGRAPHY BY DAVID MARTINEZ

LEG CIRCLES ON THE BALL

1A. Lie on the floor with your right leg on a fitness ball and your left leg extended toward the ceiling.

1B. With your abdominals tight and your shoulders on the floor, lift your hips off the floor. Keeping your hips up, point your left toe and make 8 small circles clockwise and then counterclockwise. Repeat with your right leg.

1A

1B

1

248

SINGLE-LEG BRIDGE ON THE BALL

2A. Sit on the ball, and slowly roll down until only your shoulders, head, and neck are in contact with it. Steady yourself, contract your abs, then place your left leg across your right thigh. (If that's too challenging, keep both feet on the floor.)
2B. Contract your glutes, and lift your hips toward the ceiling. Pause and lower. Repeat 8 to 12 times; then switch legs.

QUADRUPED LIFT

3A. Kneel on all fours, keeping your abdominals tight. Place a weight in the crook of your right knee.
3B. Keeping abs tight, slowly raise the sole of your right shoe toward the ceiling. Pause, then lower your knee halfway down. Repeat 8 to 12 times; then switch sides.
Trainer Tip: Use a 3- to 5-pound dumbbell for this exercise. For best results, concentrate on squeezing your glutes at the top of the movement. ■

Contributing Editor Petra Kolber is also a Reebok University master trainer. You can reach her at PetraKolber.com.

249

BODYWORK

Show Off Your *Arms*

Here's how to tone and tighten them in just four weeks.

WORKOUT BY PETRA KOLBER • PHOTOGRAPHY BY DAVID MARTINEZ

Why should you focus on your arms? Because for women, they are easy fitness targets: A woman's arms tend to be leaner than her hips, thighs, and butt, for instance, so even small muscle-firming gains are visible.

With these three moves, you can improve definition, tone, and strength. Try these exercises two or three times a week, and you'll be ready to bare your arms in as few as four weeks.

ONE-ARM BICEPS CURL

1A. Sit with your knees apart. Holding a 5- to 8-pound weight in your right hand, anchor your right elbow along the inside of your right thigh. Make sure that your abs are tight and your back is not arched.

1B. Slowly contract your biceps as you curl the weight toward your right shoulder. Pause, holding the contraction; then slowly lower to the starting position. Repeat 8 to 12 times; then switch sides.

250

SEATED TRICEPS EXTENSION

2A. While seated, hold a 5- to 8-pound dumbbell between your hands and extend your arms overhead. Be sure to tighten your abdominals in order to avoid arching your back.

2B. Keep your elbows pointed forward as you lower the weight behind your head, toward the middle of your back. Return to the starting position. Repeat 8 to 12 times.

CURL AND LIFT

3A. Stand with your feet hip-distance apart and a 5- to 8-pound dumbbell in each hand. Your arms should be at your sides, with your palms facing your body. With your abs tight and your elbows close to your sides, curl the weights up to your shoulders.

3B. Extend your arms overhead; be careful not to lean back or relax your abs. Reverse the movement to return to the starting position. Repeat 8 to 12 times. ◼

Petra Kolber is a contributing editor. You can reach her at her Web site, PetraKolber.com.

BODYWORK • BODYWORK • BODYWORK • BODYWORK • BODYWORK • BODYWORK • BODYWORK • BODYWORK

BODYWORK

The Secret to Slim *Hips*

Surprise … it's in your shoulders. Strengthen your top half, and your bottom half will look fitter, too!

WORKOUT BY PETRA KOLBER • PHOTOGRAPHY BY DAVID MARTINEZ

1B

1A

1B,
back view

One way to make your hips and thighs look smaller is to put a little more effort into toning your back and shoulders. It's a smoke-and-mirrors trick—and it may be the only workout secret shared by Miss America and Ms. Olympia contestants alike.

More definition at the top of the body draws the eye upward, and stronger muscles in that area help you stand straighter and taller. The four moves on the next couple of pages specifically strengthen the back muscles that come into play when you lift a paint can off the floor or pull weeds in the garden. All you need is a pair of 3- to 5-pound dumbbells and a resistance band, and you're one step closer to the shape you want.

SINGLE-ARM LAT PULL

1A. Hold a resistance band above your head, with your arms slightly bent and your hands shoulder-width apart. If you need more resistance, shorten the band's tubing.

1B. Without hunching your shoulders, lower your right elbow toward the floor. Focus on contracting your back muscles during the movement, and be sure to keep your left elbow slightly bent. Pause and return to the starting position. Repeat 8 to 12 times; then switch sides.

252

BALL CRUNCH WITH A TWIST

2A. Lie on a fitness ball with your heels directly beneath your knees. Bring your arms to your chest, and gently support your chin on your fists.

2B. Leading with your right shoulder, exhale and contract your abdominal muscles as you slowly lift and turn your body toward your left hip. Pause and then slowly lower yourself to the starting position. Do 8 to 12 repetitions; then switch sides.

SINGLE-ARM PULLOVER

3A. Lie on the floor with your knees bent and your feet flat. Hold a weight in your right hand directly above your shoulder, and rest your left hand on the floor.

3B. Keeping your abdominal muscles tight and your arm straight but not locked, slowly lower your right arm so that it hovers above the floor behind your head. Contract your back muscles as you return your arm to the starting position. Repeat 8 to 12 times; then switch arms.

SINGLE-ARM LATERAL RAISE

4A. Stand with your weight on your left foot, bend your knees slightly, and rest your right foot on the floor behind you for balance. Hold a dumbbell in your right hand.

4B. Keeping your abdominal muscles tight, your chest lifted, and your shoulders down, raise your right arm to shoulder height. Pause and return to the starting position. Repeat 8 to 12 times; then switch sides. ◼

Petra Kolber is a Health contributing editor and a Reebok University Master Trainer.

BODYWORK

Build Your *Beach* Body

Look better than ever in your swimsuit with these three fast, easy moves.

WORKOUT BY PETRA KOLBER • PHOTOGRAPHY BY DAVID MARTINEZ

Don't sweat summertime. These moves will help you get strong and toned, especially when it comes to that troublesome triumvirate of body parts: butt, arms, and abs. The walking lunge gets an extra kick from the friction created when you drag your foot across the floor as you stand up straight. That little bit of resistance can boost both the intensity of the move and your odds of getting the shape you want before donning that swimsuit. For the best results, start with one set of each exercise and build to three.

WALKING LUNGES
For butt and thighs

1A. Stand with your feet together and your hands on your hips.

1B. Keep your abdominals tight, and take a big step forward with your right leg, bending this knee at a 90-degree angle and keeping it aligned with your ankle; extend your left arm in front of you for balance. Contract your right glute, and drag your left toe forward as you return to the starting position. Repeat, stepping forward with your left leg. Do 8 to 12 reps with each leg.

1A

1B

1

SINGLE-ARM DIP
For triceps

2A. Sit on the edge of a bench, and place your hands beside your hips with your palms down and your knuckles facing forward. Move your feet forward, and slide your hips off the bench. Keep your shoulders down and your elbows pointed behind you. Then slowly bend your elbows to lower your hips.

2B. Lift your left arm, and use your right triceps to push back up. Pause and then return your left arm to the bench. Bend both elbows to lower your hips. Straighten both arms again, lift your right arm, and pause. Repeat 8 to 12 times, alternating arms.

Trainer Tip: If you have trouble balancing, leave your hands on the bench throughout the move. Or up the challenge by raising the opposite leg when you raise your arm.

ROLL-UP
For abdominals

3A. Lie on the floor with your hands resting at your sides and your legs straight. Flex your ankles, draw your navel toward your spine, and inhale.

3B. Exhale and bend your knees slightly. Roll up one vertebra at a time, lifting your head, neck, and shoulders off the floor in a scooping motion. Pause and return to the starting position. Repeat 8 to 12 times. ■

Petra Kolber is a Health *contributing editor and a Reebok University Master Trainer.*

BODYWORK • BODYWORK • BODYWORK • BODYWORK • BODYWORK • BODYWORK • BODYWORK

BODYWORK

Tame Your *Tight* Spots

These two-for-one moves stretch you where it hurts.

WORKOUT BY PETRA KOLBER • PHOTOGRAPHY BY DAVID MARTINEZ

Walkers and runners are especially susceptible to tight hips, calves, and hamstrings. The key to flexibility is to stretch when your muscles are warm, after a workout or even a brief walk or jog. This strategy will help you get more mileage out of your stretches and may even make you feel agile enough to walk longer or jog faster in the future. Besides, nothing says "workout over" better than a good stretch (unless it's the LED display on your elliptical trainer).

These three time-saving moves hit several muscles at once. Repeat each stretch two to three times, and you'll be done in a matter of minutes.

1

INVERTED V
For calves, Achilles tendons, hamstrings, and shoulders

1. Begin by kneeling on all fours. Make sure your abdominals are tight and your weight is evenly distributed among your arms and legs. Inhale; then exhale and lift your hips toward the ceiling. Focus on pressing your hands into the mat and lowering your heels as far as you can toward the floor. Hold 20 to 30 seconds.

CALF STRETCH
For upper and lower calves

2A. Place both hands on a wall at about shoulder height, and take a big step back with your left foot. Bend your right knee, and focus on straightening your left leg while pressing your left heel toward the floor. You'll feel a stretch in both your upper and lower calves. Hold 20 to 30 seconds.

2B. Bend your left knee slightly to shift the stretch into the lower calf. Hold 20 to 30 seconds; repeat on the opposite side.

HAMSTRING AND HIP-FLEXOR STRETCH
For the fronts of hips and backs of thighs

3A. Lie on your back, keep your left leg extended on the floor, and pull your right knee toward your chest while pressing out with your left heel. Hold 20 to 30 seconds.

3B. Extend your right leg toward the ceiling until you feel a gentle stretch behind your right thigh. Hold 20 to 30 seconds; repeat on the opposite side. ■

Petra Kolber is a Health *contributing editor and a Reebok University Master Trainer. You can reach her at PetraKolber.com.*

BODYWORK

One-Minute *Moves*

These three full-body exercises are great for fast toning.

WORKOUT BY PETRA KOLBER • PHOTOGRAPHY BY DAVID MARTINEZ

You've said you don't have time for fitness—we're right there with you, believe us—so we've whittled a total-body workout down to a blazing 60 seconds per move. These aren't your run-of-the-mill exercises either. The Single-Leg Forward Bend and the Lift and Lower each work multiple body parts at once, and the Sit-up with Leg Extension hits all of your abdominal-muscle groups (talk about multitasking). Time is precious, so give these lightning-fast moves a try—all it takes is three minutes three times a week.

SINGLE-LEG FORWARD BEND
For butt, hamstrings, abs, and back

1A. Stand with your feet hip-width apart. Bend your left knee slightly, and place your weight onto your left leg. Move your right foot behind you, resting it lightly on the floor to help you balance. With your chin up, place your hands behind your back for a chest stretch or on your hips.

1B. Keeping your abs tight and your spine lengthened, hinge forward from your hips and lower your upper body until it's parallel to the floor. Both hips should be level and your back should be straight. Pause and return to the starting position to complete 1 rep. Do 8 to 12; then switch legs.

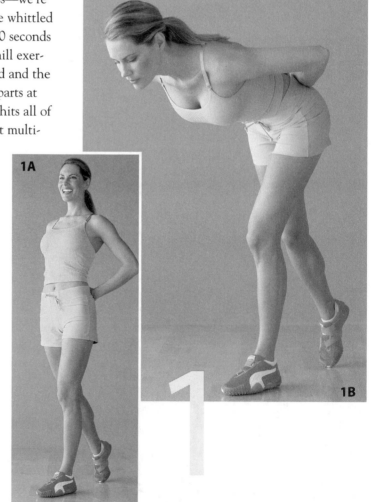

258

LIFT AND LOWER
For shoulders and legs

2A. Standing with your feet together, hold a 5- to 8-pound dumbbell in your left hand. Shift your weight onto your left leg, bending it slightly for balance. Keep your hips parallel to the floor, and extend your right leg and left arm to the side. Return to the starting position.

2B. Turn your right leg outward from the hip, and extend it forward. At the same time, raise your left arm in front of you to shoulder height. Return to the starting position to complete 1 rep. Do 8 to 12; then switch sides.

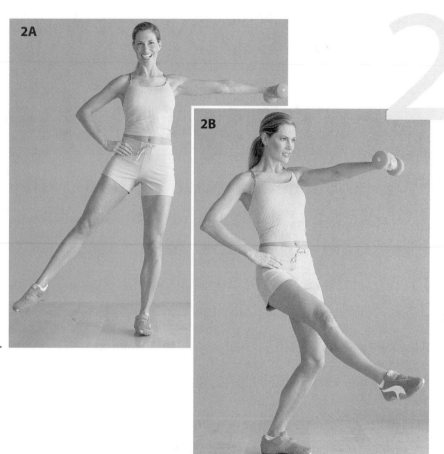

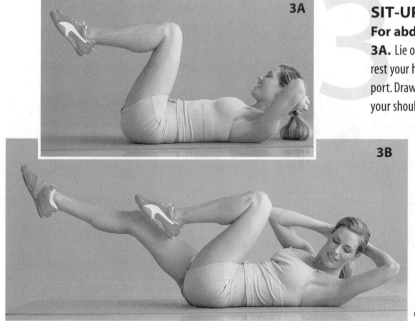

SIT-UP WITH LEG EXTENSION
For abdominal muscles

3A. Lie on your back with your knees bent, and rest your hands gently behind your head for support. Draw your navel in toward your spine, raise your shoulders off the floor, and hold.

3B. Slowly extend your right leg; then lower it as far as you can without your lower back lifting off the floor. At the same time, move your left knee toward your chest and turn your right shoulder toward your left knee. Pause and switch sides to complete 1 rep. Do 8 to 12. ■

Petra Kolber is a contributing editor and a Reebok Master Trainer. You can reach her at PetraKolber.com.

BODYWORK • BODYWORK • BODYWORK • BODYWORK • BODYWORK • BODYWORK • BODYWORK • BODYWORK • BODYWORK

BODYWORK

Fitness on the *Go*

This superfast workout is perfect when you're juggling a hectic schedule.

WORKOUT BY PETRA KOLBER • PHOTOGRAPHY BY DAVID MARTINEZ

Your to-do list is so huge that it needs its own ZIP code—the last thing you want is to add to it. But don't stress. These three double-duty moves can slash your workout time in half. For a more intense routine, do all three together. Or do one or two in spare moments throughout the day. All you need is a pair of 5- to 8-pound dumbbells.

These exercises won't sculpt you into a beach goddess, but they will stimulate your metabolism and get you moving.

LUNGE WITH TRICEPS KICKBACK

1A. Stand and position your right foot behind you. Raise hand weights to your rib cage, with your elbows also pointing behind you.
1B. Keeping your abdominals tight, bend your right knee, and lower into a lunge position while straightening your arms into a triceps kickback. Pause and push back to the starting position, keeping most of your weight on your left heel. Repeat 8 to 12 times; switch sides.

BRIDGE WITH CHEST FLY

2A. Holding a dumbbell in each hand, lie on your back with your knees bent at about 90 degrees. Keeping your elbows slightly bent, raise your arms directly over your chest.

2B. Contract your glutes, and press up through your heels into a bridge. As you push up your hips, slowly open your arms to your sides. Return to the starting position. Repeat 8 to 12 times.

2A

2B

PLIÉ BICEPS CURL

3A. Stand with your feet a bit wider than hip distance apart and your toes pointing slightly out. Hold dumbbells with your hands at your sides and your arms slightly turned out.

3B. Keeping your knees over your toes and your torso straight, bend your knees and lower your hips toward the floor. At the same time, bend your elbows into biceps curls. Return to the starting position. Repeat 8 to 12 times.

Trainer Tip: Raise your kneecaps toward your hips to work the fronts of your thighs, too. ▪

Contributing Editor Petra Kolber is also a Reebok University master trainer. You can reach her at PetraKolber.com.

3A

3B

The Ultimate
10-MINUTE
WORKOUT

BY DIMITY MCDOWELL • PHOTOGRAPHY BY DARRYL ESTRINE

Sure, you're supposed to get at least 30 minutes of exercise, five days a week. But what about those time-crunched days? Moving a little is better than not moving at all, so we asked five top trainers, "If you had only 10 minutes to work out, what would you do?" Their answer: these heart-pumping, muscle-moving routines that will lift your mood and fitness level when time is tight. Ready? Set your timer, and give that "too-busy-to-exercise" excuse a rest.

JUMP CIRCUIT

"This routine is totally portable and has a user-friendly learning curve," says Evanston, Illinois–based C.C. Cunningham, a personal trainer and educator currently working on a Ph.D. in motor learning and kinesiology. "And it doesn't allow your heart rate to drop, so you're maximizing calorie burn." In addition to a rope, you'll need a pair of 5- to 8-pound dumbbells.

1. Warm-up Jump 2 minutes

Jump at a comfortable pace, landing on alternating feet.

2. Lunge Combo 1 minute
(for butt, thighs, hips)

• **Forward lunge:** Place your hands on your hips, straighten your back, and contract your abs. Then take a big step forward with your left leg, and bend your knees at 90-degree angles, keeping your left knee aligned with your left ankle. Return to the starting position, and repeat on your right side. Do 5 reps on each side.

• **Side lunge:** With your right leg, lunge directly out to the side (see right); then return to standing position. Repeat on your left side. Do 5 reps on each side.

3. Just Plain Jump 2 minutes

Focus on landing gently on the balls of both feet.

4. Push-ups
(for chest, arms)

Get into a push-up position, either on your knees or toes, with your hands on the floor a few inches more than shoulder-width apart. Keep your back straight, and do 10 push-ups. Then move your hands directly under your shoulders so your elbows brush your sides as you lower yourself. Do 10 reps.

5. Side-to-Side Jump 1 minute

Hop from side to side with your feet together, as if jumping over an imaginary line.

6. Squat and Press 1 minute

(for butt, thighs, shoulders)

Holding a dumbbell in each hand, squat until your thighs are parallel to floor (see right). Keep your knees and ankles aligned. As you stand, extend your arms overhead (see right). Do 15 reps.

7. Double Jump 1 minute

Hop twice on your right foot; then hop twice on your left foot. Continue, alternating feet.

8. Crunch Combo 1 minute

(for abdominals)

Lie on your back, with your feet flat on the floor and your arms across your chest. Keeping your lower back on the floor, contract your abs and lift your shoulders, twisting toward your left knee. Lower and then crunch forward. Lower and then lift and twist toward the right. Return to center, and crunch forward. Repeat entire sequence 8 to 10 times.

SUPERPOWERED WALKING ROUTINE

"Walking is one of the best ways to get into shape, burn calories, and strengthen your leg muscles," says Kathy Kaehler, celebrity trainer and fitness expert for the *Today* show. Her routine, which incorporates both strength and flexibility moves, can be done on a treadmill or outside. Aim for an average pace of about 4 mph, or a 15-minute mile.

1. Warm-up Walk 2 minutes

Walk at a moderate pace for the first minute of your warm-up, then speed it up a bit during the second. If you're working out on a treadmill, bump up your pace by 0.5 mph; if you're outside, take longer strides.

2. Invisible Jump Rope 1 minute

Keep the balls of your feet on the floor, and lift your heels one at a time as you circle your wrists to turn your imaginary rope.

3. Getting-Warmer Walk 1 minute

Resume walking, using the pace you had reached during the second minute of your previous warm-up.

4. Squat-Lunge-Lift Series 1 minute

(for the butt, hips, thighs)

• **Squat:** Lower your hips toward an imaginary chair behind you, keeping your arms at shoulder height for balance (see right); return to the standing position. Repeat 5 times.

• **Lunge:** With your back straight and your hands on your hips, take a big step forward with your right leg and bend both knees at 90-degree angles (see left). Return to the standing position; repeat with your left leg. Do 5 lunges with each leg.

• **Knee lift:** Stand with your hands on your hips; then raise your left knee toward your chest (see right). Return to the starting position; then repeat with your right knee. Do 5 lifts with each leg.

5. Full-Steam-Ahead Walk 2 minutes

For the first minute, walk at the same pace you did in Step 3 of this routine. For the second, pump it up another 0.5 mph if on a treadmill; if outside, swing arms more vigorously and step faster (you can even jog if you'd like).

6. Cooldown Walk 1 minute

Slow down to lower your heart rate (if on a treadmill, decrease speed by at least 1 mph; if outside, resume initial warm-up pace).

7. Three-Way Stretch 2 minutes

March in place as you slowly reach overhead and take a deep breath. Repeat 3 times. Next, stand on your right leg, reach back with your left hand, and grab the top of your left foot. Pull your heel toward your butt to stretch your quads. Hold for 20 seconds; repeat on the opposite side. Then stretch your calves by standing on a curb or at the end of a treadmill with your heels hanging over the edge. Bend your left leg slightly as you lower your right heel toward the floor. Hold for 20 seconds. Repeat with the other leg.

PILATES-YOGA FUSION SERIES

"I like to think of the core as a tree trunk. If it's stable and strong, the wind can blow and nothing moves except the branches and leaves," explains Los Angeles–based trainer Karen Voight, creator of 18 award-winning workout videos. "If the trunk isn't solid, though, it sways and bends with the wind."

1. Gentle Stretch Warm-up 1 minute

Standing with your feet apart, twice the width of your hips, bend forward at hips. (Your abs should be tight and your back straight.) Place both hands above your right knee, and bend it slightly; hold for 20 seconds. Repeat on your left side.

2. The Bridge 1 minute

(for butt, thighs)

Lie with your knees bent and your feet flat on the floor, hip-width apart. As you inhale, squeeze your glutes and lift your hips (see right). Pause, and then lower. Do 12 reps.

3. The Bug 1 minute

(for abs, back)

Lie on your back with knees bent at a 90-degree angle and arms toward ceiling (see right).

Keeping lower back pressed into floor, lift head and shoulders as you simultaneously straighten left leg and lower right hand backward and left hand forward (see right). Hold for three breaths; switch sides. That's 1 rep. Do 16 reps total.

4. The Curl 1 minute

(for abs, back)

Lie on your back, with your knees bent and your thighs pulled toward chest. Hold your shins; exhale, and lift your head and shoulders. Keeping your lower back pressed against the floor, inhale as you extend your legs and arms at a 45-degree angle (beginners should aim for a more upright 70 degrees). Pause, exhale, and repeat 5 times.

5. The Side Plank 1 minute

(for all ab muscles)

Lie on left side, with legs stacked, weight on left forearm, elbow aligned with shoulder, and navel pulled in toward spine. Raise hip off floor; hold for 10 seconds, lower, then rest for 10 seconds. Repeat on opposite side.

6. The Airplane 1 minute

(for back)

Lie facedown, with legs together, arms extended to sides, and palms down. Exhale and contract your abs. Inhale; lift and elongate your legs, arms, and upper body. Hold for three breaths; release and rest for 20 seconds. Do 2 reps.

7. The Cat and Cow 2 minutes

(for butt, abs, back)

Start on all fours; shift weight, and lift left knee. Contract abs; bring left knee toward chest while moving forehead toward knee. Extend left leg backward, with toes pointed. Return to the starting position. Do 12 reps on each side.

8. The Twist 2 minutes
(stretches hips and lower back)
Sit on the floor with your right leg crossed over your left leg, your right knee bent, and your right foot flat on the floor next to your left knee. With your right hand resting on the floor, inhale and lengthen your spine upward. As you exhale, gently twist toward the right and bend your left elbow in front of your right knee, keeping your left forearm vertical. Inhale; then deepen and hold the stretch for 12 breaths. Repeat on the opposite side.

SOUPED-UP STAIR CIRCUIT
"This workout is a really accessible way to get a good sweat going and hit most of your major muscle groups," says creator Maureen Wilson, one of Canada's top trainers and owner of Vancouver's 20-year-old Sweat Co. Studios.

1. Climb-and-Roll Warm-up 2 minutes
Walk up and down stairs. As you climb and descend, roll your shoulders backward several times.

2. Step Push-ups 1 minute
(for chest, arms)
Place your hands on the third or fourth step and your feet or knees on the floor. With your abs tight, do 15 to 20 push-ups. For more of a challenge, put your hands on the first or second step.

3. Speed-It-Up Climb 1 minute
Go up and down stairs a bit faster than warm-up pace.

4. Triceps Dips 1 minute
(for upper arms)
Sit on second or third step. Hold on to step with elbows pointing behind you; slide hips off edge. Lift left foot off floor; extend leg (see right). Lower by bending elbows to

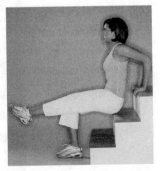

90 degrees (butt may brush floor or stairs, but use your arms to support your weight). Straighten your arms slowly. Do 10 reps. Repeat with your right leg extended.

5. Double-Step Climb 90 seconds
Take the stairs two at a time on the way up and single steps on the way down.

6. Elevated Push-ups 90 seconds
(for chest, back)
Get into push-up position so that your right hand is on the first step, your left hand is on the floor,

and your knees or toes are on floor (see left). Do 10 push-ups. Repeat with your left hand on the step and your right hand on the floor.

7. Sidewinder Climb 1 minute

Ascend the stairs sideways by lifting your right foot onto one step (see left), your left foot onto the next, and so on. Descend the stairs normally. Next time up, face the opposite direction. If you are not comfortable with this movement, simply face the stairs, and step up and down on the first step as fast as you can.

8. Single-Foot Stair Squats 1 minute
(for butt, hips, thighs)
Stand with your right foot on the first step and your left foot dangling off the edge of this step (see right). With your chest lifted, your abs tight, and your hands clasped in front of you, slowly bend your right knee and lower your hips into a squat, while keeping your right knee aligned with your ankle. Do 10 reps on the right side; then 10 on the left.

REAL-WORLD STRENGTH ROUTINE

This workout truly gets you fit for everyday activities, because "it hits every muscle in your body, not just the ones you see in the mirror," says Stephen Holt, the American Council on Exercise's 2003 Personal Trainer of the Year. "And it relies heavily on balance, so your abs are constantly engaged." Because these moves are intricate, take a few minutes to read them over before you get started. You'll need dumbbells (5 to 8 pounds for beginners, 10 or 12 pounds for more-experienced exercisers). Have a chair handy if you need to steady yourself.

1. Quickie Warm-up 1 minute
March in place or walk.

2. Curl and Press 1 minute
(for biceps, shoulders, obliques)
Hold dumbbells at shoulder height. Standing tall, press your right arm overhead while lowering your left arm to your side until it's nearly straight. In the same motion, twist your body slightly to the left (your right heel should come off the floor). Bring dumbbells back to your shoulders. Repeat on the opposite side. Do 5 reps on each side.

3. Pinkie-Toe Touch 2 minutes
(for butt, thighs)
Steady yourself on your right foot, and bend your left knee slightly to lift your foot a few inches off the floor. Bend to touch your right pinkie toe with your left hand. Return to the starting position without letting your left foot touch the ground. Do 12 reps on each side.

4. Lunge and Reach
2 minutes
(for butt, upper back, shoulders)
Begin in the lunge position, with your left foot forward, your right foot back, both knees at 90-degree angles, and dumbbells held at shoulder height. Twist your torso to the left. Bring the dumbbell in your right hand down

and across your body, reaching toward the outside of your left thigh. Pause. Then, as you straighten your left knee and push up to a standing position, bring your right arm overhead, with your right elbow bent at a 90-degree angle (see the photo at the bottom of the previous column). Pause and lower to the starting position. Do 12 reps; then switch sides and repeat.

5. Single-Arm, Single-Leg Row 2 minutes
(for upper back, butt, abs)
Stand on your right leg with a dumbbell hanging toward the floor in your right hand. Extend your left leg behind you, and tip forward from your hips so that your body forms a

straight line; avoid arching or slouching. Pull the weight upward until your right elbow is bent at a 90-degree angle, keeping it close to your body (see above). Lower the weight. Do 14 reps on each side.

6. Single-Leg Squat 2 minutes
(for butt, thighs)
Standing on your right leg, with your left toe a few inches off the floor, lower your body toward the floor by bending your right knee (keep your back straight). As you squat, slide both hands down your right quad (see left, for beginners) or your calf (for advanced exercisers).
Do 10 reps on each side. ■

The Five Best Body-Shaping Moves

Say goodbye to workout angst—these exercises are sure to shape you up!

BY CHRISTIE ASCHWANDEN • PHOTOGRAPHY BY DAVID MARTINEZ

Wading through all the new fitness products and promises to find the best is one workout you don't have to sweat through alone. Along with experts from the American College of Sports Medicine (ACSM) and the American Council on Exercise (ACE), we've compiled the best moves for your most troublesome body zones.

PUSH-UP

Target: Arms and chest

Why it's the best: "This exercise hits so much of the upper body, and it only takes a few minutes," says Norma Shechtman, M.A., M.Ed., ACE's 2003 Group Fitness Instructor of the Year and instructor and trainer at the Sports Club/Irvine (California). ACE members overwhelmingly named the push-up an exercise they can't live without.

How to do it: Place palms slightly wider than shoulder-width apart. With your arms supporting your body, extend your legs. Contract your abdominals and glutes to keep your body straight. Lower yourself until your upper arms are parallel to the floor; then use your chest and upper arm muscles to push up. Do 3 reps, and build from there.

Modifications: If a full push-up is too much at first, begin by holding yourself in the plank position—the "up" part of a push-up—and then lower yourself to the floor slowly to build strength.

You also can try a modified push-up from bent knees rather than from toes. For more of a challenge, slowly lower your body toward the floor and then hold yourself a couple of inches off the floor for a count of 5 before coming back up.

SQUAT

Target: Butt

Why it's the best: This exercise works your butt muscles (the largest in your body) and can enhance your ability to do anything that requires power, from rising off the couch and getting out of your car to skiing and hiking. ACE trainers agree; they voted the squat the best lower body exercise.

How to do it: Stand with your feet shoulder-width apart. Fold your arms in front of you, or place them on your hips. Keep your back straight, your abdominal muscles tight, and your knees over your toes. Lower your hips, stopping when your thighs are parallel to the floor. Do one to three sets of 8 to 20 reps.

Modifications: Make the exercise easier by stopping the squat before your thighs are parallel to the floor, as in the photo shown at right. For a greater challenge, hold dumbbells at your sides while you squat.

STANDING SNOW ANGEL

Target: Back

Why it's the best: This subtle yet surprisingly difficult exercise works the muscles of your middle back through a wide range of motion while simultaneously stretching your chest muscles. It's a great remedy for the slumping and slouching common among desk jockeys.

How to do it: Stand with your back resting comfortably against a wall, your arms out at shoulders, and your elbows bent, as shown above. Keeping your elbows and the backs of your hands in contact with the wall, slide your arms up until they're overhead, with your elbows straight. Lower your arms to the starting position. Perform the move in a slow, continuous motion, repeating it for 45 seconds, and work your way up to 1 minute.

Modifications: Once you can do two 1-minute sets, gradually cut your rest period until you are able to do a single 2-minute set. Aim for slower, longer sets as you progress.

BICYCLE CRUNCH 4

Target: Stomach

Why it's the best: When ACE-funded researchers at San Diego State University measured muscle activity in volunteers who performed a dozen of the most popular abdominal exercises, they discovered that the bicycle crunch required the stomach muscles to work the hardest—harder than they do with traditional crunches or such devices as the Ab Rocker.

How to do it: Lie on your back, and rest your head in your hands. Lift your upper body off the floor, taking care not to pull with your arms. Bend your right knee at about a 45-degree angle while extending your left leg 1 or 2 feet above the ground. Keep your neck relaxed and the small of your back flat on the floor. Lead with your shoulder, and move your left elbow to your right knee, as shown below; slowly reverse to the other side. Do one to three sets of 8 to 20 reps.

Modifications: If you suffer from back pain, you can support your lower back by planting your bent leg on the floor instead of alternating legs. Increase the intensity of this move by lowering your extended leg closer to the floor; to ease it up a bit, keep your extended leg at a 45-degree angle.

LUNGE 5

Target: Thighs

Why it's the best: It works all the major muscles in your legs, and you don't have to do many to feel results, says Dixie Stanforth, M.S., a group-exercise expert at the University of Texas and spokeswoman for ACE. Bonus: The lunge also activates your abdominal and back muscles.

How to do it: Stand with your feet hip-distance apart. Place your hands on your hips or across your chest. Take a step forward, landing heel first, with your left foot. Lower your right knee toward the floor. Keep your left knee centered over your ankle, as shown above; be sure your stomach muscles are tight and your chest is lifted. Push back up to the starting position; repeat on the other side. Start with 8 to 10 reps, and work up to two or three sets of 20.

Modifications: Challenge yourself further by stepping forward and lunging as if you were on a tightrope; this makes it even tougher for your thigh, ab, and back muscles to keep you balanced. Vary the move by stepping either diagonally or backward instead of forward. Whatever version you try, you can increase the load by holding a pair of dumbbells at your sides. ■

Trainer Tip: Do any or all of these moves after a warm-up or your cardio routine. For the best results, the ACSM recommends that you do this type of strength training two or three times a week.

vital *stats*

2.9
Percentage of government contract dollars (for toilet seats, plaster, paint, etc.) that go to private businesses owned by women

46
Percentage of American businesses owned by women

146 MILLION
Number of cars in the U.S. that have driver-side air bags

5,000 LBS/SQ IN
Average amount of force an air bag exerts in the first few inches of deployment

3,000 LBS/SQ IN
Amount of force that may injure an adult chest

28.8
Percentage of adults who have volunteered in the last year

2.1
Times as likely a woman is to volunteer at a hospital as a man

2.3
Times as likely a man is to volunteer at a sports event as a woman

155
Number of people worldwide who have died since 1990 as a result of birds hitting airplanes and causing them to crash

$500 MILLION
Cost of bird-related airplane damage each year

90
Percentage of bird-airplane collisions that involve federally protected bird species

26
Percentage of people who make vacation plans within 2 weeks of their departure

$2,378
Average cost of a summer vacation

$2,710
Average amount a traveler from the Northeast will spend

$2,057
Average amount a Midwesterner will spend

10
Percent chance that most adults think they have of getting a sexually transmitted disease (STD)

33
Actual percent chance adults have of getting an STD

70
Percentage of vegetarians who say they exercise regularly

38
Percentage of people who say they exercise regularly who also eat meat

98
Percentage of Americans who are meat-eaters

60
Miles per hour that a champagne cork can travel when popped

20
Percentage of all eye injuries involving carbonated beverages in glass bottles that are caused by flying champagne corks

26
Percentage of those injuries that result in blindness

50
Percentage of adults who think being physically fit is a sign of success

36
Percentage of adults who exercise once a month or never

21
Percentage of Americans who say they feel very confident about having enough money for retirement

12
Percentage who say they have consulted a financial planner in the past year

39
Percentage who say they have bought a lottery ticket one or more times in the past month

65
Percentage of party-planners who say guests behave worse now than they did 5 years ago

69
Percentage of planners who have caught guests stealing centerpieces or other decor

33
Percentage of planners who've had guests refuse to leave at the end of a party

Sources: Yankelovich; BiZBash; Intimate Matters; U.S. Bureau of Labor Statistics; Myvesta; Employee Benefit Research Institute; Scarborough Research; U.S. Small Business Administration; Center for Women's Business Research; *British Journal of Ophthalmology;* Mintel; Bird Strike Committee USA; Insurance Institute for Highway Safety; Airbag Institute—Reported by Laura Gilbert

chapter 6

healthy looks

**secrets to looking and
feeling your best**

The Eight

Biggest Beauty Breakthroughs

BY CHRISTINE COBURN

When you're in need of a lasting cure for a genuine illness, you turn to the medical profession. When you need fast fixes for problems that run only skin-deep, you turn to the beauty industry. Got flat hair, flaky skin, a pallid complexion? You can usually find a solution that will repair or at least camouflage the symptoms. They're not exactly cures for cancer, but these remedies can be pretty important if they put an end to a lifelong preoccupation, shave 20 minutes off your morning routine, or make one of your physical features look dramatically better than it did yesterday. That's why, every year, *Health* seeks out the most significant innovations in the world of beauty. Digging through heaps of merchandise and piles of press releases, we hone in on the products and procedures that deliver benefits that weren't available a year ago—the beauty boons we deem breakthroughs. Because they're brand-new, some of them may not be widely available (at least for now), and they obviously don't come with the same long-term track record as treatments that have been popular for decades.

But based on our review of scientific studies, along with interviews of industry and medical experts, these are the eight breakthroughs with the most potential to solve the beauty problems women deal with every day. Ready to be in the know? Keep reading.

FAT INJECTIONS THAT SMOOTH CELLULITE

Surprise: Fat may be the best cure for cellulite. But don't grab that Krispy Kreme just yet—this fat is injected, not ingested. Since 2003, some cosmetic dermatologists have begun injecting patients' own fat or Fascian (a naturally occurring filler, with the U.S. Food and Drug Administration [FDA] approval, that is derived from the tissue of human cadavers) to provide instant improvements for women who haven't been able to get rid of their dimples with diet and exercise. "We've found that these natural substances are very effective at filling in cellulite," says Neal Sadick, M.D., one of the pioneers of the procedures and clinical professor of dermatology at Weill Medical College of Cornell University in New York. "Because both fat and Fascian have bigger molecules than injectables like collagen, Dermalogen, and Restalyne, they can be used to fill in larger areas and depressions on the body."

The process is quick and relatively—although not completely—painless. "If the patient is using her own fat (usually from the hips, buttocks, or abdomen), we numb that area first with a local anesthetic and extract the fat with a syringe," says Barney Kenet, M.D., a dermatologist at New York-Presbyterian Hospital. "Then we anesthetize the dimpled area and use a series of injections to fill the depressions." With either injectable, the procedure takes just one visit, and the results last up to a year. But Sadick is conducting a clinical study to see whether natural fat has even better staying power than Fascian. "In my experience, some patients are seeing long-term results," Kenet says. The price? Upwards of $500 per treatment, depending on the doctor.

For a list of dermatologists who offer fat or Fascian injections, visit www.topdocs.com or www.aad.org.

LASTING COLOR FOR HARD-TO-DYE HAIR

Most women assume they can easily change their hair color if the need or the desire strikes—for instance, when they go gray a little earlier than expected or when a rough week calls for a mood-mending makeover. But that's not necessarily true. "Some women can never get complete coverage, even with heavy-duty permanent dyes," explains Amy McMichaels, M.D., assistant professor of dermatology at Wake Forest University. "Wiry, coarse, or thick and curly hair is more porous and therefore doesn't hold pigment molecules as well," she says. "The color just seeps out of the strand." The problem often affects African-American hair, which tends to coarsen as it grays. Instead of achieving a uniform brunette shade when they color, for example, women with this hair type

typically get a dull brownish tone with gray streaks, says Stuart Gavert, co-owner of and stylist at Gavert Atelier salon in Beverly Hills. Plus, the color fades rapidly, requiring touch-ups every two weeks instead of the usual six.

Recently, however, some of the best salons have found a solution with Chromatherm, a heat-activated coloring technique from Japan. "It's very similar to the Japanese thermal-straightening process," Gavert says. "You use a hot iron to melt the pigment into the strands, sealing the cuticle as you go. Because the heat literally melts the dye molecules into the hair, you don't need ammonia or peroxide, which is usually required to open the cuticle." The color also contains penetrating deep-conditioners. "Not only do hard-to-color types get vibrant, glossy color that lasts the full six to eight weeks, but also they get the added benefit of a smoother, silkier texture," Gavert says. "Most clients find that it makes their hair much more manageable and frizz-resistant." In fact, anyone looking for less damage and more shine can try this new option. It costs about $200, admittedly pricey but no more than many top salons charge for their lower-tech permanent-color processes.

To find a colorist who uses Chromatherm, log on to www.stylist911.com or www.salonlistings.com.

LASERS THAT ELIMINATE SCARS AND STRETCH MARKS

Even in this age of quick fixes, two types of flaws are notoriously difficult to remove or lighten: depressed scars (such as those caused by acne or chicken pox) and stretch marks. "In both cases, you're attempting to correct damage in the deeper layers of the skin, not just the dermis," explains David Goldberg, M.D., director of skin-laser research at Mount Sinai School of Medicine in New York City. "That's why topical treatments, including lasers and creams, are generally ineffective."

But in 2004, two lasers received clearance from the FDA for correcting these seemingly permanent problems. The first, CoolTouch, was approved to treat depressed scars after a Mount Sinai study found that three successive treatments stimulated the production of collagen around the site of the scar, "thereby filling the indentation," says study author Goldberg. More good news: The treatments were quick (less than 15 minutes), caused none of the bleeding associated with traditional resurfacing lasers, and produced no side effects. CoolTouch is effective on any skin tone. And unlike the effects of collagen injections—the most common treatment for depressed scars—the results of this laser are permanent.

Not long after CoolTouch gained FDA clearance, the ReLume laser became the first to be approved for repigmenting lightened skin, including stretch marks that have whitened with age. "This laser stimulates the production of melanin in the skin," Sadick explains. "In 6 to 12 treatments, it can return the lightened skin close to its original color—permanently." So far, it's the only laser that has consistently been able to treat pigment loss of any kind, whether it's caused by stretch marks, vitiligo, scarring, or psoriasis. And like CoolTouch, ReLume is quick, painless, and free of side effects. Sadick has only one word of caution: "I wouldn't recommend it for anyone who is in the habit of tanning, as they might have a severe sunburn reaction."

To find doctors who know how to use these lasers, log on to www.premierplasticsurgery.com or visit www.skinandhealth.com.

AN INSTANT PORE-SHRINKER

As anyone who has sat through a facial can tell you, having the gunk squeezed from your pores is not a pampering experience, no matter how gentle your aesthetician may be. And it may not produce the flawless appearance you're hoping for. "Some pores, over time, become permanently enlarged," says David Bank, M.D., director of the Center for Cosmetic and Laser Surgery in Mount Kisco, New York. "The opening can become loosened by repeated clogging and stretching over the years, or simply by the loss of collagen as you age—something that's predetermined by genetics."

New pore-minimizing lotions are high-tech cosmetic tricks. Anyone who's endured expensive (and sometimes painful) facials will appreciate their magic.

The cosmetics industry now offers an alternative to products that clean out pores but fail to address the stretching: fast-acting lotions and gels containing polymers that seem to shrink pores, at least temporarily. "Polymers, the gel-like film-formers used in many skin- and hair-care products, have been dramatically refined," says Peter Pugliese, Ph.D., M.D., director of Skin Research Laboratories in Reading, Pennsylvania. "They've become lighter in weight and more resilient, allowing companies to create products that deliver results that include firming."

One of several manufacturers using this technology is Clinique. "We've combined these ultrafine polymers with lightweight silicones to form a kind of invisible mesh that smooths the skin and tightens the pore opening," says Debbie D'Aquino, Clinique's vice president of product development.

It's definitely a high-tech cosmetic trick, notes New York dermatologist Frederic Brandt, M.D., who created his own pore treatment. "But anyone who's been fretting her way through expensive facials and serial skin-care experiments will appreciate its magic."

Try Clinique's Pore Minimizer Instant Perfector, Joey New York's Pure Pores Pore Tightener and Filler Serum, Dr. Brandt's Pore Effect, or Ellen Lange's Suede Wearable Treatment.

LIGHTER MASCARAS, FULLER LASHES

Usually, if a beauty company wants to give a mascara extra volume, the standard practice is to add more wax or bigger particles to the formula. This fattens lashes but also increases the stiffness, thickness, and weight of the product—not to mention the likelihood of clumping, smearing, and (for sensitive users) red, watery eyes. That's why the new lineup of lower wax, lighter weight volumizers is such good news for the almost 70 percent of women who wear mascara every day.

Using some of the same sheer-polymer technology recently developed to add body to hair, cosmetics makers are creating the effect of fuller lashes with formulations that are almost imperceptible to the wearer. "We're using flexolipid polymers, which

cover the hairs in an even, lightweight film that causes the lashes to push away from each other, making them look separated and fuller," explains Nancy New, senior scientist at Procter & Gamble Cosmetics. Because the mascaras gently fan out lashes, the thickness of the product becomes much less important. "These new polymers have changed our entire approach to making volumizing mascaras," says Roseanne Fama, vice president of product development for L'Oréal. "The goal now is to make the formula as light and soft as possible, because we're creating the fullness in a different way."

See if you detect a difference for yourself: Try Max Factor's More Lashes Mascara, CoverGirl's Multiplying Mascara, L'Oréal's Voluminous Full Definition Mascara, or Estée Lauder's MagnaScopic Maximum Volume Mascara.

A MORE NATURAL SOLUTION TO FINE, THINNING HAIR

Although extensions seem ideal for many women with thin or thinning hair, they're often inconvenient, expensive, and hard on the scalp. "Traditional extensions had to be braided or hot-glued into your hair at the scalp—a painstaking and sometimes painful process that took hours and put a lot of stress on the hair at the roots," says Paul Labrecque, owner of New York City's two Paul Labrecque Salons & Spas. "Even celebrity clients and models would only use them for short periods of time."

But, in 2004, hair extensions became a more realistic option thanks to cold fusion, a treatment imported from Europe. "This method involves using a lightweight polymer to bond real hair to strands of the person's own hair," says Labrecque, one of the first people to bring the technique to the United States. "Because the bonding solution is made with the same proteins found in real hair, it attaches very quickly and smoothly. A special high-frequency wand is then waved over the glue to make it adhere more securely, while the actual bond or connecting point remains completely flat."

This high-tech process causes none of the shedding, clumping, or knotting that can occur with traditional extensions. Not surprisingly, these new versions last a bit longer—up to six months instead of the usual three to four. And because there are no bulky braids or clips, the attached portion is easily hidden in even the finest hair. "In fact, we're using extensions more to camouflage thinning hair than we are for the sake of fashion," Labrecque says. "We have chemotherapy patients who are ecstatic because the results are so natural." Of course, a fuller head of hair achieved this way is going to cost you more than a can of mousse: Prices at Labrecque's salons start at around $1,500 for partial applications; expect to pay less at salons in smaller cities.

To find someone who is experienced in applying hair extensions, visit www.beautysalons.com or call 888-757-2566.

INVISIBLE, QUICK-DRYING SUNSCREENS

7

Getting serious protection from UVA and UVB rays used to mean applying thick, white, opaque lotions. But that all changed in late 2003 with the introduction of ultralight, barely there UVA-UVB sunscreens with SPFs of 30 and up. "This is a completely new generation of broad-spectrum protection," says Amy Lewis, M.D., director of the Department of Dermatology at the State University of New York Health Sciences Center at Brooklyn. "These sunscreens absorb into the skin almost immediately, leaving it silky and completely greaseless. It's a huge plus because people are more likely to apply the product correctly."

> The new sunscreens absorb into the skin instantly, leaving it silky and greaseless. Now maybe more people will use them—and use them correctly.

The ingenious ingredient in these new smooth-as-silk sunscreens is fine micronized zinc oxide, which offers sheer, blendable coverage. "Vastly different from the older zinc-oxide versions, which came in difficult-to-use opaque particles, the new microfine zinc oxide is not only more consumer-friendly, but also it's easier to use in a variety of applications," says Elaine Linker, director of product development and co-founder of DDF, a skin-care line sold in dermatologists' offices. Companies are testing the substance in fast-drying sprays, tinted moisturizers, and chemical-free sunblocks that scatter rays rather than absorb them. According to the experts we've spoken to, you will see more easy-to-use choices in the next year or so as more players in the skin-care industry switch to this improved technology.

Try Neutrogena's Ultra Sheer Dry-Touch Sunblock SPF 30 or 45, or DDF's Organic Sunblock SPF 30.

PIGMENT-FREE, ONE-SHADE-FITS-ALL FOUNDATION

8

If you can never find the right makeup to exactly match your skin tone or you're still seeking more-natural-looking coverage, then you're in luck: Invisible foundations have arrived. These colorless products involve few or no shade choices, no undertones, and—to put it plainly—no pigment. Instead, this new breed of foundation uses light-diffusing technology and face-smoothing polymers to create the illusion of a perfect complexion. For women with traditionally hard-to-match skin tones, from very dark to olive to extremely fair, this means their long search is finally over. "Instead of masking the skin with opaque pigment, we've combined the newest cosmetic and skin-care ingredients to create an optical illusion that camouflages complexion problems," explains Rochelle Quezada, director of education at Shiseido, one of the first companies to introduce this concept for foundation.

These new makeups feel a lot like lightweight versions of conventional liquid foundations, although they have a noticeably smoother, silkier texture. Once they set (in just a couple of seconds), they obscure imperfections or uneven areas with extremely fine light-reflecting particles, which act as a kind of all-day soft-focus filter for your face. And depending on the formula you choose, the foundation might help troubleshoot additional problems by using, for example, invisible micro-sponges to absorb oil and elastic powders to smooth creases. As another bonus, you never have to worry about color rubbing off onto your—or someone else's—clothes.

So if you're ready to try a fresher look, check out Shiseido's Brightening Veil SPF 24, Laura Mercier's Secret Brightener, or Prescriptives' Traceless Skin Responsive Corrector the next time you're out shopping. ■

Q + A

Mineral Makeup

I have sensitive skin, so my dermatologist recommended using a "mineral foundation." What is that?

Given today's demand for pure products, mineral makeup is becoming increasingly popular, particularly among women with sensitive skin. Available in just about every form, from foundation to lipstick to mascara, it's made from minerals taken from the earth, such as titanium dioxide and iron and zinc oxides, rather than synthetic ingredients. The advantages? No artificial colors, fragrances, or ingredients; plus, mineral products have a natural SPF. The downside is that they're intensely pigmented, making them hard for first-timers to apply. "A light touch is key," says Diane Ranger, the president and founder of Colorscience, a line of mineral makeup.

Ranger suggests patting liquid or pressed mineral foundation onto skin with fingers or a makeup sponge rather than rubbing. If you're using a loose-powder foundation, dip the brush from the side rather than straight down into the pot and shake off the excess before brushing the makeup onto skin.

Promising New Player Enters the Ongoing War Against Wrinkles

There's a new antioxidant in town, and it looks like a powerhouse. According to research presented at the recent annual meeting of the American Academy of Dermatology, idebenone (pronounced ee-dee-be-KNOWN) has the potential to be a star in minimizing wrinkles and preventing skin cancer. Like other antioxidants, idebenone helps reduce skin damage caused by environmental factors, such as ultraviolet rays, cigarette smoke, and pollution—but it works more efficiently than its counterparts, or so the preliminary studies suggest.

Researchers discovered the substance's effectiveness when they set out to compare five antioxidants that are often used in wrinkle creams: vitamin C, vitamin E, kinetin, co-enzyme Q10 (co-Q10), and alpha lipoic acid. The study's initial goal was to determine which of the five is the most useful in fighting free radicals, molecular by-products of the wear and tear of everyday life that are reputed to accelerate the skin's aging process. The scientists decided to include idebenone (a relative of co-Q10) after hearing that it was being used overseas in preservative solutions for donor organs. "We wondered if something that could keep a liver alive during a transplant could also benefit your skin, so we added it to the study," explains Joseph A. Lewis II, chief executive officer of Pharma Cosmetix Research, a research-and-development company that designed the studies (which were conducted by a third party).

The six chemicals were put through a series of laboratory tests and then graded on their ability to prevent free radical formation, UV-induced skin damage, and other processes that could affect skin's condition. Idebenone got the top score, a whopping 95 out of 100, followed by vitamin E with 80, kinetin with 68, co-Q10 with 55, vitamin C with 52, and alpha lipoic acid with 41.

But idebenone may offer more than preventive benefits. In one small study, 40 women who used a cream containing the antioxidant daily saw a 32-percent reduction in sun-related skin damage, such as fine lines, wrinkles, and hyperpigmentation. In addition, early indications show that pretreating skin with the cream, called Prevage, a few weeks before using a retinoid (such as Retin-A or Renova) may reduce the risk of irritation.

Reasons to Smile

Want prettier teeth? Check out these 10 high-tech ways to get the look you want.

BY MICHELE BENDER

For decades, it seemed that only the rich and famous spent time and money on megawatt grins. And while their teeth didn't always look real, they certainly were big and sparkling. Then came the '90s, when even people who typically avoided their six-month checkups started hopping into the dentist's chair—and not just for a good cleaning. "New technology, as well as a booming economy, made cosmetic dentistry more popular than ever," says Jonathan Levine, D.M.D., professor of aesthetic dentistry at New York University College of Dentistry and creator of the GoSmile line of whitening products. "It was a decade of dental excess, where dentists wanted to transform smiles using the latest treatments even when more conservative routes could have worked." Lana Rozenberg, D.D.S., a cosmetic dentist in New York City, adds, "You saw the same uniformly sized, Chiclet-like teeth on everyone—it looked unnatural. Today, you want someone to say, 'You have a beautiful smile,' not 'Where did you have your teeth done?'" And that's exactly the reaction you'll get with the latest advances in dental technology. Each of these

techniques will help you take your look to the next level—with less time, less hassle, and more confidence that, in the end, you'll still look like you.

SUPERFAST BLEACHING THAT LASTS

Dual whitening is the latest way to bring teeth back to the color nature intended, erasing stains caused by cigarettes, such beverages as coffee and tea, and less-than-diligent maintenance. A recent study published in *The Journal of the American Dental Association* found that teeth became eight shades brighter after a one-hour high-intensity light treatment known as power bleaching. The light activates a peroxide solution that is applied to teeth, causing it to release oxygen molecules that break down stains. But cosmetic dentists report that following this in-office procedure, whitening can regress by up to 50 percent in a month. To extend its effects, dentists now combine power bleaching with the use of an at-home whitener for one to two weeks. "Dual whitening gives you the two things you need for quick and long-lasting results: a high concentration of hydrogen peroxide in the office and high-contact time at home," Levine says. Gels and custom trays for home use are effective, but they'll run you $200 to $500 (on top of the $500 fee for your in-office treatment). For a cheaper alternative, ask your dentist to recommend a reliable over-the-counter product that will work just as well; most cost about $25 for a four-week supply.

In spite of its great results, dual whitening will not change the color of crowns, caps, fillings, and veneers. Gray stains or white calcifications may not respond well, either, because they are usually part of the tooth's structure.

COVERING FLAWS DISCREETLY

New restoration materials have made it possible to create ultrathin veneers that mask chips, worn teeth, and spaces. Older caps were bulky and opaque—an obvious sign that your smile had been overhauled by your dentist. But these custom-made porcelain coverings are only as thick as a fingernail. Despite their slender profile, these modern veneers

have stamina. The porcelain and ceramics they're made of can withstand more force and pressure than materials of old, and the new adhesives used to attach them have better staying power. "These cements work way into the tooth to attach both mechanically and chemically for stronger bonding," Levine notes. Plus, today's veneers come in colors that can be layered and mixed to closely mimic your natural tooth shade. And because they're translucent, they absorb light just like real teeth, making that flat, chalklike appearance a thing of the past.

Getting your veneers, which average about $1,000 apiece, takes at least two or three appointments. The area is numbed, about half a millimeter of enamel is removed from the front of the tooth with a high-speed drill, and an impression is made and sent to the lab. At this point, you'll get temporaries that look and function just like regular teeth. "Wearing them is like a dress rehearsal," Levine says. "You get to live in them for a week or two and see what you like and don't like." Then your dentist can make the appropriate changes. About two weeks later, your new veneers are ready, keeping your smile looking lovely for 8 to 15 years.

A natural look is important. You want people to say, "You have a beautiful smile," not "Where did you have your teeth done?"

A NATURAL LOOK FOR FILLINGS

A mouthful of metal that sparkles whenever you laugh is about as far as you can get from an au naturel grin. (It can also give away your age, since silver amalgam isn't used much anymore.) The tooth-colored porcelain and composite-resin materials currently used for fillings and crowns are stronger and more wear-resistant than ever. "Many of our breakthroughs in restoration materials use technology from the NASA space program," explains Ken Fieldston, D.D.S., a dentist in Cresskill, New Jersey.

Teeth filled with these new materials don't just look better, they *are* better.

"After years of wear, old silver fillings can cause teeth to fracture and break," says Michael Malone, D.D.S., president of the American Academy of Cosmetic Dentistry. "Today's porcelain and resin restorations have physical qualities that are very similar to enamel, so they strengthen the teeth instead of fracturing them." More good news: Less of your original tooth is removed when the fillings are put in, and liners placed beneath them prevent decay by releasing fluoride. Here's how it works: Your dentist numbs the area, removes the old filling, cleans out any decay, and then lines the inside of the tooth with a resin or cement filler. The dentist then takes an impression of the area and sends it to a laboratory, where a restoration is made. You get a temporary filling until the permanent one is glued into place in about a week or two. In some cases, the entire procedure can be done in the dentist's office, with no waiting.

FAST FIXES IN A SINGLE VISIT

Now you can have your fillings replaced and be fitted for crowns or veneers in a single visit, thanks to new equipment that makes lab services obsolete. One such example, the CEREC 3, is a combination camera, computer, and milling machine. ("CEREC" stands for "Chairside Economical Restoration of Esthetic Ceramics.") The dentist uses an infrared scan to take a digital photo of the inside of your tooth. A 3-D color image immediately pops onto the computer screen so the dentist can design your crown, filling, or veneer. Then the computer directs the milling machine to carve the restoration, which is in your dentist's hand 10 minutes later. No impression of the tooth is needed, no second shot of Novocain is required, and you've just saved that week or two of waiting for the lab to do its work.

CEREC 3 is a step up from machines of previous generations because of its more accurate calculations and 3-D technology. "With the older CEREC machines, the main benefit was creating a restoration in one visit, but the aesthetics and accuracy

weren't that good," says Daniel Deutsch, D.D.S., director of the Washington (D.C.) Center for Dentistry. "The newest machine rivals the quality and fit of what you can do in a lab."

BRACES THAT SECRETLY STRAIGHTEN

Less than five years ago, if you wanted to align crooked teeth or close unwanted spaces, your only choice was old-fashioned braces with metal brackets and wire. Though some clear-plastic brackets were available, tooth-straightening devices were still far from subtle. Industrial science has transformed all that with Invisalign, a removable appliance made from transparent plastic (similar to a retainer) that fixes your smile while keeping your vanity and natural tooth structure intact. "And because you take it out to brush your teeth and eat, food and plaque won't get trapped like they can with nonremovable braces," Deutsch explains.

A computer makes three-dimensional images from impressions of your teeth to map out the incremental movements necessary to straighten your smile. (Patients love seeing this "movie" of their teeth falling into place.) Once your doctor gives the Invisalign manufacturer the OK, a series of aligners is generated. During an office visit every six weeks, your dentist checks your progress and then gives you three new sets of aligners. You wear each set for two weeks until the six weeks is up, and the process starts again.

Invisalign can take as long to work as traditional braces (anywhere from several months to several years) and can cost just as much, too (from $3,000 to $8,000, depending on how many aligners you need). Some dentists let the devices do double duty as teeth-whitening trays by giving their patients bleaching gel to wear for an hour each day for up to two weeks, saving them the $200 to $500 they'd pay for custom trays. A potential added benefit: weight control. Taking the aligner out to eat makes you aware of what and how often you're nibbling.

ZAPPING GUMMY SMILES PAINLESSLY

Today, diode or argon lasers can vaporize excess or uneven gum tissue to make teeth look more proportioned in a matter of minutes. Dentists say the results are incredibly precise. "Cutting the gums with a scalpel causes inflammation and bleeding, which makes it harder to know exactly where the gums are going to be when they heal," Fieldston says. "The beauty of the laser is there's no inflammation, so the gum stays right where you put it."

The standard scalpel procedure requires stitches and several weeks of healing time, enough to convince many women to keep the gummy smiles they've been struggling to hide their whole lives. In comparison, the laser seems like a dream come true. After a shot of Novocain, your periodontist reshapes your gums in just a few minutes per tooth, using the instrument's very fine fiber-optic tip. Because the laser closes off blood vessels and nerve endings, there's no bleeding or stitches. Healing takes only a day or two; you may be left with a scab along the gum line, but it should flake away in about 24 hours. Of course, these perks have a price—around $1,200 for three teeth, compared with $300 to $500 for scalpel surgery on a similar-size area. Since this technology is still new and the machinery an expensive investment, only 5 percent of dentists in the United States use lasers, so finding a practitioner might take some investigating.

GIVING GUMS NEW GROWTH

Here's some groundbreaking news from the lab: Growth factors (proteins found naturally in your blood) can help replace lost gum tissue. Overzealous brushing, clenching, and gum disease can cause recession, resulting not only in teeth that look extra long but also the possibility of root exposure. It's not a pretty sight, and it can add years to your smile, since receding gums are common among older people.

"Gum grafting has corrected this for years, but the use of growth factors has revolutionized it," says

Coming to a Dentist Near You

Digital X-rays: Digital machines emit 70-percent less radiation than traditional ones, allowing a dentist to take multiple pictures of an area to yield a more accurate diagnosis. The images are instantly projected onto a screen (no more waiting 5 to 10 minutes for them to develop), and they can be enlarged to any size. Plus, with none of the lead waste and toxic solutions of conventional X-rays, this new digital technology is environmentally friendly.

Diagnodent laser: Tech-savvy dentists may use this device to easily spot a tooth defect before it can be seen with the naked eye or even on a standard or digital X-ray. The dentist shines the laser onto an area where the suspected cavity is located (decay reflects light differently than healthy enamel does), and the laser beeps if it detects a problem.

Intraoral camera: This tiny handheld camera goes into your mouth, projecting images of your teeth—magnified 20 times their normal size—onto a TV monitor. The dentist can see minuscule cracks and fractures better than she can with her eyes, so she can spot problems before repairs become costly.

Periodontal screening software: Periodontists use this computer program to check for gum disease. The specialist wears a headset with an attached microphone while measuring the depth of each tooth's pocket. A voice-activated computer uses these measurements to create a color image, displaying healthy gums in one hue and not-so-healthy areas in another.

Resources: For more information on many of these procedures, contact the American Academy of Cosmetic Dentistry (800-543-9220 or www.aacd.com), the Academy of General Dentistry (877-292-9327 or www.agd.org), or the American Dental Association (312-440-2500 or www.ada.org).

Matthew Messina, D.D.S., a consumer adviser for the American Dental Association. "Before, the procedure was done to keep gum recession from getting worse, but because we couldn't get grafted tissue to adhere to the roots, we couldn't do anything about the aesthetic aspect. Now we can put the gums back where they used to be."

The process begins with a small cut in the gums. Then a substance containing the growth factors, which are isolated and purified in a lab, is placed in and around the opening. Next, a piece of tissue is taken from a part of the palate just behind your tooth, tucked into the gum pocket, and stitched into place. (In the past, tissue was taken from the roof of the mouth, which isn't the same rosy pink as the area around your teeth, so the graft didn't blend in well.) You wear a protective bandage for a week to 10 days as the graft attaches to the exposed root. "The growth factors sort of wake up the root surface of the tooth, allowing the gum tissue to stick to it," Messina says. "Your new gums will look like they were always there."

THE LATEST DENTAL IMPLANTS

Advances in implants are welcome news for the legions of adults who lose teeth to accidents or decay. In fact, some experts estimate that a surprising 7 out of 10 adults between the ages of 35 and 44 have already lost at least one permanent tooth. A standard dental implant, which costs about $2,000, is a small titanium post that is surgically inserted into the jawbone to replace a tooth's missing root. It acts as an anchor for an artificial porcelain tooth that is permanently screwed or cemented to it.

With the newest procedure, called "immediate loading," your implant is placed in a single appointment, and a temporary tooth that looks and functions like the real thing is attached to it. That's a major improvement over the older technique, which requires a three- to six-month wait for the bone to grow around the implant before the prosthetic tooth can be connected.

"Today, improved designs and materials make implants stronger and more predictable, so they anchor better and quicker," says James Doundoulakis, D.M.D., co-director of the dental-implant department at Mt. Sinai Medical Center in New York City. Your gum tissue also looks healthier and more natural. The temporary tooth prevents the gum from shrinking back as it does when a tooth isn't immediately affixed to the implant. "Though success rates of immediate loading are approaching those of the delayed technique, there is still a slight risk of losing the implant," Doundoulakis says. There's also a sizable price difference of about $2,500 more than the cost of a standard implant.

New implants also come in a variety of shapes and sizes to closely mimic actual roots, and the abutment (the piece that connects the implant to the artificial tooth) has also been improved. "For an implant to stay in place, you have to put it in a particular spot in the bone. Sometimes, that spot causes the tooth to be at a strange, unnatural angle," says Michel Mouriavieff, D.M.D., a cosmetic and restorative dentist based in Ridgewood, New Jersey. "Now manufacturers have created custom-made abutments that have a variety of angles, so you can put the tooth restoration in the most aesthetically pleasing position." In addition, these abutments, which used to be metallic, are now constructed out of tooth-colored materials, such as zirconium, which means no more dark shadows peek through gum tissue.

PROGRAMMING YOUR PERFECT SHADE

Even the best restoration will look fake if it doesn't blend in with the rest of your teeth. To match colors the traditional way, dentists would eyeball your teeth or hold up tabs (think paint swatches made from dental materials) to find the shade that looked best with the rest of your mouth. "But the lighting in the room, wall color, or patient's clothes can change how we see color and keep it from being read accurately," says Laurence Rifkin, D.D.S., an aesthetic and restorative dentist in Beverly Hills, California, and adjunct professor of dentistry at the University of California, Los Angeles. The latest shade-matching technique uses a computer to get the perfect match. A scanner-produced image of your teeth is digitally analyzed to create what looks like a topographical map of the enamel's different hues. Software converts these colors into the equivalent shades of dental materials that should be used. The map is then sent to a technician, who builds the restoration. "This color prescription increases the chances of an excellent end result, so redoing a tooth is less likely," Rifkin adds.

A PEEK AT YOUR FUTURE SMILE

Gone are the days of wondering what you'd look like with the smile of your dreams. Cosmetic imaging has gotten so good that you can actually see how your teeth will look after an overhaul. The dentist takes snapshots of your face and teeth from a variety of angles. Via the Internet, he sends the photos, measurements of your mouth, and specifics on the procedures you're considering to a computer-imaging service that generates simulations. (Some dentists use software to do all this themselves.) If you're planning several procedures—for example, gum-disease surgery plus veneers—you can have each phase simulated at $80 to $300 a pop. Or if you're trying to choose between two different procedures, multiple simulations can help you compare your options. "There's no better way to show a patient what she'll look like," says Robert Pick, D.D.S., associate clinical professor of dental surgery at Northwestern University Medical School. "No matter how much I explain it, a picture says more than I ever could."

Michele Bender is a contributing editor in New York City. She writes regularly about beauty, fitness, and health.

Q + A
Why This Facial Workout Is Too Good to Be True

A friend of mine wants to try this gadget that supposedly erases wrinkles by strengthening muscles in the face. Could it work?

Your "friend" (wink, wink) can make her facial muscles as strong and taut as a circus trampoline, but that won't help wrinkles, says Nia Terezakis, M.D., a spokeswoman for the American Academy of Dermatology. It's not sagging face muscles that put creases on your map; it's the loss of skin elasticity that comes with aging, combined with a lifetime of sun exposure and cigarette smoking. To help repair the damage, try using facial products that contain retinoids, which are chemical relatives of vitamin A. "Only a retinoid is going to build new collagen, shrink pores, get rid of discoloration, and repair sun damage," says Terezakis, who notes that her patients who use creams containing these substances are amazed at how much better their skin appears. Prescription treatments tend to work better than over-the-counter creams, but even drugstore versions should help—just don't expect to moisturize 10 years off your face. (Look for products with the highest concentration of retinol you can find, and steer clear of retinol palmitate and retinyl acetate, which some studies suggest are not as effective as retinol.)

What Beauty Labels *Really* Mean

Preservative-free? Hypoallergenic? Here's how to decipher the all-too-confusing terminology.

BY MICHELE BENDER

Every culture has its own language, and the beauty world is no exception. But did you ever stop to think about what terms, such as *hypoallergenic,* on product labels really mean? Sure, they sound authoritative, but there are no official standards governing their use. Nevertheless, "the cosmetic industry works hard to self-regulate and be truthful," says Diane Berson, M.D., assistant professor of dermatology at Cornell University. "Honest labeling is in their best interest; if you like a product, you'll keep using it, but if you have a reaction, you'll try something else." We asked Berson and Debbie D'Aquino, vice president of global product development at Clinique, to explain the most common cosmetic terminology, plus a few labeling loopholes.

Allergy-tested: The company has conducted skin-allergy patch tests on the product. However, there are no regulations for the kinds of exams that are performed or the ways they must be carried out—one

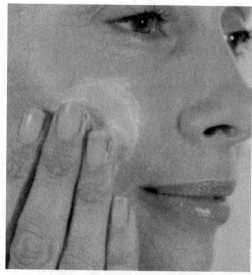

company may test on a single person, another on thousands. What's more, there's no guarantee that the procedures are always done on humans.

Dermatologist-tested: Because no rules exist that specify the kinds of research required, the testing can vary widely: A dermatologist may have taken the product home and tried it herself, or she may have conducted a large-scale study.

Fragrance- or perfume-free: No natural or synthetic scents have been added. However, a fragrance- or perfume-free item may still have an aroma, which is the ingredients' natural odor.

Hypoallergenic: These products do not contain such common allergens as preservatives and perfumes, so they are unlikely to cause allergic reactions when used.

Nonacnegenic: The formula should not irritate or inflame the skin's oil-producing follicles and therefore should not cause pimples. This is often because certain products are made without heavy oils.

Noncomedogenic: The cosmetic should not clog pores or cause blackheads and whiteheads. Usually this is because it doesn't contain heavy emollients, such as mineral oil.

Oil-free: The item contains no heavy oils, but it may contain silicones, such as dimethicone (such additives don't usually clog pores but may) to make the product feel smooth and look natural.

Preservative-free: The product was manufactured without traditional preservatives, which sometimes cause breakouts or irritation. However, it may likely contain other substances that can maintain freshness without troubling your skin. (Totally preservative-free products don't have very long shelf lives.)

Unscented: The product has no fragrance—but that doesn't mean that a masking scent hasn't been added to cover up the smell of its raw materials. If you're allergic to fragrance, you could still have a reaction.

Q + A

Shampoo Your Body

In a pinch, can I use my shampoo as a body wash?

"Why not?" asks Lisa Donofrio, M.D., an assistant clinical professor of dermatology at Yale and Tulane universities. "Most shampoos are gentle—after all, they're formulated to suds down over your eyes—so they're fine to use on your body." Some may even have added benefits: Those formulated for dry or damaged hair can substitute for shaving cream, since the extra moisturizers can help prevent razor burn. And dandruff shampoos containing the antifungal agents ketoconazole and selenium sulfide can help relieve dry patches.

But the opposite isn't always true. Many body washes are too harsh and others too heavy for hair. Unless, that is, you chose a special multipurpose product.

Q + A

Hair to Dye For

I've heard that coloring your hair can raise your risk of cancer. Is there any truth to this?

We checked with the voice of authority on the matter, Michael Thun, M.D., head of epidemiological research for the American Cancer Society. He says any link between hair dye and cancer is minuscule, if it exists at all. As he puts it, "The danger is so small that even a study of hair-dye use in over six hundred thousand women didn't turn up consistent evidence of cancer risk." If you're still worried, keep the color from touching your skin while you apply it, don't dye all the way to your scalp, and choose lighter shades (their chemicals are gentler than those in darker shades).

The Fresh Fad: *Is It for You?*

BY MICHELE BENDER

Today, looking fresh may mean keeping the contents of your cosmetics case fresh as well. Some of the creams and masks you slather on need to be treated with as much care as perishable foods. Various new products, such as The Body Deli's Botanical Facial Masques and Boscia's Willow Bark Breakout Treatment, are stamped with expiration dates and, in many cases, even require refrigeration. After examining the labels of some of the freshest cosmetics around, we tackled several questions.

The word *fresh* appears on lots of packaging. What exactly does it mean?
Not much. The government doesn't regulate descriptions on cosmetics labels, so manufacturers can use *fresh*—like *natural* and *organic*—however they want. "Those terms have nothing at all to do with how effective a product is," says Arielle Kauvar, M.D., associate clinical professor of dermatology at New York University School of Medicine.

Many of these products don't contain preservatives. That must be a good thing, right?
Preservatives have a negative reputation because

they are often synthetic, but there is little evidence that they're actually unsafe for skin, Kauvar says.

Is it important that a product contain "whole" fruits and vegetables rather than extracted enzymes or vitamins?
Some companies claim that using actual produce makes their products more potent, but so-called whole food is no more effective than food in any other form. "Each active ingredient has an ideal concentration and form that will allow the product to penetrate the skin and give you the best results," Kauvar says. That's why, for example, you won't reap any of vitamin C's antiaging benefits by rubbing an orange half on your face.

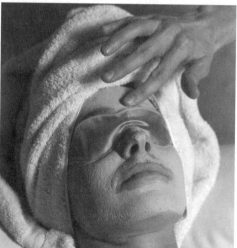

Seventy-three percent of respondents to a Health.com poll said they'd use an all-natural product even if it needed to be refrigerated and had a shelf life of just six to eight months.

Does the expiration date mean anything, or is it just a gimmick?
You should take the date seriously. Because some of these products don't include preservatives, the ingredients will become less potent after a certain amount of time or possibly irritate skin. If a mask or a cream has changed color or smells rancid, even before its expiration date, toss it. ◼

Q + A

Banish Blackheads

When I inspect my skin closely, I see blackheads. Is there any way to get rid of them without visiting a doctor?

It's tempting to engage in do-it-yourself dermatology (in other words, squeezing and popping) when you get up close and personal with a magnified mirror. But you'll probably just make matters worse. Blackheads are pores that are plugged with dead cells and oil, says Patricia Mercado, M.D., associate professor of dermatology at the University of Alabama at Birmingham. To get rid of (and prevent) them, use either scrubs that exfoliate with tiny beads or granules, or products that contain such chemicals as beta or alpha hydroxy acids. More-potent remedies, such as Retin-A, are available only from a dermatologist.

Another at-home option is a comedone extractor, a metal tool with a loop on the end. The instrument is used to squeeze out whiteheads and blackheads. "You need to know what you're doing with one of these," Mercado says. "If you use it incorrectly, you can cause scarring." Ask your doctor for how-tos before you try it yourself.

Q + A

Get Rid of Winter Red Bumps

During winter I notice red, rough, scaly bumps on the backs of my arms. What are they, and how can I get rid of them?

Those bothersome blemishes, each about the size of a goose bump, are probably keratosis pilaris (KP), an inherited skin condition that affects 40 percent of adults worldwide. The problem stems from a buildup of cells that get trapped around hair follicles, says Clark C. Otley, M.D., clinical associate professor of dermatology at the Mayo Clinic and Mayo Medical School. KP typically occurs on the backs of the arms, thighs, buttocks, or cheeks, he explains, and is often confused with acne or eczema. It becomes more severe during winter, when low humidity dries out skin.

"Keratosis pilaris usually improves with age and can go away on its own," Otley says. "If it doesn't, you can't cure it, but you can achieve temporary relief with ongoing treatment." Avoid soap, keep skin well-moisturized, and use a manual exfoliator, such as a Buf-Puf or body scrub, followed by a lotion that contains glycolic, salicylic, or lactic acid. (Try DermaDoctor's KP Duty Dermatologist Moisturizing Therapy for Dry Skin, or Neutrogena's Skin Smoothing Body Lotion.) Prescription solutions, which can be more effective than over-the-counter remedies, include Retin-A, chemical peels, or microdermabrasion. Again, remember that these results are not permanent.

Win the Dry-Skin Battle

BY MICHELE BENDER

You don't have to scratch your way through the chilly seasons. You just need to rethink some of your old habits—and the kinds of products you're using. "When the weather turns cold and humidity levels drop, the skin's outermost layer breaks down, making it dry and leaving you sensitive to products that might never have bothered you before," says Leslie Baumann, M.D., chief of the Division of Cosmetic Dermatology at the University of Miami School of Medicine and author of the textbook *Cosmetic Dermatology: Principles and Practice*. We're not suggesting that you ditch your entire beauty stash, but you may want to make a few simple substitutions until warm temperatures re-emerge.

CLEANSER

Store until spring: Gel-based cleansers. They usually contain alcohol, which dehydrates skin. (If you're using an acne or wrinkle treatment, you should definitely make the switch from a gel.)
Choose for winter: Cream-based products. They're typically milder and thicker than other formulations, so they seal in moisture more effectively. The best ones leave behind some fatty acids, nutrients that are a natural component of the skin's top layer. Look for such ingredients as honey, hyaluronic acid, and sodium lactate. Try Bath & Body Works' Pure Simplicity Fig Hydrating Shower Cream or L'Oréal's Nutri-Pure Foaming Cream Cleanser.

EXFOLIATOR

Store until spring: Mechanical exfoliators made with abrasive grains containing pumice, chopped nutshells, or fruit pits. These harsh ingredients can irritate already-dry skin. (You can still use them on stubborn spots, such as knees, elbows, and feet.)
Choose for winter: Formulas that smooth skin with mild cleansing beads. St. Ives' Gentle Apricot Scrub is an ideal body-polisher. It sloughs with tiny jojoba beads and softens with apricot-kernel oil. For the face, we like Noxzema's Daily Exfoliating Cleanser. Its scrubbers float in an emollient lotion; the menthol-and-eucalyptus scent is great for clearing sinuses.

MOISTURIZER

Store until spring: Serums or lightweight lotions. "They're typically not rich enough to hydrate winter skin," Baumann says.
Choose for winter: Thick lotions or creams; even products made for nighttime are suitable for daytime use in the colder months because of their heavy consistency. Creams and lotions that contain lipids (such as stearic and linoleic acids, sunflower-seed oil, ceramides, or cholesterol) will help replace moisture lost throughout the winter. "The cream also creates a better shield between your skin and the harsh environment," Baumann says. For facial skin, try Shiseido's The Skincare Day Essential Moisturizer Enriched with SPF 10. Eyes will appreciate Elizabeth Arden's Ceramide EyeWish SPF 10 Eye Cream, a rich lotion with light-diffusing particles that can make dark circles less obvious. And for body, slather on Origins' Calm to Your Senses Lavender and Vanilla Body Souffle. It's sweetly scented, with a frostinglike thickness, but it isn't greasy. Plus, its stearic acid and grapeseed, soybean, olive, and apricot-kernel oils help fend off flakes for hours. ▪

Wash Away Wrinkles

It sounds like something you'd dream about—then wake up laughing over: As you're cleansing your face, down the drain go makeup, dirt, and grime … along with your wrinkles. The makers of various new antiaging cleansers want you to believe your dream is actually the wave of the future. But what do the experts say?

"These cleansers may give temporary results because they contain certain hydrating ingredients (such as glyceryl stearate and propylene glycol) that can plump up dry skin, making lines less obvious," explains Tina Alster, M.D., clinical professor at Georgetown University Medical School. "But a moisturizer that remains on your skin is a better choice than a cleanser that rinses off."

Give Your Skin the Ultimate Thirst-Quencher

You've made it through winter's wrath only to find scaly, parched skin when you shed those gloves, socks, and sweaters. Fight back with this all-natural, do-it-yourself, deep-moisturizing body mask, courtesy of the beauty Web site www.substance.com. It not only hydrates the driest areas of your body, but also rids skin of dead cells. Rice bran exfoliates flaky patches, while the vitamin E and mono-unsaturated fat in avocados make ideal softeners. Other key ingredients include egg yolk, whose proteins and oils offer extra nourishment, and evening primrose oil, which contains a fatty acid that helps keep skin and nails healthy and moisturized.

MOISTURIZING BODY MASK

- 1/2 avocado, mashed
- 1 egg yolk
- 1 teaspoon honey
- 1 teaspoon rice bran (available at health-food stores)
- 10 drops evening primrose oil (available at health-food stores)

1. Stir together all of the ingredients.
2. Massage the mixture into areas that tend to become dry when seasons change: hands, feet, elbows, and knees.
3. Let the mask absorb into your skin for about 15 minutes, and then rinse. You should see—and feel—the effects immediately.

How Your Face-Washing Routine Could Be Flawed

Keeping your skin healthy is easy when you avoid these five common mistakes.

BY MICHELE BENDER

You haven't figured out yet how to blow-dry your hair like a pro, but if there's one thing you have mastered by now, it's washing your face—right? Well, don't be so sure: Most women aren't as skin-savvy as they think. We asked leading dermatologists to uncover the top five face-washing problems and, of course, help us fix them.

1. Not using water: Many people moisten their hands, put cleanser on their fingers, and apply it to dry skin. "All cleansers are designed to work with water. Water is what cleans skin, and the cleanser and soap enhance its effects," says Dennis F. Gross, M.D., a New York dermatologist and founder of the MD Skincare product line. Be sure your face is dripping wet before you start to wash.

2. Scrubbing too aggressively: Superabrasive cleansing sponges or puffs can irritate your skin as well as cause broken blood vessels, says Ellen Gendler, M.D., clinical associate professor of dermatology at New York University School of Medicine. The same holds true for mechanical facial scrubs made from nutshells, pits from such fruits as apricots, or other irregularly shaped particles; these should be used twice a week at most (or not at all if you have dry skin or rosacea, or if you are using topical prescription medications, such as Retin-A or Tazorac, which can make skin hypersensitive). The best way to buff is to put a gentle chemical exfoliant, such as glycolic or salicylic acid, on a cotton pad or your fingers and massage it into your skin.

3. Rinsing too fast: "The purpose of a cleanser is to bind to the skin's oil and debris so that it can be removed when you rinse," says Marsha L. Gordon, M.D., associate professor in the Department of Dermatology at Mount Sinai School of Medicine in New York. "If you don't rinse well, you may leave irritants on the skin." Splash your face 8 to 12 times to ensure a clean finish.

4. Treating your face the way you'd treat your body: "You'd be surprised how many people use a drying deodorant body bar or a hand soap on the face," says Valerie D. Callender, M.D., director of the Callender Skin & Laser Center in Mitchellville, Maryland. "These soaps contain detergents and chemicals that strip oils, and aren't meant for delicate facial skin." Look for gentle, soap-free cleansers or anything made just for your face.

5. Spending too much time washing up at the sink: Cleansing more than twice a day and for more than 2 minutes at a time is a definite no-no. Too-frequent washing can dry and irritate your skin or stimulate oil production, which can result in clogged pores and breakouts, Gross says. Even if you hit the gym at midday, just rinse your skin with water, and save your cleanser for morning and night. ■

The No-Surgery Face-lift

Can a new scalpel-free procedure give you the results you're looking for?

BY MICHELE BENDER

If you're one of the millions of women who want to get rid of wrinkles but aren't willing to go under the knife, then a noninvasive technique called Thermage (or Thermalift), designed to tighten tissue using radio-frequency technology, may be just what you're looking for. The procedure is now being done in the offices of 700 dermatologists, plastic surgeons, and other physicians around the country, with an estimated 500 more set to receive the technology by the end of 2004.

Here's how it works: First a numbing cream is applied to your face; then a wandlike radio-frequency tool called ThermaCool TC (short for "tissue contraction") is passed over the area that needs rejuvenating. (Although Thermage has been approved only for use on skin above and around the eyes, doctors are also using it on smile lines around the mouth.) It delivers heat into the tissue beneath the skin's surface while simultaneously cooling the topmost layer to protect against burning. "By heating the tissue, you can generate a healing response that causes new collagen to form," explains Roy G. Geronemus, M.D., director of the Laser and Skin Surgery Center of New York. The new collagen makes your face look smoother and firms sagging skin. Some experts believe the procedure can even help areas of the face that are not treated directly. "Concentrating on the skin above the brow area, for example, can enhance the appearance of the eyes, making them look less tired and more alert," explains David Goldberg, M.D.,

clinical professor of dermatology at Mount Sinai School of Medicine in New York.

The procedure takes less than an hour. You may notice some improvements immediately, but the full effect takes several months to achieve. Although practitioners say that only one treatment is necessary, new research shows that about three sessions (at around $2,000 to $4,000 a pop) spaced three to four months apart may work even better. More studies are necessary to determine how long the results will last, but a report in the journal *Lasers in Surgery and Medicine* found that 83 percent of participants experienced wrinkle improvement and 62 percent had more-lifted brows six months after treatment. Researchers are also investigating Thermage's effectiveness on breasts, stomach, arms, and legs.

Some patients say their skin felt very hot during the treatment; most women experience only mild redness and are able to return to normal activities the next day. In rare cases, swelling, scabbing, and bumps occur but disappear with time.

While this new option is exciting, it's no substitute for a surgical lift. "Though the device does tighten the skin, it's not the same degree one would see with a traditional face-lift," says Barry DiBernardo, M.D., a spokesman for the American Society for Aesthetic Plastic Surgery's Committee on Nonsurgical Procedures. "The ideal candidate is someone who needs only mild to moderate tightening." Find a doctor who performs the technique at www.thermage.com. ■

Plastic Surgery
Without the Surgeon

Are new skin-care treatments as effective as the knife and needle?

BY MICHELE BENDER

There's no question that cosmetic procedures are popular: 6.9 million were performed in the United States in 2003. But if you don't have the time, money, or stomach to take the clinical route, beauty companies are now offering products that promise to replace four of the top treatments: Botox injections, collagen injections, microdermabrasion, and chemical peels. Because over-the-counter approximations can't contain prescription-strength ingredients, we wondered if they really could replace a visit to the doctor. Here's what we found out on the do-it-yourself trend.

FAUX BOTOX

At the doctor's office: Botox is used primarily to treat between-brow furrows. This purified toxin is injected into facial muscles (at about $400 a pop, according to the American Society for Aesthetic Plastic Surgery, which provided average prices for all procedures listed here), paralyzing them so that they can't contract and cause wrinkles.

At-home treatment: Makers of most Botox-like creams claim you will see results in two weeks to two months of daily use. Typically, the active ingredient is hexapeptide-3 or acetylhexapeptide-3; manufacturers say these substances are absorbed into the muscle, reducing the production of an enzyme needed for contraction. This chemical reaction supposedly inhibits certain facial movements, as Botox does.

Examples: SCO's Topical "Botox" Infusion, Juva MediSpa's Peptide Eyelift Cream

Expert opinion: "Creams do improve your appearance by moisturizing—wrinkles are more obvious on dry skin—but none of these products can actually stop muscle movement," says Rhoda S. Narins, M.D., president-elect of the American Society for Dermatologic Surgery. "A topical cream would have to go through all the layers of the skin, the tissue and blood vessels, and then into the muscle. And no cream can go as deep as the needle." In addition, Narins and other experts say there isn't any evidence that hexapeptide-3 has paralyzing powers.

MAKESHIFT MICRODERMABRASION

At the doctor's office: Microdermabrasion uses fine crystals to polish skin, stimulating the production of new skin cells (and possibly collagen) to reduce fine lines, crow's-feet, age spots, and acne scars. Treatments cost about $200.

At-home treatment: Various grainy exfoliators are formulated with microcrystals to deliver similar sloughing action. Manufacturers claim these deep scrubs smooth skin; eliminate fine lines, wrinkles, and acne scars; help even skin tone; and make pores look smaller.

Examples: Dr. Ostad's Microdermabrasion in a Tube, Derma Pro's Microdermabrasion Scrub

Expert opinion: "These products do have the ability to exfoliate skin so your complexion is softer and smoother," says Mitchel Goldman, M.D., medical director of Dermatology/Cosmetic Laser Associates of La Jolla, in San Diego. "However, there is no similarity between the crystals in these products and the ones found in microdermabrasion machines. In fact, some of the particles in at-home scrubs are too abrasive and can even cause broken blood vessels and irritation, especially if you have sensitive skin or rosacea."

OVER-THE-COUNTER CHEMICAL PEEL

At the doctor's office: Peels (at about $800 each) use such chemicals as alpha hydroxy or trichloroacetic acid to remove the top layers of skin, giving it a fresh glow and reducing fine wrinkles, superficial sun damage, and hyperpigmentation.

At-home treatment: Some do-it-yourself options contain lactic, glycolic, salicylic, or citric acids to boost the natural exfoliating process and improve skin's tone, texture, and clarity.

Examples: Therapy Systems' Self-Adjusting Facial Peel Kit, DDF's 7-Day Radiance Peel Kit

Expert opinion: "In general, these at-home peels are safe. It's their claims of effectiveness that leave

something to be desired," says Harold Brody, M.D., clinical professor of dermatology at Emory School of Medicine in Atlanta. "You can probably get a more radiant complexion from the exfoliation. But you won't get doctor's office results. Dermatologists use stronger chemicals in higher concentrations, so the peel penetrates into deeper layers of the skin." If you decide to try a treatment at home, do a patch test first; because most products don't list the percentage of acid used, you may end up with a red, burning, irritated face.

QUASI-COLLAGEN INJECTION

At the doctor's office: Collagen, either human or bovine, is injected into crow's-feet, frown lines, and smile lines to fill them out and into lips to make them appear plumper. The cost per injection is around $400.

At-home treatment: Typically consists of moisturizers that you apply daily to the face and neck. Some products even claim to do what no injection can, allegedly ironing out deep wrinkles, helping replace collagen you've lost over the years, increasing skin's ability to retain moisture, and improving elasticity.

Examples: Aubrey Organics' Collagen TCM Therapeutic Cream Moisturizer, Joey New York's Rest-A-Line Cream

Expert opinion: "Topical collagen products can bring moisture to the skin. And if you hydrate skin enough, you can temporarily correct a wrinkle or fine line; some regular moisturizers can do this, too," says Linda K. Franks, M.D., assistant professor of dermatology at New York University School of Medicine in Manhattan. "But they cannot improve existing damage by increasing collagen content in the skin. Even prescription products proven to do that, such as Renova or Retin-A, take months or even years to work."

> In general, these at-home peels are safe. It's their claims of effectiveness that leave something to be desired
> —Harold Brody, M.D.

Hooked on the Sun

Tanning could actually be a form of substance abuse.

BY MICHELE BENDER

When we first heard about a new study suggesting that chronic sunbathers might experience the same kind of high from the sun that an alcoholic would from a vodka and tonic, we were quick to investigate. What's next, we thought, 12-step programs for "tanaholics"? But as it turns out, the study, presented at the 2003 annual meeting of the American Academy of Dermatology, might actually explain why so many women still roast in the sun and under the bright lights of tanning beds, despite the risk of skin cancer.

With the help of a psychiatrist, researchers at the University of Texas Medical Branch (UTMB) in Galveston developed two sets of questions to screen for tanning addiction, both based on standard criteria used to identify substance abusers. Then the scientists hit the beach to put sun-worshippers to the test. The results: One survey's findings suggested that 55 percent of the subjects were tanning addicts, while the other test showed that 27 percent were.

"Certainly, more work needs to be done, but this study has opened our eyes," says Richard Wagner, M.D., J.D., UTMB professor of dermatology and one of the study's authors.

Other studies may help explain the draw for sun junkies. Some researchers speculate that levels of beta-endorphin—the opium-like substance said to be responsible for the so-called runner's high—increase when skin is exposed to ultraviolet light (although this has not been proven conclusively). "It's also well-documented that sunlight stimulates the release of serotonin, another chemical that affects your mood," says Michael Holick, M.D., Ph.D., professor

of medicine, biophysics, and physiology at Boston University Medical Center and author of *The UV Advantage*. Both brain chemicals may also play a role in alcoholism and drug dependency.

The impact of research into sun addiction could be significant: In this country, more than one million new cases of skin cancer will be diagnosed this year. "We're trying to reach people educationally and tell them about the dangers of the sun, but if tanning is actually a compulsive, addictive behavior, then another strategy—like some form of psychotherapy—might be needed," Wagner says.

Are You a Sun Addict?

If three or more of the following statements have applied to you within the same 12-month period, you may be.

1. You continuously tan to keep the color from fading.
2. You feel that tanning at a salon will help you maintain the tan you've gotten outdoors.
3. When you go to the beach, you spend more time in the sun than you intended to.
4. You try other non-sun-related activities, but you find that you still like spending time in the sun best of all.
5. You tan year-round.
6. You have ever missed a scheduled activity because you decided to tan instead.
7. You spend time in the sun or in tanning beds even though you know this can increase your risk of skin cancer.

Q + A

UV Is Not an Indoor Threat

Is it true that lightbulbs emit ultraviolet rays? Do I need to put on sunscreen before I read in bed at night?

Yes, some bulbs do—and no, you should save your sunblock for the daylight hours. Fluorescent and halogen lightbulbs (but not incandescent bulbs, which are the most common type found in homes) do emit some ultraviolet (UV) rays, the same kind that are given off by the sun and are responsible for tanning, wrinkling, and skin cancer. But even if you work under fluorescent or halogen lights 40 or more hours a week, you probably don't need to worry about the levels of UV rays that you're exposed to indoors. For one thing, the plastic or glass that typically covers lightbulbs filters the rays. And even when it comes to unfiltered artificial light, "the average person will have, at worst, a minimal increase of skin-cancer risk," according to Bernhard Ortel, M.D., assistant professor of dermatology at Massachusetts General Hospital's Wellman Laboratories of Photomedicine in Boston. For your skin's sake, though, you should make sure that you protect yourself from the biggest source of UV rays: the sun. Also remember to use a sunscreen or a moisturizer with SPF 15 or higher year-round, a strategy that, incidentally, will shield you from the feeble emissions of lightbulbs as well.

Sun Protection Isn't Just for Summer

Although the Northern Hemisphere might get a little less sun during the winter months, you still risk getting sunburned when you're out on the slopes. So don't head outside without protecting all of your uncovered body parts (nose, cheeks, ears, lips) with sunscreen that has an SPF of at least 15. Gray days count, too—those devious UV rays can penetrate right through the clouds.

One More Reason to Remember to Use Sunblock

Go ahead, slather on even more sunscreen. By helping prevent skin cancer, creams and lotions with high SPFs may also stop you from getting other cancers. After crunching numbers from the renowned Women's Health Initiative study, researchers at Northwestern University recently discovered that women who had gotten basal or squamous cell carcinoma (the most common types) were more than twice as likely to develop a second, unrelated cancer as women who'd never had these two kinds. Why? The same genes that predispose women to skin cancer may also roll out the carpet for other diseases. Or it may be that solar radiation weakens tumor-fighting defenses.

Vanishing Veins

A new laser treatment can leave your legs blemish-free for good.

BY MICHELE BENDER

Up to half of all American women live with a road map of unsightly varicose and spider veins crisscrossing their legs. In March 2003, *Health* reported on a breakthrough glycerin-injection technique that almost painlessly erases spider veins (those less than 1 millimeter in diameter, or about the width of a piece of angel-hair pasta or smaller). But new research shows there's help for veins closer to the diameter of your pinkie, which plague about half of varicose-vein sufferers. These big guys are not simply unsightly; they can also hurt, cause swelling, and increase your risks of blood clots and superficial skin wounds or ulcers by 50 percent.

The standard method for treating these large veins—which result from heredity, pregnancy, hormonal changes, or prolonged standing—is to strip them out surgically. This requires general anesthesia, at least a one-night hospital stay, and often weeks of recovery; the technique can also cause scarring and postoperative pain. But that may soon be a thing of the past: The newest remedy, called Endovenous Laser Treatment (EVLT), "seems to give better results with fewer side effects than traditional surgery, and is less expensive, less painful, and faster than the high-tech treatments used in recent years," explains Neil S. Sadick, M.D., president of the American College of Phlebology and a pioneer in the use of this technology.

During the 30- to 40-minute procedure, the area is numbed and a catheter is inserted into the vein through a puncture in the skin. Next, a laser fiber about as big around as a pencil point is placed in the catheter. The laser heats the vein from the inside, causing it to close and shrink. Following treatment, patients walk around for 20 minutes to stimulate blood flow and prevent clots; after that, they can go about their day. (Wearing an elastic bandage for 24 hours and then heavy-duty support hose for a week keeps down bruising and swelling.) Veins start fading in a day or so and disappear completely after three to six months, when the vessels are totally absorbed into the body. "Because you're closing the vein off internally, there is no need for sutures, and there's no scarring," explains vein expert Mitchel Goldman, M.D., clinical professor of dermatology and medicine at the University of California, San Diego. In a study led by Sadick, published in the *Journal of Cosmetic and Laser Therapy*, the technique was successful for 98 percent of patients, with no recurrence one year after treatment.

Legs are treated one at a time; new mothers must wait two months after delivery before undergoing EVLT. The cost is comparable to that of vein-stripping surgery: $2,500 to $3,500 per leg.

You can find a vein-zapping doctor in your area by contacting the American College of Phlebology (510-834-6500 or www.phlebology.org). ■

A Cure for CELLULITE?

A new injection promises to melt away the fat.

BY MICHELE BENDER

Yet another beauty treatment is currently claiming to eradicate unsightly cellulite for good—no diet or exercise required. Skeptical? Join the club.

What is it? Mesotherapy involves a series of injections that supposedly eliminates cottage-cheese dimples and melts fat. The technique has been used in Europe for decades and is now being practiced in the States by some physicians.

What's in the injections? That depends on who's wielding the needle, but it's usually a mixture that contains one or more of the following: traditional medicines (for instance, aminophylline, an asthma drug), homeopathic remedies (such as the herb arnica), and vitamins and minerals, in addition to some sort of anesthetic to ease the pain.

How does it work? Proponents claim that the various concoctions dissolve fat and smooth the connective tissue that causes cellulite's lumpy appearance. This fat, they say, is then flushed out of the body through the kidneys.

What's the procedure like? You start with a 20-minute session during which the practitioner injects your problem areas more than 100 times (many experts use mechanical injecting machines). Because the needles are tiny and an anesthetic is used, some patients say they feel no more pain than a pinprick.

Is there a clear difference between before and after? According to patients we spoke with, yes, but they say it is a subtle change that becomes more noticeable the more treatments you have.

Any side effects? Bruising is the primary one. Aside from that, you can immediately go back to your usual routine (but you can't exercise or take hot baths for 48 hours).

What does it cost? About $450 per session; you will need an average of 10 weekly treatments. The results are said to be permanent as long as you don't gain more than 15 pounds.

The skeptics caution: There is little proof to back up mesotherapy's promises. "Because there's no standard formula for the solution, it's hard to say whether the treatment is safe or effective," warns Lawrence Reed, M.D., a plastic surgeon and a spokesman for the American Society for Aesthetic Plastic Surgery's committee on non-surgical procedures. ▪

Extreme Makeunder

There's nothing radical about the new less-is-more beauty philosophy—except for the results.

BY BARBARA GUILDEA • PHOTOGRAPHY BY MAURA MCEVOY

Unless you have been living in a cave for the past year, you're probably aware that America is in the midst of a makeover craze. You can't click the remote without coming across someone getting plucked, powdered, stretched, or styled on shows with such names as *Extreme Makeover* or *What Not to Wear*. The premise, of course, is undeniably appealing: a head-to-toe makeover, courtesy of experts working together to create a new-and-improved you. But you don't need a team of beauty pros to help you achieve an amazing transformation. In fact, most women can make big strides with small steps. Think of it as a make*under*.

We went straight to the quintessential makeunder expert—makeup artist Bobbi Brown, whose less-is-more philosophy has revolutionized the way women wear makeup—to help five *Health* readers get the most out of their beauty routines. "Beauty today is not about covering up those so-called flaws as much as it is about revealing what's unique about yourself," Brown says. "And you can easily achieve this with makeup that's pared down rather than painted on." With that approach in mind, we asked our makeover candidates to present Brown, hairstylist Nick Arrojo, and his team from New York's Arrojo Studio with their top three beauty concerns. Although the solutions to their problems required only a few minor adjustments, the results are worthy of prime time.

NICHELLE NICHOLES LEVY, 35

When I was younger, I loved experimenting with my look. But it's been ages since I've tried anything different. Yeah, you could say I'm in a beauty rut.

Makeover Goal: **No More Shiny Skin**

Nichelle battles a schizo complexion: skin that's oily in some places and dry in others. "The trick is lightening up on moisturizer and using a little more powder," Brown says. She began by using a shine-control gel on Nichelle's oily T-zone. "It forms a thin veil that actually binds moisture to the skin," Brown explains. "It also contains nylon powders, which absorb excess oil." The result is a matte surface that helps makeup glide on smoothly and evenly. Brown then applied a thin layer of oil-free moisturizer all over Nichelle's face, followed by a dusting of loose powder to lock in the moisture.

Makeover Goal: **Standout Eyes**

"Brow grooming is an easy way to instantly bring out the eyes," Brown says. She refined Nichelle's brows by plucking a few stray hairs between and beneath them; then she used a clear brow gel to keep them in place. A triple hit of eye shadow came next: a black plum powder on lids, a deeper camel tone along the crease, and a sweep of pale bone-colored shadow just below the brow bone. Navy gel liner (Brown smudged it with her pinkie to soften) along the upper lashes and a double coat of mascara finished the look.

Makeover Goal: **Healthier Hair**

If your hair is coarse, you might be tempted to use serums, sprays, and other products that add sheen, says stylist Erli Perez, but they tend to leave tresses dull and limp. All that chemically straightened hair really needs is blow-drying with a round brush and a dryer that has a nozzle attachment. Directed downward, the concentrated heat flattens the hair cuticle and helps restore sheen. If you still need a styling product, use it sparingly—a few drops of shine serum combed through hair should do the trick.

Expert Tip: Choose a yellow-based concealer to make dark skin look healthier.

Nichelle Nicholes Levy

AMY JUNGER, 39

I'm a tired working mom who's badly in need of a change but doesn't have the luxury of time. If I can swipe on Blistex in the morning, I consider it a huge victory.

Makeover Goal: **An Even Complexion**

Porcelain skin can be a blessing, but with it comes a bit of a curse: sensitivity and dryness. That's why a water-based tinted moisturizer made the most sense for Amy. It gave her a smooth look without the redness and breakouts that heavier foundations can sometimes cause. "It's also light enough to let Amy's youthful sprinkle of freckles show through," Brown says. Look for brands made with titanium dioxide, one of the most effective sunblocks around.

Makeover Goal: **A Modern Cut**

Amy's longish bob overpowered her face, and it made her look older. Stylist Arielle Meier started by trimming Amy's hair to the jawline; then she added a few long layers around the front to frame Amy's face. Next, Meier razor-cut the edges to give them a textured, piecey look. "Hair looks sexier when it's not so neat and set," she says. She kept the bangs long, explaining, "Shorter bangs are too restrictive and box in the face." To style, all Amy has to do is apply a lightweight relaxing cream before she blow-dries.

Makeover Goal: **The Right Red**

Red is a vibrant color that can make your skin glow, but it can sometimes be tricky to pull off—especially if, like Amy, you are not a natural carrottop. Colorist Jesús Hernandez decided to go with a warm shade that flatters Amy's creamy skin and clear blue eyes. "Warmer tones of honey, copper, and strawberry blond complement lighter complexions," he notes. A cool shade with greenish undertones (a burgundy or deep auburn, for example) looks great against medium or olive skin tones. First, Hernandez applied a single-process color; then he brushed on golden-blond highlights to give the new cut definition and depth.

Expert Tip: Wispy bangs flatter delicate features and add versatility. Tuck them back, or keep them straight to frame the face.

Amy Junger

ANDREA COSTA, 46

I recently divorced after 21 years of marriage. I have a whole new life ahead of me and want to show the way I feel inside: refreshed.

Makeover Goal: **A Sun-Free Glow**

For natural-looking overall color, Brown suggested that Andrea try a self-tanner and complement it with a cream blush in a warm, pretty rose. Brown also recommended topping it off with a dusting of powder bronzer to even out Andrea's skin tone. "Apply powder with a brush on the raised areas of the face where the sun would normally hit: along the forehead, at the temples, across the cheeks, and on the chin, for a sun-kissed look," Brown says.

Makeover Goal: **Fast Hair**

Andrea first needed to part with some of her length—the ends of her hair had not been cut in five years. So stylist Lina Tartamella trimmed off 5 inches, leaving Andrea's hair just a little longer than shoulder length. "Longer layers starting at the jawline brought out her hair's natural wave," Tartamella notes. Maintaining this new cut is a cinch. After shampooing, Andrea can spritz a light styling spray into damp hair at the roots; then she can let it air-dry, or blow-dry and style with a medium-size round brush.

Makeover Goal: **A Date-Night Look**

"Makeup needs to be a bit bolder and more defined at night since lighting is usually dimmer," Brown says; she suggests deeper colors or even a bit of iridescence. She applied a cocoa shadow to lids, followed by a swipe of camel color in the creases. She brought out Andrea's eyes even more with a violet gel liner along the top and bottom lashes, with the thicker line on top. Brown followed with concealer under the eyes and in the corners to brighten them, along with black mascara. An apricot-peach powder blush mirrored

Andrea Costa

the bronze tones in Andrea's skin; lip gloss in a burnt mauve, a shade similar to her natural lip color, completed the look.

Expert Tip: Trim the dry, brittle ends of super-long hair. It will look healthier and be easier to maintain.

301

Pretty Simple

Here are makeup artist Bobbi Brown's five simple steps to an all-natural look.

1 **Pick the right tools.** Brushes with natural bristles are an investment—but an important one. Because they are designed to pick up just the right amount of color and place it exactly where you need it, "they can make the difference between makeup that looks fake or makeup that looks natural," Brown explains. Resist the urge to buy brushes for every part of your face, though. You really only need four: one each for concealer, eyeliner, blush, and powder.

2 **Find your true hue.** The foolproof way to choose makeup is to select colors close to those of your skin. Look at your eyelids, and you'll see they have a definite shade. (It might be ivory or tan or slightly pink—everyone's different.) Your lips also have their own tone: rose, mauve, pink, or red. The secret is finding eye shadows or lipsticks in the same color family as yours, so they don't stand out. The right lip color, for instance, should look good even when you're not wearing any other makeup, Brown says.

3 **Beautify your brows.** "If your brows are groomed correctly, you'll actually need less makeup," Brown says. Visit a salon for a professional shaping (get a reference from someone whose brows you admire). To maintain the shape at home, be sure to use tweezers with slanted edges.

4 **Lighten up foundation.** It's supposed to even out your skin tone, not change it completely. "Foundation should look like your skin, only better: hydrated and alive, but never greasy," Brown says. "And it doesn't have to go all over the face. Just dot it on trouble spots and blend." Test at least three shades next to each other on your jaw—that's where you'll find your most natural skin color—and see which one disappears. If you're looking for something lighter, try a tinted moisturizer. "Like the name says, it 'tints' the skin and is especially good for those with dry skin or who want lighter coverage," Brown says.

5 **Play up natural lips.** "You don't have to go darker," Brown says. "A sheer shade with a hint of glimmer is a clever way to highlight lips." Stay in the same color family as your natural lip tone, and choose a product with a touch of iridescence.

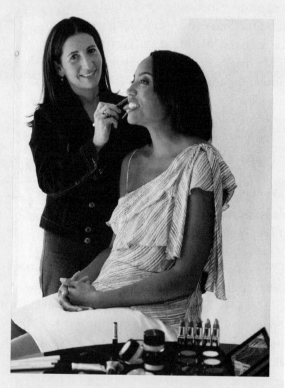

MAYA HARTY, 39

With two little girls and a full-time job, I have virtually no "me" time—and it shows. I always look thrown together at the last minute.

Makeover Goal: **Brighter Eyes**

Maya's dark circles are caused by veins that show through the delicate skin under her eyes. To combat the problem, Brown suggested a yellow-based concealer (one shade lighter than Maya's skin tone) anywhere the purplish shadows are visible—normally along the lower lashes and on the innermost corners of eyes. Brown applied concealer with a small brush, blending it gently with the ball of her finger before setting it with a yellow-toned powder. She also recommended that Maya avoid lining her lower lids; smudged eyeliner would only emphasize the darkness. Mascara, too, should go on top eyelashes only.

Makeover Goal: **A Stylish Cut**

Because her hair is full and naturally wavy, all Maya needed to give it extra body was a few inches off the ends and some smart shaping throughout. Perez added longish layers—trimming them a bit shorter and at an angle along the sides—to take weight out of her hair and make it look sleeker. Light bangs were the perfect way to play up Maya's expressive eyes.

Makeover Goal: **Thick, Curly Lashes**

It's paradoxical that Asian women, who usually have thick, lustrous hair, tend to have sparse, straight eyelashes. The first thing Brown did was introduce Maya to a lash curler. "Get as close to the roots as possible, press gently, rolling the curler slightly up, and hold for 5 seconds," Brown says. "Then move it halfway down the lashes, between the roots and the ends, and press it down again." Next came the mascara. "One way Maya can be sure that each lash is evenly coated is by rolling the wand back and forth as she strokes on the color," Brown says. A smudged line of dark brown powder along Maya's upper lids made her lashes look even thicker.

Expert Tip: For women who have little time to fuss, a layered cut gives towel-dried hair quick style.

Maya Harty

KAREN DIETRICH, 40

Fabulous and 40? Try frumpy and 40. My makeup routine is essentially the same as it was when I was in college. There's no shortage of work to be done.

Makeover Goal: **Flawless Skin**

Karen has been hit with three skin problems: enlarged pores, age spots, and a mild case of rosacea. A dermatologist can easily treat these conditions, but makeup tricks can hide the flaws as well, Brown notes. She toned down Karen's age spots and counterbalanced her ruddy complexion with a yellow-based foundation. Brown also advised Karen to be careful when she chooses blushes and lipsticks: red or hot pink would bring out the redness in her skin. Warm peach and neutral pink tones would work better with Karen's coloring. "To make pores less noticeable, apply an oil-free moisturizer with SPF 15, followed by a wax-based foundation stick," Brown notes. (Anything liquid will settle in large pores.)

Makeover Goal: **A Smarter Hairstyle**

The most workable solution for Karen, Tartamella decided, was a strong geometric cut that was shorter but not too short. She took a few inches off the ends while leaving longer layers on the top and sides. "And since her hair is longer in the front, she can brush it forward or tuck the sides behind her ears," Tartamella says. Finally, she incorporated tight layers along the sides and in back for a sleeker look.

To style, she applied a few drops of a de-frizzing sheen product to Karen's damp hair before blow-drying with a round natural-bristle brush.

Makeover Goal: **A Better Blond**

Karen needed a touch of color detox. "She had too many different shades in her hair," says colorist Jen Lusardi. She settled on a single-process permanent color—in a shade close to Karen's own light brown—that contained peroxide to cover gray and even things out. To avoid brassiness, Lusardi chose a shade with an ashy cast instead of one in a warmer tone. For vibrancy, she added highlights around Karen's face.

Karen Dietrich

Expert Tip: A concealer brush is a great age-erasing tool. It fills in fine lines and wrinkles around lips and eyes.

Q + A
Color Care: Shampoo *Does* Matter

My hairstylist told me that using a shampoo for color-treated hair could make my highlights last longer. Could this be true?

You wouldn't wash your favorite cashmere sweater in a harsh detergent, right? So why cleanse those pricey highlights with any old product?

"The main difference between shampoos made for color-treated hair and regular shampoos is detergent strength," says Mark Garrison, a hairstylist and owner of Mark Garrison Salon in New York City. "Those specially formulated cleansers contain milder surfactants (ingredients that get rid of dirt and grime) and have a lower pH, so they clean hair without stripping color."

Many of these shampoos also contain conditioning silicone polymers (such as dimethicone) that smooth hair and enhance shine, ultraviolet filters that protect hair from the sun, and fatty acids that add softness. Three of our favorites are Aveda's Color Conserve Shampoo, Charles Worthington's Results Moisture-Seal Glossing Shampoo, and

Pureology's HydrateShampoo. All are made without sodium lauryl sulfate, a detergent that's particularly hard on highlights.

Other color-keeping secrets: Wash only every other day, regardless of the product you use; avoid clarifying shampoos (the harshest of all); and use an intensive treatment once a week to keep dryness in check.

Q + A
Stick It to Unwanted Gray Hair

I recently heard about hair touch-up sticks as an at-home option for covering gray. How do they work?

Touch-up sticks—also called color sticks, crayons, or hair mascaras or powders—are like white-out (er, gray-out?) for your hair. You brush the offending strands with a shade that

closely matches your color, and let it dry for a few minutes. Most of these products wash out with your next shampoo. "They're perfect for women who want a quick way to cover gray before they decide to go for more commitment-heavy formulas," explains Todd Fox, a colorist at Frédéric Fekkai Salon and Spa in New York. "They're

also good for people who want to cover their roots between color appointments."

We like ColorMark's new Instant Professional Hair Color for Gray Roots. Its sponge-tip wand is easy to use. If you're blond, Retro Root Dual Hair Powder is available in two natural shades: Blonde and Honey.

Q + A — Why You Shouldn't Worry About This Wrinkle Myth

If you tend to sleep on one side more often than the other, will you get more wrinkles on that side of your face?

Surprise—there is a bit of truth to this old cosmetic legend. What dermatologists call the nasolabial fold, the "smile line" that stretches from the side of your nose to the corner of your mouth, does tend to be slightly deeper on the side you favor for sleeping (though in most cases it would take a long, rude stare for someone to really notice the difference). Wrinkles on any other parts of your face aren't affected by your sleeping habits, so trying to give equal time to each side is liable to leave you more sleep-deprived than smooth-skinned.

A better tactic is to pay close attention to the biggest wrinkle-causer of all: the sun. Use sunscreen liberally (even during the winter), and you can sleep with your face pointing in whichever direction you prefer.

Can Bottle Blonds Go Straight?

Attention, (un)natural blonds: You may be able to smooth your locks with thermal reconditioning, the hottest offering to hit salons. Women who have gone blond or gotten highlights generally shouldn't straighten their hair. But there's been some progress on the flat front. New York salon owner Paul Labrecque, for example, has developed a method that he claims gives the single-process blonds out there (i.e., those with highlights or permanent/semipermanent color) sleek strands without the risk of damage. The technique is similar to that used on non-color-treated tresses: Chemicals along with a flatiron are used to permanently break the bonds that make hair curly. The big difference, Labrecque says, is his careful pretreatment with protective creams, oils, and proteins that are custom-mixed to suit each client's particular needs. (Prices for the procedure range from $750 to $1,500.)

To find out if Labrecque could live up to his promise, Beauty and Fashion Editor Colleen Sullivan put her head in his hands. A highlighted blond, she longed to give up her unhealthy 20-minute-a-day drying routine, but she feared her already-fragile hair would fall out after a thermal-reconditioning session. Happily, she ended up shaving precious minutes off her a.m. routine, and her hair looks healthier, sleeker, and shinier than before.

If you want to give thermal straightening a try yourself, make sure you go to someone who has experience with bottle blonds (Labrecque is now training other stylists in his technique). Keep in mind that you may be turned away if your hair is overprocessed and in danger of breaking.

Q + A — Stop Cold Sores

How can I prevent the cold sores I get when I'm stressed?

Cold sores, blisterlike blemishes usually found on or near the lips, are often confused with canker sores, located inside the mouth. Nonprescription medicines can help the pain and speed the healing of cold sores, which are caused by a herpes virus. But only prescription medication can halt an outbreak altogether or at least shorten its duration to a few days. Take the medicine (either in pill or topical form) as soon as you feel the tingling or burning sensation that starts a day or two before sores appear. Remember that cold sores are highly infectious, so no kissing or sharing dishes or utensils.

Five-Minute Makeup Tips

1. Liven up your lip color.
Exchange your subtle gloss for a bold lipstick, suggests Boston makeup artist Debra Macki. We like Rimmel's Lasting Finish Lipstick in Red Hot.

2. Get bold with blush. Cheek enhancers add a little extra glow to your complexion. Clarins' All Over Base gives your eyes and cheeks just the right amount of liquid shimmer.

3. Choose a dramatic eye shadow. Pick your favorite color, and slightly dampen the applicator before sweeping it across the palette. This makes the colors deeper and richer, says Chanel makeup artist Susan Sterling.

4. Line your eyes. Gold-tone eyeliner applied along lower lashes instantly brightens your face. (Stick with basic black along your top lashes.) We like Clinique's Shimmer Cream Eye Crayon in Gold Lights.

5. Jazz up your nail polish.
Glitter and iridescence are big trends, and nails are an excellent place to try some sparkle. Revlon Nail Enamel in Riveting Russet is a festive red sprinkled with gold.

6. Draw some attention to your décolletage. A cream that has sheen captures light as it softens skin. For a hint of glimmer with a sensual scent, we suggest Estée Lauder's Beautiful Fragrance Silk.

Q + A

I plan on changing my hair color soon. How can I get my brows to match?

Actually, you don't want them to match exactly. "Eyebrows are naturally a half-shade to a shade darker than your real hair color," says Eve Tobin, a colorist at Lépine New York salon. "Keep that balance in mind when you change the shade of your hair." You'll get the best results if you have your brows tinted at the same time you have your hair colored. Just keep in mind that brow hair grows faster than the hair on your head, so you may have to stop at the salon between appointments for a quick touch-up (many hair colorists will do this at no charge).

If you dye your own hair at home, though, leave your eyebrows alone. "Applying the solution yourself is tricky, and it's dangerous for the chemicals to get too close to your eyes," Tobin warns. Instead, you'll have to rely on a few makeup tricks. A gel in a shade close to your new hair color is easy to apply and looks natural

Making Brows Match

(try Revlon's Brow Fantasy). Start by applying the gel to the area of the brow closest to your nose, brushing the hairs up and following the natural shape of your brow as you go.

To achieve the most authentic look using a pencil, make sure you use a product made specifically for the brows (we like Laura Mercier's Brow Pencils) rather than eyeliner or shadow, either of which can be too soft. Celebrity makeup artist Sue Devitt advises keeping the pencil sharp so that the strokes are very fine.

The Faces of Health

The winners of our fourth annual contest share how they keep their minds, bodies, and spirits healthy.

BY KATHY PASSERO • PHOTOGRAPHY BY CEDRIC ANGELES

True health is about more than looks. It's about the way you look at life, as the five winners of this year's Faces of Health contest prove. Each has encountered obstacles—including serious illness and the loss of a loved one—but all have learned to channel them into resilience and optimism. Here, in their own words, these women share their secrets for an upbeat outlook.

STEPHANIE SCOTT, 34

Singer, actress, and songwriter in Santa Monica, California

On living healthy: I eat a balanced diet, weight-train, and run 5 to 6 days a week. I also indulge in monthly massages. A little pampering goes a long way toward combatting stress.
On surviving setbacks: In 1989, I developed anorexia and went from 145 to 101 pounds in 4 months. It took months of reading about the long-term damage I was inflicting on my body to help me start eating normally. It was much harder to determine the underlying roots of my disease. Faith, prayer, and patience helped me get healthier.
On self-image: I spent a long time feeling like I didn't live up to the world's beauty standards. But anorexia taught me how dangerous it can be to buy into that philosophy. Now I'm trying to use my experience to help others lead healthier, more fulfilled lives.

Stephanie's secrets
for inner and outer beauty:

Throw away your scale. I know from experience that you can lose weight and not feel healthy. Instead of a number, learn to pay attention to how you feel and how your clothes fit.
Mix strenuous workouts with leisurely ones. You don't have to knock yourself out every time you exercise. A walk on the beach can count as part of your fitness routine if you enjoy it.

Health is about taking care of yourself so that you can be a blessing to others.
—Stephanie Scott

Real living means learning to accept yourself—stretch marks, self-doubts, and all.
—Diana Patton

DIANA PATTON, 36

Corporate diversity leader in Toledo, Ohio

On living healthy: After years of working at a job that required lots of travel, I got my priorities straight and accepted a job offer closer to home. Evenings are family time, so I set my alarm for 5:15 every morning and usually exercise before work. Sometimes I throw on sneakers and go for a run or do an exercise video in my pajamas. I strive to cook every night—mostly healthy meals, though we occasionally have pizza or a chocolate dessert. It's not living if you don't give yourself treats.

On surviving setbacks: My youngest brother committed suicide 10 years ago. The only way I could deal with the tragedy was to draw on my faith in order to create something positive from it. So I founded a high school scholarship in his honor. Kids ostracized him, so this award is for the child who goes over to talk to that kid standing alone on the playground, the one nobody wants to play with.

On self-image: I modeled professionally for about 10 years, but I feel more beautiful today because I'm happier.

Diana's secrets
for inner and outer beauty:

Highlight your best feature with makeup. I always play up my lips with liner and colored gloss—M.A.C. and Bobbi Brown are my favorites—and keep everything else on my face understated. That way my makeup never looks overdone.

Think positive. A negative attitude shows on your face, in the way you walk, the way you speak to other people—the way you do everything.

MYRNA MALIMBAN, 37

Stay-at-home mother of three in Springfield, Virginia

On living healthy: Being a home-schooling mom to 5-, 7-, and 9-year-old kids and running a household can be mentally, physically, and emotionally demanding. Setting aside a small amount of time to exercise, read, and eat healthy gives me the energy and mental clarity I need. My kids have an hour of quiet time each day, which I use as private time to nap or to read.

On surviving setbacks: I've been fortunate that I haven't had any traumatic events in my life, but going from the business world to being a home-maker was a big adjustment. I know this is the most important work I can do right now, so I channel my enjoyment of learning into teaching my children.

On self-image: Today, my happiness isn't tied to my weight or age. I see getting older as an adventure.

Myrna's secrets
for inner and outer beauty:

Read up on fitness facts. You don't need to invest in a personal trainer if you read health and fitness magazines. I constantly find workouts that challenge new muscle groups in a cost-efficient way.

Use a tinted moisturizer with sunscreen. Neutrogena's Healthy Defense Daily Moisturizer SPF 30 evens out my skin and protects it from sun.

Health isn't about beauty or age; it's about keeping an open mind.
—Myrna Malimban

BONNIE NOBEL, 64

Co-owner of a graphic design firm in Berwyn, Pennsylvania

On living healthy: I eat a lot of whole grains, vegetables, and lean proteins, and I walk 4 miles a day through the rolling hills around the studio where my husband and I run our business. Each morning starts with my own sort of meditation—I watch the birds outside the kitchen window. It makes me happy to be surrounded by nature.

On surviving setbacks: When I was in my 30s, I was bedridden for 3 months with mononucleosis and hepatitis. After getting better, I felt completely reborn. Being sick made me realize how precious life and health are. I've worked hard to stay in shape and to remember that when life takes us in a different direction than we'd originally planned, we're probably going to end up benefiting from that unexpected experience.

On self-image: My energy keeps me young. I try not to worry about every new wrinkle. The best makeup for me is a healthy diet, exercise, and sleep.

Bonnie's secrets
for inner and outer beauty:

Wear a hat when you leave the house. I keep a big collection of hats near the door so that I can always grab one as I walk out the door. That and sunscreen have saved my skin.

Live like a kid. My 3-year-old granddaughter is a great teacher because she's totally focused on whatever she's doing at that moment. I try to be more like her and not let my mind worry about what I have to do tomorrow.

Wrinkles are a road map of where you've been. There's nothing wrong with them!
—Bonnie Nobel

CHERYL TAWIL, 45

Stay-at-home mother of two in Los Angeles

On living healthy: When I was 20, I was diagnosed with Crohn's disease, a chronic intestinal illness. Eating a healthy diet, getting enough sleep, and minimizing stress are essential to keeping my disease in check, so I make time to indulge in hobbies that nurture my soul, such as reading, sewing, and quilting.

On surviving setbacks: My experience has made me a more compassionate person. When I start feeling down, I remind myself of how this illness would impact a homeless person with no access to a doctor.

On self-image: I was a chubby kid, so for years I had a preoccupation with being thin. Then I got sick and lost 30 pounds. When an old friend told me I looked great because I'd dropped so much weight, I was shocked. I realized thin doesn't always mean healthy.

Cheryl's secrets
for inner and outer beauty:

Stretch after exercising. It increases flexibility and melts away tension.

Stay hydrated. I sneak water into my diet through fresh fruit juices and clear low-sodium soups. When I get enough fluids, my skin looks better.

It's important not to lose touch with what's really valuable: living in the moment.
—Cheryl Tawil

vital *stats*

27
Percentage of women who eat the recommended amount of fruits and vegetables every day

15
Percentage of women who eat chocolate every day

11.6
Pounds of chocolate the average American eats per year

4
Pounds of chocolate the average person in Japan eats per year

34
Percentage of American women who are obese

3
Percentage of Japanese women who are obese

83
Percent increase in spending on vet bills since 1996

50
Percent increase in health-care spending since 1996

37
Percentage of doctors who say they don't think medical school prepared them well for their profession

89
Percentage of workers who snack on the job

16
Percentage of people who admit to stealing snacks from their co-workers

80
Percentage of Americans who have not made any medical preparations for an emergency, such as a terrorist attack

30
Percentage of Americans who say they would face serious problems if their families had to go without medications for three to five days

37
Percentage of singles who have cut a date short because of "scary" home decor

31
Percentage of Americans who say a date's kitchen reveals more about his or her personality than any other room in the house

3
Percentage of home-buyers who gave their kids the final word when deciding on a new house

45
Percentage of Americans who say they live in households where anger and stress are a problem

63
Percentage of adults who deal with stress by taking a walk or a break

13
Percentage of adults who use medication to lift their mood

554
Number of calories a 140-pound woman burns per hour downhill skiing

252
Number of calories a 140-pound woman burns per hour playing table tennis at the ski lodge

 2
Number of U.S. cities named Valentine: Valentine, Nebraska (pop. 2,820); and Valentine, Texas (pop. 187)

64
Percentage of men who don't make romantic plans for Valentine's Day

56
Percentage of working women who say they have no time or energy to pay attention to themselves

32
Percentage of working women who think of leaving their jobs at least once a day

31
Percentage of hotel guests who say the first thing they do when they get to their rooms is adjust the temperature (the number-one answer)

3
Percentage of hotel guests who say the first thing they do when they get to their rooms is check out the minibar

Sources: Ensure/American Association of Working People /Institute for Health and Productivity Management/ American Society of Health-System Pharmacists; U.S. Census Bureau; Candy USA; Centers for Disease Control and Prevention; Chocolate Manufacturers Association; International Obesity Task Force; Packaged Facts; Centers for Medicare and Medicaid Services; Sedona Training Associates; National Consumers League; GLS Consulting; Trane Home Comfort Institute; HealthStatus calorie calculator; Lavalife; Century 21; Medscape poll—Reported by Lisa Lee Freeman

relationships

the keys to success for love, family, and friendship

No More
Boredom in the Bedroom

Recent books and TV shows claim that lack of desire is epidemic among married couples. But is it?

BY SUSAN ORENSTEIN

The story of sex has a variety of era-defining plotlines: The '50s featured the obliging housewife who served dutifully in suburbia, while the '70s heroine studied herself in a hand mirror. But at the dawn of the 21st century, the best seller is about what women aren't doing, and every day seems to bring new coverage of the sad state of sex in today's marriages.

Alarmed, life strategist and TV host Dr. Phil was moved to declare an "undeniable epidemic" of marital malaise at his Web site. The "not tonight, dear" message is even delivered via TV sitcoms, where, for example, everybody loves Raymond—except his wife, Debra, on sex night. The listless couple also became the subject of a popular book, *The Sex-Starved Marriage: A Couple's Guide to Boosting Their Marriage Libido*. After its debut, author Michele Weiner Davis ~~came~~ so busy with media appearances that she ~~but~~ having had no time for sex herself. ~~as~~ to be this incredible fascination with ~~opening~~ behind closed doors," she says.

Is the sexless marriage just another pop-culture myth? As always, when it comes to sex, the story gets complicated quickly.

On one hand, the swirl of day-to-day life would seem to leave little room for the average couple to be romantic. (As one of my friends puts it, sex can feel like one more task she needs to perform.) So it's very easy to see how a term like DINS—dual income, no sex—would gain currency. Yet research doesn't support a new trend. Janet Hyde, Ph.D., professor of psychology and women's studies at the University of Wisconsin, has found that even demanding jobs do not diminish sexual frequency. And data from the well-respected National Opinion Research Center at the University of Chicago consistently shows that husbands and wives have more sex than single people. Married couples' average—approximately 67 times a year—has stayed about the same for 10 years.

David Schnarch, Ph.D., a noted sex therapist and the author of *Passionate Marriage: Keeping Love and Intimacy Alive in Committed Relationships*, refutes the notion that people are too stressed for sex with the fact that pornography is more popular than ever, and both men and women are having plenty of affairs. "When an article tells us 'The reason is we're too busy,' as opposed to 'Our partner wouldn't touch us with a 10-foot pole,' " he says, "we like that explanation better."

At present, the sexless-marriage story taps into a collective mood, a gnawing dissatisfaction that goes beyond the bedroom. Real culprits—like a kid-centric ethos that, according to *Atlantic Monthly* writer Caitlin Flanagan, means that she goes to far more birthday parties than cocktail parties—detract from wedded bliss. Then, too, the role sex plays in matrimony has changed profoundly. "Women no longer see sex as something they are supposed to do to 'service' their husbands," says Peggy Vaughan, author of *The Monogamy Myth*.

By the same token, our unrealistic expectations about marital sex are fed by images of lusty movie sirens and Viagra ads that promise hours of passion in one gulp. In truth, "if you have movie-quality sex once a month, you're a really lucky couple," says Barry McCarthy, Ph.D., a therapist and co-author of *Rekindling Desire: A Step-by-Step Program to Help Low-Sex and No-Sex Marriages.*

I've learned from my relationships that the thrill of discovering someone can yield to routine, both in and out of bed. But that's not all bad; I like it when my lover orders for me in a restaurant or reads my moods.

Richard E. Fischer, Ph.D., a New York couples therapist, says, "Married couples have to work hard to create some fantasy." Advice about introducing novelty skirts the problem. Risk is harder the more invested you are in a relationship, because you face exposure or rejection. "But," says Heidi Berrin Shonkoff, a therapist in Berkeley, California, "all change requires us to tolerate fear and discomfort."

That's certainly been my experience. The first time I tried to be more playful with a long-term

boyfriend (think candles and a scarf), he looked puzzled and even a bit defensive. I felt a twinge of school-yard fear that he might laugh. He didn't, and although the moment was far from movie-quality, things did improve.

Plumbing the experts, I learned that sexual stumbling blocks are not only normal, but also opportunities. "You've got to figure out what arouses you and be willing to communicate that," says Patricia Love, Ed.D., author of *Hot Monogamy: Essential Steps to More Passionate, Intimate Lovemaking.*

"It is normal to feel anxious and even disappointed," Shonkoff says. It's also important, she notes, to be honest about the choices that keep you from having sex, rather than be a victim of your schedule. "If sex

> Sexual stumbling blocks are not only normal, but also opportunities to learn what arouses you.

is great, you find time to do it," Schnarch says. "It's a lot more fun to complain about the lack of intimacy than to work on it."

At times, I've crammed my life full to avoid confronting problems in a relationship. But recently, I made a different move. I gave up some Saturday runs with my sports club so that my boyfriend and I could spend a few lazy mornings together at home. It was a small gesture—hardly a sexy story line—but at least I was taking a step toward the closeness I want. ▪

Susan Orenstein is a freelance writer based in San Francisco.

Sex by the Numbers

Average number of times per year heterosexual couples have sex:

Never married—62
Married—67
Remarried—72

When It's
TIME to TALK

Here's how to handle those tough conversations that leave you tongue-tied.

BY SUSAN FREINKEL

Discussing a glowing job review, thanking a friend for something kind—conversations like these are a cinch. But when it comes to confronting someone, demanding a change in behavior, or ending a relationship, we'll do almost anything to avoid these tough talks, even at a cost. Is it possible to have the hard heart-to-hearts without unacceptable casualties? Absolutely, says Bruce Patton, co-author of the book *Difficult Conversations: How to Discuss What Matters Most* and deputy director of the Harvard Negotiation Project, which studies conflict resolution.

Whether you're assertive or timid by nature, you can navigate the rockiest conversation, provided you are guided by a few basic points. Be clear about your feelings and what this problem means to you. Also, be open to the other person's perceptions—instead of casting blame, explore how you both may have contributed to the situation. "The most important thing is to not measure a conversation's success by the other person's response, but by how well you did in saying what it is legitimate for you to say," Patton says.

We asked Patton how to handle three common types of difficult encounters. Here's his advice.

"ALWAYS LATE FOR EVERYTHING" FRIEND

Situation: You invite a friend to see a movie, but she's so tardy you miss the beginning. This is a habit with her. In the past you've said nothing about her lack of punctuality, but this time you're steamed.
Solution: Ask yourself why you're so upset. You probably feel disrespected, as if your friend is saying your time isn't as important as hers. But on further reflection, Patton says, you might realize "the world is fairly evenly split between people who are very cognizant of time and those who aren't. There's no fault here. It's just a difference." Recognize, too, that you've contributed to the problem by waiting so long to confront her. You can't hold her responsible for something that you haven't told her about.

Acknowledge that you should have mentioned your feelings about it earlier and that you are still uncomfortable discussing it, but tell her that you need to talk about the issue because it is affecting your friendship. Explain that while you know she doesn't intend to insult you, you feel slighted. Tell her you would appreciate her being more considerate of your time. Then ask, "What's your reaction?"

"What often happens at this point is that the friend says, 'I'm sorry, but I think you're too sensitive about this time thing. You've got to chill out,'" Patton says. Be firm, though. Remind your friend that this isn't just about being on time but also about respecting each other's needs. Then ask her again whether she can accommodate yours. If she says no, she's not necessarily a bad friend, just an honest one. "Plan accordingly. Get over it, or plan to see her less," Patton says.

If she says she'll try to be on time but still runs late, you can bring up the subject again (most folks trying to change need a few reminders). If she still leaves you waiting, it probably means she can't or won't change. It's up to you then, Patton says.

You can't hold a friend responsible for something she does that annoys you if you haven't told her about it.

PASSED OVER FOR A PROMOTION

Situation: A co-worker hired after you gets the promotion you feel you deserve. You decide to talk to your boss about it.

Solution: To have this conversation, you need to be open to the possibility that others may think less of your performance than you do. So don't charge into the boss's office demanding, "Why did you promote some whippersnapper over me?" or "Are you trying to get rid of me?" Patton says, "If you go in assuming you should have gotten the promotion, it will get you into trouble."

While you might have deserved to be promoted, it's more likely your boss sees the situation differently. If the reality is indeed Machiavellian—that your supervisor is trying to deep-six you—you'll probably get more valuable information using a less-confrontational approach.

Tell your boss you want to talk about your career path. Acknowledge your surprise at being passed over for the promotion, citing your positive reviews, experience, managerial skills, or whatever. But also open the door for her to give you an explanation. You might ask her if your self-assessment is off or if you've done anything to anger the higher-ups. Tell her you'd like an opportunity to work on your weaknesses so you'll be considered for the next promotion. Then see what she has to say about your idea.

If your boss's answer doesn't make sense—say, she claims you aren't putting in enough time when in fact you've clocked more hours than anyone else—point that out and keep digging, asking for concrete examples of problems in your performance. Work on correcting any legitimate concerns she identifies. Then schedule follow-ups to monitor your progress and any commitments you may have discussed.

If you decide to talk to your boss about a missed promotion, be prepared for the possibility that others may think less of your performance than you do.

Patton notes that if your manager is the sort who dreads conflict, be aware of that and focus future talks on things that are easily discernable as valid issues. But don't discuss the situation with co-workers; these conversations are gossipy and could well backfire.

DISSED BY YOUR HUSBAND

Situation: In the year since you were married, you've noticed that whenever your husband discusses politics, he tends to belittle what you have to say—even in front of friends.

Solution: You want your mate to know that his barbs frustrate you and make you feel like an also-ran. But when you're dealing with someone you love, the most productive approach is to try to understand what this behavior is all about.

Point out that since it's early in your marriage, the two of you are still learning each other's strengths and vulnerabilities, as well as how to talk with each other. Then describe the way his pattern of dismissing your opinions makes you feel, and help your husband explore why he's doing it.

Keep in mind that there may be various explanations for his behavior. Your mate may think he's merely bantering, Patton says. "Schoolboys use [this technique] to show connection and affection. You only do it to people you care about." Or he may be repeating old family patterns; perhaps this is the way his mother was treated. If so, you can remind him that you're not her and that you won't accept such treatment. But remember that you're there to help probe, not preach. "You get in trouble if you say, 'Hey, buddy, here's the truth about you that you didn't see,'" Patton says. He calls this the godlike voice and adds, "it's extremely annoying to other people." The only thing you can talk about with absolute authority is the way your husband's behavior is affecting you.

Chances are he never meant to hurt you, Patton says. So give him examples of less-hurtful discussion styles. Rephrase one of your husband's put-downs, for instance, so that it's not belittling. The key is to treat this not as a chance to criticize but as an opportunity to learn more about each other. This approach usually works to resolve problems. "Most times just getting it out on the table and talking about it brings you closer, because you don't have these kinds of uncomfortable conversations with people you don't care about," Patton says. ■

Susan Freinkel, a freelance writer and former Health *staffer, lives in San Francisco.*

Broken Up over Breakups

Don't underestimate the toll a fizzled romance can take on your mental health. New research from Virginia Commonwealth University shows that humiliating experiences—particularly those involving a romantic breakup—are nearly as likely to cause major depression as a serious loss, such as the death of a loved one. Loss plus humiliation is even more devastating, says psychiatric geneticist Kenneth S. Kendler, M.D., who led the study. For example, if your marriage breaks up, well, then that's a loss. But if your ex moves into a house a few doors down with a woman half his age and shows her off to your friends and family, that's loss combined with humiliation. The combo was twice as likely to lead to depression as loss alone, Kendler says.

Blurter + Brooder = Domestic Disaster

Why are some couples perpetually starry-eyed while others are constantly unhappy? A new study shows that the interplay of certain verbal-communication styles can create "precarious couples" who lack intimacy and feel persistently dissatisfied.

A major factor is "blirtatious-ness," or how likely a person is to impulsively speak his or her mind, says William Swann, Ph.D., who led four studies of a total of 1,372 adults. When the results were combined, he found that relationships were rockiest when highly blirtatious and critical women were paired with reserved men. (When the traits were doled out the opposite way in men and women, the couple got along just fine, perhaps because "men don't really feel all that comfortable when they are being verbally dominated," Swann says.)

If the precarious pattern describes your relationship, be concerned but don't despair. While verbal-communication style and criticalness are not likely to change, a couple can learn to deal with mismatched characteristics, says Swann, a professor of psychology at the University of Texas at Austin.

"It's important for the man to be aware of the need to express himself. If he doesn't,

he'll become resentful and withdrawn, which will make the woman try to draw him out more, which will make him more resentful and withdrawn," Swann says.

At the same time, the female blirtatious critic should launch fewer tirades and, thus, give her partner some precious airtime to encourage communication where it typically breaks down, says Samuel Gosling, Ph.D., another author of the study. Just don't push your partner too far, he warns: Some people simply need more psychological space.

Not sure if you're a blurter or a brooder? You can find out by taking the BLIRT test (that's the Brief Loquaciousness and Interpersonal Responsiveness Test) at www.outofservice.com.

How Little Things Can Hurt Relationships in a Big Way

Which lasts longer: the agony caused by an infidelity or the aggravation of looking at a big pile of dirty dishes? Most people believe it's the intimate betrayal. But a study conducted by Harvard University psychologist Daniel Gilbert, Ph.D., suggests otherwise. "When the pain of the psychological insult gets big enough, we do something about it," he says. So if your spouse is disloyal, you might enter couples counseling, but you wouldn't suggest therapy because he leaves crusty dishes sitting in the sink overnight. The paradoxical result, Gilbert says, is that "the wife's anger about her husband's disorderliness may actually outlive her anger about his philandering."

In Gilbert's study, a "victim" was given an insulting written analysis of his personality. Then bystanders were allowed to read the same profile. Researchers found that five minutes later, the bystanders, who merely read the negative assessment, disliked the offending writer more than the actual victim did.

Why? When insulted, people "go through a process of unconscious rationalization: 'It must be a mistake,' 'What do psychologists know anyway?'" Gilbert says. "When you observe someone insulting someone else, it's not so awful that the psychological defenses kick in." And because the targets of insults tend not to deal with their hurt on the spot, he explains, they feel worse longer.

Five Simple Ways to Say NO

Nobody wants to be a doormat. Here's how to stop others from taking advantage of you.

BY VANESSA GENEVA AHERN

Your co-worker asks you to cover for her when she leaves early ... again. Your neighbor begs you to cat-sit. Your friend wants you to donate to her latest favorite charity. And you? You either say yes when you really don't want to, or you make an excuse—and then you end up feeling like a doormat or a weasel.

Why is saying no so hard? Harriet B. Braiker, Ph.D., never thought it had to be. Braiker, a clinical psychologist in Los Angeles and the author of several best-selling books on stress and well-being, died in January 2004, after the publication of her book, *Who's Pulling Your Strings? How to Break the Cycle of Manipulation and Regain Control of Your Life*. *Health* had the chance to speak with her before her death.

The desire to please others at your own expense "has to do with a greatly inflated value of niceness, the idea that you have to be nice at all costs," Braiker said. "A pattern of compulsive people pleasing sets you up to be easily manipulated."

Furthermore, it can backfire. "One reason you say yes when you really want to say no is because you are afraid the other person will get mad," Braiker said. "In fact, you're the one who gets angry—at the other person for asking and at yourself for saying yes."

Chances are you know that you can turn people down without upsetting them or coming off as cold-hearted and selfish. It's just that, when push comes to shove, you can't always think of the right words for "no." Here are five effective ways to say it.

> **One reason you say yes when you really mean no is because you are afraid the other person will get mad. In fact, you're the one who gets angry—at the other person for asking and at yourself for saying yes.**
>
> **—Harriet B. Braiker, Ph.D.**

322

THE "NO, BUT ..." RESPONSE

Use this when: You're willing to negotiate.

Example: Your new assistant asks for a personal day during your busiest week.

You say: "No, but we may be able to work something out if you can come in for a few extra hours the week before."

Why it works: "You're saying no to the initial request, but you're also showing that you are willing to change your mind if the other person can meet your requirements," says Stephen Schoonover, M.D., president of Schoonover Associates, a human resources and leadership-development consulting firm in Falmouth, Massachusetts.

THE NO SANDWICH

Use this when: You'd like to help, but you can't.

Example: You're dressing for a long-awaited romantic dinner with your spouse when your sister calls and says, "Our baby-sitter canceled at the last minute, and we have tickets to a concert. Would you mind watching your nephew tonight? He's been asking about you."

You say: "You know I love him, but I've already got plans. Why don't you try so-and-so? And tell Johnny that I'll make a special date with him next week."

Why it works: You're placing the "no" between two positive responses. "The sandwich technique works well if you're worried about staying on good terms," Braiker said.

THE "IT'S FOR YOUR OWN GOOD" NO

Use this when: Saying no will actually benefit the questioner.

Example: A friend who is unemployed is desperately looking for a job and hears that the company where you work is hiring. You really don't think

he'd be the right person for the position, and he asks, "Would you mind putting in a good word for me?"

You say: "I'm not sure you'd find your niche there. You're great at coming up with creative ideas, but we need number-crunchers."

Why it works: Your friend needs honest feedback, Braiker said. "If he isn't a good match for the company, then you're saving him from wasting their time—and his."

THE "BUTT OUT" NO

Use this when: Someone asks a nosy question.

Example: A close co-worker is hoping for a raise. While you're in the ladies' room she asks, "What are they paying you?"

You say: "I really hope you get the raise, because you deserve it. However, I prefer not to discuss my salary."

Why it works: "It's often easier to say no if you first empathize. The other person is usually less likely to argue your answer," says Greg Markway, Ph.D., co-author of *Painfully Shy: How to Overcome Social Anxiety and Reclaim Your Life*.

THE REDIRECTING NO

Use this when: You need to address an underlying problem.

Example: Your friend wants to get all the kids together for a sleepover—at your house. Trouble is, she has yet to reciprocate.

You say: "Kate loves spending time with your daughter, but that night isn't good for us. Plus, I think the kids sometimes get bored at our place. Maybe we could have the sleepover at your house sometime."

Why it works: "You're saying no," Markway says, "but you're also steering the conversation toward the real problem." ■

Wanted:
More Female Friends

Women need confidantes more than ever—but it's hard to find them. These simple strategies can help you make connections that last.

BY MARLA PAUL

When I moved to a Chicago suburb a few years ago, my biggest worry was whether my daughter would make friends in kindergarten. Would her classmates already be paired off in a Noah's Ark of best friends? I wasn't even remotely concerned about myself. True, I wasn't working in an office anymore, so there'd be no instant work friends. But I'd hang out with my new neighbors, grab coffee with the mothers of my daughter's new classmates, meet women in my yoga class. No problem.

My daughter made friends easily. I, on the other hand, sat in my car in the grammar-school pickup line pretending to read a magazine because I didn't feel welcome in the knot of moms yakking outside the school door. God, I hated pickup time.

It wasn't as if I hadn't tried. I'd invited women out to lunch, become a room mom, and had the local librarian over for tuna salad. But nothing took. People were happy to get together when I called, but nobody ever called me. I was mystified, frustrated, and lonely as hell.

So I did what writers do: I wrote about my problems. I aired my wallflower status in an essay in the *Chicago Tribune*. But I was uncomfortable with my revelation; I was sure I was the only one struggling to find pals. Within days, though, letters filled my mailbox. A lot of women were hitting dead ends as they searched for friends, it seemed, and they all feared the problem stemmed from a personal flaw.

After that, I began writing a column on women's friendship. Over the past few years, I've talked with hundreds of women and a raft of psychologists and other experts, and I've come to understand that there's nothing wrong with us. The climate for friendship has simply turned icy, like January in Chicago. Women are so busy juggling work, family, and aging parents, they're barely able to wedge in old friends, let alone embrace new ones. Yet they need new ones more than ever. Women work, and then they ditch the office to stay home with their kids. They hopscotch from town to town to nab a promotion. They marry, divorce, remarry. With every significant change, they're likely to leave old friends behind. And while making new friends seems effortless for kids thrown together in school, for adults it's an awkward dance whose steps they can't quite remember. It can feel weirdly pushy and needy for one woman to pursue another as a friend. It's easy to give up if things don't fall into place fast.

But even if making new friends is difficult for women, I found that they're not destined to go without forever. The researchers I spoke to had insights; so did women who, through work, clever strategies, and patience, eventually found confidantes. Here are some of the most important things they shared; keep them in mind if you're trying to snare new companions.

It can feel weirdly pushy and needy for one woman to pursue another as a friend. It's easy to give up if things don't fall into place fast.

FIND COLLEAGUES—EVEN IF YOU DON'T HAVE A JOB.

Lynda Lemisch's closest buddies had always been her co-workers in the hospitals where she had worked as an occupational therapist. She had only casual acquaintances in Media, Pennsylvania, a suburb of Philadelphia where she'd lived for four years. "It's hard to meet people—you come home, you're tired," Lemisch says.

Then she had a baby and quit her job. "It was very isolating," says Lemisch, now 42. "I said to my

husband, 'I talked to the cashier at the grocery store today. That was my big adult conversation.'"

Lemisch desperately needed the mom equivalent of colleagues—sleep-starved women with whom she could swap tales about the vicissitudes of caring for an infant. But as a slightly older first-time mother, she struggled to find others like herself, a former career woman adjusting to motherhood. So Lemisch cast a wide net. "I talked to anybody who walked by with a stroller, anybody whose grocery cart had a car seat in it," she says.

She and her child joined a tumbling class for babies and frequented story time at the library; Lemisch also went to gatherings of a local chapter of Mothers & More, a national group for moms who are balancing careers and kids.

Lemisch's persistence paid off. She made one friend at the market: "I had a plastic gadget that covered the grocery-cart handles so my son couldn't chew on it. She asked about it—we're both germphobes with our firstborns." At the baby tumbling class, she clicked with some other older moms, and at Mothers & More, Lemisch met a pediatrician who became a pal.

Having made friends who share her background or interests and who understand the strains of new motherhood has made her life much more enjoyable. Lemisch remarks, "When somebody says, 'This is hard—aren't you tired?' it's a validation of what you feel."

PRIORITIZE FRIENDSHIP.

Toni Kayumi was working four jobs in Fort Wayne, Indiana: During the day, she was a TV station account executive; nights and weekends, she ran an advertising agency from her home, recorded voice-overs for a radio station, and acted in a theater troupe. "I was the single workaholic," she says.

The needle on her days edged past the full mark, but her life felt oddly empty. She yearned for the counsel of pals, and she missed the fun of her childhood gang, giggling into the early hours at slumber parties. "I had a boyfriend, but it wasn't the same as being with female friends," she confesses.

Kayumi casually knew three other women through work and church. They had a lot in common: Three were in radio; none had kids or a serious romantic partner. One Monday night they got together for dinner. After a few hours of animated conversation and raucous laughter, they made another date. By the third dinner, it struck Kayumi that she had been laughing more and feeling less stressed since she'd been seeing these women. "I realized, 'Here's what's been missing,'" she says.

The women decided to meet every week. It was a big commitment to friendship for Kayumi. She used to spackle friends into the odd spaces in her life, but now she was carving out territory just for them. That meant shoving aside her ad-agency business for a night and saying no to dates with the guy she was seeing, even if he felt jealous.

Two years later, those Monday dinners have a sacred space on her calendar, says Kayumi, now 40. She credits her friends with giving her the confidence

> In order to meet new friends I talked to anybody who walked by with a stroller, anybody whose grocery cart had a car seat in it. —Lynda Lemisch

to close the agency and accept a promotion to marketing manager at her TV station. They have each others' keys, drop off medicine if someone is sick, feed each other's cats if one of the group is out of town. They even vacationed together in Mexico.

And when Kayumi got married in February 2003, her friends were there. They've promised each other that marriage won't fray their friendship. "It's important to make sure you make time for it," Kayumi says, "even as life changes."

AFTER PLAN A, TRY PLANS B, C, AND D.

I eventually found friends, too. I look back now and realize that my first efforts to make friends were pretty awkward: Being a room mother exposed me to only a few women, and taking yoga introduced me to lots of people who weren't interested in talking right then. But I kept trying. I volunteered to help lead a writing workshop at my daughter's school and met another writer who's become a close friend. When a woman moved in across the street, I welcomed her with a plate of brownies and discovered a warm companion. None of these relationships sprang to life effortlessly. They germinated like seeds, needing sun, rain, and a long growing season.

I think these relationships finally took because we were good matches. But I also learned a few things that helped. A friendship has to develop in its own time. If you try to rush things, you can scare someone away.

If something serious is bothering you, air it. If you don't, the relationship may wither needlessly. That almost happened with one new friend. I was always the one calling to get together, and after six months it was beginning to make me uncomfortable—which I nervously told her one day over lunch as my stomach cartwheeled. She admitted she wasn't good at picking up the phone. We resolved that issue by setting up monthly lunches, eliminating the issue of whose turn it was. If I hadn't spoken to her about it, I might have begun to feel so hurt and resentful that I'd have stopped calling.

Finally, I learned to cut people more slack. I try to keep my eye on what's important and make my peace with small disappointments in a relationship. If others do the same for me, I know we'll be friends for a long time.

Marla Paul, author of The Friendship Crisis: Finding, Making, and Keeping Friends When You're Not a Kid Anymore, *writes a column on friendship for a nationally syndicated section of the* Chicago Tribune.

Smart: The New Sexy

Good news for non-supermodels: When it comes to picking a mate, men are paying more attention to a woman's education and earning potential—and a little less to her looks.

In an analysis of engagement announcements spanning 22 years in the local newspaper, researchers at Grand Valley State University in Michigan looked at the education (and therefore the prospects for well-paying jobs) of the men and women planning to wed. Over the decades, the percentage of women who were better schooled than their future husbands jumped from about 20 percent in 1980 to 30 percent in 2002. Only 20 percent of the marrying men in 2002 were more educated than their prospective spouses.

"In the United States, women have traditionally cared more about a man's income potential, because the female is usually the dependent spouse," says lead researcher Sonia Dalmia, Ph.D., an assistant professor of economics at Grand Valley. "But the earning potential of a woman is gaining in importance, especially in economic downturns when jobs are at risk."

Does that mean a woman's looks are now less of a lure? Not so you'd notice, says Dalmia, who had college

students rate the attractiveness of the brides and the grooms pictured in announcements. Across the 22-year test period, women continued to "marry down" in terms of appearance. Although the number of unions in which the bride was more fetching than the groom did decline from 65 to 59 percent. While there's still a strong male emphasis on looks, Dalmia says, "interest in earning potential has gone up."

The mixed result may predict an increase in egalitarian relationships. "I hope so," Dalmia says. "I hope this will lead to more people marrying not just for financial security, but because they really want to. And maybe fewer divorces, too."

Why Women Respond Differently Than Men to Depression

Why do nearly twice as many women as men suffer from depression? A recent study suggests that the gender gap might not be as wide as previously thought.

Researchers have found that women were approximately three times as likely to be labeled as depressed by family members as male relatives with the same symptoms. And a woman's depression is generally attributed to internal causes, such as moodiness, for which she is more likely to seek professional help. But when a man displays similar types of behavior, the blame is typically assigned to external forces he has no control over, such as unemployment or divorce—issues that he probably would not see a doctor about.

Because reports from family members are sometimes used to make an initial diagnosis, explains study co-author Jessica Brommelhoff, M.P.H., "the discrepancy in depression rates may not be as great as some of the literature suggests."

These Girls Gotta *glide*

This unusual coffee klatch proves that it's never too late to skate.

BY KIM WONG • PHOTOGRAPHY BY ANGELA WYANT

It's cold enough in the ice rink to refrigerate a side of beef, but for these women spinning around on skates, the temperature is just fine. "We've been going through menopause together, and there's no better place to be when you're having a hot flash," 63-year-old Velita Worden says with a grin.

When Skatetown Ice Arena first opened in Roseville, California, six years ago, women in their 40s and 50s signed up for lessons one by one. Many, including Worden, had never laced up a pair of skates, so at first they clung to the boards or wobbled along tentatively. And despite more than a few humbling spills, they returned every week, forming lasting friendships and eventually working their way up to such feats as spins, jumps, lutzes, and salchows. Today, the 12 women gather as much for each other's fellowship as they do for the exhilaration of being on the ice.

Karen O'Brien with coach Jayne Throckmorton

We've been going through menopause together, and there's no better place to be when you're having a hot flash.

—Velita Worden

"It's my lifeblood now," says Worden, who started skating at age 58 because she thought it would be an activity she could enjoy with her grandchildren. The kids quickly got bored with it, but Grandma was hooked. She now drives 90 minutes each way just to get her skate fix.

The class is known as the Coffee Club because it ends with java and a chat. "This group is just like my family," says Margaret Wade, nicknamed "The Comeback Kid" because she quit skating at age 16 and picked it up again at 52. The retired pharmacy technician took on a part-time job to pay for lessons. "We've been skating and going through life changes together," Wade says. "I know I can come here, and no matter how hectic my day's been or how stressed I am, there's a sense of support."

That's essential because learning to skate is a tall order at any age. Falling, standard practice for both novices and experts, can be particularly hard on older bones. "I know this is a risk, but the experience is well worth it," says Karen O'Brien, a 55-year-old partner in a professional development firm who was diagnosed with osteoporosis last year. "I don't do foolish things that would put me directly in harm's way, but I realize that I take a chance each time I step on the ice."

O'Brien persists in skating the fine line, taking private lessons and meeting her pals a couple of times a week for the class and the coffee talk afterward. A few of the women have entered small competitions and have placed—in part, they say, because so few women their age enter. And last

(left to right) Karen O'Brien, Velita Worden, Nancy Donovan, Madeleine Levy, Pat Travis, Janet Rosenfield, Margaret Wade

This group is like my family.

—Margaret Wade

winter, most of them performed in their rink's Christmas show.

On the heavy side as a child, O'Brien longed to skate. Now slender and fit, she is making up for lost time. "The women I skate with have inspired me so much," she says. "When I think about how I identify myself these days, I'm a skater. It's in my bones." ■

Scoring Points with Her Son

Through roller hockey, a mom and her teenage son build a bond that any parent would treasure.

BY KERRI WESTENBERG • PHOTOGRAPHY BY FRAN GEALER

As the sun begins to set, Lori Basch glides across the concrete rink on her inline skates, a hockey stick in her hand. Her son, Aaron, flicks the puck her way. He's helping his mom work on launching it into the air toward the goal, and it's not going well. "Keep the puck on the stick, and follow through," the 17-year-old prompts.

Lori tries again. This time, she manages to get the disk a bit higher, but it still falls just short of the net. "Is that better?" she asks. "No, not really," Aaron replies. Well, at least he's honest.

It's obvious from the first meeting that Lori, 44, and her son, a high school senior, are anomalies—and not simply because they're decked out like National Hockey League players (without the extra insulation). Their ease with each other doesn't stop when they swap their pads and skates for street clothes. While Lori and Aaron, of Calabasas, California, a suburban community just west of Los Angeles, suffer the same growing pains as other teenage sons and their single moms, these two say that their teamwork in the rink has helped their relationship survive and even thrive.

Teammates: Lori Basch and her son, Aaron, take a break from practice.

From the beginning, their roles were reversed. "The first time I went skating, Aaron had to show me how to put on the safety equipment, and he was only 8 years old. I didn't know a thing," Lori says.

That was back in 1994, but before long she was inline-skating three or four days a week on a beach-side path in nearby Santa Monica. "Skating became an obsession," Lori says. "I loved the way it made me feel."

The next summer, she and Aaron enrolled in an inline skating camp together. On a whim, Lori signed up for a hockey class and quickly knew she had found a game that could keep her enthralled. "Hockey is a great workout. You don't realize you're sweating because you're just concentrating on following the puck around," Lori says.

Her hockey fever was infectious, and Aaron soon got the bug. At age 12 he joined his first team; Lori served as coach. Now, when he's not presiding over the math or sailing clubs, Aaron is playing hockey on his high school team and with his mom in a coed YMCA league.

The shared pursuit has helped keep this mother and son close, even when Lori divorced Aaron's father in 2001. "We can relate a lot through hockey," Aaron says. Lori adds, "We strategize before games and analyze afterward, and that helps us keep our communication about everything else open, too."

And Lori does more than just play the sport; she has also turned her love of hockey into a business venture. After she competed in her first tournament in 1998, she searched the vendor booths in vain for an appealing memento of the experience. All Lori could find were men's T-shirts and tank tops. But she returned home with something more valuable than a tchotchke: a new career.

In 1999, Lori, who until then had been a stay-at-home mom, started Rinky, which sells hockey paraphernalia for women. The company's inventory includes fitted cap-sleeve T's with such slogans as "Chicks with Sticks," baseball caps that say "Hockey Hair," and flashy leopard fur–covered hockey gloves. (The products are available at her Web site, Rinky.com, and at sporting-goods stores across America.) The company also sponsors girls' teams and makes its products available at wholesale prices to teams who sell the items during fund-raisers.

But Rinky's biggest philanthropic endeavor is Stick It to Cancer, an ice-hockey competition for women that is held in Minnesota every April to benefit the Susan G. Komen Breast Cancer Foundation. In 2003, the event raised $18,000.

Even more satisfying to Lori, though, is skating with her son. In a recent game, Aaron passed the puck to his mom, the left wing with golden curls sneaking out of her helmet. She slapped the puck in for a goal. "Way to go, Mom!" yelled Aaron as he rushed over with a hug. Score one for parenthood. ■

> **We strategize before games and analyze afterward, and that helps us keep our communication about everything open.** —Lori Basch

Pass the puck: Team Basch works on shooting skills.

331

Ask Ali

Discover expert advice about new babies, drug addiction, home life, and work environment.

Psychologist Ali Domar, Ph.D.

WHEN IT IS (AND ISN'T) TIME FOR ANOTHER BABY

I have two kids and desperately want a third. My husband doesn't. Who wins here?

First of all, don't think you're alone on this—I see the situation all the time. I've heard it called the "kindergarten syndrome": The youngest child enters preschool, and all of a sudden Mom realizes she wants another baby.

There's no one right answer here, but asking yourself some questions can help. Did you and your husband discuss from the beginning how many kids you wanted to have? If you're changing your mind, you should start the discussion with why and go from there. Are you financially stable enough to have another child? If you agreed that you'd stay home until the kids were in school, could you be afraid to re-enter the workforce? Or do you think the financial burden is weighing on your husband's shoulders? He might be ready to share that responsibility or want to get a job he likes more without worrying so much about the pay. Finally, do you want a bigger family because you came from a large one yourself? Even though your siblings are the best things that ever happened to you, that doesn't mean your children are going to feel the same way about theirs.

You and your husband should try to approach these questions as a team. You don't want to resent him for denying you a third child, but you don't want to force an unwanted baby on him either. He is likely to grow to love another child; still, it's definitely a risky situation. I've seen cases like this where the father is not as attached to the youngest child. If you really get stuck, you might want to see a counselor to talk out the pros and cons of having another baby.

HOW TO SHOW SUPPORT FOR A POSSIBLE DRUG ADDICT

My friend had a pill habit, but she managed to kick it a few years back. She was recently in a car accident, though, and was prescribed pain medication by her doctor. Now she's acting erratically, and I'm starting to worry that she's gotten addicted again. How can I be supportive but help her see that she's slowly losing control?

I would be careful not to jump to any conclusions. Addiction is an enormous problem in this country, but so is undermedicating pain—a lot of physicians do this out of fear that their patients will become dependent. It could be that your friend's doctor is aware of her history and has been undermedicating her for that very reason, leaving her to deal with pain. She also could be suffering from post-traumatic stress disorder or experiencing stress because of financial burdens the accident may have caused.

All of that said, I am a big believer in gut feelings. If you think you should bring up the issue, you might casually say, "I am still so impressed with how you got yourself healthy a number of years ago, and I'm sure you're concerned now that you are on pain medication again." This could help open the door. Just remember that it's not your responsibility to handle her erratic behavior. Be as supportive as you can be, while at the same time protecting yourself.

WHEN THE NEW HOUSE DOESN'T FEEL LIKE HOME

My husband and I recently moved out of the house our children grew up in, and I can't seem to think of our new place as home. I really miss the old house. What can I do to adjust?

I think anytime people move out of the house where they raised their kids, they are bothered by more than just the new surroundings; they are disturbed by the fact that their roles have changed, too—in your old home, you were the mom, the matriarch. I had a very hard time when we moved out of our first home, even though my daughter was only a year old. People tend not to remember the bad things, like the leaky faucets and the faulty air conditioner; they remember the baby cutting her first tooth and taking her first steps.

If it's the memories and not the actual house that you're having a hard time letting go of, then there are a number of things you can do to make the new place yours. Pick out some old photos, have them enlarged, and display them. Get rid of that pristine and perfect look, which makes a house feel very cold. I guarantee that the home you just left, if you

raised your kids in it, didn't look perfect. You may even want to decorate a room to resemble one in the old house (cluster knickknacks the same way, or paint the walls the same color) to make the space feel more familiar.

But the most important thing that you can do is to generate new memories. Have more gatherings, carry on old traditions, and create new ones.

And give it time. In the future, there may be grandchildren breaking the new house in for you.

MESSY DESK? WHY YOU SHOULD KEEP IT CLEAN

I'm a hard worker and I do a good job, but I can't seem to keep my desk clean. Even though I know where everything is, co-workers make jokes about the mess—and so does my boss. Should I be worried?

Quite frankly, yes. If your desk is messy and cluttered, people will think that you're the same way. A recent study suggests that people are, in fact, judged by the way their surroundings look. There was also evidence in this study that conscientious, hardworking people really do have cleaner desks.

Obviously, your boss is noticing your work space. In fact, it wouldn't surprise me if he or she walked around after hours inspecting the area. I'd take these comments seriously, and sit down and figure out how I could keep my desk as clean as possible. Buy "in" and "out" bins; prioritize, organize, and throw away. At the very least, try straightening up before you leave each day. It will make your life easier because you'll be able to find things faster. And it may get you a promotion sooner. ▪

Alice D. Domar, Ph.D., is a Harvard Medical School assistant professor and director of the Mind/Body Center for Women's Health at Boston IVF, Department of Obstetrics and Gynecology, Beth Israel Deaconess Medical Center.

How Family Ties a Feminist and Supermodel Together

BY MEREDITH MARAN • PHOTOGRAPHY BY JOE PUGLIESE

The first time I saw my favorite (and only) niece, Josie, she was just 2 hours old. Wrapped in a politically correct, gender-nonspecific blankie of many colors, she nursed energetically at her mother's breast while her proud papa, my baby brother, beamed. "Beautiful," I gasped. I felt I'd never before truly understood the meaning of the word.

The first time I saw Josie on the cover of *Glamour*, she was 19 years old. I was on a story assignment, dashing past an airport newsstand, when the sight stopped me in my tracks: a whole wall of Josie's cleavage topped by the headline "Lust Lessons: Teach Them Tonight!" I wanted to buy every copy and pass them out to everyone I saw. And I wanted to buy every copy and burn them, so no one would see.

Five years and four *Glamour* covers later, not much has changed. Josie's still a supermodel, and I'm still alternately bragging and wincing about it. "That's my niece," I often feel compelled to point out to super-market clerks, to my dentist's receptionist, even to strangers in drugstores. "How do you feel about that?" my feminist friends ask sympathetically when Josie bares nearly all in a *Sports Illustrated* swimsuit issue.

"Mixed," I say. But "mixed up" is more like it.

Being a journalist, I make it my business to research issues that perplex me. Being a feminist, I find one of those issues is the persistence of the beauty myth. The more barriers women break through, the more heavily the image of female beauty seems to weigh on them, as Naomi Wolf wrote in 1991 in her book *The Beauty Myth*. Women may be getting more powerful, but

they're also getting more cosmetic surgery (there were 80 percent more facial procedures done in 2002 than in 1997, according to facial plastic surgeons). And for decades, eating disorders have steadily become more common among young women.

As our family's designated gadfly, I tend to inflict my values—as well as my confusion—on my relatives, including my beloved niece, who has become quite a wealthy young woman thanks to the beauty industry. "When I was your age," I find myself muttering at Josie—well, at Josie flickering on my TV screen—"I was doing useful things. Picketing the Miss America pageant. Writing diatribes against sexism. Growing my armpit hair. How could you have turned out this way?"

When I see Josie in the flesh, I strive for a more tactful approach. "I'm glad for your success," I told her recently over a platter of sushi. "But I'm worried about the impact of what you're doing—on you, and on girls and women."

"I'm good at what I do. That makes me happy," Josie countered. "You get to be creative with your writing, Mer. I get to be creative with my work."

"But doesn't it bother you," I pressed on, "to be reinforcing a standard of beauty that 99 percent of women can't fit?"

"I know modeling puts out this stereotype that the so-called beautiful woman is skinny and tall and looks like Barbie," Josie answered. "But I've never believed you had to look like that to be happy."

"Easy for you to say, Size Zero," I thought, trying and failing to resist comparing my 50-year-old body to hers. Sure, I believe that people should be judged by the quality of their character, not by the attractiveness of their skin, eyes, or highlights. And sure, I know that someday Josie's taut flesh will droop, her streaked hair will dull to gray, and her rosebud lips will pale and pucker—and I will still think she's beautiful.

But knowing that doesn't help when Josie and I are thigh-to-thigh. And it didn't help when I went to see my editor at *Glamour* a while ago and sat waiting beneath a larger-than-life-size poster of Josie. "Don't stand next to the pretty girl," the teen magazines of my girlhood warned. Forty years later, my

editor glanced from me to Josie, then back at me. "I, um, see the family resemblance," she murmured and mercifully led me to her office.

Watching Josie devour a California roll, struggling to separate my envy from my ethics, I swallowed an estimated 45-calorie bite of unagi and confessed, "I lost 15 pounds 5 years ago during the worst time of my life, and I've never been as happy with my body as I was then. Now I'm having the happiest time of my life, and I've gained weight, and I beat myself up about it every day."

"Don't stand next to the pretty girl," the teen magazines of my girlhood warned. Forty years later, my editor glanced from me to Josie, then back at me. "I, um, see the family resemblance," she murmured.

"You look great, Mer," Josie said.

"For a 50-year-old, you mean?" I sniveled.

Josie regarded me steadily. "You look great, period," she repeated. I squinted at her suspiciously, then had what *Ms.* magazine used to call a "click" moment of truth. "I'd rather be thin than happy. Some feminist role model, huh?" I said, and we both burst out laughing.

Later I thought about the serious side of my admission. I thought about the formative years that my friends and I had spent poring over magazines, yearning for bodies like Josie's, and the years we've spent since, starving, exercising, and punishing ourselves in a million different ways to try and get one. Even as we have built our big fat "postfeminist" lives—with careers and passions our mothers weren't allowed to have and relationships they couldn't even imagine—we have kept running on a parallel track of self-loathing, the size of our thighs always counterbalancing the more important gains we were making. No matter how satisfying our successes, there is always this: We are never as beautiful as we could be, as beautiful as we want to be—as beautiful as Josie is.

"Isn't the goal of feminism to give women the same rights as men? And the same luxuries that men

have?" Josie asked me recently as we climbed into her Escalade.

"To give women the control over their lives that you have, yes," I agreed. "But don't you feel manipulated, diminished, by people relating only to how you look?"

"I don't feel manipulated. I feel lucky," Josie shot back. "I'm what America thinks is beautiful. I fit into society easier than a lot of people because of my looks."

What could I, loving aunt, self-appointed mentor, committed feminist, say to my niece? Yes, I'm critical of the beauty industry, pained by the damage it does to females, including me and possibly—now or later—Josie. But as her feminist aunt, I also ask myself what it means to support a young woman I love and respect, even if what she's doing doesn't follow my script for her life, even if what she's doing alternately awes and disturbs me. Josie is living her own dreams, not mine or anyone else's. What could be more feminist, or more beautiful, than that?

"You're right. You're lucky," I said. "My question is, what are you going to use that good luck for?"

"I'm sure my beautiful aunt will stay on my case till I get off my ass and do something good for the world," Josie answered, flashing that million-dollar smile.

"Flattery will get you everywhere," I told her, my arms wrapping around her twice, it seemed, as I hugged her.

I passed by another airport newsstand the other day and saw a wall of Josie on a new magazine cover. I plucked a copy for my collection, told the cashier reflexively, "This is my niece," resisting the urge to hold Josie's face next to mine to help her see the family resemblance.

"Beautiful girl," the cashier responded, as people always do.

"She is a beautiful girl," I said, and I meant it. ■

Meredith Maran is the author of the book Dirty: A Search for Answers Inside America's Teenage Drug Epidemic.

Do You Have Skewed Views?
You could harbor unconscious prejudices and not know it.

Who's a bigot? If you think "Not me, but I know one when I see one," think again. According to two recent studies, those traits that are often used as evidence of tolerance—egalitarian beliefs and a college education, for example—may predict how a person genuinely sees herself. These traits don't, however, measure the underlying prejudices that influence our behavior, even that of people who view themselves as racially tolerant.

Researchers in both studies used the Implicit Association Test (IAT) to measure the participants' unconscious prejudice. Each subject was asked to match both negative and positive words with names stereotypically associated with Americans of either African or European descent. The IAT response rate is considered a measure of hidden bias: The more implicitly prejudiced a person is, the more likely he is to match negative words with stereotypically black names and positive words with stereotypically white names.

In a 2003 study, 24 whites watched movies of faces that morphed from neutral to hostile. Biased viewers were more likely to perceive a black person as angry even if his countenance was neutral. The more prejudiced the viewer, the quicker and longer he sensed hostility. In other words, a person who believes the stereotype that blacks are angrier than whites is more likely to perceive enmity in blacks. This held true whether or not the subject was aware of his bias.

In a follow-up study, participants were shown photos of racially ambiguous faces with hostile or neutral expressions. Biased individuals were more likely to identify the faces with blatantly angry expressions as black. Study co-author and Northwestern University psychologist Galen Bodenhausen, Ph.D., says that based on the findings of both of these studies, even well-educated, tolerant thinkers who claim not to be prejudiced in fact *were* when it came to associating race, emotion, and stereotypes. This does not mean that all such people are racists. "You might genuinely have egalitarian attitudes and beliefs but still have a conditioned association in your mind that affects the way you perceive people's faces," he says. And simply knowing the association exists may be the first step toward changing it.

Why Moms Earn Less Money

Children are priceless, but they cost a lot. They're especially expensive for working moms, who pay a "motherhood penalty" in the form of an average salary that is significantly lower than that of childless women. You'd think the gap would have narrowed over the past 20 years as more women have started working. But according to a new study in the *Journal of Marriage and Family,* the penalty is still stiff.

Moms earn up to 13-percent less than their childless peers, says study co-author Pamela J. Smock, Ph.D., probably because they switch to part-time, settle for jobs closer to home, or choose positions with more flexible hours. "Just because women have made an entrée into the workforce doesn't mean they've been able to make an exit from family obligations," says Smock, associate director of the Institute for Social Research at the University of Michigan. In fact, other researchers have found that women report doing 37 hours of domestic labor per week, compared with the 18 hours men report. "You have women with more education, greater work experience, and higher aspirations still stuck taking the kid to the doctor," Smock says. One solution: A more equal division of parenting responsibilities. "If we change what's going on inside the home," she says, "we'll see changes across the board."

Queen of the Board

One woman shares how windsurfing helped her take care of her aging parents—and herself.

BY TERESA WILTZ • PHOTOGRAPHY BY LORIE SHAULL

It was clear early on that she wouldn't be able to continue like this for much longer. Her parents—brilliant, complicated, accomplished people—suddenly were no longer able to cope with even the most routine aspects of life. They needed help making dinner, paying bills, going to the bathroom. They needed another pair of hands, another pair of eyes, another pair of legs. But more than anything, they *needed*.

And Helen Van Gelder devoted herself to them and their needs. She quit her job in Northern California and, in 1997, at the age of 59, moved back home to Baltimore. She became her parents' legs, hands, and eyes. She cooked meals and counted pills for her mother, Miriam, who was going blind. She reassured her father, Philip, who was suffering with Alzheimer's disease, that he hadn't been abducted by Mexicans. She did all of this lovingly. Still, round-the-clock caregiving exacted its price. "I'm a trained family therapist," Van Gelder says with a rueful laugh, "and I know. You don't live with this kind of stress. Twenty-four hours a day, seven days a week was going to make me crazy."

Sanity came in the form of a sailboard that her older brother loaned her. He'd taken her out a few times and taught her the basics several years before. The first time out, Van Gelder hoisted the sail up, fell over, picked it up, fell over. Every time she fell in the water, she giggled. It became a game, one in which the outcome didn't much matter. What did matter was being outside, face to the sun, splashing in the water, playing. On the water, she could let go.

At age 65, Van Gelder has the tightly wired frame of a dancer, a relic of the modern-dance training she'd had as a child. Still, she says, she had never been much of an athlete. Anything that required team effort and a ball eluded her. She'd always felt like such a klutz, the slowpoke who fell behind everyone else. But on the water, with her sailboard, Van Gelder could move at her own 60-something pace. On the water, she always felt young, a feeling that translated to life on land as well.

She hired home-health aides to help out with her folks during the day, and this gave her a much-needed respite. The decision made sense to her, but her parents found it harder to accept. Her mom and dad both had become bedridden, though, and Van Gelder knew she couldn't handle it all on her own. At first the aides came for only a few hours at a time. After a while, they stayed 8 hours a day, with Van Gelder taking over at night. During the day, whenever she could, she would drive nearly an hour to Gunpowder River and resume her routine of picking up the sail and falling over. Finally, she says, "I stood up on the board long enough to sail a few feet. I was totally thrilled. I thought, 'This is great; this is really fun.' Of course, I was hardly moving." But it was a start.

Windsurfing (and a little yoga) kept her body fit for the physical demands of caring for two ailing parents. But more importantly, she says, it kept her emotionally fit through her parents' many falls, heart attacks, seizures, and life-threatening infections. Being on

the water, Van Gelder says, "was such a high for me that two or three outings a week would keep me peaceful for the rest of the time."

The sport also gave her a life after her parents passed away, her father in 1999 and her mother a year later. After her mother died, Van Gelder, who had taken a hiatus from her career to care for her parents, formally retired. She felt unmoored in their absence and in need of a focus for her future. And then she realized that she already had a focus: windsurfing. So she decided to carve out a life for herself doing what she loved most.

Van Gelder moved in with her beau, Bill, a retired engineer and fellow windsurfing fanatic whom she had met a few years back. Eight months out of the year, they live in Annapolis, Maryland, where together they chase the wind and play in the water. When the weather gets cold, Van Gelder heads back—alone—to Northern California, where she catches up with old friends.

And while she still doesn't care if she falls in the water, these days she's gotten a bit better at staying afloat. In 2001, the Baltimore Area Boardsailing Association (BABA) awarded her first place in the Women's Novice Class. The following year, she took first place in the Women's Class Mid-Atlantic Series Regatta, a feat she repeated in 2003. That year, she also placed first in BABA's Women's Class.

With windsurfing, Van Gelder muses, "you always feel triumphant. It's reviving, revitalizing. I'm not perfect yet. But on the water, I'm perfect. On the water, I'm perfect." ■

Teresa Wiltz covers arts and culture for The Washington Post.

Give New Acquaintances a Longer Look

If you find yourself gazing deeply into someone's eyes across the room but you're not quite sure that you like what you see, try staring just a little longer—it could tilt the scales in their favor. According to a recent study, whether you like a person is partly determined by the amount of time that you spend sizing him or her up. When researchers increased the amount of time a study volunteer spent looking at one face over another, the one that got more "face time" won out in a likability rating. The influence goes both ways: Looking longer led to liking better, and vice versa. "Gaze is a critical component for humans," says study author Shinsuke Shimojo, Ph.D., of the California Institute of Technology in Pasadena, "and by playing gaze 'catch-ball,' we can increase friendliness, attractiveness, and intimacy."

Monkey Research Suggests Nature Wins One over Nurture

Not quite sure if you got your sharp tongue from listening to your parents bicker or from their genes? An Emory University study tilts the scale to the nature side of the nature-versus-nurture debate.

Researchers gave infant monkeys to adoptive mothers just after birth, and then studied the babies' behavior over the course of three years. The young monkeys displayed behaviors that mirrored those of their biological mothers: If a mom was aggressive, so was the infant—even when the adoptive mother was a friendly type—and vice versa. This study is the first to suggest that such behaviors are inherited in primates, says author Dario Maestripieri, Ph.D.

Caution: Online Buddies Are Not Therapists

An online chat is definitely not the same as therapy. In a recent study conducted in Europe, at least 40 percent of people who visited depression chat rooms were suffering from major depression, and half were receiving no professional care. Wheras, a computer offers access to information and the ability to air feelings in privacy, experts say, it simply can't do the job of a trained therapist.

Dilemma for Parents of Fall Children:
School Them Early or Hold Them Back?

If you're the parent of a child born in the fall, you may know the question echoing through preschools everywhere: Can he (or she) start kindergarten, or should I hold my child back? Apparently, being the youngest in the class by even a few months can have a surprisingly significant effect.

In the study, researchers in Great Britain surveyed the parents and teachers of more than ten thousand schoolchildren ages 5 to 15, asking them about the kids' emotional well-being and behavior; the pupils were also queried. No matter the age group, the scientists found, children in the youngest third of the class were about 20-percent more likely to have a mental-health problem, such as anxiety, attention deficit hyperactivity disorder (ADHD), or "oppositional disorder," which is pretty much what it sounds like.

The results don't mean all young-for-their-grade kids carry a burden, explains study leader Robert Goodman, M.D., Ph.D., a professor of brain and behavioral medicine at King's College in London. But they do suggest that teachers could decrease the net suffering of students by being more sensitive to age. Teachers often forget to make allowances for their youngest charges; it might help, the researchers say, if they called roll by birth order or grouped kids by age.

Parents need to be sensitive to their child's development as well. To test where yours stands, take the quiz used in this research. Visit www.youthinmind.com (your child must be 4 to 17). The site gives parents a report in lay language, plus a more technical assessment that they can take to the doctor.

Should you hold your child back if he or she was born in autumn?

Kids in the Classroom:
Just Monkeying Around?

The theory put forth that girls and boys learn differently has always been controversial, but supporting evidence may lie in—of all places—the animal kingdom. Among wild chimpanzees in Tanzania, young females learn to forage for termites—and become much better at it—more than two years earlier than their young male counterparts. Scientists have deduced that the females carefully copy their mothers' methods of using vegetation as tools to snare more bugs for their supper. Male chimpanzees spend their time monkeying around, eventually developing their own less-efficient foraging styles. "Teachers say, 'Wow. This is exactly what I see going on in my classroom. Boys are more active, and girls are in small groups talking or playing teacher,'" says researcher Elizabeth Lonsdorf, Ph.D., of the Jane Goodall Institute's Center for Primate Studies at the University of Minnesota.

Rites of Renewal

Struck by loss, these women share the creative strategies that helped them heal, regain strength, and move on.

BY JANE MEREDITH ADAMS • PHOTOGRAPHY BY LESLIE WILLIAMSON

Loss is like a bad car crash: It's often unexpected, and you're not sure if you'll survive. When a loved one dies, funerals and black clothing help: They give you a ritual to cling to and something to do; they tell the world you are grieving, and they invite others to comfort you. But when you're devastated by divorce or miscarriage or injury, there is no predetermined path to renewal, and you're left to deal with the grief on your own.

Some women create new rituals that not only mark their loss, but also help them move forward and find happiness again. Intensely personal, these rites range from saying a prayer to planting a tree or crafting art. Such actions honor the past and deliver the message "I survived, and I'm stronger."

Getting stuck in grief can damage your health, says psychologist Dorree Lynn, Ph.D., a leading national trauma expert and author of *Getting Sane Without Going Crazy*. "These rituals not only say good-bye to the trauma, they say hello to what's next," Lynn says.

Here are three women who endured loss and found creative ways to get past it.

REENIE RASCHKE, 41
Oakland, California

In 1999, my husband of 12 years decided I didn't 'glow' anymore—and he left me. I was a full-time mom taking care of our 5- and 7-year-old children. I felt overwhelmed and scared and angry about the prospect of making the mortgage payments and

supporting my family. So I broke stuff: dishes and tiles my husband and I had collected. It was a tremendous relief. I could let go and breathe. I kept the broken pieces to make a wall mosaic.

Since I didn't know anything about mosaics, I checked out a how-to book from the library. It was physical work; I threw out my back and sliced my fingers. The harder it got, the more I thought, "I'm going to finish something really difficult." And I did.

After my husband left, I turned my hobby, photography, into a business. I started taking pictures of children and families and weddings. And I met someone else, Greg Fieler.

The 12- by 20-foot wall mosaic is in my home office. I call it "The Wall of Broken Dreams" because my images of married life were shattered. Even so, I made something new and beautiful out of it—just like my new life.

CRYSTAL BAILEY, 21

Maylene, Alabama

In May 2003 I was 5 months pregnant. I went to the doctor for an ultrasound, and the technician couldn't find the baby's heartbeat. I was devastated. The next day, the doctors induced labor. After more than 30 hours, I had a little boy. My entire family

came to the hospital, and we held the baby and took pictures. He weighed 14 ounces and was 10½ inches long. We named him Samuel. We had him cremated so he could be home with us.

In the following fall, some of the nearby hospitals sponsored a Walk of Remembrance, an annual ceremony for people who've had a miscarriage or lost a baby. About 100 people came. Before the walk began, each of us lit little candles to remember our babies. The walk ended at the Little Ones Memory Garden, which is part of the Birmingham Botanical Gardens in Alabama. The memorial garden is a clearing in the middle of the woods where people who've lost babies plant trees. I go there to be by myself and talk to my son. I tell him I love him.

My husband, Shonn, and I have a 3-year-old daughter, ShyAnne. She keeps asking when she's going to have a baby sister. I tell her, "Mommy's trying."

SARAH MASTRO, 47

Seattle

In 1985 I slipped on some ice and broke my right leg. The fracture was symbolic of how badly my life was splintering apart. My husband at the time had recently moved away from our home in Alaska to the Bay Area to receive treatment for a knee injury. My three children, who were then 3, 4, and 8, stayed with my mother while I was in the hospital,

but no one could look after our house, which was way out in the bush. The pipes froze up, the house became uninhabitable, and we quickly lost ownership of it.

It turned out that my leg was in even worse shape than I thought. I had six fractures of the fibula; a dislocated knee; and damaged ligaments, tendons, and nerves. I had bolts and plates put into my leg. Because of my injury, I couldn't work to support myself, let alone my children.

Two months after I fell, my husband and I divorced. Still, I wanted our children to be closer to their father, so once I was strong enough, we moved to Bend, Oregon. I became a real-estate agent and was very successful. I had a second surgery on my leg to take out the plates and bolts, and then, about 10 years later, I had a third surgery to repair the vascular damage. I was left with 150 staples and an 8-inch scar that reaches down my leg.

I wanted to visibly mark both my physical and emotional triumphs, so I looked into getting a tattoo. I really liked the spiritual approach of Vyvyn Lazonga, a tattoo artist who lives in Seattle. I went to see her, and we came up with a design that would cover my scar: a phoenix surrounded by images of fire and water. It symbolizes resurrection and rebirth and the fire inside you that continues to burn even through tragedy.

After I got my tattoo, I moved to Seattle and met a man, Charlie Mastro, online. We got married last year. My husband, who is an avid fly-fisherman, got his first and only tattoo—a wedding band

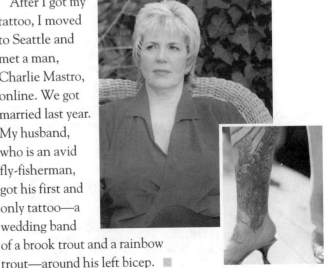

of a brook trout and a rainbow trout—around his left bicep. ∎

vital *stats*

10.7
Number of times per hour cigarettes or smoking appeared in top-grossing movies during the 1950s

4.9
Number of times per hour cigarettes or smoking appeared in the early 1980s

10.9
Number of times per hour cigarettes or smoking appeared in 2002

4
Percentage of women working in clerical jobs who are problem drinkers

14
Percentage of women working in executive jobs who are

20
Percentage of people who said they heard a homophobic comment at work in 2003

34
Percentage who heard a sexually inappropriate comment

7
Percentage of women who say that they feel discriminated against on a weekly basis because of their gender

---

24
Percentage of all adults who have tried a low-carb diet since 2002

12
Percentage currently on one

20
Average number of pounds participants lost on a low-carb diet in 12 weeks

17
Average number of pounds participants lost on a low-fat diet in 12 weeks

25,200
Number of additional calories each low-carb dieter ate over the 12 weeks compared with the low-fat dieters

44
Percentage of women who feel guilty for eating ice cream

30
Percentage of men who do

1 TON
Average amount of ice cream Americans eat in their lifetimes

1 TON
Approximate weight of a baby elephant

38
Percentage of women who say they worry about developing heart disease

82
Percentage of Americans over age 40 who are at risk for heart disease

1.5
Percent drop in cancer death rates among men each year since 1998

0.8
Percent drop in women's cancer death rates

20
Percent increase in black women's risk of death from cancer versus white women's

37
Percentage of white teenage girls who have used a tanning booth at least once

80
Percentage of UV damage that occurs before age 18

1
Rank of melanoma among cancers in women ages 25–29

92
Percentage of women who use prescription medicines regularly

22
Percentage of people who cut back on prescribed dosages because of the expense

$73.04
Monthly cost of individual health coverage for members of Congress in 2002

$212.71
Average monthly premium for individual HMO coverage in the United States

13
Percentage of people who say they sleep better when their partners are away or in different beds

14
Percentage of e-mails that involve lies

27
Percentage of face-to-face conversations that do

 37
Percentage of phone calls that do

Sources: Sanofi-Synthelabo; Opinion Dynamics; Harvard School of Public Health; National Cancer Institute–American Legacy Foundation; University of Minnesota–West Virginia University; Associated Press–Ipsos; Occupational and Environmental Medicine; Leflein Associates Inc.; American Cancer Society–CA; Archives of Pediatrics and Adolescent Medicine–University of Michigan Health System; Unusually Stupid Americans; Physiology and Behavior; Fat, Dumb, and Ugly; Elephant Encyclopedia (www.upali.ch/elephant_encyclopedia.html); Cornell University; Novations–J. Howard & Associates; Gallup Poll—Reported by Laura Gilbert

chapter 8

mind & spirit

**how to release stress and enhance
emotional well-being**

The Power of a Positive Spin

A new approach to psychology offers a specific
prescription for happiness that doesn't cost
a penny ... but it may require a little practice.

BY PETER JARET

After years of focusing on what goes wrong
when people become anxious or depressed,
a growing number of psychologists are saying it's high time to look on the bright side. "Our
interest is emotional well-being, in what goes right
for people who are happy and well-adjusted," says
Christopher Peterson, Ph.D., a professor of psychology at the University of Michigan and a leader in
the field of positive psychology, a new approach to
the discipline. "What are the traits that allow people to lead fulfilled lives? What are the strengths
and virtues that contribute to happiness?"

If that sounds more like the stuff of greeting cards
than serious science, consider this: In March 2004,
the distinguished Oxford University Press published
*Character Strengths and Virtues: A Handbook and
Classification*, an 800-page scholarly text that
categorizes and analyzes the 24 key traits
associated with mental health and happiness.
Edited by Peterson and Martin E.P. Seligman,
Ph.D., a University of Pennsylvania psychologist who is considered the guru of
positive psychology, the book celebrates

such characteristics as love, prudence, creativity, and
leadership. It's intended to be a counterpart to the
traditional text of psychiatric medicine, the *Diagnostic
and Statistical Manual of Mental Disorders*, with its
gloomy chapters on troubling conditions, such as
obsessive-compulsive disorder and schizophrenia.

Analyzing the bright side was not as easy as you
might think. Peterson and Seligman spent three years
working with a team of experts to identify traits that
are shared and valued across cultures. (Persistence just
happened to end up on the list.) During that time,
they pored over not only psychiatry journals, but also
the works of philosophers and classic religious texts.

Practicing another important ideal on their trait
list—humility—Peterson acknowledges that the
classification system in *Character Strengths and Virtues*

> Becoming aware of your own
> strengths and virtues can help
> you make the most of them.
>
> —Christopher Peterson, Ph.D.

is a work in progress. "Our goal was to get the conversation started, to encourage people to begin to look at the strengths and virtues that contribute to emotional well-being," the psychologist says.

But the authors have higher aspirations, too (motivated, perhaps, by two more of the virtues they selected: kindness and leadership). They would like to help make everyone a little happier. To achieve this goal, Peterson and Seligman, who is also the author of *Authentic Happiness: Using the New Positive Psychology to Realize Your Potential for Lasting Fulfillment*, have created a 240-item questionnaire designed to identify strengths and virtues. (You can find this and other quizzes by visiting www.authentichappiness.org.) The duo hope to spread their gospel to mental-health practitioners around the world.

"Becoming aware of your own strengths and virtues can help you make the most of them," Peterson explains.

If you know that love of learning, kindness, and leadership are among your strong points, you might flourish in a job that involves teaching, for instance. If creativity and the appreciation of beauty and excellence are your virtues, you are likely to make the most of them with a career or hobby that gives you an opportunity to express yourself.

Research shows that you can also enhance certain character traits. In their new classification system, Peterson and Seligman weighed the available evidence for each of the 24 attributes that they examined.

There's not much data to support the idea that you can become more prudent (one of the key virtues) or kinder, sad to say. But other qualities can be cultivated, sometimes by doing something as simple as taking a walk in the park, counting your blessings at the end of the day, or sitting down and writing a letter you may never send. ■

Award-winning writer Peter Jaret is a contributing editor.

Think Yourself Healthy

Researchers have known for a while that emotions can affect health. But it hasn't been clear how feeling blue could lead to feeling fluish. Now, with the help of some nosy questions and an EEG machine, scientists at the University of Wisconsin-Madison have uncovered at least part of the explanation.

In the study, lead author Richard Davidson, Ph.D., asked 52 participants to think about the best and the worst times of their lives. While the men and women called up these memories, the researchers closely monitored the activity in the parts of the brain that are associated with positive and negative emotions. Then the volunteers were given a flu vaccine.

Six months later, the scientists measured flu-antibody levels. Participants who experienced particularly intense negative emotions (according to their brain activity) had fewer antibodies, the researchers found. In fact, the subjects who felt the worst made 50-percent fewer antibodies than those who were the least disturbed by their painful memories. That's quite a sizable difference, according to Davidson, a professor of psychology and psychiatry—big enough that if everyone got flu shots, "people with negative emotional styles would be more likely to develop the flu."

This dynamic works the opposite way as well. "It's absolutely likely that positive emotions can improve your immune function," Davidson says. Indeed, in another recent study of his, people who were trained in meditation for eight weeks showed increased activity in the brain's "happy" side; they also produced more antibodies after receiving a flu vaccine than people who didn't meditate.

10 Essential Traits for a Happy Life

Can you build a better character? Absolutely, say proponents of positive psychology. You are likely to be happier, healthier, and more fulfilled if you become aware of and work toward enhancing your signature qualities. We've chosen 10 of the 24 traits outlined in *Character Strengths and Virtues*. See which ones apply to you and how you can make the most of them.

1. Love of Learning: *A fervor for acquiring new skills, satisfying curiosity, and building on knowledge.* Follow your inquisitiveness. Make a list of three things you enjoy or value, and choose one you'd like to know more about or be better at. Having a practical purpose can often be a big motivator. Always wanted to learn Italian? Sign up for a language course, and plan a trip overseas to put your new skill to use.

2. Creativity: *A flair for producing something new, surprising, or unusual.* The key is to let your inhibitions go. Whether you try painting, writing, playing music, or dancing, do it with a playful spirit. Also, try new things just for the fun of it, and don't judge your work.

3. Humility and Modesty: *Recognizing the true measure of your abilities and achievements and appreciating those of others.* Write down the names of three friends whom you most admire; then list the traits you most appreciate in them. Put a plus sign beside the characteristics you share and a minus sign beside those you wish you had.

4. Humor: *The ability to find something to laugh at even in* times of trouble and a knack for helping others do the same. Watch a funny movie or sitcom. Read an amusing book. Laugh at yourself by identifying three of your goofiest quirks and describing them in a journal.

5. Persistence: *The strength to work toward a goal in the face of obstacles, difficulties, or discouragement.* If you've tried and failed at something that matters to you—whether it's losing weight or keeping your New Year's resolutions—think about what didn't work and how to do better next time. Research shows that people who take responsibility for both their successes and failures are most likely to persevere.

6. Gratitude: *A sense of thankfulness.* Count your blessings. Think of three things you're grateful for that happened during the day: a friendly word, good news at work, any small success. Set aside a few minutes once a week to give thanks for what you've got.

7. Forgiveness: *The capacity for letting go of hurt and anger.* Write a forgiveness letter. First, think about someone who hurt you and the anger you feel about what happened. Then write a letter explaining your feelings and stating that you forgive the person. Don't send it—just the act of writing the letter, experts say, will jump-start the healing process.

8. Appreciation of Beauty and Excellence: *The ability to recognize and take pleasure in the good things in life.* Stop and smell the roses—literally, if there happens to be a garden in bloom nearby. Set aside a morning or afternoon to do nothing but savor something: Walk in the woods, listen to music you love, or visit an art gallery.

9. Spirituality: *The belief in a transcendent dimension of life.* You don't have to go to church to tap your spiritual side. Devote 10 minutes a day to meditation, first thing in the morning or just before bed; this can be prayer or quiet contemplation that allows you to go beyond yourself.

10. Vitality: *A feeling of energy and aliveness.* Get up, and do something. Nothing enhances your sense of vitality more than some physical activity. Even an exhausting gym workout can be exhilarating. Don't like the gym? Go for a hike, take a bike ride through the park, or do a circuit of the neighborhood.

What Your Heartbeat Has to Do with a Negative Mind-set

It seems that a little sensitivity is a good thing. But in a recent study at University College London, people who were closely attuned to their own hearts beating also tended to experience more feelings of anxiety, as well as other negative emotions. Volunteers were asked if their heartbeats were synchronized with a series of musical tones. Those who were highly aware of their heartbeats were more apt to report negative feelings. But take heart, says psychiatrist Hugo Critchley, M.D., Ph.D., the study's lead author: "Not only are those with better inner awareness likely to benefit from therapies, such as relaxation drills, but also they tend to experience positive emotions more acutely."

Be Bold—You'll Feel Better

Curiosity may have killed the cat, but it saved the rat—at least it did in a University of Chicago study that found bold rats lived longer than scaredy rats. When psychology researcher Sonia Cavigelli, Ph.D., put the rodents in cages filled with interesting things to explore, some went at it with gusto, while others hung back. Blood tests showed the timid rats had significantly higher levels of stress hormones in their blood immediately after the new experience. They also died 20-percent sooner than their braver counterparts. The reason isn't clear, but researchers speculate that higher levels of stress hormones might alter immune function. It's too early yet to translate this study to humans, who may be able to gain a greater benefit from being cautious. So if you're a wallflower, don't start worrying about losing your bloom early.

Boost Your Creativity with the Power of Flowers

To impress your boss, get to work early—and don't forget the flowers. According to researchers at Texas A&M University, foliage adds oomph to creative thinking. In a study of 101 volunteers, performance on creativity tests increased 15 percent on average when plants or flowers were in their offices. But be warned: Greenery didn't do a thing for productivity on detail-oriented work (like proofreading or number crunching).

Take a Breath of Fresh Peace

This mini relaxation exercise is like a booster shot for the soul. You can do it any time of day and in virtually any location—your car, a bus, the office. Sit quietly, and focus on your breathing. Slowly inhale through your nose, visualizing your lungs filling with oxygen. As you exhale slowly through your mouth, relax your shoulders; then stretch or yawn. Repeat this two or three times. Next, slowly say to yourself "I am" as you inhale and "at peace" as you exhale. Feel a sense of tranquillity settle within you. Repeat this a few more times, visualizing your heart filled with peace. When you're ready, take a few deep breaths and shift your awareness back to your environment.

349

Your Personal Antistress Strategy

Find out how to cope, using a plan tailored to your personality type.

BY NANCY STEDMAN

You would think that with the deluge of articles and books promising to shine a light on the path to calm—Amazon.com alone offers 6,445 volumes on stress—America would have become the Zen capital of the world by now. So how is it that, according to a recent national survey, 78 percent of Americans say they are still searching for ways to relax? Is all that advice wrong, or are you just a lost cause?

"Incomplete!" is the word that psychologist Naomi Quenk, Ph.D., would use to describe the most familiar methods of handling tension, which focus on generic relaxation techniques. Instead of following one-size-fits-all advice, Quenk says to tailor strategies to your personality. In her book *Was That Really Me? How Everyday Stress Brings Out Our Hidden Personality*, she discusses the different ways people experience stress.

Quenk's approach, the product of decades of research, helps you determine what she calls your "stress personality type," based on the classic Myers-Briggs Type Indicator. This test, developed in the 1960s and now widely used to help people find their ideal careers, classifies individuals according to the

> There's no need to toss a plate when people defy your expectations. Try to ease up on your ideals to keep stress in check.

ways they go about gathering information (whether they trust their intuition or need solid facts), where they direct most of their energy (toward other people and things in the case of extroverts, toward inner thoughts and ideas for introverts), and other elements. It's these differences that make one woman feel overwhelmed if she's got plans every night of the week, while another woman feels exhilarated by all her social engagements.

Having a basic understanding of your personality, Quenk asserts, will help you pinpoint exactly what stresses you out, recognize how you typically respond, and develop specific techniques to cope.

Based on suggestions from Quenk and other experts, we've created this personal antistress guide to help you develop a game plan designed for you. We describe eight distinct personality types—one of which you should identify with—and give detailed tips for each. (Don't think you're Sybil if you see yourself in several types; that's completely normal. Just try a few more coping mechanisms to find the combination that works best.)

Feeling a bit anxious? Read on.

THE TAKE-CHARGE TYPE

Your defining traits: You love to coordinate events and supervise people. Office party? Neighborhood barbecue? You probably volunteered to head it up. Others may view you as a control freak or feel that you are micromanaging them. But you believe it's your responsibility to get things done right—and right now.

Your stress personality: Because you need to feel competent and in control, you get stressed-out in chaotic situations (a poorly run business meeting could push you over the edge). You also become aggravated when it seems that other people are slacking off. And woe to those who interrupt you and prevent you from finishing the task at hand.

Under stress, you try even harder to organize everyone and everything, often annoying people around you. You become hypersensitive and may accuse others of not appreciating you. Keep some tissues handy, because you're prone to emotional outbursts.

Your special stress-busters:

- "Relax from the demands of having to be in control by going to a place where someone takes care of you, such as a spa," Quenk advises. "Trust your body to the hands of a masseuse."

- To regain a sense of worth, try the Eastern practice of active meditation, suggests Paul Wilson, a well-known stress lecturer. "Concentrate all of your attention on whatever task you're doing, even something as simple as washing the dishes, and put 100 percent of your effort into it," he says.

Your biggest day-to-day challenge: Letting go of control. "Slowly begin to delegate tasks to the people you supervise and to family members. You will be easier on yourself and others when you realize that most people can become competent once given a chance," Quenk says.

THE RESERVED IDEALIST

Your defining traits: You hold strong notions about how people, including yourself, ought to be treated. You're very tolerant of other people's quirks, and you normally focus on the good in people. As a result, friends—and even strangers—often confide in you. Yet it takes a while for you to become really comfortable around new people, and you keep your sensitive side to yourself. Your own feelings are easily bruised.

Your stress personality: Spending your days in situations that go against your values, such as being a doctor who doesn't have enough time to care adequately for patients, makes you feel trapped. Because you have a hard time making new connections with people, you panic when you might lose someone you hold dear, such as a relative who is seriously ill or a friend with whom you're fighting.

Understanding your personality can help you pinpoint what stresses you out—and how to handle it.

When stressed, you are likely to criticize and yell at others. You become convinced that you are stupid and, perhaps, even unloved or unlovable. You tend to grow irritable, sarcastic, and fidgety. Steer clear of china: Under extreme tension, you may become physical and break things.

Your special stress-busters:

- When you're feeling down about yourself, lift your self-esteem with a pep talk. Susan M. Lark, M.D., a preventive-medicine physician in Northern California and author of the *Anxiety & Stress Self Help Book*, suggests that you remind yourself each day on the commute home of your accomplishments at work.
- Take a breather from the emotional drama of your life, and try to reconnect with a higher purpose by following an online labyrinth, such as one of the two at www.stonecircledesign.com (click on "Discovery" and then "Interactive Labyrinth Walks"). Labyrinths, a metaphor for life, are circular paths that since ancient times have been believed to soothe and heal. Following one may sound a bit far-out, but other Reserved Idealists say the technique works.

Your biggest day-to-day challenge: Easing up on your ideals. If you experience the same kinds of disappointments over and over (no man is ever attentive enough; no boss is ever fair enough), then it's time to re-evaluate what you want from people and situations. "Get real," Quenk says. "Try to lower your expectations for yourself and others."

THE FLEXIBLE REALIST

Your defining traits: People are attracted to you because you have a knack for finding the fun in life. Typically easygoing and optimistic, you enjoy material possessions, good food, music, art, exercise, and many friends. You don't dwell much on the past or future, and you're sometimes accused of having Peter Pan-ish "I won't grow up" tendencies. But you're not all fun and games: When things go awry at home or at the office, you're the perfect person to have around—you solve problems quickly and efficiently.

Your stress personality: Because you thrive on adapting to change, you feel frustrated if you have little freedom to do things your own way and at your own pace. Deadlines make you anxious. Confronting decisions that will affect your future,

such as whether to switch careers, can send you into a tailspin.

The future becomes an especially scary prospect when you're stressed. You grow despondent and fear that something terrible is about to happen to you. Sometimes you seek out solace by becoming involved with mystical philosophies or groups.

Your special stress-busters:

- Choose a particularly supportive friend from your large circle of pals, and call on that person to reassure you that a tragedy won't happen and that you'll be OK.
- Because you take great pleasure in physical objects, distract yourself from worry by inhaling and exhaling slowly as you focus on a small personal object that you like a great deal. "It might be a jeweled pin or a flower from your garden," Lark says.

Your biggest day-to-day challenge: Learning not to fear the future. "Come up with contingency plans," Quenk says. "Tell yourself, 'If I lose my job, I'll move in with my mother or another relative.' "

Flexible Realists are known for their optimistic nature and generally have lots of friends.

THE THEORETICAL VISIONARY

Your defining traits: You concentrate single-mindedly on projects and pay more attention to what's going on in your head than what's happening around you. "You are the most intellectually independent of the types," Quenk says. "You have a theory to explain everything, prefer innovative solutions to established ones, and are adept at seeing situations from an unusual perspective."

Your stress personality: Because you like envisioning the big picture, you become frustrated when you're forced to deal with lots of tedious details and facts. Your desire for completion means you have trouble coping when unexpected occurrences interrupt your thoughts and projects.

Of all the introverted types, you are the one who is most agitated by overstimulation from crowds; too many social commitments; noisy, busy environments; and what you see as invasions of your personal space.

Under pressure, you get easily irritated with people and tend to lash out at them. You may even rant at an object like a door that you accidentally bump into. You also fixate on one or two details that you can't stop thinking or talking about, such as your weight or a pimple. Such obsessiveness carries over into your behavior, as you lean toward excess in eating, drinking, cleaning, exercising, watching television, you name it.

Your special stress-busters:
- Get out of your head by doing something active, such as cooking or taking a hike, Quenk says.
- More than any other personality type, you need to reserve time for yourself to regroup and regain your mental energy. Make a point of scheduling some downtime on your calendar—in ink.

Your biggest day-to-day challenge: Becoming more tactful. You create additional friction when you express an opinion so forcefully that it sounds like a dictum. "Practice talking with modifiers, so that you start a statement with 'This is the way it seems to me,' rather than blurting out your ideas," Quenk suggests.

THE ENTHUSIASTIC PEOPLE PERSON

Your defining traits: You're upbeat, and you like to make sure everyone gets along. The keys to your personality are sympathy and camaraderie, and you thrive in work environments where you feel part of a team. As the extroverted cousin to the Reserved Idealist, you are careful not to hurt others' feelings and are sensitive to indifference. You risk overextending yourself because you don't want to disappoint people by turning down invitations or requests for favors.

Your stress personality: Conflict and negativity, even if the situation doesn't directly involve you, make you squirm. You feel distressed when you think that you are not trusted and appreciated by others, or when you are criticized tactlessly. Your anxiety level rises when you're forced to do things that you suspect will hurt people or that go against your values.

Stress often causes you to withdraw and become critical. You turn pessimistic and negative, seeing the worst in everything and everyone—including yourself. In a frantic search for calm, you may devour self-help books.

Your special stress-busters:
- Write your thoughts and experiences in a journal. "You are usually so focused on other people that it's easy to lose track of your own feelings," Quenk says. "Putting them on paper forces you to notice that you resent, for instance, doing almost all the housework. It also makes you see just how much you're doing—and overdoing."
- Because you tend to avoid people when you're stressed, inanimate objects are a more reliable source of comfort. "Rekindle positive feelings by taking on a new but manageable project, like painting a room or organizing your closet," Quenk suggests.

Your biggest day-to-day challenge: Becoming more assertive about articulating your own needs. Because you tend to worry about hurting others' feelings, try to voice your opinions tactfully, says Allen Elkin, Ph.D., director of New York City's Stress Management and Counseling Center. For example, if someone interrupts you, Elkin suggests a kind response: "Hang on. I'm not finished yet."

THE LOGICAL THINKER

Your defining traits: You pride yourself on being analytical, fair, and objective. You enjoy coming up with ways to improve procedures and systems. Intellectual and mechanical topics fascinate you. And while you are generally quiet and uncomfortable around people, you can talk endlessly about the ideas that matter to you. You find it easier to demonstrate affection through actions—such as buying your husband a coveted camera—than through words.

Your stress personality: You have problems when the people around you seem incompetent, act lazy, or try to micromanage you. You dislike having your abilities questioned. You also become unnerved when other people express strong emotions, especially if these feelings are directed at you. Like other introverted types, you may find a hectic social life to be a burden.

In times of stress, you may misplace such things as house keys and become unable to focus. You also tend to misread people's simple actions and become slightly paranoid. If a friend fails to invite you to a party, for example, you may jump to the conclusion that she hates you, when in fact this might be a get-together only for her relatives. You may become too logical, obsessively arguing about trivial details that might prove to be irrelevant.

Your special stress-busters:

- Reassure yourself that others do care about you by organizing a simple outing with close pals, such as a picnic or a pedicure, Quenk says. Even less gregarious types need comfort from old friends.
- Stimulate your logical side in a nontaxing, relaxing way by reading a novel or assembling a jigsaw puzzle, she suggests.

Your biggest day-to-day challenge: Developing a better grasp of how other people feel. Instead of jumping to conclusions when you think you've been slighted, do some investigating. "Ask yourself, 'Do I really have enough evidence to support my beliefs?' " Elkin says. "If the answer is 'no,' reconsider your case and hold off coming to any premature conclusions and reactions just yet."

THE ENERGETIC DOER

Your defining traits: You dislike routine and love trying all things new and different. You have the creativity and initiative to hatch a plan, as well as the energy to put it into action. You may be interested in so many things that you have trouble deciding where to focus your attention. You jump from project to project as soon as the initial challenges have been met. Because you tend to get involved in many things, you risk burning out.

Your stress personality: You want maximum freedom to pursue your impulses, and you feel stymied by rules or people who get in your way. Details, deadlines, and routines sap your energy.

When you're stressed, you're likely to become withdrawn and depressed. You lose your optimism about the future. Getting bogged down in the moment, you see your present situation as endless and may obsess on a thought, such as "I'm alone now and will always be alone." Without diversionary projects, you may focus on your body, sometimes imagining that a minor symptom is a sign of serious illness.

Your special stress-busters:

- As a creative person, you can easily take a mental vacation just by imagining yourself in a place you associate with carefree times. "Most people will just recall something visually, but the image is more vivid and more appealing when you can remember other sensations, such as the sound of a waterfall and the piney smell of a forest," says Edward A. Charlesworth, Ph.D., director of Willowbrook Psychological Associates in Houston.

• Keep your calendar full, with events to look forward to (even a simple dinner with friends counts), and think about them whenever you start to obsess about the future or your health, Quenk says.

Your biggest day-to-day challenge: Learning to pace yourself. "Do a little advance planning so you can avoid an impossible time crunch," Quenk says. If Wednesdays are usually hectic at work, don't book a game of tennis that evening.

MS. QUIET AND DEPENDABLE

Your defining traits: You enjoy dealing with facts and fine points in an efficient and systematic way. Hardworking and conscientious, you often play a behind-the-scenes role that sometimes leaves you feeling underappreciated. You respect tradition and are uncomfortable with change. Your immediate reaction to new ideas is usually negative.

If stress sends you straight to the department store, rely on a friend instead of a credit card next time you feel overwhelmed.

Your stress personality: As an orderly person, you become stressed when chaos surrounds you, when work piles up, when people interrupt you, or when procedures are constantly being revised. A born worrier, you become particularly distressed when other people ignore problems that are obvious to you. You may come unglued by new experiences, such as visiting a city for the first time.

You are usually quite careful, but stress can cause you to do something impulsive, such as buying an expensive piece of jewelry you can't afford. You tend to imagine all kinds of potential personal disasters, which only compounds your stress.

Your special stress-busters:

• To reduce your anxiety about new experiences, think of earlier scenarios that are somewhat similar to the ones you're facing (such as the last time you went to a party where you didn't know many people). "The situation will seem less scary once you discover how much is already safe and known," Quenk says.

• Although you may need help with overwhelming tasks, you dislike asking for it because doing so makes you feel like a failure. Offset those negative feelings by reminding yourself how often you have willingly helped others without judging them.

Your biggest day-to-day challenge: Getting a grip on reality. Try considering the worst possible outcome of a situation that worries you. Will you really end up on the dole if you get fired? By exaggerating the consequences, you can actually put your genuine risk in true perspective. Elkin says, "We all have that second voice of reason that talks back to our worried voice."

Depression + Job = Poor Work Performance

Women who are depressed say that their mental state is a major barrier to workplace success—an even greater obstacle than child- or elder-care responsibilities, sexual harassment, pregnancy, or sexism. A recent survey, sponsored in part by the National Mental Health Association, found that depression led women to avoid contact with their co-workers, leave work early, make more mistakes, and lose motivation to finish projects. The good news: Once the women sought treatment, 9 out of 10 said that their outlook improved—and so did their work performance.

Seven Steps to Help You Face Up to FATIGUE

Get your energy back with this eye-opening advice from the experts.

BY KATHERINE ELLISON

Feeling especially rundown these days? Join the club. More than half of American women ages 18 to 49 complain of tiredness and a lack of energy, according to a recent survey by HealthFocus International, a research firm that tracks health and eating trends. That's a virtual epidemic, one that medical professionals are starting to take seriously.

"Fatigue is a symptom people dismiss because nearly every human being experiences it," says Anthony Komaroff, M.D., a professor of medicine at Harvard Medical School and a leading chronic-fatigue specialist. After all, ours is not a restful age, especially for women, whose typical day is a mad relay race. Still, Komaroff warns, exhaustion can be a sign of a hidden medical problem, mild or serious.

If you have such a condition, getting a diagnosis may not be easy: Doctors, like the rest of us, don't always give reports of overtiredness the attention they deserve. But the good news is that fatigue often stems from an easily treatable condition. So any energy you spend finding and fixing what's wrong may lead to energy gained. If you're ready to recover your vitality, here are seven steps worth taking.

CHECK THE MENU.

You know that a balanced diet doesn't mean you split your allegiance between Häagen-Dazs and Ben & Jerry's, right? "If you're living off ice cream, with no fruits or vegetables and grains, you're missing antioxidants from vitamins and minerals that form the foundation of energy building," says Pam Peeke, M.D., a Pew Foundation scholar in nutrition and metabolism and an assistant professor of medicine at the University of Maryland. These nutrients help the body break down and process fuel, she explains. So eating from a plate rather than a vending machine is your first line of defense.

If that's obvious, another common mistake isn't. Simple dehydration can be a real energy drain, says Munsey Wheby, M.D., president of the American

College of Physicians and a professor of internal medicine at the University of Virginia. This is especially true if you exercise outdoors in warm weather and neglect to replenish fluids or consume enough salt. Perspiring heavily lowers your blood volume. That means oxygen isn't delivered to your tissues as efficiently as it should be, depleting your muscles and brain. There's an easy cure, of course. Pour yourself plenty of water.

Meanwhile, you may want to try pouring less of something else: alcohol. That extra glass of Chardonnay with dinner might help you ease into dreamland at bedtime, but it can also spoil your rest in the wee hours, say experts at the National Institute on Alcohol Abuse and Alcoholism. Even a drink or two as early as happy hour can later disrupt the brain-activity patterns linked to restorative sleep, making you feel woefully groggy the next day. Women, who have been shown to absorb alcohol more readily than men do, are particularly at risk.

Drinking alcohol can also impair your sleep by causing chronic heartburn and chest pain. The syndrome, known as gastroesophageal reflux disease, or GERD, is at its worst for many people at night. Although the causes are uncertain, culprits may include drinking, overeating, smoking, obesity, and pregnancy. The disorder generally occurs when a valvelike ring of muscle at the bottom of the esophagus doesn't close fully, allowing liquid from the stomach to leak back. Occasional heartburn is not necessarily worrisome, but if you suffer from it more than twice a week, you should have it checked out.

The risks of ignoring acid reflux include ulcers, gastric bleeding, and even increased susceptibility to cancer. Home treatments range from raising the head of your bed several inches (place wooden blocks under the legs) to taking common antacids and using the proton pump inhibitor omeprazole (Prilosec), newly available over the counter.

MIND YOUR MEDICINES.

Be careful when you open your medicine cabinet: Many common drugs can leave you aching for an afternoon nap. The list includes most sleeping pills, which can cause hangovers when used nightly. More surprising medications to watch include many nonprescription pain relievers and supposedly nonsedating antihistamines, as well as some drugs that regulate blood pressure (such as beta-blockers), lower cholesterol, stabilize heart rhythm, and control seizures.

Antidepressants and antianxiety drugs can also cause fatigue, though newer ones, such as Prozac and Celexa, are less likely to make you tired, explains Lauren Broch, Ph.D., director of education and training at Cornell University's Sleep-Wake Disorders Center in White Plains, New York. The drowsiness is sometimes only a start-up side effect that will disappear within a few days or weeks. If you experience continual and debilitating fatigue, consider a different drug or a lower dose; you also may want to take it at a different time—right before bed, for instance.

TALK TO YOUR PARTNER.

Ask your bedmate: "Do I snore really loudly every night?" And encourage honesty. If the answer is yes, you might have sleep apnea, a serious disorder in which breathing momentarily stops hundreds of times a night. This frequently leads to lethargy during the day. Apnea is often accompanied by unusually loud snoring—as high as 78 decibels in one study, certainly loud enough to wake a partner (an outboard motor runs at 80 decibels). In some people, muscles in the throat and tongue relax during sleep, blocking the upper airway. Another cause is obesity, which also can restrict air intake.

Sleep apnea afflicts some eighteen million Americans, according to the National Sleep Foundation, but experts believe it may be underdiagnosed, particularly in women. Most doctors have little training in sleep disorders and often think of this condition as a man's problem. "It's more common than we'd ever envisioned," Wheby says. Both apnea and a milder problem called upper airway resistance syndrome are most common in women after menopause. Treatments include surgery to remove excess tissue and using a mask that blows a continuous stream of air through the nasal passages.

357

4 MAKE A SYMPTOM CHECKLIST.

Several conditions with distinctive symptoms can be at the root of fatigue. Ever have a crawly, tingling feeling in your legs that makes it hard to sleep? You may have a little-known neurological condition called restless legs syndrome. One in seven adults surveyed by the National Sleep Foundation in 1999 reported feeling unpleasant sensations in their legs a few nights a week or more, but just 3 percent said their doctors told them they had the disorder. "People generally know they have it but may not know it by name, and so they may not bring it up with their doctors," says Margaret Moline, Ph.D., director of the Cornell Sleep-Wake Disorders Center.

No one's sure what causes the syndrome. It seems to be at least partly genetic, although some sufferers with low iron stores have found partial relief by taking supplements prescribed by a doctor. (Be careful, though—iron can be toxic at high doses.) The National Center on Sleep Disorders Research says several drugs seem to make sleeping easier. They include some used for treating Parkinson's disease, as well as sedatives and narcotic painkillers. But it's best to start with low-risk therapies. The Restless Legs Syndrome Foundation suggests walking, stretching, taking hot or cold baths, and getting massages, which can temporarily relieve symptoms. Alcoholic beverages, cold and allergy medicines, and most antidepressants appear to make the disorder worse.

Don't have restless legs? Perhaps ordinary pain is wearing you down. "From arthritis to premenstrual cramps, any painful condition can keep you awake and cause daytime sleepiness," Moline says. Occasionally, fatigue can also result from an infection, whether it's a run-of-the-mill virus or even an untreated dental abscess. In such cases, you can blame the exhaustion on your system's defenses. When the body recognizes a virus or other invader, the response is an immune-cell counterattack, says

Benjamin Natelson, M.D., professor of neurosciences at the New Jersey Medical School and director of the New Jersey Chronic Fatigue Syndrome and Fibromyalgia Center.

"The cells release substances called cytokines, which make you feel sick while they're trying to kill the virus," Natelson says. "The way cytokines work is not totally understood, but they produce fever, malaise, and chills, and they make you feel achy and lousy."

> Sometimes doctors begin a long set of diagnostic tests when it's not necessary. Often what's really to blame is the pace of your life.
> —Anthony Komaroff, M.D.

Even menopause, with its annoying hot flashes and night sweats, can disrupt sleep and make you tired during the day. Many women have been frightened away from the most effective remedy—menopausal hormone therapy (HT), previously known as hormone replacement therapy (HRT)—by recent studies linking it to increased risks of breast cancer, heart disease, and stroke. Those risks appear real, but the verdict is still out on HT prescribed for short-term relief of hot flashes and other symptoms during menopause's transitional stage. Many experts call such use reasonable.

"A lot of women get better with estrogen supplements," says Ted Friedman, M.D., Ph.D., an associate professor of medicine at the University of California, Los Angeles, and a fatigue specialist in endocrinology at Charles R. Drew University. Friedman commonly prescribes the hormones in low-dose gels and patches. Because the drugs enter through the skin, they're not processed by the liver; this lowers risk, compared with oral HT.

5 SIGN UP FOR A BLOOD TEST.

Among the first things that a doctor should suspect when you complain of constant fatigue is a problem with your thyroid—a small, butterfly-shaped gland wrapped around your windpipe, at the base of your neck. It controls your metabolism, or the rate at which you turn food into energy, so a malfunction can leave you flat out of gas.

A simple blood test can tell you if your thyroid is flagging. And there's a good chance that it is: According to the American Association of Clinical Endocrinologists, as many as 10 percent of women have hypothyroidism, a disorder in which an underactive gland pumps out scant amounts of thyroid hormone. The problem is five times as common in women as it is in men.

Researchers now believe more than twenty million Americans have some form of thyroid disease, twice as many as previously thought. In 2003, endocrinologists endorsed a more narrow range for normal thyroid functioning, making millions of people newly eligible for treatment.

Unfortunately, many physicians haven't caught up with the latest standards, says Leonard Wartofsky, M.D., professor of medicine at Georgetown University School of Medicine and an authority on thyroid problems. That means many sufferers likely remain undiagnosed. Once the condition is identified, however, the remedy is simple: You just take a thyroid-hormone supplement.

MONITOR YOUR MOOD.

Callously dubbed "the common cold of mental illness," depression can in fact leave you deeply lethargic. And even though there's growing awareness of the problem, experts say doctors still fail to treat it effectively. "Doctors are notoriously bad at diagnosing depression," says Michael R. Clark, M.D., director of the Chronic Pain Treatment Program in the Department of Psychiatry and Behavioral Sciences at Johns Hopkins University School of Medicine. "They miss it, they underestimate its severity, and they don't treat it for a long

Could You Have Chronic Fatigue Syndrome?

For 16 years, Laura Hillenbrand, author of *Seabiscuit: An American Legend,* has struggled through episodes of fatigue so disabling that at times she could barely even lift a pen. Now Hillenbrand has gone public with her difficulty, becoming a very visible face of chronic fatigue syndrome (CFS). Once widely dismissed as the "yuppie flu," because many seeking help for unexplained exhaustion were well-educated women in their 30s and 40s, the disorder is gaining wide recognition as a real—and serious—condition.

The Centers for Disease Control and Prevention (CDC) estimates that at least five hundred thousand Americans suffer from the syndrome or a similar condition, although some medical specialists and patient advocates believe CFS is gravely underdiagnosed. The principal complaints, which vary from patient to patient, always include fatigue that persists or recurs for six months or longer, along with at least four of the following symptoms:

- Severe memory loss or an inability to concentrate
- Tender lymph nodes
- Muscle pain
- Joint aches (without swelling)
- Sore throat
- Headaches that are new or unusual
- Poor sleep
- Daylong exhaustion after physical exertion

Sufferers alternate between illness and relative well-being, sometimes recovering but sometimes growing worse. No one knows the cause.

Therapies designed to help patients regain comfort and function include antihistamines and anti-inflammatories. Cognitive-behavioral therapy also shows promise.

If you want more information about CFS, the CDC and National Institutes of Health have helpful Web sites: www.cdc.gov/ncidod/diseases/cfs/ and www.niaid.nih.gov/factsheets/cfs.htm.

enough time." One reason, Clark notes, is that the majority of people suffering from depression or its equally enervating cousin—anxiety—complain of other symptoms, such as pain, dizziness, or fatigue.

"Over a lifetime, something like 15 percent of the population could be diagnosed as clinically depressed," says Bonnie Strickland, Ph.D., professor of psychology at the University of Massachusetts and past president of the American Psychological Association. Among women, one in four will be seriously depressed during her lifetime.

A common symptom of both depression and anxiety is disrupted sleep. Depressed people obsess over the past, Strickland says, and often wake up in the middle of the night or early in the morning, finding it hard to get back to sleep. Overly anxious people worry about the future and have trouble falling asleep. Either way, sufferers are likely to find themselves dragging during the day.

But once correctly diagnosed, both problems are relatively easy to treat. Getting more exercise or increasing social contact can improve mild depression, Strickland says. Meanwhile, the expanding array of mood drugs on the market can ease severe cases of depression and anxiety. "Properly treated, two-thirds of folks recover within three or four months," she notes. And, thankfully, more and more doctors are learning to ask patients troubled by tiredness (and reluctant to discuss their moods) whether they're feeling blue or anxious.

KEEP AN EYE ON THE BASICS.

As important as a medical checkup is, a real-life check-in can't be ignored. Don't forget the obvious. "Sometimes doctors begin a long set of diagnostic tests when it's not necessary," Komaroff points out. "Often what's really to blame is the pace of your life." A few easy changes can make all the difference. Make sure you spend enough hours in bed. Read up on time management. Or develop another incredibly energizing skill: the ability to just say no. Now, really, who could ever be too tired for that?

Katherine Ellison is a Pulitzer Prize–winning former foreign correspondent and author of The New Economy of Nature: The Quest to Make Conservation Profitable. *She is writing a book about how women's brains change when they become mothers.*

Rev Up Your Energy in a Flash

It's 4 p.m., and you're wondering how you're going to muster enough get-up-and-go to finish the day. The next time you start crashing, just try one of these tips from four of the nation's top spas.

1. Slather yourself with citrus scents. They're said to enhance your energy level and boost your mood, so look for products infused with lemon, lime, or orange essential oils.—*Citrus Salon and Day Spa, Blue Bell, Pennsylvania*

2. Run your hands under cool water for 20 seconds. Then close your eyes and, using the middle finger of each hand, tap each of the following areas five times: between your eyebrows, the tops of your cheekbones, your chin, and the area just under your nose. This quick and simple routine stimulates the nerve endings in your face, giving you an allover pick-me-up. —*Aria Spa and Club at Vail Cascade Resort and Spa, Vail, Colorado*

3. Walk or run up two flights of steps (about 20 stairs) twice. Land on every other step going up; hit every step going down. It gets your heart rate and circulation going. —*The Broadmoor, Colorado Springs, Colorado*

4. Soak a clean cotton washcloth in water that has been infused with a few drops of lavender or mint, put it in the refrigerator, and let it chill for 10 minutes. Place the washcloth over your face, and breathe deeply.—*Spa Ojai, Ojai, California*

How to Get the Greatest Grief Medicine

Walk—don't run—to grief counseling: Therapy for people who have lost a loved one is often unnecessary, according to a report from the Center for the Advancement of Health. Almost 80 percent of people feel much of their sadness lift within six months of the death of a close relative or friend, researchers say. Counseling may still be helpful, though, for people who suffer traumatic or "complicated" grief after losing someone to violence or in a tragedy, such as with the September 11 attacks, or for those survivors whose intense sadness lingers long after the loss.

It's Not Easy to Turn a Frown Upside Down

Winning the lottery might give you a great high, but it probably won't last. According to one theory, while overall happiness may be temporarily affected by life's ups and downs, it always returns to a genetically fixed set point. But a new study suggests that losing your job may have a more permanent negative impact on your happiness level that lingers even after you rejoin the workforce. A positive spin? Maybe your temperament isn't dictated solely by your genes after all.

What's Best for the Blues?

A new study suggests why talk works for some and drugs are better for others.

For someone who's depressed, deciding whether to try drugs or the talky approach known as cognitive-behavior therapy poses a bit of a dilemma: Some 60 percent of people who undergo either treatment get better, but that leaves 40 percent still suffering. And there's no way to know whether a given patient would have done better on the therapy he or she didn't try.

"There is no data on the planet that says what kind of treatment is best for a particular person," says Helen Mayberg, M.D., a professor of psychiatry and neurology at Emory University. Her new study doesn't yet answer the question, she says, but it "shows that drug therapy and cognitive therapy do not affect the brain in the same way, so it's not just a flip of the coin."

Mayberg and her colleagues used positron-emission tomography (PET) scans to measure brain activity in 14 depressed patients before and after cognitive-behavior therapy (which focuses on changing unhealthy thinking patterns). The researchers compared the scans to others previously done on patients taking antidepressants. People in both groups showed similar rates of improvement, but there was a twist.

Those who'd received talk therapy showed "top down" changes, with decreased activity in the reasoning part of the brain. In patients treated with drugs, however, the limbic system—where the deeper centers of emotion reside—was damped down. This, Mayberg says, may be why people on drug therapy often notice improvements in mood and sleep before changes in coping and self-perception occur.

The researchers next plan to compare PET scans of patients within each group. Because drugs can have serious side effects, Mayberg says, the goal is to determine which patients can do well without them.

16 Ways to
Beat the Winter
BLAHS

These simple strategies will keep your energy level soaring all season long.

It seems to happen every January. That holiday adrenaline carries you into the new year, and then—*bam!*—you've got nothing left to look forward to except the darkness of winter. You scowl at your alarm clock in the morning; during the day your energy sags; and by quitting time all you want to do is go home, eat dinner, watch TV, and get in bed.

Diagnosis: the winter blahs, or what doctors call seasonal depression. This malaise, scientists say, is likely caused by a decrease in the amount of daylight you're exposed to in winter's shorter days. Over half the population notices some seasonal mood changes, says Michael Terman, Ph.D., who directs the winter-depression program at the New York State Psychiatric Institute and Columbia University College of Physicians and Surgeons in New York City.

Women seem to be more likely than men to suffer seasonal lows; some studies say as much as twice as likely. Researchers speculate that this increased vulnerability is due to normal hormonal fluctuations that increase a woman's sensitivity to light changes.

And while the blahs aren't life-threatening, "they can compromise work productivity and quality of life for up to five months," Terman says.

Luckily, you don't have to live in lethargy. We asked the nation's leading experts on winter depression, diet, and exercise what they do to raise their spirits. Follow their advice, and you may not feel the need to hibernate during those cold months.

LIGHT UP YOUR LIFE.

Light therapy is the first-line treatment for seasonal affective disorder (SAD), and scientists say it is also an effective remedy for its milder cousin, the winter doldrums. But even if you're not wild about the idea of basking in front of a bright lamp every day, there are simple ways to get a lift by lightening up.

1 **Expose yourself to superbright light:** Years of research have shown that light deficiency is a leading cause of the winter blahs. When it's dark, your brain secretes more melatonin, a sleep-related hormone associated with SAD, so shorter days can make you feel sluggish.

Light therapy is the standard treatment for SAD. Studies prove that when your eyes are regularly exposed to a lamp specially designed to be 10 to 20 times as bright as ordinary indoor lighting, melatonin levels in your blood drop and energy increases. The tricky part of light therapy is matching the amount to your circadian rhythm, the internal clock that tells you when to wake up and when to sleep. The dosage involves three factors: the intensity of light, or lux; the daily duration of exposure; and the time of day that you're treated. "There's no cookbook formula for light therapy," Terman says. "You need to dose for your individual needs."

To help you determine your optimum light prescription, take the Automated Morningness-Eveningness Questionnaire at the Center for Environmental Therapeutics' Web site (www.cet.org). You may notice an improvement after a few days of treatment.

2 Change your bulbs: Deborah Burnett, a Tennessee-based interior designer, may not have to shovel mounds of snow, but she still feels the effects of less light in winter. "From the end of August until the end of April, I sit under a full-spectrum, high-intensity fluorescent lamp at night while I watch TV," says Burnett, who specializes in lighting and color.

If you don't want to invest in special equipment, a few simple lighting changes can make a difference. "Things look better in the correct light, and you feel better when you're well-lit," says Burnett, author of *Comfortable Living by Design*.

The best change that you can make, she says, is to switch the bulbs in overhead lights in the two rooms women tend to frequent: the kitchen and the bathroom. Look for a fluorescent tube with a minimum of 4,100 degrees Kelvin (a measure that tells you whether the light will have a warm or cool appearance) and a color-rendering index, or CRI (a scale that is used to describe the tone of light on objects),

of at least 85. The higher both of these numbers are, the closer to natural light the bulbs will be. (Sometimes the numbers aren't listed on the box, so ask a salesperson.) If your overhead light fixtures can't accommodate fluorescent tubes, Burnett

> Over half the population notices some seasonal mood changes due to the decreased daylight during winter's short days.

suggests screwing bright white halogen bulbs into recessed or decorative fixtures. You can also try inserting compact fluorescent lights into your table lamps; these bulbs aren't as bright as the tubes, but Burnett says they can improve your point of view.

3 Sit near the window: Lamps aren't the only source of mood-brightening light. Even something as simple as moving your desk near a window can help, Terman says. Or run errands during your lunch break; even a cloudy day offers far more light than indoor spaces.

4 Create rainbows: Living in the Southwest, environmental psychologist Janetta McCoy, Ph.D., doesn't have to endure long winters, but she still makes a point of using light to improve her state of mind. "I like to hang a crystal in a window facing south to capture the sun and produce colorful rainbows around the room," says McCoy, assistant professor in the College of Architecture and Environmental Design at Arizona State University. "You can't feel moody or sad in a room of rainbows."

ENERGIZE YOUR SPACE.

Design can be good preventive medicine. Rearranging your space can help stop you from sliding into a funk, says McCoy, who has investigated the effects of environment on stress and creativity. The trick, she says, is creating an atmosphere that relieves energy-sapping tension. Here's how to make your surroundings work for you.

5 **Enjoy the view:** Natural landscapes seem to have a mood-elevating effect, McCoy says; plants and natural materials may, too. But you don't necessarily have to spend your days gazing out the window or drive miles to a particularly scenic spot. Interior views, created by incorporating earthy touches into your space, can be just as soothing, McCoy says. Arrange the furniture at home or in your office to take advantage of the elements around you: exposed wood floors, indoor plants, a vase of flowers.

6 **Add color with affordable accessories:** Of course, an occasional jolt of caffeine can get you going. But "you can't get through winter with just Starbucks," says Mimi Cooper, a principal in the Cooper Marketing Group, a color-consulting firm that helps retailers and manufacturers select palettes based on decades of tracking people's responses to different shades. "Color is the easiest and cheapest way to make a visual and emotional change," Cooper says. For an espresso-size jolt, she suggests accessorizing with vibrantly colored socks, scarves, lingerie, pillows, towels, or sheets. When Cooper is feeling particularly glum, she pulls out her own secret weapons: patterned socks, a red bag, and bright yellow underwear.

7 **Decorate with plants:** In feng shui theory, winter is governed by water—the deep abysmal kind, not the Caribbean blue type. It's no wonder that people feel gloomy during the first months of the year, says national feng shui expert Stephen L. Field, Ph.D. The dark forces of water are tempered by elements from the earth, so placing plants in clay or terra-cotta pots in the sunny southern portions of your house "might be an effective counter for the winter abyss," says Field, professor of Chinese and chair of the department of modern languages and literatures at Trinity University in San Antonio.

8 **Eat by candlelight:** Fire strengthens Earth's mojo, giving it an added edge against the energy-zapping effects of water, according to feng shui. Field recommends lighting candles at dinner to fuel the fight against the forces that drag you down.

9 **Clean house:** You take cues from your environment. So even if you devour all the self-help books at Barnes & Noble, you'll probably still lack the motivation to get off your butt if your house is in shambles. "I make sure that my refrigerator is clean, I get rid of clutter, and I clear the space under my bed," Burnett says.

10 **Charge the air:** Ever experience an all-natural high while walking on the beach or standing beside a mountainous waterfall? It could have been the fabulous scenery—or all the negative ions in the air, Terman says. Levels of these charged particles tend to be lower in airtight, heated spaces, such as those in the typical winter home. If, like most people, you can't sit out winter on a beach, a machine called a negative ionizer may help. "We've explored this therapy in three separate controlled clinical trials with impressive results," Terman says. "Negative air ionization proved just as effective as light therapy or antidepressants." The reason for the effect is still unclear, but some researchers believe negative ions increase levels of the mood-lifting brain chemical serotonin.

11 **Take control of the thermostat:** Nothing sours your outlook like a room that's either too hot or too cold, McCoy says. At home, experiment with the thermostat to find the temperature that feels best to you. (If your husband protests, tell him your health depends on moving the needle a few degrees.) When you venture out, adopt the old layering strategy to counter the effects of an ice-cold theater or a broiling restaurant.

> Boost your mood with bright colors. Try accessorizing with vibrantly colored socks, scarves, lingerie, pillows, towels, or sheets.

GET MOVING.

Studies have shown that a good walk or run can chase away the dumps as effectively as antidepressants, says James A. Blumenthal, Ph.D., professor of medical psychology at Duke University Medical Center, who has researched the connection between mood and exercise. Consider these ways to stay active.

12 Go for a test run: Don't expect an overnight attitude adjustment. Blumenthal advises that you'll probably need to exercise regularly for several weeks before the therapeutic effects kick in. Studies have found that 30 minutes of aerobic activity three times a week should do it, Blumenthal says. "Data suggest that strength training can improve mood, too," he adds. How? "One of the more prominent theories is that exercise may influence brain chemicals, like serotonin, that control mood," Blumenthal says. Another explanation: "Exercise may make you feel better because you've accomplished a task you once thought was difficult."

13 Take a spin in the mall: Not up for facing the cold—or the stale gym air? Expand your definition of the track: Blumenthal suggests a brisk walk around the mall.

14 Work out in style: When it's time to update your winter attire, don't forget to spruce up your fitness wardrobe as well. "Even buying a jogging bra with a red stripe can give you an edge," Cooper says.

15 Dream it, do it: The power of imagination can help you find an activity you'll enjoy enough to stick with no matter what the season, says Jay Kimiecik, Ph.D., an associate professor in the Department of Physical Education, Health, and Sport Studies at Miami University in Oxford, Ohio, and author of the book *The Intrinsic Exerciser: Discovering the Joy of Exercise*. Visualize yourself in motion: Are you speedy and quick? Maybe you should take up running. Or are you more the rhythmic type? Try biking or swimming. Methodical and mindful? Go for yoga. "When you stop focusing on external reasons for exercising, like weight loss or living longer, and start focusing on the vision you have for yourself, you're more likely to really enjoy physical activity," says Kimiecik, who puts on a flotation belt for buoyancy and "runs" laps in the pool in nasty weather. When you enjoy exercise, he explains, you're more likely to creatively handle obstacles—such as weather, family, or jobs—that can get in the way of workouts.

16 Sleep in later: Even early-birds struggle to make crack-of-dawn workouts when it's still dark as midnight outside. "Don't fight human nature," advises Gregory Florez, CEO of an online health-coaching service called FitAdvisor.com. "During the winter, try to schedule late-morning, lunchtime, or after-work workouts instead." ■

Are You SAD … or Just Blue?

It's one thing to subsist on DVDs and takeout food over a cold and dreary weekend, but it's another to hole up for three or four months at a stretch. If during the winter not only your appetite (specifically carb cravings) shoots up, but also you gain weight, have trouble concentrating, and become irritable easily and often—not to mention you feel like camping out in bed 24-7—you may have seasonal affective disorder (SAD) or even depression. If a combination of these symptoms persists for longer than two weeks, see a doctor.

Are you not sure whether you should get medical help or self-treat? Then take the Personal Inventory for Depression and SAD questionnaire at www.cet.org, the Web site of the nonprofit Center for Environmental Therapeutics, which is overseen by SAD expert Michael Terman, Ph.D.

Why Women PANIC

Women are twice as likely as men to have an anxiety disorder. The good news is there's help.

BY ANNDEE HOCHMAN

It happened one Saturday night amid the clatter of a Greek restaurant. My friends and I had ordered appetizers, and the waiter had poured each of us a pale glass of retsina, that pungent, resiny Greek wine.

Suddenly I began to feel as if the walls were edging in. My palms grew damp, my heart drummed, my stomach churned. I had only one shrill thought: If you don't get out of this restaurant immediately, you are going to faint—or die.

I mumbled that I didn't feel well, and then I raced for the door. The night was clear and cold outside; I gulped air until my pulse finally quieted. Shaky, relieved, and mystified, I got into my car and drove myself home.

I'd had my first panic attack.

I began to avoid restaurants, but then my panic started to percolate in other venues—hair salons, movie theaters, elevators, tunnels. My work, which involved teaching and public speaking, became a nightmare of nausea, sweaty palms, and heart palpitations. Ashamed, I told no one. I covered my increasingly antisocial behavior with a fistful of excuses (I was broke; I wasn't hungry; I'd seen that movie before). My world shrank to a slim corridor of safe places. Once, when I panicked at home, I wrapped myself in a quilt to smother the trembling and berated myself: Just snap out of it.

After ruling out a medical problem, my doctor prescribed Xanax. But I didn't want a pill; instead, I tried self-help, support groups, therapy, relaxation tapes, meditative breathing, and wishful thinking. Months passed. My panic attacks didn't.

It might have helped if I'd realized just how much company I had in my increasingly constricted world. Research has shown that women are twice as likely as men to suffer from panic attacks. And recently it has become clear that women's vulnerability is even greater than previously thought. The disorder, it seems, can strike older women and very young girls, as well as the women in their teens and 20s known to be most at risk. What's more, it now appears that panic attacks not only hit women more often than men, but also that they hit women harder.

Why are women more prone to panic? It may be due in part to fluctuating hormones that shape the way the brain processes stress, says Kamila S. White, Ph.D., who directs the behavioral-medicine program at the Center for Anxiety and Related Disorders in Boston. Estrogen in particular affects the availability of serotonin, the brain's "calming chemical."

Whatever the reason for the difference, it shows up early. A recent study found that by age 6, girls are twice as likely as boys to have an anxiety disorder. The gender difference is also evident in what happens after the problem develops, says Kimberly Yonkers, M.D., who has collaborated since 1990 on the Harvard/Brown Anxiety Research Project. "Women relapse at a threefold higher rate," she explains. "When men recover, they tend to stay well."

So that's the bad news about anxiety. But there is also good news. Panic disorder is highly treatable, responsive to both medication and cognitive-behavioral therapy. There's even a new twist on the latter treatment that promises rapid relief for those who can tolerate its intensive approach.

It was cognitive therapy that finally cured me, in 12 sessions designed to defuse my panic attacks through relaxation, reassuring self-talk, and gradual reintroduction to restaurants. My therapist gave me homework: Go to a diner alone, and eat three bites of French toast. Join a friend for lunch. Have dinner at a fancy restaurant. Breathe through the cantering heartbeat, the swimmy sense of unreality. Permit the symptoms to pass.

For years, R. Reid Wilson, Ph.D., associate clinical professor of psychiatry at the University of North Carolina School of Medicine, treated his anxiety-ridden patients with this "permissive" approach. But he and a handful of other cognitive therapists now believe they have a quicker, better way, what Wilson calls the "provocative" stance of actually exacerbating panic symptoms.

Wilson may take a client into the very places she fears—a restaurant or a supermarket, for instance.

> **Studies show that even as early as age 6, girls are twice as likely as boys to have an anxiety disorder.**

When she begins to feel signs of anxiety, he encourages her to try intensifying the sensations rather than attempting to relax through them. The symptoms often start to dissipate after a few minutes. Wilson says, "We ask people to notice what they're feeling and tolerate that. What they begin to discover is, 'I can manage these feelings.'"

Others use a similar approach, but in the less threatening atmosphere of the therapist's office. If a person suffers shortness of breath during attacks, the therapist may instruct her to breathe through a straw; if dizziness is a concern, she'll be told to twirl rapidly in a chair. People with anxiety disorders overreact to their physical symptoms of distress, says White, of the Center for Anxiety and Related Disorders. "We expose them to the symptoms until they no longer see them as dangerous but as boring, bothersome, or annoying."

For Wilson, the new twist in treatment is primarily about attitude: The idea is to welcome panic as a kind of martial-arts adversary instead of taming it with breathing techniques and relaxation mantras. "It's a mental game," he says. "You want to go toward your symptoms instead of away from them."

It's been 15 years since I had my first panic attack, but thinking about Wilson's method tosses me right back to that Greek restaurant—clammy palms, coiled stomach, and all. On the other hand, perhaps his confrontational approach would banish my fear of attacks forever.

I go to restaurants now, often and eagerly. I ride elevators to the 47th floor. And I breeze through the Lincoln Tunnel. But I still carry a dog-eared card that got me through some of the worst episodes of panic. "You will survive this," reads the faded print. "You always have." I keep it folded in my wallet, just in case. ◼

Anndee Hochman is the author of Everyday Acts & Small Subversions: Women Reinventing Family, Community and Home.

Q + A

Prevent Panic Attacks

Recently I experienced a sudden, overwhelming fear for no apparent reason, and my heart felt like it was going to explode. My doctor says I had a panic attack, and I'm afraid of having another one. How can I prevent them?

The best strategy for eliminating panic attacks is to get over your fear of them. Recurring attacks are self-perpetuating; the anticipation of another one can make the episodes more frequent and severe. Cognitive-behavioral therapy can break this cycle. During treatment by a psychologist or a therapist, you're taught to understand the disorder and its causes (the cognitive part), and you learn ways to deal with it (the behavioral part). After about 12 sessions, many patients stop having attacks or have them very rarely. (Some people may also require medication.) You can contact the American Psychological Association (800-964-2000) to locate a qualified therapist in your area. Incidentally, panic disorder is more common than you might think, affecting an estimated 1.6 percent of the U.S. population and, for unknown reasons, striking twice as many women as men.

The proper treatment can free you from panic attacks.

Researchers Discover a Biological Root to Panic Disorders

For many of the 2.4 million American adults stricken by panic disorder (PD) each year, feelings of shame compete with irrational fears. Now there's new evidence that the fears reflect a biological problem, not a failure of courage. In a recent study, brain scans showed that PD patients were short on receptors for serotonin in certain areas of their brains, especially the parts involved in controlling anxiety.

How Photos Could Cause You to Have False Memories

Some trauma therapists use photographs to dredge up what they believe to be repressed memories in their patients. But although pictures may cue accurate memories, they can also backfire, says psychologist D. Stephen Lindsay, Ph.D., of the University of Victoria in British Columbia. In his study, researchers asked psychology students to recall details about three experiences they'd had in grade school—two real, the third invented by the researchers. Half were also shown a class photo. Of the participants who'd been shown a class picture, two-thirds recalled the pseudo-event, versus only one-quarter of those who didn't receive the visual prompt. "Using a photo as a way to help people remember may be risky," Lindsay warns.

Watch Out for the Emotional Cost of a Car Crash

There's nothing like it: the squeal of brakes, the unholy grinding of steel on steel, and finally the silence after a car wreck, when all or nothing is possible. Frequently, what follows is post-traumatic stress disorder (PTSD). "Approximately 25 percent of those injured in a vehicle accident will develop PTSD," says Edward B. Blanchard, Ph.D., director of the Center for Stress and Anxiety Disorders at the State University of New York at Albany and co-author of *After the Crash: Assessment and Treatment of Motor Vehicle Crash Survivors.* In fact, according to Blanchard, motor-vehicle accidents are the leading cause of PTSD in the United States.

People with this disorder can have a variety of symptoms, including psychological numbing of emotions, anxiety, poor concentration, and insomnia. There is no sure-fire way to predict who will develop PTSD, but some factors stand out, says Edward J. Hickling, Psy.D., a psychologist and the other author of *After the Crash.* Experiencing severe fright or feelings of unreality during the accident bump up the odds, he says, as does prior depression. If someone was killed or seriously injured, that may also increase the risk of PTSD in survivors. Being female triples the risk, he adds, though no one is certain why.

Two-thirds of people with postcrash PTSD get better on their own within a year, Blanchard says. But if you were in an accident a while ago and still have symptoms, you should seek professional help. Hickling and Blanchard have a Web site (www.afterthecrash.com) that offers a cost-free online assessment. Fill out a questionnaire; Hickling and Blanchard will review your answers and respond with customized recommendations.

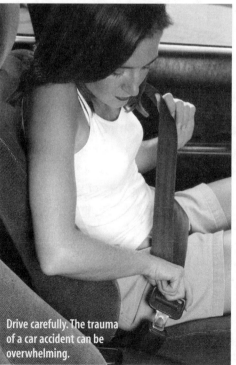

Drive carefully. The trauma of a car accident can be overwhelming.

Looking for Satisfaction?
You May Need to Take a Reality Check

Perhaps Mick Jagger couldn't get any, but the folks in Colombia are just brimming with satisfaction. The recent World Values Survey canvassed people in over 80 countries on their feelings of happiness and general life satisfaction from 1999 to 2001. Colombia topped the list, while the United States staggered in at a somewhat surprising 16th place. The former Soviet Republic of Ukraine came in last—a fact that doesn't surprise survey director Ronald Inglehart, Ph.D., of the Institute of Social Research at the University of Michigan. "Declines in living conditions do more damage to subjective well-being than having it all or never having had much at all," he says. So what is Inglehart's prescription for happiness? Always keep your expectations fully in line with reality.

When Perfectionism *Fails You*

There's nothing wrong with high goals. Impossible ones are another matter.

BY INGRID WICKELGREN

When Emily Wilson (not her real name) showed up at the eating disorders clinic at the University of North Carolina in 2002, she seemed like a person with almost everything under control. She had a tendency to micromanage her weight through excessive exercise, but she was a successful event-planner who was able to pull off complicated projects and keep her clients calm throughout the process.

It quickly became clear, though, that Wilson's eating disorder was a symptom of a bigger problem.

Wilson didn't feel like a success at all, says psychologist Cynthia Bulik, Ph.D. Even the smallest quibble in a client's glowing evaluation would totally devastate her. And when she received a professional award, Wilson explained to Bulik that the competition was weak.

Recently divorced, Wilson felt that she had to look perfect to find the right guy. She'd spend 2 to 3 hours on her hair, makeup, and clothes before going on a date. Then, if she didn't look good enough, she'd cancel her plans.

There's nothing wrong with a person wanting to excel, but over the past few years, researchers have become increasingly aware of the damage that perfectionism like Wilson's can cause. At its worst, it can set you up for serious problems, including eating disorders, clinical depression, anxiety, even suicide. But even milder forms of perfectionism can eat away at happiness.

Because perfectionism comes in degrees, it's impossible to figure out exactly how many people struggle with it. Even so, the problem appears to be widespread. Florida State University psychologist Thomas Joiner, Ph.D., estimates that as many as half of all women are somewhat perfectionistic; up to 10 percent are so much so that depression, suicide, and eating disorders are serious worries.

"It's a contemporary epidemic," says Golan Shahar, Ph.D., assistant professor of psychiatry and psychology at Yale University. "Our society is so encouraging of achievement."

The problem with perfectionism is not the relentless striving to do well. Perfectionists don't just set high goals, experts say; their objectives are so unrealistic that they almost guarantee failure. "A perfectionist has really high standards, never meets them, and then beats up on herself for that," Bulik says.

Even success can bring sadness to a perfectionist: Her reaction to reaching a goal is often "So what?" followed by "What's next?"—with nary a pause for "I did it!"

The psychological fallout of perfectionism can be dramatic. In 1996, Paul Hewitt, Ph.D., a clinical psychologist at the University of British Columbia in Vancouver, and colleague Gordon Flett, Ph.D., a psychologist at York University in Toronto, studied the development of depression in 103 people who were also rated on levels of perfectionism. Flett and Hewitt found that people who scored high on so-called self-oriented perfectionism (they demanded perfection of themselves) were more likely to become depressed or more depressed than they were already.

Perfectionists who believed that others required them to be perfect were more likely to make serious attempts at suicide, the researchers found. In a study of alcoholics, Hewitt and Flett found that "socially prescribed" perfectionism was a better predictor of a suicide attempt than either depression or hopelessness.

Although perfectionists might be admired for their tireless pursuit of success, they are not always high achievers. The drive for perfection can lead to procrastination and to endless, fruitless agonizing.

"If the boss tells you, 'Yeah, you do great work, but you're completing one assignment every 3 months, and we expect four,' maybe you need a different approach," says psychiatrist Murray Enns, M.D., of the University of Manitoba in Winnipeg.

Perfectionism is equally hard on relationships. A perfectionist may be so preoccupied with herself that she ignores her social life, Shahar says, or she may be reluctant to make friends who could discover her flaws. A perfectionist also may judge her partner, friends, and family according to her own impossible standards—not a recipe for satisfying connections.

For all the unhappiness it causes, perfectionism is a hard habit to shake. Shahar and Yale psychoanalyst Sidney Blatt, Ph.D., both of whom treat seriously depressed perfectionists, believe the best way to reduce these tendencies is through intensive therapy. It takes time for a perfectionistic patient to trust a therapist, Shahar says, but only then will he or she be able to explore other ways of dealing with the world.

> A perfectionist may be so preoccupied with herself that she ignores her social life, or she may be reluctant to make friends who could discover her flaws.

Other experts, such as Bulik and Enns, say many perfectionists can benefit from cognitive techniques that can help them identify distorted thoughts and replace them with healthy ones. For example, black-and-white thinking—the belief that only perfection equals success—should give way to shades of gray, such as "What was right about my work, and what could be improved?" Instead of concluding that one mistake means you're a failure, put it in context: You may have been laid off, but the master's degree that got you the job is still an achievement.

> It takes time for a perfectionist to trust a therapist, but only then will he or she be able to explore other ways of dealing with the world.

While coaching patients to think in new ways, Bulik asks them to practice being imperfect. A supermom, for instance, might be assigned to order in instead of cooking or to leave work at 5 instead of 7.

Bulik's first assignment for Wilson: Go shopping with an imperfect hairdo. "No one gave her bumpy ponytail a second glance," the psychologist recalls, "and once she got involved in window shopping, she forgot about it, too."

After six months of psychological therapy, Wilson finally began to relax a little bit. "She learned to come home from a job, kick off her shoes, and say, 'Wow, that was a lot of work today, but the client was satisfied,'" Bulik says.

Nobody would call Wilson easygoing, but she can now assess her work more realistically and pat herself on the back when she does a good job. She worries less about her appearance, Bulik says. "She's now able to say to herself, 'A guy who only wants a perfect-looking woman is not the type of guy I want!'"

Ingrid Wickelgren is the author of The Gene Masters: How a New Breed of Scientific Entrepreneurs Raced for the Biggest Prize in Biology.

Are You Feeling Blue? Try Animal Therapy

How's this for an alternative therapy: Petting an animal may cause levels of serotonin and other mood-lifting hormones to rise, according to preliminary results of an ongoing study at the University of Missouri–Columbia. Dog-owners appear to benefit most from petting their own canine comrades, while folks who don't own dogs can get a mood boost from playing with other people's pets. The research was funded by the VPI Skeeter Foundation, a group whose slogan is "Prescribe Pets, Not Pills."

1mind & spirit: in depth

Mend Your Heart and Mind with This Medicine

BY EVA MARER

I f you have high cholesterol, you know that drugs called statins can do your heart a favor. Now it seems that the same medicines might work wonders for your mood as well, staving off depression and reducing anxiety.

That's a good thing, of course, especially since some previous studies have suggested a link between aggressive lipid-lowering and increased risks of depression and suicide. (The brain needs cholesterol to function properly, and some experts have worried that reducing levels too much could disrupt serotonin metabolism.) But according to a recent study in *The American Journal of Cardiology*, heart patients who took statins actually fared better psychologically than the patients who took them irregularly or not at all.

In one study, patients who regularly took statins had a 30- to 40-percent lower risk of feeling depressed, anxious, or hostile.

Researchers tracked about six hundred patients for an average of four years; some of them used the drugs continuously, some intermittently, and some not at all. Every year, the participants filled out standard psychological questionnaires. The results were striking: Those who regularly took statins had a

30- to 40-percent lower risk of feeling depressed, anxious, or hostile. Patients had to have been on the drugs for a year before the mood benefit began to show, but the odds of psychological distress continued to fall with each additional year they were on the medication.

The results were so dramatic, they made the researchers a little nervous. "We almost hesitated to publish," says Yinong Young-Xu, Sc.D., who co-authored the study while a postdoctoral student at Harvard School of Public Health. Other research published around the same time yielded similar findings. (It will take a randomized, controlled study to answer the question definitively—one is currently under way.)

It's unclear exactly how statins might boost mood, Young-Xu says. But whatever the explanation, the report helps dispel concerns about the psychological side effects of taking them to lower cholesterol. And with 36 million people meeting the criteria for needing the drugs, according to the National Institutes of Health, the news comes as a welcome relief. ■

Solve Problems in Your Sleep

Research suggests that you do some of your best thinking while you're dreaming.

BY ANNDEE HOCHMAN

Dreams are much like foreign movies without subtitles: It's hard to make sense of what's happening. Some are thrilling (you are flying effortlessly over the Rocky Mountains), while others are perplexing (your third-grade teacher morphs into a bullfighter with a crimson cape). Almost all leave you wondering, "What did that mean?"

Skeptics may dismiss the nighttime mini-flicks in your brain as "only a dream," but many experts across the spectrum—from the most pragmatic neuroscientists to the more spiritual New Age gurus—say that if you pay attention, you can find the keys to life decisions both monumental and small. Should you have a baby? Enroll at a cooking school in Tuscany? Splurge on that Marc Jacobs handbag? Dreams may even hint at conflicts or questions that percolate just beneath the surface of your awareness, and then bubble up when daytime defenses are down.

"My belief is that the purpose of dreaming is almost the same as the purpose of waking and thinking: to solve problems," says Deirdre Barrett, Ph.D., clinical assistant professor of psychology at Harvard Medical School and editor-in-chief of the academic journal *Dreaming*.

The newest twist in dream work is the notion of lucid, or cognizant, dreaming. The idea is that if you are aware of the experience, you can act as a director, guiding your dreams to help you confront big issues or, at the very least, ensure that the plot unfolds the way you wish.

Whether you're preoccupied by a difficult relationship, a workplace struggle, or a health concern, sleeping on it just might yield a solution (and, no, you won't wake up exhausted—or at least any more so than you normally feel). Here's how to turn your dreams into reality.

RECALL YOUR DREAMS

Everyone dreams, but most people have a hard time remembering the details once they wake up. During different cycles of sleep, the level of brain activity responsible for memory decreases, and that may be why even your most elaborate dreams fade before you punch the snooze button. But don't despair: Experts say that anyone can improve dream recall, the first step toward understanding and using your dreams. The more you can remember, the larger your cache of problem-solving possibilities.

Get a good night's sleep. This ensures longer stretches of dream-rich REM (rapid eye movement) sleep, which varies from about 10 minutes at the start of the night to as much as an hour by morning. To set the stage for REM sleep, take a warm bath, play soothing music, or read something light-hearted, advises Rosemary Ellen Guiley, Ph.D., author of *The Dreamer's Way: Using Proactive Dreaming to Heal and Transform Your Life*, as well as more than 20 other books on dreams and intuition.

Use self-suggestion. Yes, it might sound like psychobabble, but experts say (and we can personally attest) that the simple act of telling yourself "I will remember my dreams" several times during the day and again at bedtime aids dream recall.

Take time to remember. In the morning, lie still and try to recollect everything you possibly can about your dream. (Of course, this works best on weekends or during vacations, when you can actually linger in bed.) If the memory seems to vaporize, shifting into your usual sleeping position—say, curled up on your left side—can help unleash more details, explains Patricia Garfield, Ph.D., co-founder of the Association for the Study of Dreams, an international research organization. Even if you recall only fragments (a blue convertible, your grandmother's chicken-noodle soup, a tranquil beach in Maui), repeat those images to yourself to fix them in your mind. An event or a feeling during the day might jog your memory and enable you to fill in the details.

Write it down. Keep a notepad and pen or a voice-activated tape recorder by your bed so you can document your dream while the memory is still fresh. Tell it to your significant other, or e-mail it to a friend so that you don't forget it. "Some research has shown that just recalling dreams, telling them to a friend, or writing them down has therapeutic value," says Alan Siegel, Ph.D., a psychologist at the University of California, Berkeley.

Keeping a journal can help you recognize patterns and recurring images that may help you figure out what your dreams are trying to tell you.

DREAM ANSWERS TO YOUR QUESTIONS

Ever have that exhilarating feeling in the morning when you think you've just dreamed a brilliant plan to end world hunger? Your partner might simply roll over when you recount your nighttime brainstorming sessions, but scientists will listen.

When Harvard dream researcher Barrett was conducting studies for her book *The Committee of Sleep: How Artists, Scientists, and Athletes Use Dreams for Creative Problem-Solving—and You Can Too*, she asked 76 college students to try using their dreams to solve more-mundane quandaries (for instance, how to rearrange the furniture in a new, smaller apartment). She instructed the group to use dream-incubation techniques—that is, to choose a pressing problem, phrase the dilemma succinctly, and think about it before bed each night. Within a week, half of the students had dreams that directly addressed their concerns, and in many cases those nighttime visions offered realistic answers. "Dreams sometimes come through with dramatic solutions to a chemistry problem or a golf swing," Barrett says.

A similar study, published in the December 2003 issue of *Dreaming*, showed that people who used these strategies to help resolve real-life issues reported that after 10 days their problems seemed more manageable and less distressing. The subjects also reported less daytime anxiety and depression compared with a control group. You can learn and practice the same techniques yourself at home.

Frame the question. Guiley recommends wording the problem as a specific one-line question: Should I pursue an MBA? What's the best way to approach my angry neighbor? How can I make more time for exercise? "I don't think there's anything you can't ask dreams, from major things to small things," she says. Reflect on the question several times during the day and again for 5 or 10 minutes before you go to bed. If after three nights your dreams don't yield insight, Guiley advises rephrasing the question: Instead of asking "How can I stop being so busy?" you might ask "What can I do to have more fun?"

Learn your own dream language. While they may contain archetypal symbols common across the globe, dreams more often use a highly individualized vocabulary built on your personal and cultural experiences and associations. For instance, the color white signifies purity in some societies, death in others; to you, however, it may evoke the potential of a blank canvas.

Keeping a journal can help you recognize patterns and recurring images so that you can figure out what your dreams are trying to tell you. Garfield, who has kept a dream diary for more than 50 years, advises jotting down a few notes about experiences and emotions in your daily life as well. "Then you're able to connect the dream pictures to the waking life events and better understand them," she says. Barrett notes that dreams are especially good at revealing solutions that lie outside the box. "There's less censorship during dreaming," she says. "The dream goes in a direction that the waking mind would not."

Get a second opinion. While you are the ultimate authority on your own dreams, you can nevertheless glean insights from talking to a friend or to a therapist, or even through participation in a dream group (like book clubs, but for dreams), either in person or online.

Turn metaphors into reality. Once you've compiled your personal dream dictionary, you're ready to put the entries to use. Disturbing images of being chased or attacked may point to inner turmoil, Guiley says. "The dream is saying, 'This is how I'm feeling—I'm dying in this job; the relationship is killing me,' " she says. "They are truth-oriented." Garfield tells of a woman she knew who once dreamed that her house was being squeezed out by high-rise buildings. The woman, a lawyer, realized that she resented being overlooked in her firm. She told her boss she was overdue for partnership and was soon promoted. "One dream shouldn't make you change a relationship," Siegel says, but a pattern of very powerful recurring images may nudge you into action.

CONTROL YOUR DREAMS

If you can train yourself to be conscious while you're in the midst of a nighttime fantasy—the hardest part of lucid dreaming—you can stage-direct the plot: You might decide to visit ancient Babylon or to star in a blockbuster movie, all in a good night's sleep. "These are symbolic actions that show you are transcending your usual sense of what is possible," says Stephen LaBerge, Ph.D., a long-time researcher in the Department of Psychology at Stanford University and founder of the Lucidity Institute, a research center. That sense of empowerment and possibility can carry over into your everyday life, prompting you to switch careers, learn a second language, or train for a marathon. The key is to first cultivate your ability to sleep, dream, and pay attention all at once; then use this awareness to get the most out of your dreams.

Practice during the day. Spend some time in your waking hours visualizing something you would like to do in a lucid dream, such as skydiving. Then, right before you go to sleep, tell yourself, "The next time I'm dreaming, I will be aware that I'm dreaming."

Control your dream destiny. If you are able to be conscious that you're dreaming, then you can learn to take charge of the action. LaBerge says a special advantage of lucid dreaming is that you can use it to tame a troubling nightmare. For example, if you think of the dragon, monster, or burglar in your dream as the parts of yourself you might find unpleasant or frightening, he says, confront these images. "People can say to themselves, 'The next time the nightmare happens, I want to turn around and hit the assailant,' " Barrett adds. "They benefit more than if they just try to suppress the dream or wake up. They get a certain sense of mastery."

Rewrite the script. Use lucid dreaming to explore new ways of relating to people in your life. You can have a conversation with the guy who broke your heart 20 years ago, the colleague who dismisses your ideas, or a dead relative you were close to.

People can also use such dreams to deal with their performance anxiety or shyness—for instance, by rehearsing a speech before an imagined audience or trying out cocktail-party conversation with an idealized listener who delights in your witty banter. "You can practice in a dream state without fear of the consequences," LaBerge says. Because brain activity during a dreamed action (a swan dive or a pirouette, for instance) is the same as during the real event, dreaming may actually help you prepare for a performance outside of your bedroom.

Even if you never come close to competing in the Olympics or dancing with the Joffrey Ballet, you may carry a sense of accomplishment across the border from your dreams to your waking life. Dreams provide inspiration "to start us down new paths, to understand what is possible," LaBerge says. ■

Anndee Hochman, a freelance writer based in Philadelphia, frequently dreams about facing a final examination in French literature without ever having read the book.

Your Brain on Dreams

For decades dream theory was all just speculation. But now technology, such as positron-emission tomography (PET) and magnetic resonance imaging (MRI), allows scientists to spy on the dreaming brain—seeing which parts buzz with activity and which ones cease their neuronal chatter.

Researchers once believed that dreaming occurred only in REM (rapid eye movement) sleep, when parts of the brain are busy, the body is slack, and your eyes dart behind closed lids. People cycle through sleep stages every 90 minutes, with stretches of REM growing longer throughout the night. Now scientists believe that dreams occur in all phases of sleep but that REM dreams are particularly, well, dreamy. "[These] dreams are more visual, more bizarre, and longer" than those in other sleep stages, explains Matthew Walker, Ph.D., a psychiatry instructor at Harvard Medical School.

The source of this dreaminess lies in both the hardware and software of the brain. As you drift into REM sleep, certain parts of the brain—chiefly the prefrontal cortex involved in decision making and memory—seem to turn off, while the limbic system and amygdala, both associated with emotion, rev up. The brain continues to send messages to major muscles, but they're blocked at the spinal cord (otherwise you'd be up at 2 a.m., acting out that dream of winning an Olympic gold medal).

"Scientists think that the reason our dreams are so completely bizarre and illogical is because of the shifting-down of that prefrontal lobe, the logical control center that keeps your line of thinking safely on track," Walker says.

In addition, the brain's chemical brew changes dramatically in REM sleep; levels of serotonin and norepinephrine (which help sustain focused attention and concentrated thought) drop precipitously, while levels of acetylcholine (which in high concentrations may foster illogical associations) rise higher than in waking.

"It may just be that the dreaming brain is set up to put things together in odd, unusual combinations, ways we never would when awake," Walker says. "But why? That's the next real question."

From Shy to Shining

Do parties make you tremble? There's no need to be a wallflower. Here's how to put your jitters on ice and learn to enjoy yourself at social functions.

BY SALLY LEHRMAN

Whenever I walk into a party, I morph into my preteen self at my first school dance. As I cross the threshold, I realize my dress is too short. A moment later, I sense a pimple on my forehead. Everywhere I look, people are huddled in impenetrable cliques. I overhear merry laughter, clever insights, and witty stories, and I want to slink into a corner. The chances are pretty good that when holiday festivities roll around, you feel the same way, judging from the research of Stanford University social psychologist Philip Zimbardo, Ph.D., who's known as the father of shyness research. The pressure most of us feel at parties to seem happy and connected, often with people we barely know, can be overwhelming, explains Zimbardo, author of *Shyness: What It Is, What to Do About It*. No matter how confident we look, most people have felt like awkward teenagers at some point.

> **People with social anxiety think everybody is as interested in their faults as they are. They're not.**
> —Angela Neal-Barnett, Ph.D.

In fact, of the more than ten thousand men and women Zimbardo has surveyed, interviewed, and tested since 1972, nearly all described themselves as shy at least some of the time. A full 40 percent consider themselves "dispositionally" shy—they identify the trait as a basic part of who they are and struggle with it on a daily basis. Additional research suggests that about 4 percent of adults feel so self-conscious that they have trouble in ordinary situations, including such everyday circumstances as going to work. These fearful folk, who grapple with what's known as extreme social anxiety, start limiting their contact with others while still young and often avoid going to college or choosing an ambitious career.

But even the supershy can learn to open up, says Zimbardo. And the techniques that help them can work for the rest of us, too.

Clinical psychologist Lynne Henderson, Ph.D., a colleague of Zimbardo's, has run a clinic for hard-core wallflowers for three decades and has watched hundreds bloom. The shyest people aren't constitutionally different from others, Henderson and Zimbardo contend; they're just wilting from lack of practice. The less often you take risks in social interactions, the more your self-esteem drops and the worse your shyness becomes, creating a self-perpetuating cycle. So in the treatment groups, Henderson simply helps people develop their "social fitness."

Clients in weekly Shyness Clinic sessions role-play frightening situations, such as speaking up in a meeting. Then they head out with assignments to do each day, exercises akin to sit-ups or endurance-building jogs around the block. The tasks are simple: Smile and say hello to a passerby on the street. At

the gas station, go inside to pay the clerk instead of using your credit card at the pump; start a conversation with the person behind you in the checkout line at the market.

These encounters may seem trivial, but they're not, Zimbardo says. The feedback that they offer is crucial—for the exceptionally shy folks at the clinic and for everyone else, too. As people rely more and more on high-tech communication tools, such as e-mail and cell phones, face-to-face contact diminishes. That's a setup for interpersonal problems, says Zimbardo, who thinks his next survey may well show the shy population growing.

"If you don't learn through practice and observation, social interaction becomes awkward, and you start to avoid it," he says. "You have to practice in little ways every day."

Here's the no-sweat approach:

Start small. Make the first party you attend one given by a friend. Or try a low-risk business reception, and stay only a short while.

Warm up your social muscles. Before worrying about such details as what to wear, shoo away that internal critic and remind yourself that you are a successful, interesting person. "People with social anxiety think everybody is as interested in their faults as they are. They're not," says Kent State University psychologist Angela Neal-Barnett, Ph.D., author of *Soothe Your Nerves: The Black Woman's Guide to Understanding and Overcoming Anxiety, Panic, and Fear.*

Exercise your "social fitness": Say hi to passersby, pay in person when you fill up your car, chat with a co-worker at the coffeepot.

Remember to breathe. You may find your heart pumping wildly and the perspiration beginning to trickle as you walk up to the door of the party. That can make you more nervous and get your heart beating even faster, says Neal-Barnett, who works with anxious and shy patients. To break the cycle, calm your body by breathing deeply and counting to 10.

Try a favorite party trick. Not the lampshade-on-the-head kind, but the hover-in-the-hall variety. People gather near doorways for a reason: It's easy to say hello when someone passes, and there's less pressure to sustain a conversation.

Act like you're a friendly person. Pretending to be comfortable will make you feel more comfortable, Zimbardo says. You don't even need to say a word. Try some nonverbal cues: Smile, keep your arms uncrossed, nod, lean forward.

Ease your way in. It's tough to make a grand leap into a group conversation. Sidle up to a small pack, and just listen. When the discussion lags, introduce yourself. The talk will continue—and you'll be part of it.

Don't try to entertain. Attempting to be witty will just make you stiffen up. Instead, capitalize on the fact that people love talking about themselves. Ask about your companions' interests, work lives, or families. Then you can bond over things you share, and they'll remember you with pleasure.

Help the next guy. At least 40 percent of your fellow partygoers feel as awkward as you do. Make an effort to put them at ease, and your discomfort will start to evaporate.

Attempting to be witty will just make you stiffen up. Instead, capitalize on the fact that people love to talk about themselves.

Do it again. When it's all over, ask your family or friends whether you really sounded as insipid as you thought. (Be sure to let them know that no is the right answer.) Make plans for things you'd do differently next time. And above all, make sure you keep exercising your social skills. "Success is the best cure for shyness," Zimbardo says. ∎

Don't Be Shy—It Just May Lead to Heart Disease

A little-known personality type may be just as dangerous as the oh-so-familiar type A, and doctors are getting closer to understanding why. In a recent study at the University of British Columbia, a researcher posing as a lab tech verbally harassed students as they tried to do a math problem. People with type-D personalities—who have a tendency to be negative and shy—were most likely to experience spikes in blood pressure and release the stress hormone cortisol. Both of these reactions signal an increased risk of heart disease, the same problem linked to type-A traits, such as impatience and hostility. The results expand on previous findings that Ds are more likely than other type personalities to suffer a fatal second heart attack. Counseling or antidepressants may reduce this risk.

Proof That the D-O-G Personality Really Does Exist

Who could ever doubt that Lassie had a sweet nature? Well, scientists could. Not all of them are convinced that dogs or other animals have personalities. But now research buttresses what every dog-lover has suspected: A recent study in the *Journal of Personality and Social Psychology* found that dogs do, in fact, have plenty of the P-word. When a dog-owner and someone acquainted with both the owner and the pooch rated the dog's personality, both humans reached pretty much the same conclusions. To check the accuracy of such ratings, the researchers also had the owner and his or her acquaintance rate the owner's personality. What they found: "In terms of personality, we agree about dogs as much as we agree about humans," says Samuel Gosling, Ph.D., professor of psychology at the University of Texas at Austin and an author of the study.

In addition to making your dog happy, studies such as this one may someday help scientists identify genes in humans that play a role in personality.

Got Pain? Illuminate It

If your nurse opens the curtains when you ask for pain meds, don't call a lawyer. A dose of strong sunshine can be effective in treating postoperative pain. A recent study found that patients who recovered in sunny hospital beds felt better and healed faster than those in darker rooms.

University of Pittsburgh professor Bruce Rabin, M.D., Ph.D., and his team sought inexpensive methods that hospitals could use to reduce inpatient stress and to speed healing. Sunlight, a proven mood-elevator, was a logical candidate. The researchers randomly assigned patients to rooms on the shady side of a surgical ward or to another side flooded with 46-percent more natural light. Subjects in sunny rooms experienced 20 percent less stress and 20-percent less discomfort; they also used less medication and saved 20-percent on their pharmacy bills. "I didn't expect to get this dramatic effect," Rabin says, but it made sense. "When it's bright out, you feel good. And when you feel good, you think, 'Hey, I forgot it hurt.'" Next, you get active, which reduces complications (such as blood clots) and speeds recovery. Given these results, finding ways to let the sunshine in may be the next trend in hospital design.

How Age Tinkers with Your Traits

Can your personality really keep changing—and *improving*—long into adulthood? New research says yes.

BY EMILY SOHN

In her 20s, life was easy for Nina Abbott (not her real name), and she was easygoing. She had a good job and a relationship headed toward marriage. Then, at age 28, Abbott got pregnant. When she decided to keep the baby, her boyfriend left. Everything was changing—and she changed, too.

Now 38, the corporate analyst in Cape Cod, Massachusetts, is much more assertive than she used to be. She's less agreeable and more outspoken; she thinks about what she wants and then goes after it. Where she used to be happy-go-lucky, she's now a bit of a worrier. And she's not so free with her time anymore; what was once a large social group has now been whittled down to a few close friends. "I'm a different person than I was 10 years ago," Abbott says. "It's pretty dramatic."

And she might continue to evolve. Psychologists used to think that major personality traits were set, if not in stone, then in concrete; they could change and

> **You're neurotic? Just wait. New research holds out the possibility that you'll become calmer, less emotional, and more secure as you get older.**

develop, but only through childhood and adolescence. Shrinking violet or social butterfly, ne'er-do-well or nose to the grindstone—by the time you hit 30, you are who you are, said influential studies in the '80s and '90s, which showed that people remain stable throughout adulthood. Researchers believed genes and biology defined your personality from the get-go. Any changes were programmed into your genes as well.

But that thinking has changed. According to an increasing number of studies, many of the traits that define you are more malleable than ever imagined. It now seems your personality continues to evolve throughout adulthood, into your 40s, 50s, and beyond.

Psychologists hope that understanding when and how you change will lead to better therapies for such personality disorders as anxiety, paranoia, and antisocial behavior. For everyone else, the research could fuel new faith in New Year's resolutions: Perhaps you truly can become the person you want to be after all.

In one of the latest studies to shake conventional notions, psychologist Sanjay Srivastava, Ph.D., now at Stanford University, and colleagues used the Internet to question more than one hundred thirty thousand American and Canadian men and women between ages 21 and 60. The researchers pegged each respondent in terms of what psychologists call the "Big Five" personality categories: neuroticism, agreeableness, extroversion, openness, and conscientiousness.

On every trait, the scientists found, the older participants tended to score differently than the younger ones, suggesting that people change as they age. Older respondents were more conscientious and agreeable than younger ones. Women tended to become less emotional with age; they got calmer, too—less neurotic, more secure.

Longitudinal studies, which follow individuals over time instead of comparing people of different ages, point in the same direction, says psychologist Brent Roberts, Ph.D., of the University of Illinois at Urbana-Champaign. His review of such research has found variability from person to person, but the tendency is toward becoming more conscientious, stable, and agreeable, and less open. "We're not boats without rudders, changing with every shift in the wind," Roberts says. "Still, we change."

All this raises an obvious question: Can you guide the changes? Some researchers think not. Psychologist Robert McCrae, Ph.D., of the National Institute on Aging, believes changes in adulthood are either so small as to be insignificant or completely out of your control. People evolve in consistent ways across drastically different cultures, from China to Russia to the United States, he says. On the other hand, they don't tend to change much after such major shake-ups as divorcing, getting fired, or moving to a new state. Such findings suggest genes and biology, not culture or choices, determine who you are, McCrae says.

By and large, most researchers agree that genes can explain only about half of the ways you differ from your next-door neighbor. The rest is probably open to influence, says psychologist Dan Mroczek, Ph.D., of Fordham University in New York. In one study, Mroczek followed more than sixteen hundred men for 12 years. "If you're shy, you're not going to become some raving party animal swinging from the rafters," he says. "But you can become less shy."

How? Science provides no answers so far but offers clues. Acting "as if" might shift your personality in a desired direction, says Ravenna Helson, Ph.D., a psychologist at the University of California, Berkeley, and until recently director of the Mills Longitudinal Study. Helson has been following more than 100 women since they graduated from college in the late '50s and early '60s. Her research indicates that

Most researchers agree that genes can explain only about half of the ways in which you differ from your next-door neighbor.

people who take demanding jobs tend to become more disciplined, she says. Other studies have shown similar changes, suggesting that if you want to become a nicer person, you should start volunteering; if you would like to be more outgoing, try joining a club. People should invest themselves in raising a family or in work they like, Helson says. "A certain amount of personality change comes from making that investment," she adds.

Amy Lieberman figured that out for herself. Ten years ago, the 46-year-old paralegal from Edina, Minnesota, had a job she liked, a happy marriage, plenty of friends, and two healthy children ages 6 and 8. But she constantly worried that terrible things might happen. "I didn't have the confidence that I could handle what life was going to dish up," she says.

So Lieberman began what she calls an interpersonal journey. She took up yoga, embraced religion, and read books about spirituality. She quit her job to spend more time with her kids and started volunteering. Gradually, she began to feel more self-confident, stronger, and less fearful. When five family members fell ill in a short period of time, she was prepared to meet the challenges and handle the stress. "I really have found a whole new life," Lieberman says. "The world has expanded in a direction I wasn't expecting."

If you're interested in making some changes, Roberts suggests putting your resolutions on a 10-year plan. (The shifts he sees in his research happen slowly.) And expect good things. Judging from another study of Helson's, this one with women in their 60s, over time you'll likely become less anxious and frustrated. "The trend is toward a better adjusted, more mature personality up until late adulthood," she says. "This is very much bringing people toward the kind of people they want to be."

Nina Abbott is looking forward to the changes to come. Ten years from now, she'll be 48; her son will be 19. With an early retirement on the horizon and her son out of the house, she'll have more time and fewer responsibilities. She'll be able to take bigger risks without worrying so much about the consequences.

In many ways, Abbott hopes, her 50s will be just like her 20s: happy-go-lucky and carefree. If you didn't know better, it might seem that she hadn't changed at all. ■

How Your Town's Name Can Affect You

If your town's name sounds even remotely medical, nutritional, or psychological, watch out: Researchers may soon be knocking on your door. In an effort to draw attention to their work, scientists are choosing small communities with suggestive monikers as the settings for new studies.

To test the idea that dietary calcium can help control weight—a notion supported in earlier research—obesity expert James O. Hill, Ph.D., director of the Center for Human Nutrition at the University of Colorado, recently had townsfolk in Calcium, New York (population 3,300), boost their dairy intake to three servings per day. Result? The weight came off (go figure): Participants in the study dropped an average of 14 pounds.

Meanwhile, in Mt. Healthy, Ohio (population 7,000), researchers employed by a supplement manufacturer had residents take the company's vitamin-C pills for 50 days in a row. At the end of the study, most participants reported feeling (what else?) healthier. Three-quarters never got a cold, 86 percent had no indigestion, and roughly half said they had more energy.

No word on which towns are now in scientists' crosshairs. But we think residents of Hygiene, Colorado; Looneyville, West Virginia; and, um, Climax, Georgia, should keep their eyes and ears open.

vital *stats*

27

Percentage of people who have received mental-health treatment in the last two years

63

Percentage of those who are women

39

Percentage of people who haven't received mental-health treatment because it's too expensive

80

Percentage of people who have received treatment who say it was effective

37

Percentage of mothers of teens who think condoms effectively prevent pregnancy

47

Percentage of fathers who do

23

Percentage of those moms who think teens are capable of using condoms correctly

33

Percentage of fathers who do

97

Percent of pregnancies prevented by condoms, when used correctly

37

Percent fewer errors doctors who play video games frequently make when performing laparoscopic surgery compared with non-gaming surgeons

27

Percent faster doctors who play video games complete surgery compared with those who don't play

8

Average number of first dates that single professionals have each year

12.5

Percent chance that a woman's date will call her for a second date if she hasn't heard from him within 24 hours of the first meeting

30

Percentage of men who say they have trouble finding jeans that fit

58

Percentage of women who do

3 to 4

Average number of new pairs women buy annually

66

Percentage of teen girls who are concerned with weight gain

33

Percentage of teen boys who are

60

Percentage of women who say they are on a diet or are going on one in the next few months

44

Percentage of men who say they are

5.6

Millions of bottles of Nair sold annually

2

Olympic-size swimming pools that amount of Nair could fill

69:67

Ratio of the average height of an American male to a Dutchman in 1850, in inches

70:72

Ratio today

36

Percentage of people who say they eat leftover pizza the next day, even if it hasn't been refrigerated

2

Hours leftover pizza can stay at room temperature before it goes bad

34

Percentage of food poisoning outbreaks traced to food storage temperature, the most common reason

69

Percentage of Americans who say that green vegetables are the most nutritious

7

Percentage who say orange, red, or yellow ones are

0

Amount of difference a vegetable's color makes in its nutritional content

Sources: John Komlos, Munich University, Nair, Mintel, It's Just Lunch!, Green Giant / American Dietetic Association, Harris Interactive, Beth Israel Medical Center, Alan Guttmacher Institute, American Dietetic Association/ConAgra Foods/ Idaho Food Protection Program, DietDirectives.com/ BuzzBack Market Research—Reported by Laura Gilbert

Index

scanners for, 57
women's feelings about,
126–129
Broccoli, 65
BSE. *See* Mad cow disease.
Bt (pesticide), 181–182
Burgers, 196–200
Butter, dairy, 191, 218
Butterbur root, 89
Butters, nut, 188–190

C
CA125 protein, 117–118
Caffeine, 56, 115, 185
Calcium
in dairy products, 140, 187
and travelers' diarrhea, 191
and vitamin D, 79, 137, 140
for weight loss, 384
Calories
in restaurants, 178–179
role in dieting, 157–159
speedy low-cal lunches, 178
tips for burning of, 222–224,
314
Cancer
in African-Americans, 344
anticancer drugs, 13, 15
and artificial sweeteners,
202
breast, 41, 43, 56–57, 117, 128,
130
cervical, 16
colon, 13, 55, 195
from CT scans, 66–68
and diet/nutrition, 148
emotional aspects of, 63,
116–118, 120–125
by gender and race, 344
from hair coloring, 285
music/meditation for, 48
online information, 23, 63
ovarian, 116–118, 121–125
overtesting for, 63
prostate, 63–65
skin, 54–55, 68, 220, 344
sleep for treatment of, 68
vaginal, 125

Carbohydrates
for body fuel, 151, 223
daily requirement of, 152
effect on blood sugar, 151–153
high-fiber choices of, 159
low-carb diets, 150–154,
156–157, 203, 220, 344
Car crashes, 369
Cardiac bypasses, 13–14
Cardiovascular system
changes with aging, 138–144
heart, 12–14
varicose veins, 42, 296
Cars, airbags in, 270
Cashews, 188–190
Cataracts, 85
Cauliflower, 65
Celery, 149
Celexa, 357
Celiac disease, 155
Cellulite, 272–273, 297
Cerebrovascular accident (CVA).
See Stroke.
CEREC 3, 280
Cervical cancer, 16
Cervix
cancer of, 16
Pap smear for, 16, 63, 125
Cesarean section, 109
CFS. *See* Chronic fatigue
syndrome.
Chasteberry, 41
Cheeses, 88, 108, 201, 216
Chemical peels, 293
Chemotherapy
"chemo-brain" from, 122–123
nausea and vomiting, 46–48
tumor-starving for, 13, 15
and vitamins, 50
Chi, 244–245
Chicken, 17, 210–211
Children
alternative therapies for, 44–50
brain scans for babies, 67
decision to have, 332–333
echinacea for, 37
gym programs for, 246

held back in school, 341
parenthood in midlife, 135–136
and parent's sex life, 317
Chinese medicine, 245
Chiropractic/chiropractors, 44,
92–93, 95, 100
Chlamydia pneumoniae, 61
Chocolate, 88, 100, 195, 314
Cholesterol
and cinnamon, 219
drugs for lowering, 18–19,
60–62, 81, 373
and garlic, 39–40
and heart disease, 102–103
high-density lipoprotein (HDL),
61, 193–194
low-density lipoprotein (LDL),
61, 81, 147, 149, 193–194
and supplements, 144
tests for, 61
Chondroitin, 40–41
Chromatherm, 273
Chronic fatigue syndrome (CFS),
359
Cinnamon, 219
Clarinex, 75–76
Claritin, 74–76
Cleansers, skin, 288, 290
Cod liver oil, 80
Co-enzyme Q10, 89
Coffee
decaffeinated, 185
Fair Trade Certified, 184
shade-grown, 184
and sperm mobility, 115
Cognitive behavioral therapy, 359,
361, 367–368
Colas, 137
Cold sores and canker sores,
306
Colds/upper respiratory
infections
echinacea for, 37
vitamins for, 36–37, 384
Colon
cancer of, 13, 55, 195
colonoscopy, 55–56, 67–68

antacids, 77, 357

antibiotics, 17, 49, 62, 72–73, 114, 136, 178

anticancer, 13, 15

antidepressants, 25–26, 30, 89, 100, 357, 361

antiemetics, 107

antifungal, 115

antihistamines, 75, 77, 107, 183, 357, 359

anti-inflammatory, 16, 60–61, 96, 240, 359

for anxiety and panic, 366

beta-blockers, 89

cholesterol-lowering, 18–19, 60–62, 81, 373

for chronic fatigue syndrome (CFS), 359

combinations of, 76

corticosteroids, 75

cost of, 74–76, 344

decongestants, 77

for high blood pressure, 60–62

illicit use of, 167, 332–333

for impotence, 317

interaction with herbs, 38

for irritable bowel syndrome (IBS), 30

microchip delivery of, 20

for multiple sclerosis (MS), 15–16

over-the-counter (OTC), 87, 94, 96

for pain, 46–47, 87

phosphate binders, 17–18

for restless legs syndrome, 358

side effects of, 16, 19, 30, 46–47, 76, 357, 361

for sleep, 34

for stress, 314

triptans, 88, 89

vaccines, 16, 347

Dual-energy X-ray absorptiometry (DXA), 143

DXA. See Dual-energy X-ray absorptiometry.

Dyslexia, 51

Ears

acupuncture of, 46–48

infections in, 44, 48, 77

Eating disorders, 162–173, 335, 370–372

Echinacea, 37

ECT. See Electroconvulsive therapy.

Edamame, 43

Education/school, 327, 341, 347, 348

EEG. See Electroencephalography.

Elavil, 30

Electroconvulsive therapy (ECT), 24–27

Electroencephalography (EEG), 347

Emotions. See also specific emotions.

about body image, 243

effects of negative, 349

effects on body, 140, 347

gender differences in, 344

and obesity, 162–173

pain of, 96

from past memories, 347

satisfaction with life, 369

therapy for, 346–348

Employment/work

and alcohol use, 344

and allergies, 220

effects of depression on, 355

environments for, 333

ergonomics at, 91

exhaustion from, 314

income/pay from, 100, 144, 220

loss of, 361

and marriage, 220

promotions at, 319–320

sleeping on job, 100

stretching at, 91

vacation time from, 52

Endometriosis, 58

Endovenous Laser Treatment (EVLT), 296

Energy

afternoon slump in, 360

chi as, 244–245

exercise for, 348

ginseng for, 154

lack of, 150–154, 356–360

renewal of, 353

Ephedra, 50

Epinepherine, 183

Ergonomics, 91

Estorra (zopiclone), 34

Estrogen

for bone health, 137

effects on personality, 114

effects on serotonin, 367

EVLT. See Endovenous Laser Treatment.

Exercise. See also Bodywork.

aerobic and anaerobic, 94, 141, 228, 229

anxiety/fear of, 226–227

benefits of, 93, 125, 140, 229, 231–232

body fuel for, 151, 223

body-shaping moves, 267–269

for calorie burning, 222–224

cross-training in, 223, 231, 237

dancing for, 223

deep breathing with, 48

for energy, 348, 360

environments for, 226–227

fitness balls for, 94, 248–251, 253

and happiness/peace, 52, 349, 360, 365

headaches after, 88, 233

hydration during, 106, 114, 233, 246

machines for, 94, 223

for memory, 98–99

to music, 224–225

pain caused by, 239

of pelvic-floor muscles (Kegel), 112–113

retro workouts for, 225

and sleep quality, 228

strenuous, 91–95, 236, 240–241

for stress reduction, 314

stretching after, 142, 313

swimming for, 81

tools/accessories for, 94, 231, 248–253, 259–261

steroidal, 50, 98
stress hormones, 153, 349
Hormone therapy (HT), 41, 43, 358
Horse chestnut seed extract, 42
HPV. *See* Human papillomavirus.
HRT. *See* Hormone therapy.
HT. *See* Hormone therapy.
Human papillomavirus (HPV), 16, 125
Humility/modesty, 348
Hydration/dehydration, 106, 114, 233, 246, 356
Hydroxytyrosol, 51
Hyperemesis gravidarum (HG), 106–108
Hypertension. *See* Blood pressure, high.
Hypnosis/hypnotherapy
  for irritable bowel syndrome (IBS), 28–30
  for pain relief, 32
  self-hypnosis, 33
  for smoking cessation, 32
  for tissue healing, 31–33
Hypothyroidism, 358–359
Hysterectomy, 58, 125

IBD. *See* Inflammatory bowel disease.
IBS. *See* Irritable bowel syndrome.
Ibuprofen
  for back pain, 96
  with glucosamine, 76
  for knee injuries, 240
Ice skating, 328–329
Imitrex, 88, 89
Immune system
  emotions effect on, 347
  and infections, 72–73, 358
  and stress hormones, 349
  and vitamin D, 80
Imodium-AD (loperamide), 30
Incontinence, 112–113
Infections
  from herpes virus, 306
  and immune system, 72–73, 358

in middle ear, 44, 48, 77
  and sepsis prevention, 72–73
  sexually transmitted, 136, 270
  of urinary tract, 72–73, 114
  yeast (vaginal), 115
Inflammation
  and heart disease, 69
  inflammatory diseases, 16
  and multiple sclerosis (MS), 15–16
Inflammatory bowel disease (IBD)
  drugs for, 16
  hypnotherapy for, 28–30
  and vitamin D, 80
Injuries
  from airbags, 270
  from car crashes, 369
  to eyes, 270
  to knee, 238–241
  from overuse, 240–241
  from running shoes, 233
Inline skating, 330–331
Insomnia, 40
Insulin, 153, 185
Integrative medicine. *See* Alternative therapies.
Introversion, 353–354
Iron, 154, 358
Irritable bowel syndrome (IBS), 28–30
Isoflavones, 41, 43, 137

Japan/Japanese, 71, 136, 273, 314
Jazzercise, 225
Joints
  arthritic changes, 40–41
  knee problems, 238–241
  pain in, 79

Kale, 148
Kegel exercises, 112–113
Keratosis pilaris (KP), 287
Kidneys
  dialysis of, 17
  stones in, 67, 73
Knees, 238–241
KP. *See* Keratosis pilaris.

Labels/labeling
  of cosmetics, 284–285
  of genetically modified foods, 180, 182–183
  hypoallergenic/fragrance-free, 284–285
  for organic foods, 181–183
  words *fresh* and *whole* on, 286
Labyrinths, 352
Lactic acid, 228, 233
L-arginine, 42
LASEK. *See* Laser subepithelial keratomileusis.
Laser-assisted in situ keratomileusis (LASIK), 82–84
Laser subepithelial keratomileusis (LASEK), 84
LASIK. *See* Laser-assisted in situ keratomileusis.
Lavender, 360
Laxatives, 55
LDL. *See* Cholesterol.
Lead, 49
Legumes, 149
Leptin, 173
Libido, 42, 136, 316–317
Lifestyles
  and blood pressure, 62
  healthy changes in, 60–61, 69
  and heart disease, 60–61, 146
  for longevity, 146–149, 232, 349
  and obesity, 163
  sedentary, 235–236
  and stroke, 146
Light. *See also* Sunlight.
  definition of, 362–363
  natural, 363
  sensitivity to, 88
  types of bulbs for, 295, 363
Light therapy, 362–363
Listeria, 108
Longevity, 146–149, 232, 349
Lotronex (alosetron), 30
Lutein, 146
Lycopene, 65, 149, 183

Tinidazole, 136

TM. *See* Transcendental meditation.

Tofranil, 38

Tomatoes, 65, 149, 183, 220

Topamax (topiramate), 89

Transcendental meditation (TM), 33

Trichomoniasis, 136

Triptans, 88, 89

Tumors. *See* Cancer.

Tylenol (acetaminophen), 56

Ultraviolet (UV) rays, 294–295, 344

Urinary system. *See also* Bladder, urinary; Kidneys.
  infections in, 114, 119
  sepsis of, 72–73

Urinary-tract infections (UTIs), 114, 119

Uterus, 58

UTIs. *See* Urinary-tract infections.

UV rays. *See* Ultraviolet rays.

Vacations, 52, 270

Vaccines
  for cervical cancer, 16
  for flu, 347

Vagina
  cancer of, 125
  yeast infections, 115

Vaginal discharge, 136

Valerian, 40

Varicose veins, 42, 296

Vegetables. *See* Produce.

Vegetarians, 179, 270

Veins, skin, 296

Viagra, 317

Vinegar, balsamic, 216–217

Vision
  auras in, 88
  contact lenses for, 83–84
  corrective surgery for, 82–84
  power of gaze, 340
  with presbyopia, 85

  sensitivity to light, 86, 88
  with starbursts, halos, or glare, 82–84

Vitamin A, 183

Vitamin B complex, 41, 89

Vitamin C
  for colds, 36–37, 384
  in genetically modified foods, 183

Vitamin D
  with calcium, 79, 137, 140
  deficiency in, 78–80
  sources of, 80

Vitamins
  and chemotherapy, 50
  for cold prevention, 36–37
  deficiency in, 78–80
  for headache relief, 89
  for sexual enhancement, 42

Volunteerism, 270

Walking, jogging, and running
  for business owners, 233
  for exercise, 111
  programs for, 234–236, 263–264
  in water, 222, 230
  for weight loss, 157

Walnuts, 194

Warts, 33

Water
  amounts to drink, 247
  benefits of exercise in, 222, 230
  bodily need for, 356–357
  buoyancy of, 231
  in feng shui theory, 364
  jogging in, 222

Web sites. *See* Online information.

Weight loss. *See also* Diets/dieting.
  and artificial sweeteners, 203–204
  calcium for, 384
  from eating disorders, 370–372
  exercise for, 133, 157, 236
  false expectations of, 160, 165, 308
  five strategies for, 158–161
  fruits and vegetables for, 158–159

  gender differences in, 385
  grapefruit for, 155
  hyperemesis gravidarum (HG), 106–108
  hypnotherapy for, 33
  from illness, 313
  and insulin resistance, 153
  keeping off, 156–157, 170, 173, 235
  and pregnancy, 111
  Solution for, The, 168–173
  surgery for, 162–167
  and teenagers, 385

Weight training, 142

Weight Watchers, 158, 170

Wheat, 183

Windsurfing, 338–339

Wine, 88, 109, 147, 177

Work. *See* Employment/work.

Workouts. *See* Exercise.

Wrinkles, 277, 289, 292, 306, 312

Xanax, 366

X-rays/imaging techniques
  for back injury, 95
  CT scans, 66–68, 233
  mammograms, 56–57, 63, 100, 129
  MRI, 27, 130
  PET scans, 21, 361, 377
  radiation from, 66–68
  rTMS, 27

Yeast, 115

Yoga
  Anusara, 242–243
  mindfulness practice, 365
  principles of, 243
  for self-confidence, 384

Yogurt, 187

Zantac, 77

Zelnorm (tegaserod), 30

Zinc oxide, 55, 276–277

Zofran, 107

Zoloft, 37–38

Zyrtec, 75–76

Contributors

Jane Meredith Adams
Vanessa Geneva Ahern
Karen Ansel
Hilary Beard
Leigh Beisch
Ben Brown
Jessica Brown
Michael Castleman
Rick Chillot
Michelle Dally
Paula Disbrowe
Catherine Dold
Anne Driscoll
Sharon Edry
Paul Elledge
Katherine Ellison
Anne Enslow
Darryl Estine
Christine Fellingham
Lisa Lee Freeman
Susan Freinkel
Fran Gealer
Debbie Geiger
Laura Gilbert

Jodie Green
Andee Hochman
Bob Holmes
Ray Kachatorian
Wayne Kalyn
Susan Katz-Miller
Alice Lesch Kelly
Maureen Kennedy
Brian Lavendel
Sally Lehrman
Wendy Lichtman
Diane Mapes
Meredith Maran
Eva Marer
Linda Marsa
David Martinez
Maura McEvoy
Jennifer Nelson
Susan Orenstein
Kathy Passero
Margie Patlak
Aviva Patz
Marla Paul
Kate Powers

Carol Prager
Linda Rao
Suz Redfearn
Tracy Seaman
Joel N. Shurkin
Fran Smith
Emily Sohn
Lisa Spindler
Nancy Stedman
Loren Stein
Jacqueline Stenson
Barbara Stepko
Wendy Lyons Sunshine
Danny Turner
John T. Ward
Rebecca Webber
Kerri Westenberg
Ingrid Wickelgren
Leslie Williamson
Teresa Wiltz
Marion Winik
Kimberly Wong
Stacey Grenrock Woods
Amy Young

Editorial Advisory Board

William Berger, M.D.
Steven Blair, P.E.D.
James Blumenthal, Ph.D.
Mark Blumenthal
Lisa Donofrio, M.D.
James Duke, Ph.D.
Elsa-Grace Giardina, M.D.
Linda Giudice, M.D., Ph.D.
Jo Hannafin, M.D., Ph.D.
David Heber, M.D., Ph.D.
David Katz, M.D.
Marianne Legato, M.D.
Julius E. Linn, M.D.
Richard Lipton, M.D.
Susan Love, M.D.
JoAnn E. Manson, M.D., D.P.H.
Bess Marcus, Ph.D.
Vivian Pinn, M.D.
John S. Williamson, Ph.D.

Contributing Editors

Christie Aschwanden
Michele Bender
Maureen Callahan, M.S., R.D.
Kerri Conan
Alice D. Domar, Ph.D.
Dorothy Foltz-Gray
Timothy Gower
Brett Hill
Peter Jaret
Alexis Jetter
Petra Kolber
Dimity McDowell
Nancy Ross-Flanigan
Robin Vitetta-Miller
Liz Weiss